The Civilization of the American Indian Series

The MODOCS *and Their* WAR

JOE BEELER

The MODOCS *and Their* WAR

BY KEITH A. MURRAY

NORMAN AND LONDON
UNIVERSITY OF OKLAHOMA PRESS

Buku ini di-edit oleh Baniamin Joebhaar waktu ia mendjadi tamu dari University of Oklahoma Press dalam bulan Agustus-September 1958, dibawah pimpinan Rockefeller Foundation di New York.

The Modocs and Their War is Volume 52 in The Civilization of the American Indian Series.

LIBRARY OF CONGRESS CATALOG CARD NUMBER: 59–7488
ISBN: 0–8061–1331–6

8   9   10   11   12   13   14   15   16

TO MY BEST FRIEND
Olive Murray
who is also my wife

FOREWORD

THIS BOOK IS THE RESULT of an interest in the Modoc Indians which dates back to my college days, when I read a graphic, though inaccurate account of the murder of General Canby by Captain Jack. In the summer of 1954, and again in the summer of 1956, this interest was stimulated when the National Park Service employed me as a seasonal Ranger-Historian at the Lava Beds National Monument, near Tule Lake, California. Here I could study the Modoc War battlefield first-hand and interpret it to visitors to the Monument who asked me far more questions than I could answer.

When I tried to learn more, I found that the information available was widely scattered, and nowhere was there a single, chronological account of the war and its causes which made use of all the primary materials available. The older stories were usually eye-witness accounts written in many cases years after the event by men or women who had seen only part of the conflict, while the later accounts were inadequate because they leaned much too heavily on the pioneer reminiscences with all of their usual weaknesses.

I wish to express my gratitude to Superintendent Robert R. Budlong of the Lava Beds National Monument, who encouraged me to write the complete story of the war, and made available the records and files which had been collected by the National Park Service relative to the Modoc War. Particularly do I want to thank Supervisory Ranger Raymond G. Knox for his personal interest in this work. He was the first person to take me into Captain Jack's Stronghold and to point out the actual spots where many of the events of the war took place.

In the three years that have passed since this study began, I have had considerable help from a number of people. I should like to thank the Bancroft Library of the University of California for permission to quote from manuscripts in the Pacific Manuscripts collection. Mr. O. C. Applegate, Jr., has been most generous in granting the use of the Applegate Papers pertinent to the study of the war. Mr. Ronald Todd of the University of Washington Library has helped in finding materials. The entire staff of the California State Library assisted me to find items in their collections not available elsewhere. The county clerk of Siskiyou County also helped me find records available only in Yreka. There were many helpful people who came to the Monument when they heard I was working on this project and gratuitously offered me information they had retained since childhood, or gave me of their time taking me to some spot where a significant event of the war had taken place.

To Professors Angelo Anastasio and Herbert C. Taylor, Jr., of the Western Washington College of Education anthropology department, I would like to express my gratitude for their valuable comments on the material relating to the culture of the Modocs. I should also like to thank James O'Brien of the Western Washington College English faculty for his editorial work on the manuscript.

KEITH A. MURRAY

Western Washington College of Education
Bellingham, Washington

CONTENTS

ILLUSTRATIONS

The MODOCS *and Their* WAR

I

THE SETTING

IN THE MIDST of a forbidding plateau, along the shore line of an ancient lake bed in northern California, stands a cairn of lava rocks surmounted by a rough wooden cross. For three-quarters of a century this crude monument has served to mark the spot where a general officer of the United States Army met his death. The inscription on the cross-arm reads: "General E. R. S. Canby, U. S. A., Murdered by Modoc Indians, April 11, 1873."

Canby's death belongs to the same chapter in the history of the West which records wars with the Apaches, the Nez Percés, and the campaign against the Sioux that reached its climax at the Little Big Horn River with the "Custer Massacre." The Modoc Indian War of 1872–73, in which Canby died, was a far more difficult campaign than Custer's, and considering the shortness of the war and the number of Indians involved, was the army's most expensive Indian war. Although the colorful and controversial George Custer has inspired a wealth of books, articles, and scholarly studies, students have tended to neglect the conflict in northern California that ended only three years before Custer's death.

This Indian war was fought by an army which had been almost entirely demobilized after the end of the Civil War. What soldiers remained on active duty were not only stationed in the Deep South, but were scattered in small detachments throughout the western plains, Arizona, and along the Pacific Coast. Only a handful of soldiers, mostly raw recruits, were stationed between the Sierras and the Rocky Mountains. The widely separated army posts were expected to support the Indian agents and to keep the peace among Indian bands. The military was also expected to prevent conflict between the red men and the steadily increasing number of white miners, stockmen, and farmers who entered the Great Basin between 1850 and 1870. The settlers insisted that they be permitted to enter areas where there was water which could be used to irrigate crops or streams where placer mining could be attempted. They impatiently demanded the complete and immediate removal of all Indians from desirable land so that there could be additional settlement and development of the western states and territories. Some of the settlers who came west after the Civil War were quiet, industrious workers, but others were unruly and reckless. Sometimes this group was on the right side of the law, and sometimes it was not. These men accepted lynch law, were not unduly shocked by murder, and believed that dead Indians were a vast improvement over live ones. The difficulties for the army in the conflicts between Indians and settlers proved too great for army leaders to handle.

The Modoc Indian War was the final desperate resistance to the impact of white man's culture on the ancient Indian folkways. It marks the concluding stages of the decline in vigor and numbers among a fierce people, beginning in the early years of the nineteenth century and ending when a band of beaten and spiritless prisoners were forced aboard a Central Pacific Railroad train bound for exile on a tiny reservation in Oklahoma.

The present story takes note of the cultural background of the Modocs, the changes in their way of life that came after their first contacts with white men, the nature of the land where they lived, and its peculiar features which made it possible for them to defend it so ably. The story also concerns itself with the fundamental reasons for the conflicts between the Indians and the white ranchers and miners, as well as the immediate causes of the war itself.

This account also considers the disputes in Grant's cabinet over the settlement of the Indian problem, and the part played by well-meaning, but ill-informed eastern humanitarians, whom the scornful western settlers called the "Lo!-the-poor-Indian" reformers. It tells about the Modocs themselves, of Old Schonchin who lived in peace

4

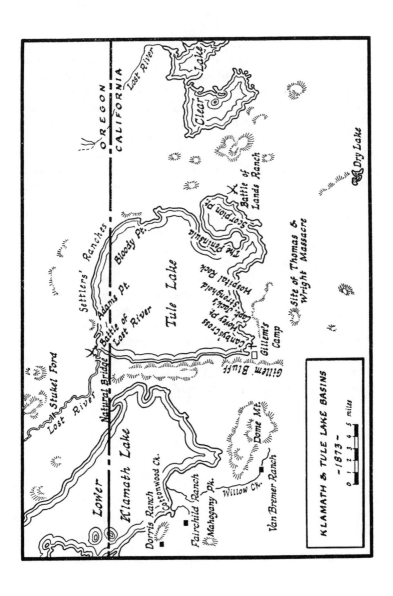

KLAMATH & TULE LAKE BASINS
—1873—

0 1 2 3 4 5 miles

with the white men; who signed a treaty and lived on the reservation where he was sent. It tells of his rival, Captain Jack, who denounced Schonchin and led a band of dissident Modocs against the federal government, its agents, and their treaties and reservation system. This story also tells of Curley Headed Doctor, the religious leader, who used magic and fanaticism to support the followers of Jack in their five months' fight against the army and the settlers. It also tells of other Modocs who killed more white men than their own forces numbered. These Indians so bewildered the enlisted men opposite them that the private soldiers became almost worthless as fighters. They even confounded the strategy of officers who had taken part in victorious campaigns in Virginia, Georgia, and Tennessee. As diplomats the Modocs completely outclassed the commissioners who were sent to deal with them; yet these same Indians, in a burst of irresponsible violence, brought about their own ruin by treacherously murdering General Canby, the one man who might have solved their problems fairly and brought about a just peace settlement.

The memory of the stirring events of the winter and spring of 1872 and 1873 is preserved in a national monument where trails may be found leading to and through the chief battle areas. Here, too, is the simple tribute to Canby erected by a comrade-in-arms ten years after the General's death, still telling in silent eloquence of an almost forgotten catastrophe in the settling of the West.

II

PRELUDE TO HOSTILITIES

THE ENTIRE HISTORY of the bands of California Indians
known now as the Modocs is closely related to the geography and
topography of their hunting grounds. The center of their hunting
range and the scene of the Modoc Indian War was their defensive
stronghold located in the lava beds of the Tule Lake and Klamath
Lake basins. These flows were the result of tremendous volcanic
activity in the ages past. From time to time during the past several
thousands of years, eruptions of lava or pumice have covered most
of what is now northern California and southern Oregon. These
eruptions have, naturally, forced any human inhabitants to adapt
themselves to live with volcanic activity. The fact that the Modocs
were able to survive in the great lava flows along the south shore
of Tule Lake in 1872–73 causes one to believe that they and their
ancestors had done that sort of thing more than once before.

The reasons for the fanatical defense of their land and stronghold and their hostility to other Indian peoples or white emigrants
are intimately bound up with their tribal history, especially with the
history of their first contacts with Americans.

From the 1820's until after the Civil War, the contacts between
white men and the Modocs were intermittent, but they produced
a crisis in Modoc society that had to be resolved. White miners
crossed the Indian hunting range. White miners disturbed the
streams. White traders changed their economic way of life. White
settlers fenced the meadows along the lakes. White religious teach-

ers upset the traditional Modoc system of ethical behavior. By the time the different white groups had become well established, such a tight noose had been drawn around the Modocs that the Indians had to struggle for their cultural life. This was nothing strange to American history. Cherokee, Creek, Iroquois, Shawnee, and Mandan had all gone through the same experience. To the Modocs, however, it was something new, and something terrible, though Indians had been in the region for centuries.

Archaeologists tell us that the first inhabitants of the Klamath–Tule Lake basins came there between seventy-five hundred and nine thousand years ago. Remains of their dwelling sites have been found near Lower Klamath Lake. These Indians were not Modocs, but were only part of the tremendous migration of wandering hunters who populated North and South America thousands of years ago. New volcanic activity which produced the cinder cone of Schonchin Butte and the lava flow known during the Modoc War as "Black Ledge," probably put an end to human activity in the Lava Beds for many centuries. Much more recent settlements have been discovered, dating from about 2000 B.C., along the shores of Lower Klamath Lake. These, too, were probably abandoned about the time Columbus discovered America, for volcanic activity in the Medicine Lake highland would certainly have made living conditions almost impossible. One effect of these eruptions can still be seen immediately south of Tule Lake, for it produced the flow locally known as the Devil's Homestead.[1]

Not long after the end of the volcanic activity of the fifteenth century, the ancestors of the Modocs and Klamaths drifted into the Lakes district of southern Oregon and northern California. At first the Klamaths and Modocs were closely associated with each other, but about the time of the American Revolution, the Modocs separated from the Klamaths. Ethnologists find that villages which are distinctly Modoc began about 1780. For political purposes, the two groups of Indians worked together for another hundred years, but when white men first came into the Tule Lake Basin, the Modocs

[1] Robert J. Squier and Gordon L. Grosscup, "Preliminary Report of Archaeological Excavations in Lower Klamath Basin, California (1954)," U.S. Department of the Interior, National Park Service, typewritten report.

were clearly a separate group of people. Their numbers were not great. Reliable estimates claim that there were from four hundred to eight hundred of them before 1800, although one guess says there were several thousand.[2] The Modocs were spread over considerable territory, about 5,000 square miles of hunting range. They had at least twenty semipermanent villages, the farthest north of which was located on the present site of Klamath Falls. There was a village at Hot Creek (now Willow Creek) on the west, four along Lower Klamath Lake, four on Lost River, seven along the shores of Tule Lake, and three as far east as Sprague River. Most of these villages were very small. When the Modoc War began, the initial attack was made on two villages across the Lost River from each other, neither of which had more than half a dozen lodges. These villages, of more or less permanent dwellings, were used only in winter.

In the summer, the Modocs wandered from Goose Lake to Mount Shasta, a distance of roughly one hundred miles. They were hunters of deer, antelope, and mountain sheep. From bones found near their settlements we learn that they ate rabbits, marmots, and ground squirrels, all of which are plentiful in the area. They also gathered roots and seeds, which they made into a crude flour or used as a kind of cereal when mixed with water and boiled. Probably their most common food was the seed of the wocus, a species of pond lily. Ideally these were gathered at the time the seeds ripened and the pods cracked. Since this practice did not guarantee an adequate supply, the Modoc women usually gathered unripe pods and dried them, storing them until they were needed later in the year. While the pods were being ground and preserved, other Indians were catching fish to be dried and ground.

Before 1800, the Modocs had a Stone-age technology. They ground their food in mortars of basalt or rough lava. For hunting they used an extremely wide wooden bow sharply tapered at the ends with a narrowed center for a hand grip. Their weapon points were made of obsidian, readily available from Glass Mountain, a dozen miles south of the Lava Beds. Sometimes they carried a cross-hilted knife of this material. Some of their chopping or cutting

[2] William M. Turner, "Scraps of Modoc History," *Overland Monthly*, Vol. XI, No. 1 (July, 1873).

blades were made of fine-grained basalt, but their favorite material for these purposes was obsidian. What clothing they wore in aboriginal times was made from grass or tule fiber, or animal skin, decorated with shell beadwork or a belt of braided grass.[3] By midnineteenth century, they had adopted European styles of clothing, but they usually made their clothes themselves.

Before 1800, the permanent living quarters of the Modocs consisted of lodges known as wickiups which were set into shallow excavations from six inches to four feet deep, and about twelve to twenty feet in diameter. A framework of willow poles was then erected and overspread with tule matting. The whole was covered with earth, with a kind of stairway over the outside leading to a hole in the top which admitted the occupants who descended by a rawhide ladder attached to the center pole.[4] Somewhat later, when the coming of American authority cut down the raids from their enemies, they built a more solid structure with hewn or even squared timber, but still covered with tule mats and earth.[5] The appearance of these dwellings could be described as an "inverted bird's nest." These were the kinds of buildings in the camps of Captain Jack and Hooker Jim when the cavalry attacked them in 1872.

For transportation, the Modocs walked from place to place; on the rivers and lakes they used either crude log dugout canoes, or else "balsa" rafts made from bundles of tules tied at the ends and lashed firmly together.[6] The horse was not introduced among the Modocs until the end of the first quarter of the nineteenth century.

The Modocs probably did not have the remotest idea of the coming of the white fur traders and explorers, and if they did hear of them, they would have considered it no concern of theirs. Nevertheless, the trips of these white men profoundly affected the lives of most Indians in the Pacific Northwest, even those living many miles

[3] Rachel Applegate Good, *History of Klamath County, Oregon: Its Resources and Its People*, 32.

[4] Alfred B. Meacham, *Wigwam and War-path, or the Royal Chief in Chains*, 311; John Charles Frémont, *Memoirs of My Life*, 296ff.; Good, *Klamath County*, 10.

[5] Frederick S. Dellenbaugh, *The North Americans of Yesterday: A Comparative Study of North American Indian Life, Customs, and Products, on the Theory of the Ethnic Unity of the Race*, 215.

[6] Alpheus Hyatt Verrill, *Our Indians: The Story of the Indians of the United States*, 208.

from the seacoast or the Columbia. The expeditions of Mackenzie, Fraser, and Lewis and Clark brought in other traders and they, in turn, changed the system of barter and exchange of the Indians of the Great Basin. Within twenty years, white man's trade goods had spread through the whole region, creating new wants among the Indians.

The first direct contacts the Modocs had with traders occurred about 1825 or 1826 when a Hudson's Bay Company brigade from Fort Vancouver, under the leadership of Finan McDonald, made a trading sweep through parts of Idaho, Utah, Nevada, and Oregon. During the next fifteen years, other brigades directed by Peter Skene Ogden and John Work left Vancouver for California and Oregon trading points. These brigades must have made an imposing sight with their well-armed traders and their tremendous number of pack and saddle animals. The Modocs were not immediately affected by the traders because, before they could profit from such enterprise, they were almost destroyed by a natural disaster from which they recovered very slowly.

About 1830 there was an unusually severe winter in northern California. The food caches of the Modocs were lost beneath the deep drifts that formed in the lakes and river valleys. Severe storms kept the Indians in their lodges for days at a time, and at the same time obliterated landmarks which they used to find the location of their food supplies. Game animals could not be found. Weakened by cold and hunger, a heavy proportion of the Modocs died. The rest were saved only when a herd of antelope trying to cross Tule Lake on the ice, got too close inshore, broke through, and drowned directly in front of their village.[7]

They were still a weakened tribe of Indians when, in 1835, a party of French-Canadian trappers came into the Basin. The identity of these men is not known. They may have been connected with the Hudson's Bay Company, or they may have been free-lance traders. Once again they introduced the Modocs to European trade goods, and several of the Modocs were taken to the international and intertribal trading center of the Pacific Northwest, The Dalles

[7] Turner, "Scraps of Modoc History," *Overland Monthly*, Vol. XI, No. 1 (July, 1873).

of the Columbia. Here they beheld the wonders of an Indian economy which had been trading with the white men for almost a generation. Horses seemed particularly to have aroused their interest. Almost at once, horses became the symbol of wealth and prestige among the Modocs. Possession of these animals also greatly increased their mobility and aided their hunting during the usual summer wanderings.

The Modoc Indians did not have any acceptable commodity for trade at The Dalles with the "horse Indians" living north of the Columbia and in the Snake River Valley. Since they were not a fur-gathering people, the Modocs had no animal skins to trade. Quickly, however, they learned that the Indians to the north were willing to trade horses or trinkets for slaves. Northern Indians would pay a particularly high price for girl slaves, whom they might use for concubines or employ gainfully as prostitutes.

It was during the next ten years that the Modocs acquired their reputation as fearsome and merciless raiders, preying on their neighbors for stock or captives. Most of the slave raids seem to have been made at the expense of the Pit River or the Shasta tribes, although occasionally the Modocs would raid the Paiutes or the upland Takelma.[8]

The only direct account of such a raid came from a survivor among the Shastas who hid during the affair. As a child he witnessed a sudden, vicious Modoc attack. The adults of his own village had gone into a sweathouse near their rock-shelter dwelling when the Modocs struck. The children of the village were unharmed, but their parents were ruthlessly slaughtered as they dashed out of their bath. The youngsters and young women were seized, tied to the backs of horses, and taken north.[9] The male children brought a price of about one pony each. Small girls commanded a somewhat higher price, while adolescent girls or mature young women could be traded for as much as five ponies, depending on their personal attractiveness.[10]

---

[8] Philleo Nash, "The Place of Religious Revivalism in the Formation of the Intercultural Community on Klamath Reservation," in *Social Anthropology of North American Tribes* (Fred Eggan, ed.), 381.

[9] Rufus Steele, "The Cave of Captain Jack, "*Sunset*, Vol. XXX, No. 5, (May, 1913), 566.

The Modocs seldom went to The Dalles themselves. They traded their captives to middlemen, such as the Klamaths or the Warm Springs Indians. Every few months during the trading season, which usually started in April, the Modocs and Klamaths would meet near Yainax Butte for a "fair" where captive girls could be traded for horses. The occasion was a social one; gambling and horse racing went on day and night, and sometimes marriage alliances might be contracted during the celebrations.[11]

Before these trading operations and raiding expeditions began, the most important man among the Basin Indians might be the shaman, a combination of priest and doctor. These were commonly older men, whose prestige and experience were so great that they stayed at home while the younger men raided, traded, and traveled.

When the coming of the white men changed the trading habits of the Basin Indians, the prestige of these shamans was undermined. The younger men who had always deferred to their elders were the ones who visited The Dalles, learned the Chinook jargon, and brought home new styles in clothing. Suddenly their prestige, in a prestige-conscious culture, became greater than that of the old shamans. When the whites came to sign treaties and recognize "chiefs," they would take the younger men, whom they knew, while the practitioners of magic who had held much of the real power before were now either ignored or actively opposed.

The Modocs were more slowly affected by the new value system than were the Klamath and Warm Springs Indians. Fewer of their young men went to The Dalles than those of their neighbors to the north. Accordingly, the shamans among the Modocs remained powerful longer than they did among the Klamaths.

Direct contact between the Americans and the Modocs did not come through trade. The first American known to have come through the Great Basin was John Charles Frémont, who visited northern California and southern Oregon in December of 1843 as the commander of an exploring expedition. His first meeting with

[10] Albert Samuel Gatschet, *The Klamath Indians of Southwestern Oregon,* lix–lx.

[11] Samuel A. Clarke, "Klamath Land," *Overland Monthly,* Vol. XI, No. 6 (December, 1873), 550.

the Klamath-Modoc was uneventful.[12] This was not the case, however, on his second expedition three years later.

In the spring of 1846, Frémont was in California as an official explorer for the United States government. In March, he was ordered out of Spanish territory by General Castro, the military commander at Monterey. For three tense days Frémont toyed with the idea of defying Castro with his tiny army, then changed his mind, quietly pulled out of his fortified camp, and moved slowly up the Sacramento and Pit River valleys. Castro was happy to see him go and permitted Frémont complete freedom of movement in northern California.

When Frémont had gone as far as he cared to up the Pit River (then known as the east fork of the Sacramento), he moved across to Clear Lake and then down to Tule Lake, which he reached on May 1. Later in May, his party traveled up the Lost River toward Klamath Lake, and while he was watched closely by the Modocs, he was not attacked. He camped finally in the Klamath marshes, north of the lakes.

While Frémont was camped here, Lieutenant Archibald Gillespie of the United States Marine Corps arrived in Monterey. Officially Gillespie was a messenger of the government of the United States; unofficially he was a bearer of private messages from the expansionist senator from Missouri, Thomas Hart Benton, to his son-in-law, Frémont. Gillespie hired the famous Peter Lassen as a guide, and the two started north to deliver Benton's message to Frémont. The two Americans presented no threat to the Modocs, but their horses tempted the Indians who tried to steal the animals. Lassen and Gillespie escaped, however, with both their lives and animals. They reached Frémont and delivered the message that was to turn him south toward fame and the conquest of California.

The very night Gillespie arrived, Frémont's small camp, consisting of three white members of his expedition, himself, the two messengers, and five Indian guides, were attacked by Klamaths and three of the party were killed. Another was so badly wounded that he died shortly afterward. The dead were buried; and the horses—the prime objects of the raid—were driven back and forth over their

[12] Frémont, *Memoirs*, 296–99.

graves to prevent the Indians from digging up the bodies and muti-
lating them as trophies of their attack.[13]

When the tough little mountain man, Kit Carson, rejoined the
main group of Frémont's party, he returned with fifteen men and
made a retaliatory raid on the village beside Klamath Lake. The surprised Indians fled, and Carson burned their town, rejoining Frémont before he marched south.

Carson's raid alerted Indians throughout the entire Klamath
country. The Modocs were as fearful of whites after Frémont left
as the Klamaths were. Americans planning to begin regular trips
across Modoc lands were, unknown to the Indians, even then leaving
the Willamette Valley for northeastern California.

These Americans came because it was highly desirable to find a
shorter and easier route from Fort Hall to Oregon than the difficult
and hazardous one along the Oregon Trail through the Blue Mountains and the Columbia Gorge. Almost invariably the weary wagon
trains would arrive at this part of the road late in the summer with
their equipment worn and their animals weakened by the long,
2,000-mile trail behind them. If a more level route could be found,
hundreds of wagons would use it. The thing a southern route needed
most was a good supply of water and forage along the way between
the Humboldt River and Goose Lake. This gap was largely unex-
plored. The Willamette settlers chose for the leaders of the exploring party Lindsay and Jesse Applegate, who had crossed the plains
over the northern Oregon Trail three years before. The expedition
consisted of fifteen men, who left Dallas, Oregon, on June 20. They
worked their way down the Willamette and crossed the divide into
the Rogue River Valley without trouble from the Indians there.
From the Rogue, they crossed through the Cascade Mountains, and
reached Lower Klamath Lake on July 4.

Now in Modoc country, the Applegate party noticed Modoc
signal fires as far as they could see. They did not know why their
presence disturbed the Indians. They found pieces of newspaper at
a campsite, and they surmised by the litter they found that white
men had been there not too long before. The Applegates said that

[13] *Ibid.*, 480–96; Harry L. Wells, "Frémont and the Modocs," *The West Shore*,
Vol. X, No. 3 (March, 1884), 79.

they also found evidence of horses having been driven back and forth over the campsite. Later, when they heard of Frémont's trouble with the Klamaths, they assumed that their party had been camped at the same place as Frémont's battle, though probably they had not; for Applegate's men were in California, while Frémont's fight had been at Rock Creek, near Upper Klamath Lake.

Two days later, the Applegate surveying party reached Tule Lake by way of the high ridge separating Klamath Lake from the Tule Lake Basin. One member who was hunting for fresh meat became separated from the main party, and rode into the Lava Beds. His presence further alarmed the Modocs, who were convinced that the whites were going to attack them. To the astonishment of the Applegates, the Modocs put their families and movable possessions into canoes and paddled furiously for their island refuge north of Scorpion Point. Doubtless the Modocs were vastly relieved when the Oregonians turned northwest, looking for a crossing point where they could ford the Lost River.

A few miles from Tule Lake they met an Indian, who, though frightened by the white men, was persuaded to show them a crossing point. He indicated that the Stone Bridge, about four miles upstream from the point where the river flowed into the lake, was the usual ford. This amazing formation was a ledge of lava which acted as a natural bridge. Water flowed under and over it to the depth of about eighteen inches, but the bridge was wide enough to accommodate a wagon or to support easily a man on horseback. For several years this was the main crossing point for the white man's emigrant trains. By the time of the Modoc War it was no longer in use, for the depth of water gradually increased over the years.

On July 8. Applegate's men reached Goose Lake and passed out of Modoc country, but the result of their work was to affect profoundly the future of the Indians of the Great Basin, for it brought emigrants directly to Modoc country. Actually, the use of the South Emigrant Road was a disappointment to its sponsors. While it was given considerable use, most cross-country travelers still continued to use the northern route, for it was much better known.

The Applegates arrived at Fort Hall in time to convince a band of emigrants from Missouri that they should try the new route.

Several members of the Applegate exploring party acted as guides from Fort Hall to the Willamette.[14] These wagons crossed the Modoc summer range and frightened away the game upon which the Indians depended for subsistence. The Modocs were not a people to accept this intrusion without retaliation. They attacked the next wagon trains and tried to run off the horses or cattle as opportunity permitted.

It is impossible to state accurately how much damage was done to the trains. Since the Modocs did more damage than any of the other northern California Indians, legend later ascribed many killings to them that never took place. Claims of damage were often based on the wildest of rumors. Killings to the number of 350 were laid at the door of the Modocs, but this number included people killed well outside of Modoc territory—along the coast, in the Umpqua and Rogue River valleys, at the head of the Deschutes, and even on the Columbia. Frontier literature was filled with accounts of Indian atrocities. Tales were told and widely believed that men had been killed and mutilated, that children had their heads struck against a rock or had been carried into captivity, and that maidens had been ravished and then burned at the stake over sagebrush fires by cruel captors. The legends ran the gamut of the popular "down-with-the-redskin-varmint" tradition. In the minds of the frontiersmen, the Modocs were the worst of all Indians for depravity.

An anonymous sick emigrant was supposed to have been killed "in Modoc country" in the fall of 1846, and twenty-four men were said to have been killed between Goose Lake and Tule Lake in 1847. It is impossible to know how many deaths actually took place.

Between 1847 and 1849, the Modocs gave emigrant trains little trouble because in the fall of 1847 contact with the whites brought one of its usual results: smallpox struck the Great Basin Indians, and many Modocs were included among the victims. It is impossible to describe the effect of such a calamity on a culture. Western European civilization has known of no epidemic that killed more than a

[14] Lindsay Applegate 'Notes and Reminiscences of Laying Out and Establishing the Old Emigrant Road into Southern Oregon in the Yead 1846," *Oregon Historical Quarterly*, Vol. XXII, No. 1 (March, 1921); Hubert Howe Bancroft, *History of Oregon*, I (1834-48) (vol. XXIV of *History of the Pacific States of North America*), 546; Frances Fuller Victor, *The Early Indian Wars of Oregon*, 87.

quarter of all people since the Black Death of the fourteenth century. We do not know how many Modocs died, but other peoples to the north lost from 25 to 50 per cent of their inhabitants, and some bands in the Columbia Valley were wiped out entirely. The heaviest mortality fell on the sick, the very young, and the old people. The elders of the village had always been the leaders, and now they were dead. A catastrophe of this kind, coupled with the arrival of the more advanced civilization of the white settlers, almost completely changed the culture patterns of the Modocs. Hereafter, the young Indian men preyed upon the wagon trains about as any group of bandits might, since they lacked much of the capacity to survive in the old ways.

While the epidemic raged, naturally the South Emigrant Road was open and safe.[15] Throughout the next year, the Modocs kept away from their Indian enemies and the white men's wagon trains. After two years, however, the Modocs recovered enough to raid those who were using the trail. A government report issued several years later asserts that eighteen whites were killed in 1849 as notification that the Modocs were back in business.[16] These were killed at a place that came to be known as "Bloody Point." Here the Emigrant Road first touched Tule Lake after its long descent from the highlands around Clear Lake. After the road left Clear Lake, it wound across a high, rocky, wooded plateau, then passed just north of Horse Mountain, turning north through what are now grain fields. Between two rim rocks the road next crossed a bench which appears to have once been the bottom of the lake before some geological upheaval elevated the shore thirty or forty feet above the lake level of the 1850's. It then turned down a hill to the lake. Since the water was frequently reached at the end of a hard, dry day, it became customary for the travelers to camp off the road at the edge of the lake. From the bench, there is about a quarter of a mile of gradually descending country, and the lava outcropping grows correspondingly higher. Huge boulders have sloughed away from the cliff formed by the rising land, and in these boulders within a hundred yards of the old lake, the Indians would conceal themselves. Many attacks were made here, until emigrants grew wary and camped farther to the west where they could see their enemies if they were going to be attacked. There was no legend about Bloody Point. It was all too true, and except for some confusion about its exact location and the number of people killed there, it is probably the grimmest spot in the history of emigrant travel along the southern route.

There is a legend of a massacre in Fandango Pass, east of Goose Lake, which may be related to the 1849 killings. The story is told that a party of emigrants, possibly of Mexican ancestry, stopped here to celebrate their successful crossing of the Nevada desert. The Indians are said to have killed every one of the emigrants on the first evening after they crossed Surprise Valley. Their identity remains a mystery, however, and there is no proof that there ever was either a Mexican emigrant train or a massacre; but the name of Fandango Pass is still used to describe the route they were supposed to have followed.

When gold hunters began to use the Emigrant Roads, the Indian's fate was sealed. In 1849, thousands of emigrants crossed the plains to reach the placer deposits in the little river valleys that ran from the Sierras into the Sacramento and the San Joaquin. Most of these gold seekers entered California farther south than Fandango Pass and Bloody Point, giving very little disturbance to the Modocs. There is no report of trouble in 1850.

By 1851 every stone was almost literally turned over in the search for gold. Some of the prospectors entered the valleys of the Klamath and Shasta rivers. In March of 1851, Abraham Thompson (who had come north to check on a rumor that John Scott had found gold on Scotts River) found gold on Greenhorn Creek near the present town of Yreka. Immediately, several thousand miners rushed there and staked claims near Shasta Butte City and along the Shasta River. By summer, the miners needed forage for their stock, and some began to cut their hay on land which the Modocs claimed. There was trouble at once from both the Modocs and the Shastas who were their neighbors immediately to the west.

In the late summer of 1851, the Modocs or Pit Rivers (some even say the Paiutes) raided a pack train headed for the gold fields and ran off with forty-six mules and horses. It makes little difference who organized the raid. The Modocs eventually got the horses, and a searching party discovered that the whites would need reinforcements to get them back. Under the urging of the owner of the stock, one Augustus Meamber, a small force of some twenty men were organized in Yreka to teach the Indians respect for white man's property.[17]

One member of this vigilante party became the nemesis of the Modocs, and they remembered him for generations. He was a young man who had arrived in Yreka only a few weeks before; a well-known mountain man and Indian fighter named Ben Wright. This man's career, while brief, was so spectacular that almost twenty years after his death his actions both on this campaign and during the next year were claimed by the Modocs to be a major cause for their fight against the whites.

Wright was born in Indiana twenty-three years before his arrival in Yreka. His parents were religious people; one source says they were Quakers, another says he was the eldest son of a Presbyterian minister.[18] When he was eighteen his mother died, and he left home. A fight with his first employer caused him to go to Leavenworth, Kansas, where he joined a wagon train headed for the Willamette Valley. On the way west, the train was attacked, and the young daughter of the wagon captain lost her life. Perhaps this Indian attack transformed Wright into an Indian-hater. More probably he was only another of those restless young spirits that acted as the cutting edge of the frontier movement. He could have become an outlaw as some did and gone down in history as California's Billy the Kid. He chose, instead, to stay on the proper side of the law, but he was himself lawless, reckless, and violent. Many such men were in the mining camps of the early 1850's.

When Wright arrived in Oregon City in the fall of 1847, the Cayuse War was just beginning, to revenge the murder of Dr. Marcus Whitman and his wife. Wright enlisted and got his baptism of fire in this campaign. When the war ended, he found that farming

[17] Harry L. Wells, "The Modocs in 1851," *The West Shore*, Vol. X, No. 5 (May, 1884), 132–33.

[18] Don C. Fisher, "Ben Wright," unpublished typewritten MS, Lava Beds National Monument, Tulelake, California.

did not suit his fancy, and for the next four years he hunted beaver and Indians. Like all of his kind he became more Indian than the Indians themselves. He let his naturally curly hair grow long—Indian style. In his fights with the Indians he copied the deeds of his enemies and mutilated the bodies of his victims. He took scalps (which custom, of course, had been introduced among the western Indians by such white men as he). He boasted of the fingers and noses he had cut from the bodies of dead and wounded Indians. His reputation grew as time went on, and by the time he was twenty-three, he was the acknowledged champion Indian fighter in northern California.

His arrival in Yreka when the expedition to recover stock was leaving seemed almost providential. He was offered the leadership of the party, but he refused on account of his youth and his recent arrival in town. Nevertheless, he went along, and as a result of his advice, the whites won a decisive victory over the Indians.

The hunt for the stock led the Yreka men across the natural bridge on Lost River to the east side of Tule Lake. They passed a Modoc village and rode carelessly on as though they had nothing in mind except a horseback ride. They made a noisy and ostentatious camp a few miles beyond the Modoc village, and pretended to settle down for sleep. During the night, however, fifteen of the men under Wright's leadership, sneaked back to the Modoc camp and at first light attacked it.

The attack was a complete surprise. The Modoc women and children were captured at once, and the men who were not captured were chased from the village into the marsh and Tule swamp between the village and the edge of the water. Several Indians were killed, and the rest gave up. They surrendered the stock—or some stock—which satisfied the white men, and Wright and his posse rode back to Yreka in triumph. No further trouble came from the Modocs that winter.

In the Shasta valley the next May, a miner named Calvin Woodman was killed. A band of hemp-happy white men from Yreka promptly hanged an Indian named Scarfaced Charley—a Shasta—though actually he was himself looking for the murderers when the whites met him. Their ghastly error did not prevent the Yreka men from continuing the search, and two other Indians were eventually found who seemed responsible for the killing. One was hanged; the other, surprisingly enough, was able to establish his innocence, and the whites released him.

As the search party which had punished Woodman's murderer returned, one of them, John Ornsby, received a letter from his uncle, who was with a party coming to Yreka by way of the South Emigrant Road. The miners of Yreka knew how much in need of supplies they would be after the long trip, and they raised supplies to aid these newcomers in reaching the mining fields. A small band under Charles McDermit went out to convoy the train through the dangerous Modoc country. The group they were looking for had already passed the Lost River Bridge when McDermit reached them, so this train was in no danger. Its captain reported to McDermit that they had been "annoyed" by the Modocs, but no harm had been done, and also that they knew of several other trains and pack columns that were behind them. McDermit's men decided to go as far east as Goose Lake to warn the others to be on guard when they passed Bloody Point. Within a few miles, the Yreka men met a small band of packers and warned them of possible danger ahead. The packers scoffed at the warning and were attacked at Bloody Point. All but one packer, known as Coffin, were killed. He escaped only by cutting the pack from the animal he was hobbling, jumping on its back and dashing toward the attacking Indians; they were so surprised by his maneuver that he broke through the encirclement before they knew what he was trying to do. He rode into Yreka, and Ben Wright promptly raised a party to reinforce McDermit. If there was going to be trouble in the Modoc country that summer, Wright wanted to be in on it.

Meanwhile, three of McDermit's men, Coats, John Ornsby, and James Long, rode back to see how the packers were faring. The Modocs saw them coming and ambushed these three, killing them all. McDermit's depleted force did not know that the Modocs were in a killing mood when they started back for Yreka.

At Bloody Point, McDermit's party found the Modocs attacking another wagon train which was defending itself under the command of Trail Captain Morrison. McDermit's warning had reached Morrison's party before the Modocs arrived. The Indians faced a corral of wagons when they fired from the rocks and the tules along the lake shore. Although temporarily frustrated, the Indians settled down for a siege, for they thought it was only a matter of time until the emigrants ran out of water or ammunition; and the Modocs could be patient.

To hurry matters along, the Indians set fire to the grass surrounding the six wagons. As soon as he saw the fight, McDermit hurried to the rescue, but he was not strong enough to drive the Modocs away. All he could do was to join those in the corral. The whites saw horsemen approaching in the distance and feared they were Modoc reinforcements, for wagon trains did not travel from west to east. One can imagine Morrison's and McDermit's delight when they discovered the horsemen to be Ben Wright and his rescue party from Yreka. When the miners arrived, the Indians fled, though Wright was able to kill some Modocs before they could escape. When the emigrants arrived at their destination, their gratitude was fervent, and their praises of Wright were loud.

News of the fighting went, also, to the gold camps springing up in the Rogue River Valley of Oregon. If the Modocs were attacking and killing emigrants, they were certain to raid the unsuspecting wagon trains known to be on their way to Jacksonville over the South Emigrant Road. The miners there immediately outfitted an escort party under the leadership of John E. Ross to get the emigrants through. Ross was a huge man physically, and his very appearance inspired confidence in his judgment. His force arrived only a few days after that of Wright and the Californians. Together they scoured the country and were horrified at what they found.[19]

Apparently there had been other wagon trains before McDermit's little escort force left Yreka. In the area of Bloody Point a number of bodies and the remains of burned wagons were discovered. How many lost their lives in these Modoc attacks will never be known. When Tule Lake was drained in the 1930's, however, a number of charred wagons were found during the digging of the drainage ditch around Bloody Point, and from time to time a part of a human skeleton is still found there.

[19] John E. Ross, "Narrative of an Indian Fighter," Jacksonville (Oregon), 1878, MS in Bancroft Library.

It is commonly believed that there was a particularly terrible massacre at Bloody Point in late August or early September, 1852. A description of the alleged massacre, however, makes it clear that actually it referred to a composite of many attacks and killings. Further, Wright and Ross were in the area during most of both months and did not report such a massacre, but they did report dead emigrant victims of Modoc raids. They buried their bodies where they found them.

Wright claims to have discovered twenty-two bodies of those slain by Indians that summer. Ross reports that his men buried fourteen. Some of these reported burials probably were duplications, for the two parties were working together. Accounts have varied. Some say the Modocs killed thirty-three, others thirty-six, and some lurid accounts have put the number as high as seventy.[20]

The condition of one body infuriated the whites. It was that of a young woman[21] who had been chased almost a mile and a half from the point of attack. Whether she had almost succeeded in escaping along the road to the west or whether the Indians played a sadistic cat-and-mouse game with her will, of course, never be known. When they finally tired of chasing her, they closed in, overpowered her, cut her throat, stripped the clothes from her body, and mutilated it shockingly.[22]

Many of the angry men in the rescue force were, like Wright, in their early twenties. Women of any description were exceedingly scarce in the mining camps, and "good" women of marriageable age were almost nonexistent. To find one brutally killed by Indians made them act as if they were a group of thirsty desert travelers who found someone wantonly throwing away their water supply. By fair means or foul, Wright's men were determined to punish the

[20] Pacific MSS, "Statement of Inhabitants of Southern Oregon and in Northern California in Regard to the Character and Conduct of the Modoc Indians. Also a Statement of General Joel Palmer on the Same Subject While He Was Superintendent of Indian Affairs in Oregon," Statement by W. S. Kershan, 48, Bancroft Library; Hon. John H. Mitchell, *Indian Depredations in Oregon*, 19; Meacham, *Wigwam and War-path*, 296; *Report of the Commissioner of Indian Affairs, 1863*, 58.

[21] *Report of the Commissioner of Indian Affairs, 1863*, 58.

[22] Colonel William Thompson, *Reminiscences of a Pioneer*, 77; William S. Brown, "The Other Side of the Story," *Overland Monthly*, Vol. LXXXII, No. 4 (April, 1924).

Modocs and to recover the property which had been taken from the wagon trains before the wagons were burned.

Wright and fifteen men remained on the "peninsula" below Bloody Point for almost two months trying to induce the Indians to give up the things they had taken from the emigrants. They also hoped that they would have an opportunity to attack the Indians. The Modocs were quite aware of Wright's intentions, however, and refused either to give up the property or to give him a chance to kill them.

The presence of the white men prevented any further attacks on wagon trains during the fall of 1852, and by the end of October it was clear that all emigration for the year was at an end. One by one, Wright's men drifted away, and although replacements came out from time to time, it was unmistakably clear that Wright would have no men left by spring. Wright did not want to return to Yreka without avenging the murdered emigrants and recovering the property. As time went on, the Indians began moving into their permanent winter villages, and their number increased relative to Wright's small force. The dread the Indians felt for the whites turned to contempt, and they became increasingly insolent.

One Indian, in a burst of bravado, revealed that two white girls in their very early teens were held captive by a band of Modocs in the Willow Creek valley, about thirty miles west of Wright's camp. The Indians seized them during a raid on a train south of Lower Klamath Lake. No one knows for certain who they were, but they have been identified by some as the daughters of a murdered emigrant named Reed.[23] When Wright heard about them, he promptly added the return of the children to his list of demands on the Indians.

In early November, Wright's party at the peninsula camp ran short of supplies. Four men were sent to Yreka for food and ammunition. They arrived just before election day, however, and thought it would do no harm to vote for Pierce and get drunk. They must have had a monumental spree, for they were many days in returning. For six days Wright's men were almost out of food. The white men were preparing to kill their horses when the supplies came in.

[23] James Michael Allen, *Wi-ne-ma.*

25

When the food arrived, Wright invited the Indians to a feast. The main body of Modocs refused to come, for they were suspicious of his motives. One story is that they had heard that one of Wright's men had gone to the local doctor while in Yreka and asked for strychnine to poison the Modocs. Whether this demand was the raving of a drunken man or whether Wright actually told him to buy poison is one of the most controversial points of the history of the relations between the whites and the Modocs. In any event no strychnine was actually sold to Wright's representative.[24] During the Modoc War the apologists for the Indians repeated this legend constantly. In later years, Wright's men quite freely admitted that they planned treachery, but they insisted they intended to shoot the Indians, not to poison them. By their code of ethics, poison would have been unsportsmanlike.

Only two Indians accepted the invitation, and since the whites wanted more victims, these two were fed, given presents, and allowed to leave. Forty more Indians came closer with great caution, but never did all of the Modocs come in to Wright's camp at the same time.

The white leader then moved his camp west to the Lost River Bridge. By this time it was past mid-November, and he knew he had to bring matters to a conclusion at once or give up his scheme for that year. Fenning, one of Wright's men, had taken an Indian woman for a mistress while he was camped in the Tule Lake Basin, and she told her man that the Indians were going to "jump" the white men's camp in the next day or two.[25] This was possible, for the population of the Modoc camp had been growing steadily, and the men in it now outnumbered Wright's party almost three to one.

Wright decided to wait no longer. He told his friends that he was going into the Indian village by himself and would settle things once and for all.

The Indian encampment was on a low bench just above the river. Directly behind it was a bluff rising perhaps another twenty feet. During the night, Wright put ten of his men on the high bank over-

[24] Nash, *Revivalism*, 383; Meacham, *Wigwam and War-path*, 298; Harry L. Wells, "The Ben Wright Massacre," *The West Shore*, Vol. X, No. 10 (October, 1884), 314ff.
[25] Yreka *Union* (April 26, 1873).

looking the Indian camp and six more across the river, which at this point was about sixty feet wide. Early in the morning, Wright walked boldly into the camp of the Indians, who were drying meat for their winter food supply. They scowled at him, but made no move to harm him. Wright was dressed in his ordinary clothes with his head sticking through a hole in a blanket which he was using as a crude overcoat. The blanket also served to conceal a pistol he held in his hand.

He had told his men that he was going to make one last demand for the property taken from the emigrants. He would also demand the return of the captives. If he was refused, he would shoot the Modoc leader. Thereafter, he would immediately throw himself flat on the ground while his concealed followers were to open fire to cover him so that he could scramble away.

Since Old Schonchin, the headman, was absent, Wright went to the man who was next most important and made his demand. When he was curtly refused, Wright fired twice through the blanket; the Indian fell dead, and the white men on the banks opened fire as their leader withdrew from the Indian camp. The Modocs were in a panic; some tried to seize their bows, but many just ran. They were hunted ruthlessly. Some fled into the water and were shot down when they came up for air. Others in the sagebrush were rounded up and destroyed as soon as they were found. The Indians said later that only five of the forty-six Modocs in the village escaped Wright. One of these, however, was Schonchin John, brother of the chief, and during the Modoc War, second in command to Captain Jack.

The white men scalped their dead enemies, mutilated their bodies as the Indians had those of the emigrants, and returned to Yreka, dirty, shaggy, brown, and noisy, waving the scalps as they came. Wright was a hero. The miners took a week off, and for seven days the town staged a wild carousal. The drunken fights grew so fierce and so much furniture was broken that the cooler and soberer citizens began to restore order. Little by little the celebration let up. The volunteer company was discharged on November 29.[26]

[26] Brown, "The Other Side of the Story," *Overland Monthly*, Vol. LXXXII, No. 4 (April, 1924), 157; John B. Horner, *Oregon: Her History, Her Great Men, Her Literature*, 185–88; Pacific MSS, Statement by W. S. Kershan, Bancroft Library; Meacham, *Wigwam and War-path*, 300; Thompson, *Reminiscences*, 78–81.

The triumph of the Americans, however, caused bitter resentment among the Modocs. They never forgave, and they did not forget.

Wright really gained very little from the affair except the fear and hatred of the Indians in the whole Shasta and Siskiyou country. No property was returned. The captive girls remained in the possession of the Modocs. When the girls grew up, they became a lucrative source of income for their captors, who made them prostitutes in the Modoc camps. Business was so profitable that the older girl was killed when two men quarreled over ownership of her. One of them in a burst of fury cut her throat and threw her body over a cliff, where its remains were found in 1873, by one of the Oregon volunteers who had been told of its whereabouts by a Modoc. What happened to the younger girl is not known. Modoc women said later that she, too, had been thrown off a cliff above Cottonwood Creek by the jealous Indian women because she had become too popular with their men. There is no way of proving this, and the story may well have been one of the lurid rumors started by Indian-haters who used it to justify their demands for total extermination of the Modocs during the war.

In the summer of 1852, while Wright was killing Modocs in the mountains, gold was discovered on the ocean beaches of southern Oregon. Shortly afterward, coal was discovered near Marshfield.[27] Once again there was a swift population increase of unattached, violent, and irresponsible young males, eager to make a fortune. In a matter of months, their prospecting on Indian lands succeeded in stirring up the Umpqua and Rogue River tribes to the point that the possibility of an Indian war could not be disregarded.

Inevitably, a white prospector was found murdered. Because it was generally assumed that he had been shot by an Indian, a retaliatory raid was made on the Rogues. There were never any formal declarations of war, or even of intent to fight. The first warning the Indians got was the sound of the shot from the gun of an irate white man. The Americans rationalized their methods by pointing out that this was also the way that the Indians killed whites. It is doubtful whether a higher standard of morality should have been expected of

[27] Bancroft, *History of Oregon*, II 329–42.

whites who had practically "gone native" than of the natives themselves. In any event, attacks on Indians far removed from western Oregon spread the trouble through the Shasta country to the edge of Modoc lands.

When a white man was killed near Scott's Bar, west of Yreka, Ben Wright, who was living with a Shasta woman at the time, came to Yreka with a group of Shasta Indians to help find the killer. They were joined by Elisha Steele, a Yreka lawyer, who had come to the gold fields from New York by way of Wisconsin in 1850. His mining ventures had been unsuccessful, and his store-keeping operations also failed. When he returned to his practice of law, however, he found his professional services in demand, and he remained as lawyer, judge, and state political leader until his death. He was not popular in Oregon, nevertheless, for he had taken a leading part in trying to carve out a territory from northern California and southern Oregon. The Oregonians felt that such a move would delay their own statehood.[28] Steele and Wright were successful in finding the murderers, who were given a fair trial rather than a lynching. The Shasta Indians learned to respect and trust Steele; they even permitted him to talk them out of further depredations, and he persuaded them to move to Fort Jones, southwest of Yreka, in custody of the army during the Rogue River war. It was not long before other Indians were also turning to him for advice. On the other hand, while they understood Wright well enough, they did not trust him.

The troubles during 1852 and 1853 that broke out into full-scale warfare in 1854 in the Siskiyou Mountains and coasts of Southern Oregon pushed freight rates to Jacksonville and Yreka so high that prices became almost prohibitive. Freighters flatly refused to go through hostile Indian country unless they were well paid for the risk.[29] A clamor arose to force them to give up their free-ranging habits and to concentrate all Indians where they would give no further trouble and could be kept under the watchful eye of the army.

[28] John Golden, "Political Factions Among Three North American Indian Tribes; The Hopi; Klamath-Modoc; and Fox," typewritten MS, University of Chicago, 1951.

[29] Letter, Joel E. Palmer to B. F. Dowell, Salem (Oregon), December 17, 1857, Palmer Statement, Pacific MSS, Bancroft Library.

It was assumed that a few plowing lessons would change the Indians from hunters and root gatherers to farmers.

The army's part in the Rogue River War was conducted by the old Mexican War veteran, General Wool, in charge of the military division of the Pacific, who was extremely unsympathetic with the views of the settlers. In his opinion there would be no Indian troubles if the whites would leave the Indians alone. His belief was probably true, but it was also unrealistic in view of the usual impact of gold fever on the ethical values of white men. The army was not sympathetic towards the miners, and General Wool and Colonel George Wright, in charge of military activities in the Northwest, agreed that it was the Indians who needed protection and not the whites.[30]

The settlers were furious at the army's attitude. Accordingly, a soldier guarding a group of Indians accused of murdering a white man was himself killed by settlers. In retaliation, other soldiers opened fire on the whites and killed three settlers. Feeling was so strong that any wandering Indian was liable to be shot at sight, and many Indians voluntarily gathered under the protection of the army, who established a daily roll-call to make sure that no Indian was out where he could get into trouble.

In January, 1854, the trouble spread as far east as Lower Klamath Lake, and there was fear that the Modocs might join the fighting. That month four men were killed on the Emigrant Road, and in June a pack train in the Siskiyous was attacked by Rogues. One man was killed in this raid and the ammunition in the train was captured by the Indians. The frontier was beginning to panic. Obviously something had to be done.

The Interior Department did not agree with the War Department's view of the war. It turned to the one man whom they knew both Rogues and Modocs feared. Joel Palmer, Indian superintendent for Oregon, appointed Ben Wright to the position of Indian agent in charge of all tribes south of Coos Bay. To these Indians, his appointment was tantamount to a declaration of an extermination policy. To his credit, however, it should be said that Wright apparently tried to quiet things down and to prevent further raids either by whites or Indians. On several occasions he was able to settle

[30] Bancroft, *History of Oregon*, II, 344.

Indian troubles simply by threatening to arrest those responsible for disorder.

Had he been a more temperate man in his behavior or habits, Wright might have made a real contribution to the development of southern Oregon and northern California. Unfortunately, he was extremely intemperate. He was drinking very heavily by this time, and with him drink was a prelude to violence. Even the hard-bitten miners of Port Orford were scandalized when one night the drunken Wright compelled the government interpreter, an Indian woman named Chetcoe Jennie, to strip herself naked while he whipped her through the streets of the little town.[31]

Jennie was furious and plotted vengeance. There were plenty of Indians who were willing to co-operate with her in getting rid of Wright, including a former guide from the Frémont expedition named Enos. Enos was now working for Wright. On February 25, 1856, a dance was held at Whaleshead at the mouth of the Rogue River. A group of Oregonians had imported a number of Indian and half-blood girls for partners, and a considerable body of jealous Indians gathered across the river. Wright heard that trouble was brewing and went there to keep order. When he arrived, he was told that Enos was inciting the Indians to violence, and at once Wright crossed the river in company with a citizen named Poland. Both white men were promptly seized and killed. It was claimed that after Wright had been mutilated, his heart was cut from his body, and that Jennie ate part of it in revenge for his treatment of her.

Wright's death was the signal for an attempt to slaughter any American that could be caught, and several were. Palmer, who was superintendent for all Indians in Oregon, appealed to General Wool for military help in removing any peaceful Indians from the Rogue Valley so that the settlers could be more efficient in exterminating the hostile ones. Wool responded with a violent letter denouncing the whole affair. To Palmer, he wrote: "The future will prove that this war has been forced upon those Indians against their will, and that, too, by a set of reckless vagabonds, for pecuniary and political objects, and sanctioned by a numerous population who regard the treasury of the United States a legitimate subject of plunder."[32]

[31] Pacific MSS, Statement by Rev. Josiah L. Parrish, Bancroft Library, 82.
[32] Bancroft, *Oregon*, II 395–97.

The trouble continued for another year while volunteer armies from both California and Oregon marched and countermarched through the Rogue and Klamath valleys. In the summer of 1856, a band of Californians attacked the Modocs on Tule Lake for good measure.

By April of 1857 the war was over. The murderer of Wright was captured and, on April 12, hanged. Enos, who had helped engineer the affair, was lynched at Battle Rock. What happened to Jennie is not known. The sullen and beaten Rogues were forced to live on the Siletz Reservation, where their confinement brought about a heavy mortality.

Emigration along the South Emigrant Road stopped completely in 1857 when the news of the Rogue River War reached the east. Since the road was not used, there was no Modoc trouble that year.

The following year a military expedition marched through the Indian country east of the Cascade Mountains for the purpose of overawing the tribes there. The soldiers did not pass through Modoc country; hence Modocs were not impressed by American might. As the Modocs gained in numbers after the smallpox epidemic of the decade before, they became more truculent rather than more subdued.[33]

That fall the trouble along the road broke out again. In September, a wagon train passing Goose Lake was attacked, and Felix Scott and seven others were killed by Modocs. In June, 1859, another small wagon train was attacked at Bloody Point, the men and women were killed, and the children were taken captive to the "peninsula." The approach of another stronger train caused the Modocs to kill their captives to prevent rescue.[34]

Emigration was small in 1860. The only recorded travel through Klamath-Modoc country was that of the cattleman, Steen, who searched that summer through the mountains of southeastern Oregon now bearing his name, looking for a place to pasture his stock.

In 1861, the Civil War began, and all regular troops were withdrawn. Soldiers marching east reported all quiet in the Klamath lakes country. Their departure, however, left the protection of the

[33] Nash, *Revivalism*, 383.
[34] Bancroft, *Oregon*, II, 478.

wagon trains and the control of the Indians to the volunteers. Almost no men from the Pacific Northwest went east during the war to fight for or against the rebellion. They felt that their main job was to stay home and protect their families from Indians. Probably they also felt they needed to support their cause in case a small-scale civil war should break out among themselves. Southern sympathizers were both numerous and vociferous. The mining camps were not unanimous in support of the Union.

Shortly after Lincoln took office in 1861, Lindsay Applegate, the leader of the exploring party which laid out the original South Emigrant Road, was appointed special agent for the Lakes Indians. He thought his prime duty was to guard the Emigrant Road. He promptly raised a volunteer force of forty-three men and left for the Modoc country to protect the wagon trains using the southern route. Applegate left western Oregon on August 19. His party did not reach the Lakes country quite in time, for on the twenty-seventh of August, a wagon train was attacked near Goose Lake; three men were killed and one wounded. The volunteers, however, did arrive at Bloody Point in time to prevent another tragedy. A train surrounded by Modocs was in dire peril as the relief party came in sight. The Indians promptly broke off their attack, and the wagons went through safely. Over nine hundred head of stock, however, were taken by the Modocs that year.[35]

The next year, 1862, was a dark year in the history of the Siskiyou country and all of Oregon. The winter was unusually severe. In January, the Columbia River at Portland was completely blocked by ice. When the cold and snow stopped, heavy rains fell. Over seventy-one inches of rain were recorded near Portland between October, 1861, and March, 1862.

The weather was not the only thing that was bad. The dark emotions rampant during a civil war surged through the whole West. The army was in the East and disloyalty among the miners became more and more unrestrained. A considerable number of the young men from the Southern States made no attempt to conceal their sympathy for the Confederacy. So many of them migrated to the new mineral discoveries in Idaho that the Unionists became

[35] *Report of the Commissioner of Indian Affairs, 1863,* 59.

alarmed. In the California gold fields the situation was not much better. Oregonians were generally much more loyal and looked on their neighbors to the east and south with ill-concealed hatred.

The foreign affairs of the United States were also in a sorry state, and these matters affected the West directly. French troops were in Mexico, and if war came between France and America, the fighting would give Maximilian's army an excuse to move into California and Nevada to seize the great mineral wealth available there. The British government was also just barely polite in its relations with Lincoln's diplomats, and a small island in Puget Sound, claimed by both England and the United States, was actually occupied jointly by troops of both nations in garrisons located at opposite ends of the island. A declaration of war, momentarily expected, would plunge British troops and a naval force into the interior of the Pacific Northwest. The Indians sensed the insecurity and uneasiness of their white opponents and accordingly became more and more restless. The Modocs were especially affected by the cleavages between Oregonians and the Californians.

Although there had never been any treaties signed by the United States government with the Klamath, Modoc, Shoshone, or Bannock Indians, and no treaty negotiations had ever taken place, treaties were necessary because the decade-old pattern of intermittent Indian attack and volunteer rescue parties could not be allowed to continue. Further, the habits of the Indians themselves were changing. No longer was it necessary to go slave raiding and to follow the slow and difficult trade with The Dalles. Now trade could be carried on directly with Yreka. While the miners looked with considerable suspicion on the Modoc men, they looked with quite different eyes on their women. Young Modoc boys could also find employment from time to time as house servants where they could learn both the English language and the vices of the white man. Little by little the younger Modoc men came to be accepted as customers for drink or merchandise, which they could pay for in money or horses obtained by doing odd jobs. They also did a thriving business peddling their wives and sisters to the miners, who paid the Indians in gold or horses.

Yreka was a mining camp very much like dozens of other small gold camps in California during the Civil War. The streets were narrow; the buildings spread from near the foot of the hills at the eastern side of the valley and sprawled over the bench to the west. Dust was everywhere. It was hot in the summer and cold in the winter. To the Indians, it was exciting and colorful, and they made the most of it. The Modocs did not feel any need for a reservation when their young men and young girls could wander about the Yreka mining district whenever and however they pleased.

The leader of the Modoc group who adjusted best to the new ways in Yreka was Keintpoos, dubbed, for a joke, by Judge Steele as "Captain Jack" because of an alleged resemblance to one of the miners of that community. Jack's whole way of life conflicted with that of the Oregon settlers, who wanted title to land for farming and stock raising. As long as the Indians roamed their traditional hunting grounds, there was always the possibility of conflict. Farmers had no time to fight, and they did not want their wives and daughters to live in constant danger. They demanded, as a result, that the Indians be put on a reservation where they could be watched by the army when it should once again be stationed along the frontier. Old Schonchin was willing to yield to the pressure of the Oregonians, to forsake his wandering ways, and to settle on a reservation. This Jack would not do, and he and his young men were encouraged by the old shamans, who felt their power slipping as more and more white man's ways were taken up by the Indians. Over the basic issue of whether or not to go to a reservation the rivalry between Jack and Old Schonchin began.

In 1863, the settlement of the Modoc question could be put off no longer. George Nurse took a claim on Link River, just below Upper Klamath Lake. The Applegates also took a claim at Clear Lake. They reported the entire area admirably adapted to cattle and sheep raising. It was only a matter of time until settlers would locate along the shores of Tule Lake. Old Schonchin was not as vulnerable to settler pressure as Jack. His band was in the Sprague River Valley which was in no immediate danger of settlement, but Jack's band roamed the Lost River and Tule Lake country, where people had seen and reported good land available for enterprising white stockmen.

When things began going better with the eastern war, an army post was established at Fort Klamath in 1863 by Major C. S. Drew, First Cavalry. His garrison was small, and because of the Civil War, he depended largely on Oregon volunteers to keep it manned.[36] In September of that year, Lincoln appointed Elisha Steele Indian agent for the tribes of the Yreka region. Steele reported that when he took office, he found the Klamaths, Modocs, and Shastas at war with each other, and the Indians along the California coast completely destitute. He claimed that he relieved the destitution and induced the inland Indians to make peace with each other.

But Steele did not hold his position long. Politics were more important than a good Indian policy. California's senator, John Conness of Sacramento, disliked Steele and asked Lincoln to remove him. This Lincoln would not do, so legislation was passed which made it impossible for Steele to remain in office. He was replaced by Austin Wiley.[37]

Destitution was not confined to the coastal Indians. Captain William Kelley, who was in charge of the army garrisons in Oregon, found the Indians in the Klamath area so poverty stricken that he gave ten tons of beef and six tons of flour to the Indians to keep them from starving. Subagent Rogers of the Oregon superintendency construed this action as a reflection upon his work, and he quarreled so bitterly with the army and complained about the soldiers so constantly that the Indians themselves became confused.

Accordingly, on St. Valentine's Day of 1864, Jack's band of Modocs, along with a few Klamaths and Shastas, went to the man they knew and could trust: they asked Judge Steele to draft a treaty for them, even though they were no longer under his agency. Steele knew that his jurisdiction no longer extended to the Modocs and Klamaths and, furthermore, that he had no authority to negotiate treaties with any Indians. Nevertheless, he felt that an informal treaty was better than none, especially when the Indians themselves asked for one. He thought he could turn over to the new superintendent a *fait accompli*. By the terms of this treaty, the Modocs and others who signed it promised to stop stealing stock and to refrain

[36] Bancroft, *Oregon*, II, 504.

[37] Jeff C. Riddle, *The Indian History of the Modoc War, and the Causes That Led to It*, D. L. Moses, 1914, Letter from Judge Elisha Steele to his brother, 253ff.

from further child stealing. They agreed to quit selling their women to the miners, though marriage by purchase to other Indians was permitted. They also agreed to cease quarreling among themselves. They conceded the right of soldiers to punish them if they broke the agreement. In return, they were given permission to trade, to act as guides, and to operate ferries for a fee. They also agreed to get permission from the soldiers at Fort Klamath whenever they wished to leave a reservation that would be set up for them. Steele promised, bound only by his own word, to try to get a reservation for Jack's band just west of Tule Lake along the Lost River.[38]

Bureaucracy fumbled badly on this occasion. Because they were jealous of Steele, the heads of the Office of Indian Affairs ignored the treaty signed by him. Although it was necessary to set the whole machinery in motion once more, the Indian Office preferred to arrange for a second treaty that they had worked out than to take one already arranged, even though it might bring peace to the Modoc country. Jack might have broken Steele's treaty. No one can know, for what he had agreed to voluntarily was never put into force. Rather, Jack was told that he was bound by another treaty that he did not like, that he did not want, and that he signed only because of the pressures brought to bear on him.

The basic objection to Steele's treaty, as far as the Oregonians were concerned, was that it did not compel the Indians to remove themselves from the Tule Lake Basin or to stay on a reservation. It made specific provision for the manner in which the Indians were to be allowed to leave the reservation. Jack said he was willing to accept its terms, even though it was never put into force and was never submitted to the Senate. This meant nothing to the settlers. They gave the feeble excuse that since Steele's treaty did not involve any money payments to the Modocs for land cession outside of the Lost River, the treaty was invalid.

Indian Superintendent J. W. Perit Huntington was authorized by the Commissioner of Indian Affairs to negotiate a treaty with the Modocs that would remove them from Lost River and put them on a reservation somewhere else. On June 22, Congress made a $20,000 appropriation to cover the cost of a treaty with the Indians of south-

---

[38] *Report of the Commissioner of Indian Affairs, 1864.*

eastern Oregon. Because Agent Wiley of California was unable to attend, Huntington went alone to negotiate for a meeting date where he could make an agreement with the Modocs, the Klamaths, and a band of Paiutes called by the Oregonians the "Yahooskin Snakes." Some of the Indians agreed to meet on October 8, and Huntington went home.

By the ninth of October the representative of the government arrived at "Council Grove" about a mile north of Klamath Agency. Over one thousand Indians were also present for the treaty making. Of these, 710 were Klamaths, 339 were Modocs, and only 22 were "Snakes." The treaty was based on the premise that all of these Indians were much alike and could live in harmony on the same reservation.

The treaty of 1864 was a standard Indian agreement. It provided for the cession of all land claimed by these three groups and allowed them to keep part of the Klamath range on Upper and Middle Klamath Lakes. The Indians were to receive $8,000 worth of supplies for the first five years, $5,000 worth for the next five years, and $3,000 worth for the third five years after the treaty was ratified. Presumably they would be self-supporting after fifteen years. To help them, the government promised to build shops and mills and to establish schools for the teaching of mechanics and agriculture as well as reading and writing.[39]

The Klamaths were willing to accept Huntington's treaty, but most of the Modocs and Paiutes signed "reluctantly." The entire reservation was located on former Klamath land. No Modoc or Paiute was allowed one acre of his traditional hunting grounds.[40] In spite of Modoc reluctance to sign, Old Schonchin gave an impressive promise to abide by his signature. After he had made his mark, he stood facing the south, placed one hand on his heart, and slowly moved the other hand from left to right, indicating by this sign that as the sun moved from east to west, so would his word be true.

A major reason that the Lakes Indians were willing to sign, even though many were dubious about doing so, was that another group of Paiutes, called the "Walpape Snakes," under the leadership of

[39] *Ibid., 1865,* 104.
[40] Nash, *Revivalism,* 385–86.

their headman, Paunina, was raiding both Klamaths and Modocs as well as attacking any white man who came through the Silver Lake–Summer Lake country about fifty miles north of Goose Lake. A military expedition under Colonel Drew marched through Paunina's land, but the Indians avoided the soldiers. The soldiers then camped at Fort Klamath until June 28. While they were there, a group of prospectors from the Shasta Valley were attacked near Silver Lake in eastern Oregon about one hundred miles east of Fort Klamath, and were rescued only after a forced march from the fort. Modoc and Klamath enemies of Paunina saw that the army might be a strong ally in their own fight against the Paiutes.

In October, as the commissioners were on their way to the Columbia Valley following the treaty making, the whites were immensely fortunate in surprising Paunina's family with no guards in camp. The Indian women and children were promptly seized, and word was sent to Paunina that his wives and children were to be held as hostages for his good behavior until he signed a treaty. The next year, on August 12, 1865, he gave up, and he and some of his followers were allowed to settle at the "upper end" of the Klamath reservation.

All of the Indians agreed to one thing. If Judge Steele could not be their agent, they wanted another man who knew them and whom they felt they could trust. Lindsay Applegate was one such man. By unanimous decision, they asked Huntington to appoint him. This was done, and Subagent Applegate took office in September, 1865, although the United States Senate had not yet ratified the treaty under which he operated. He visited the Indians in the fall of 1865 and issued some rations to them. In the spring of 1866 he returned and selected an agency site a few miles north of the present location of Klamath Agency. This was in the heart of the permanent winter settlement area of the Klamaths. His plan was for the agency to be separated from the army post, and both to be separated from the civilian settlement of Linkville (now Klamath Falls), which was growing around the George Nurse claim below Klamath Lake.

In the winter of 1865–66, all Klamaths living at the "upper end" moved down to Applegate's agency, for in spite of the fact that Paunina had signed a treaty, they did not trust him. No supplies were given the Paiutes, and these Indians became fearful that they could not live through the winter on the reservation. Although a few stayed with Paunina, after a little time most of his band moved north off the reservation and re-established themselves around Summer Lake. In the spring of 1866 their leader joined them. Troops were sent north to compel him and his followers to return to the reservation, but he decided to fight.

Paunina eluded the soldiers, and during the next few months he raided mines and emigrant trains in Idaho, and his Indian enemies in eastern Oregon. The army and volunteers attempted to capture the raiders. Soldiers set up Camp Bidwell in Surprise Valley, Camp Alvord east of Steen's Mountains, and "old" Camp Warner, north of Lakeview, using these posts as bases from which they might operate against Paunina and the Paiutes.

On the Fourth of July, 1866, Lieutenant R. F. Bernard, a former army blacksmith who had risen out of the ranks to become a cavalry officer and a leader in the Indian wars for the next decade, was in charge of an expedition against the Paiutes. With thirty-four cavalrymen, he tried to catch those Paiutes in the Owyhee River Valley who had attacked miners and teamsters there. While he was out, Paunina turned the tables on the military by attacking Schonchin's band of Modocs in the Sprague River Valley. With considerable energy for a seventy-year-old man, Schonchin pursued the Paiutes. The wily Paunina concentrated his warriors near Goose Lake and swept down upon the agency. Applegate, reservation Indians, and a few troops barely managed to drive the hostile Indians away.

Klamath reservation Indians were ordered discharged by the brusque Secretary of War Stanton. With magnificent inconsistency, he then demanded that Warm Springs Indians be recruited under the leadership of W. C. McKay and attached to the army as scouts. These Indians joined the fray with enthusiasm and promptly murdered fourteen prisoners who had fallen into their hands. In retaliation, the Paiutes captured a whole wagon train of whites in western Idaho and killed every emigrant in the party. The killings of this "Ward Party" along the Oregon Trail shocked the whole American people. Not all had been fortunate enough to be killed in the direct attack. It was discovered later that the wounded and the captive women and children were put to death after savage torture. This fact was thoroughly publicized.

The Paiute War lasted until July, 1868, and the time between the Ward massacre and the end of the war was spent in hunting Paunina ruthlessly. When the leader was finally killed, his followers were found to be starving. They had eaten all their horses, they had very little ammunition left, and in dejection they quit fighting and returned to the reservation.

During the Paiute War, Jack continued to be at odds both with Schonchin's band and with the agency. By the summer of 1867, the split among the Modocs over the leadership of their tribe was made clear. The United States authorities, and particularly the Applegates, favored Old Schonchin because he was willing to co-operate with them. To Jack, such favoritism was intolerable. He repudiated his signature to the treaty of 1864, and in 1865 he left the reservation and returned to Lost River. When he got there, he sold ammunition and guns to Paunina's band in order to show his independence of both Schonchin and the American authorities. Klamath Indians, under the leadership of a "chief" appointed by Applegate after an election and named David Allen (promptly dubbed Allen David by the Indians), checked the source of hostile armaments and traced them to Jack's Modocs. When Jack found his work was exposed, he became a bitter enemy of Allen David.[41]

When Jack returned to Lost River, he found that Americans had moved into his tribal grounds, even though the 1864 treaty had not yet been ratified and was not yet in force. The Oregon settlers were frightened when Jack came back to live beside them, and they petitioned the authorities at Fort Klamath to force Jack to return to the reservation. Captain McGregor, the commanding officer, tried persuasion, but Jack refused to go, and McGregor did not feel he could handle another Indian war on top of the one he already had. In 1866, Lindsay Applegate went out to Lost River, also, to try to persuade Jack to return to the Klamath reservation. Jack was polite but firm in his refusal. In 1867, Superintendent Huntington came to Klamath with the first annuity goods. Jack would have none of

[41] Letter, Lindsay Applegate to Stephen B. Thoburn, Fort Klamath, September 19, 1869, Applegate Collection.

them if receiving them meant coming back to the reservation. The superintendent tried to threaten Jack. The Modoc's answer was pointed. He took his band across the river and told Huntington that he would open fire if he were followed. Since the white man had no soldiers, Huntington did not pursue, but after he returned to Fort Klamath, he requested soldiers to help punish Jack. The commander refused to send them.[42]

During the whole three-year period Jack was off the reservation, he continued to visit Yreka, to trade, to drink, and to ask advice of Judge Steele, or Steele's partner, Judge A. M. Rosborough. It was customary for one of these men to give the Indians a "pass" certifying their identity and good character. It usually took the following form:

April 6, 1868

Charlie, the Indian to whom I give this paper makes a living for himself and family by farming, driving teams, etc., and wants me to give him this paper certifying to the fact that he is a civilian Indian and not a wild Indian—that he is an independent freeman entitled to the protection of life, liberty, and pursuit of happiness by the laws of civilization.

A. M. Rosborough,
County Judge of the
County of Siskiyou, and
State of California[43]

It takes no student of Indian affairs to see that by the beginning of 1869 nothing had been settled about the Modocs. The whole Indian policy naturally needed a complete overhauling, but, like other matters at the end of Johnson's stormy term of office, it waited for the new administration to take over and end the bickering that had marked all phases of governmental activity between 1865 and 1869.

[42] Nash, *Revivalism*, 388; Bancroft, *Oregon*, II, 515–62.
[43] Applegate Collection.

Captain Jack, leader of the renegades, subchief of the Modoc Indians residing on the California-Oregon border. From a painting by Henry H. Cross (Courtesy National Archives).

Miner Street, Yreka, Siskiyou County, California (Courtesy National Archives).

Ben Wright, Indian fighter (Courtesy National Park Service).

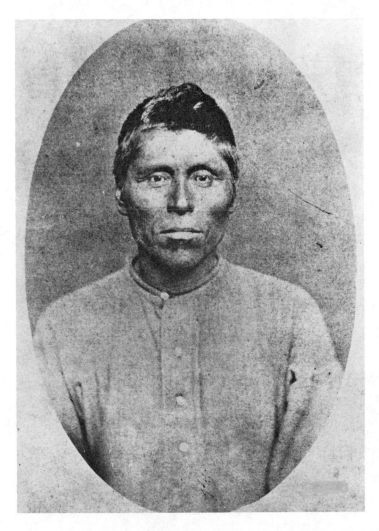

Curley Headed Doctor, the shaman (Courtesy National Archives).

General E. R. S. Canby, commander on the Pacific Coast, peace commissioner. From a painting by Henry H. Cross (Courtesy Gilcrease Museum).

III

A PEOPLE IN DISTRESS

THE PROBLEMS OF THE MODOCS were made much greater by political events and unskilled political appointments three thousand miles away at the nation's capital. The situation was not helped by the blundering of army officers or Indian superintendents in Oregon or California.

On March 4, 1869, U. S. Grant was inaugurated president of the United States. When an administration changes, new appointments are the order of the day. In Grant's day, when cabinet officers changed, the minor officials, under the spoils system of the time, changed as well. On May 1, Huntington was succeeded as Indian superintendent for Oregon by a stalwart Republican workhorse named Alfred B. Meacham. Meacham was known in Oregon as a supporter of President Grant.

Historians have castigated Grant for his appointments, and much of the criticism was well deserved. There is no doubt, however, that the appointments were well meant. Like the proverbial highway, his Indian policy was paved with particularly good intentions. The policy failed, however, because of the dishonesty and incompetence in the Office of Indian Affairs.

Grant's main difficulty was that he was incapable of taking a strong stand amid the conflicting ideas for running Indian affairs. There were at least three policies advocated. Department of the Interior officials were guided by the belief that the agent was more important than the Indian. The workings of this policy had been anything but an outstanding success; in fact, it led to disaster before it was abandoned. The War Department, on the other hand, believed that it was cheaper to feed an Indian than to shoot him. Since the army had the job of finishing the Indian wars, its leaders concluded cynically that all Indian wars were started by white men. A third policy was urged on the President by nongovernmental citizens, a policy presented by Meacham, and sometimes called Grant's "Quaker Policy." Probably its name comes from the fact that some Philadelphia humanitarians had persuaded the President to turn the Indians over to missionaries of various religious denominations. These men were convinced that if the Indians adopted Christianity, they would also change their habits, their folkways, their economic system, and then would become peaceable and self-reliant. The main difficulty in this policy was that the well-meaning men who were put into positions of authority knew almost nothing about Indians and were far more concerned with religious statistics than in the building of mills or schools. In spite of its failings, the "Quaker Policy" might have succeeded if the Interior and War departments had not been at odds. As it was, poor temporizing Grant decided to try the ideas of all three groups at the same time. The consequent division of authority and different points of view could not help bringing disaster.

Meacham, who had been in Oregon since 1863, qualified under the "Quaker Policy" because he was a member of the Methodist church. He first lived in the Grande Ronde Valley and operated a toll road and hotel on the route between Walla Walla and the Idaho gold fields.[1] In 1844 he had helped remove the Indians from Iowa to the west; hence, in the eyes of the Oregon congressional delegation, he was qualified as well for the job of Indian superintendent for Oregon, a position which required him to move all Oregon Indians to reservations. President Johnson knew that Meacham was no admirer of his and refused to appoint him. When Grant announced his new "Quaker Policy," Meacham called on the President to offer his congratulations. It was a strategic move, for Grant was already considering his visitor for the office of superintendent. At the conclusion of their interview, Grant offered Meacham the job.

[1] T. A. Bland, *Life of Alfred B. Meacham*, 3-6.

Almost before Meacham had returned home and had taken office, Grant and his advisers decided to allow each idea to have a chance to prove itself. The Indian Bureau worked out no pattern or plan, and almost by chance some superintendencies were placed under the Department of the Interior, some were made practically autonomous, and some were put under the control of the War Department. Oregon agencies were at first handed over to the army.

When Meacham was ordered to turn over his office to an army officer, such a protest went up from his friends that a compromise was worked out whereby Meacham was retained as superintendent; Ben Simpson and Charles Lafollette represented the old Indian policy and were retained as agents at Siletz on the coast and Grand Ronde in northeastern Oregon. The rest of the Oregon agencies were then turned over to the army. Captain O. C. Knapp, a veteran of the Union Army, promoted twice for gallantry and meritorious service in action, was made agent of the Klamath reservation.[2] Even on the military and Interior Department reservations, however, missionaries were encouraged to organize religious work among the Indians.

When Meacham first began to visit his agencies, he was shocked at the conditions he found. Human nature was revealed at its worst; he learned that regardless of the ideas his employees represented, they were inefficient and sometimes dishonest in their dealings with the Indians. He was also scandalized at their morals. He reported one of his agents as saying "that he thought the best way to civilize Indians was to *wash out* the color," an expression implying that interbreeding between the whites and Indians was the solution to the Indian question. Meacham observed dryly that some of his agents "had accomplished what they were able to in that line."[3]

When he arrived at Klamath, his first job was to induce treaty Indians to return to the reservation. His efforts to persuade the roving Paiutes to return were only partially successful. General Crook, Department of the Columbia commander, would not force them to go back with the use of troops, and only a few came down to Yainax station. Even these kept drifting off the reservation, complaining

[2] Riddle, *Indian History*, 38.
[3] Meacham, *Wigwam and War-path*, 162.

that they could not live there. Meacham's successors later set up a new reservation of over two thousand square miles near Malheur Lake. Much later yet, when they were too weak to protest, the Malheur reservation was closed and the Paiutes were moved to Yakima, although one band under Winnemucca went to Nevada and stayed there.[4]

Meacham was appalled at conditions at Klamath. Almost as soon as he took office he issued regulations against polygamy, gambling, or slaveholding by any Indian in Oregon. He also directed that any white man on a reservation living with an Indian woman had either to marry her or give her up. He found considerable need of such an order. He states that there were "children of every shade" at the agency. The white officers at Fort Klamath took Indian women quite openly, even from their husbands. He was distressed, moreover, to find that their husbands would not take them back after the officers gave them up. He complained that one officer gambled with the Indians in spite of his regulations and had won thirty-seven horses in his gambling. Meacham found Klamath women going to the fort commissary to buy goods, and since they did not have money for payment, they acquired it by acting as prostitutes for the enlisted men. In spite of trouble on the reservation, he blamed the army and kept the Applegates on the job. He cleared them because they practiced no "mixing of blood," kept their promises, and lived without smuggling whiskey on the reservation as some of his agents did. In spite of his clearance, however, Meacham complained that the Applegates had promised the Indians a sawmill four years before, and while the Indians had in good faith begun to cut logs, there was still no mill built. The mill appropriations had been spent for other things. There was no dishonesty involved, but the Indians did not have their mill.

The administrative policy set up by Meacham provided for adequate food and clothing for the Indians, the introduction of democratic political institutions, and the establishment of agriculture as soon as feasible. He also determined to stamp out native shamanism.

At first there was a concerted effort to carry out the plans formulated. Supplies were sent and received without too much delay.

[4] Bancroft, *Oregon*, II, 553.

Transportation was difficult from The Dalles, but wagons could and did get through. Although Indians accepted the food furnished them by the agent, they used the government wheat and beef only as a supplement to their customary wild foods. The expectation was at first that the Indians could be taught to plow, but they broke so little ground and showed themselves so indifferent to this manner of obtaining food that the agents despaired, although they tried for four years to produce some kind of a crop. Their efforts were continually frustrated by midsummer frosts.

Eventually the agents decided to make the Indians herdsmen of cattle. This worked somewhat better than urging them to cultivate cereal grains, but even so it was only indifferently successful, and more and more Indians came to depend on the agents for their subsistence. The Indians did not know how to build log cabins, and the agents were determined that they should live in houses instead of their traditional wickiups. The Applegates patiently showed them how to put logs together. The Indians, however, would not work without an overseer, so the school teacher was sent into fields with the boys, ostensibly to show them how to farm, but actually to try to get some work out of them. This extracurricular duty of the teacher was perhaps more practical than his attempt to teach the Indians to read and write, but it was not quite what the government had in mind when it appropriated money for a school.

Jack watched the proceedings on the reservation closely, and the more he saw of things, the more convinced he became that he should try to live as his ancestors had. He felt his way of life to be much more adequate for his band than that of Schonchin. Many reservation Modocs also began to have doubts about their ability to live by the white man's ways.

Among these white man's ways were elections and democratic government. In the summer of 1869 the Applegates held the first elections among the Klamaths for the office of "chief." Allen David, one of the old slave traders, was victor over "Blow." Eight subchiefs were also selected. A court was established with Indian sheriffs, and each subchief was made a "sergeant." Obviously, by holding an election, the Applegates—and, through them, the U. S. government—totally ignored the Indians formerly holding power. The first trial

under the new officials was held in December, 1869. The Indians had
so much fun that for a while normal activity was almost suspended
while courts decided any and all kinds of cases. Eventually the
agents had to reduce the court sessions to one a month in order to
get any other agency business done.[5] The "chiefs" and "subchiefs"
acting as de facto magistrates soon acquired great prestige. They
were supported by the government partially to reduce the authority
and prestige of the shamans.

The anti-shaman campaign was a deliberate act to shatter the old
culture patterns of the Indians. In addition, since many of the agents
were zealous workers for their religious denominations, the prac-
tices of the shamans in the direction of paganism was intolerable
competition. Subagent Knapp, for example, under Meacham's orders, had Link River Doctor, a Klamath Indian medicine man,
arrested, tried, and imprisoned on the charge of practicing "spiritual
medicine." Meacham issued a direct order in the fall of 1870 forbidding all shamanistic activities.

The shamans fought back. They threatened ritual killing of the
agents, but the agents defied them, and nothing happened. Failure
to kill their enemies further reduced the influence and prestige of the
Indian doctors. In the complex of this struggle for prestige, an expert
diplomat was needed to persuade Jack to return to the reservation
and adopt the new system of values, the new ways of life, and the
authority of Old Schonchin. Meacham had his work cut out for him,
but he was determined to try.

In the early fall of 1869, Meacham and Knapp held a consultation on how best to approach Jack. In due time, a messenger was
sent to his camp on Lost River, and Jack promptly sent back the
reply that he did not want to see them, either Knapp or the superintendent, but if they wanted to talk to him, they would have to
come to his camp. He would not come to their headquarters. This
was another move in the struggle for prestige. The party to a dispute who could induce the other to come to him was, by elementary
logic, the more powerful. Knapp and Meacham knew this, but decided to ignore it. They first asked for troops from Fort Klamath,

[5] Fred Lockley, "How the Modoc Indian War Started," Overland Monthly,
Vol. LXXXI, No. 7 (November, 1923), 12.

but they found this was impractical. The morale of the men at the fort was very low. Desertion rates were high—Meacham with some hyperbole asserted that half of the troops were needed to guard the other half, and to wait on the officers of the fort. He did not like the army, and told with some satisfaction that a group of men detailed to search for deserters themselves joined the first group in abandoning their duty. Finally, Klamath Indians were sent after the soldiers, and all the deserters were brought back. This kind of soldier would do little good in forcing Jack to come to the Klamath reservation.

In mid-December, a motley collection of negotiators started for the Modoc country. It consisted of an unstated number of soldiers, Meacham and Knapp, W. C. McKay, Old Schonchin, Frank Riddle and his wife Toby, two Klamath women, Ivan Applegate, George Nurse, and several other civilians used as teamsters. The soldiers were ordered to stop at Link River, and the rest of the little expedition moved south to the Lost River.

The party reached Modoc country on the twenty-second of December. The Indians had kept abreast of developments, and were aware of Meacham's plans. Accordingly, when he had reached a point about five miles from the Modoc camp, he was met by four mounted Modocs who told him that Jack would not see him and that he might as well go back. After a short talk, Meacham pushed on past the Indians and began to gallop for the Indian camp. Seeing that Meacham could not be intimidated, the Modocs rushed ahead of him and beat him into Jack's village by a small margin.

They apparently gave the alarm, and when Meacham arrived, not an Indian was to be seen except the four he had first met. The village was small—only thirteen lodges. One of the Indians rushed up the outside stairway leading into Jack's wickiup and disappeared through the hole in the top. When, after a moment's hesitation, Meacham prepared to follow, an English-speaking Indian appeared and gave the order, "One man come! No more!"

Meacham had gained a victory, although he later admitted that he was so frightened at the thought of entering an Indian dwelling alone that he didn't think of much else. The Indians had conceded his right to talk to them, even though they had at first refused. In the game for prestige, the agent had taken the first trick.

Inside, Jack was flanked by a number of his men. His attitude was cold and unfriendly. He refused to shake hands, to speak, or to smoke. After he had lit his own pipe, Meacham had sense enough to remain quiet, thus taking the second trick by forcing the Indians to speak first. Scarfaced Charley, a young Indian who had frequented Yreka enough to know English pretty well finally broke the silence in a short speech of mingled English and trade-language jargon. Scarfaced Charley asked Meacham why he had come when they did not want him.

Meacham, thus invited to speak, told them that he was the new white "chief" sent to them by the President. He vowed friendship and asked for a hearing. Then he invited Jack to speak. Jack broke his silence by accusing all white men of being swindlers and liars, but he conceded Meacham the right to make a proposition and said that the Modocs would listen. Meacham asked whether his friends might come in while he talked, and Jack gave permission.

Jack next produced papers which he valued highly, papers written by Steele and Rosborough and others in Yreka. These notes attested to his good character. Meacham handled them as though they were original copies of the Declaration of Independence, while most of the other white men who had seen them had shrugged them off. Jack was pleased by the superintendent's consideration, and Meacham was on his way.

Once it was obvious that the negotiations would take a little while, the Modoc leader had a small camp prepared for Meacham's party. The Indians even gathered some fuel and furnished the Meacham party with a fish for the evening meal.

The next day wagons came down from Linkville, and Meacham prepared a return meal. The Indians suspected treachery, or Meacham read into their actions what was not there; at least, they would not eat until Meacham had first sampled the food. He considered this proof that the Modocs had been told that Wright was going to poison them seventeen years before, and that they had never forgotten it.

After the meal the formal council began. The interpreters were Frank Riddle and his Modoc wife, Toby, a couple who played an important role in the Modoc War. His wife was later given the name of Winema, and she is more commonly known by this than by her original name. When Meacham went on lecture tour after the war, he took both the Riddles with him, and he gave her the name, though there is no evidence that she was ever called by it before she was twenty-five years old.

The Riddles were employed by the government, as the best interpreters available. Frank Riddle had gained his knowledge of the Modoc tongue from his wife, with whom he had been living for about six years. He had left Kentucky before he was eighteen and moved to the California gold fields. He took a mining claim at Yreka and worked it for a few months before he met Toby. She was a girl of only twelve, but she was taken into Yreka to be peddled to the miners by her father, a brother of Captain Jack. When she was first brought to Riddle, he refused to deal with the Indian, but several days later, when she again was brought to him, he decided to let her stay. Apparently he was not interested in a casual and temporary arrangement, for he bought her outright from her father for the sum of several horses. In this way, Riddle became a "squaw man" before he could vote, and his companion was little more than a child. Before he was twenty, Riddle fathered a child by his Indian mistress; the little boy was named Jefferson C. Davis Riddle. (Inasmuch as the baby was born during the Civil War, it is obvious where Riddle's sympathies lay.) Mining did not pay, and Riddle moved to the Upper Gap on Lost River in 1868, where he became a trapper of bear and a hunter of elk and deer. The next year Meacham's order to free Indian slaves, directed at the Indians, and an order directed at the whites either to marry or to give up their Indian women applied to Frank Riddle. He chose to keep Toby, and so she became a legally married wife. For this she was grateful to Meacham and became his friend. Riddle seems to have been an easy-going fellow who did not resent Meacham's interference in his domestic life. Accordingly, the Riddles worked with Meacham whenever he needed to deal with the Modocs, and they were present at the Lost River Conference in late December, 1869. They not only interpreted for Meacham, but also advised him how to answer.

In the conversations that occurred during the morning and afternoon of December 23, Jack at first denied that he had ever signed the treaty of 1864. He told Meacham that if he could be shown where he had made his mark at the treaty, he would go to the reservation. Meacham's luck held out. He had brought one of the original copies of the treaty with him, and he showed Jack where he had made his mark. Since Old Schonchin and McKay, the Indian scout, were there and both had seen Jack make the mark, they were able to prove that it was his signature and that they had seen him make the mark. Nonplussed, Jack stopped talking about Lost River and began to ask where he would be sent if he did go to the reservation. Meacham had almost won. He told Jack that he could have any unoccupied land that suited him. After a silence, Jack finally stated that if he could live near a friend named Link River Jack, he would go.

At this point the Modoc shaman, Curley Headed Doctor, jumped to his feet and said in the Modoc language, "We won't go." Doubtless, Curley Headed Doctor had been following the proceedings with growing misgivings. If Jack's band went to the reservation and accepted the leadership of Old Schonchin and the Indian agents, his authority and prestige would be drastically curtailed. The shaman's abrupt statement threw the conference into confusion. All the Modocs leaped to their feet, and many of them drew pistols. Jack immediately deferred to the medicine man and announced, "I am done talking."

According to Meacham, at this stage of the proceedings, Riddle and Toby took matters into their own hands. There was no time to stop for interpretation and a rapid exchange took place in the Modoc language. Toby is reported to have cried out, "Wait! Wait! until I talk. Don't shoot! Hear me!" Then she and her husband urged the Modocs to accept Meacham's proposal and not to start bloodshed.

McKay warned Meacham to be on his guard, but in the intense excitement this warning was hardly necessary. Meacham attempted to dominate the situation again by telling Jack that wagons were already there to carry the Modocs to the reservation. Like a small boy, Jack asked Meacham what he would do if the Modocs refused to go. Meacham replied that his party would fight until they were all dead, and when they could fight no more, other white men would come and kill the Indians until all the Modocs were dead. This was the kind of talk that Jack could understand and respect. When Meacham demanded that Jack either agree to go to the reservation or fight and insisted that the Indians could have the right to decide which they wanted to do, Jack retired in a sober mood, while the whites separated from the Indians.

Meacham's people realized that if Curley Headed Doctor won, they would probably be killed, but they also knew they had to appear courageous. Under the pretext of sending out a man to find their horses, they sent a messenger to Linkville and the soldiers, asking them to move during the night to a point within gunshot of the Modoc camp, but not to allow the Indians to know they were there. In that way, the whites could put up a bold front and still could feel that if they were forced to fight, they might escape alive.

In Jack's lodge, Curley Headed Doctor urged the assassination of the envoys with all the persuasiveness he could command. Jack demurred. The argument went on into the night, some Modocs favoring one point of view, and some the other. The argument gave the soldiers time to arrive.

Instead of staying out of earshot, however, the soldiers charged the camp with wild yells and clanking sabers. Meacham, a strong temperance advocate, was scandalized to confirm his suspicions that the entire troop had been spending its time in Linkville at the local saloon bending their elbows in company with "forty-rod" whiskey; every man in the outfit was roaring drunk.

Their arrival broke up the discussion in Jack's lodge. The Indian leaders hurried away when they heard the noise, for they thought that a major force was upon them. They fled to the Lava Beds on the south shore of Tule Lake, but there was no fighting.

Knapp went outside and quickly restored order among the men. He assigned each soldier to sentry duty around the camp until he sobered up, which took the balance of the night. None of the women and children got out of the camp, and in the morning Meacham assured them they would not be harmed. The original offer still stood, but all the muskets of the Indians would have to be delivered to the army. While the Modocs grumbled, the departure of their leaders left them no choice, and they turned over their guns.

At daylight, the disgusted Indians saw how few soldiers there were, but now they were weaponless. In their difficult position, the Modocs could do little more than make professions of good will and state their willingness to do what Meacham suggested. Jack's sister, Mary, who had learned fairly good English as mistress to five or six miners in Yreka prior to 1869, asked Meacham for permission to go to the Lava Beds to induce her brother to join the party headed for the reservation. Jack agreed to come with the others only on the condition that Meacham would make the Klamaths promise not to ridicule him for having run from so small a force of cavalrymen. Meacham solemnly promised, and Jack joined his band.

Meacham was no mere observer and recorder of customs. To his horror, he learned that when the Indians left their village, they had abandoned an old woman, by the primitive logic which sentences a person to death by neglect when he is no longer strong enough to make a contribution to the group welfare. He gave orders that the woman was to be brought in, and when the Indians asked for a fee for doing it, he indignantly refused to pay. Under his insistence, they brought her in, even though they thought the errand foolish.

When the entire Indian band had assembled, Meacham's convoy left for Linkville, where they arrived on December 27. On the next day, they arrived at Modoc Point on the Klamath reservation. The weather was cold and it had just stopped snowing,[6] but the Klamaths were there in force to see Jack's people come in.

Meacham at once issued orders against gambling, for he believed it would lead to a saturnalia. In his own words, "Much confusion of property and domestic relation would have ensued." By this he meant that, if stick games were permitted, men might stake their own children or even their wives on the result. At least they had been known to do that. Instead of a gambling spree, Meacham proposed to substitute a ceremony of reconciliation between Allen David and Jack. These two were still enemies on account of David's exposing the Modocs of Jack's band for selling arms to the Paiutes. The pageant-loving Indians were satisfied with the compromise, and the next day, December 29, was set for the affair.

Jack came to the reservation with only forty-three people, but

[6] Letter, Ivan Applegate to his brother, December 25, 1869, Applegate Collection.

the number of Modocs was increased when some of Schonchin's band joined them. In addition, fifteen additional Modocs were later brought in by the soldiers.

The ceremony must have been colorful, and doubtless Meacham felt well satisfied with himself as he witnessed it. He drew a line to mark the boundary between Klamath and Modoc bands and placed each group on his own side of the line. The Klamaths arrived early, and Allen David took his position in front of them and almost at the line. The Modocs came more slowly, and Jack took his position facing Allen David. Meacham made a short speech urging them to live together as neighbors. Then, an axe, used for a formal "bury the hatchet" ceremony, was placed on the ground, and David and Jack met at the line, laid a pine bough upon the axe, placed their feet on the bough, and in silence they shook hands. In turn each subchief and headman came forward, placed his bough on the axe, and shook hands with his opposite number. When all had finished, Allen David gave a brief speech, and Jack responded with an expression of good will toward both Klamaths and white men.

Goods were then distributed to Jack's band in honor of his coming to the reservation. The children were seated on the ground in a semicircle; behind them were the women, and behind them were the men. The important men sat in the center and the others at either end. Blankets, shirts, cloth, thread, needles, and buttons were thus given out, and the Modocs went home to their own camp. Each Indian group then ate a great feast prepared from beef ordered slaughtered by Knapp when he heard that the Modocs were coming.[7]

The mellow glow created by good food and presents lasted for some time beyond the first day. Klamaths and Modocs were permitted to mingle, and in spite of Meacham's injunction against it, gambling soon began again. In addition, "fraternization" between the young people of both tribes took place.

On New Year's Eve, Meacham was still at the reservation. He had a huge pine fire built, and all the Indians gathered around it in the chilly winter night. Meacham talked to them, explaining that this was the last night in the year 1869. They asked him how he

[7] Letter, O. C. Knapp to Ivan D. Applegate, December 24, 1869, Applegate Collection.

knew this, and he tried to explain to a blank-faced audience of five or six hundred Indians some of the intricacies of astronomy and time-keeping. He held up his watch to them, saying that when the hands met at the top of the dial, it would be 1870. Allen David proposed that he fire a pistol at the exact moment of the New Year. The suspense was almost painful as Meacham indicated the passing of the last few seconds; then the silence was broken by the pistol shot. All the Indians were standing, and they shouted toward the west in honor of 1869. They then turned toward the east in honor of 1870, and again raised a shout toward Klamath Lake, officially accepting the New Year.

Meacham left the reservation, elated with the success of his mission. Knapp seemed to be a competent man to leave in charge, and Jack was safely on the reservation and out of the way of the settlers. The Paiutes were quiet, and the settlers were free to take up claims along the Lost River. Emigrants might travel the road around Bloody Point, or along the shores of Goose Lake without fear. It seemed that an auspicious decade had dawned.[8]

Unfortunately, the good will evidenced in the last week of 1869 did not last. Like most human beings, these red men had a regrettable habit of reverting to their normal cantankerousness whenever the stimulus to good behavior was removed. The Klamaths were much more numerous than the Modocs, and their more rambunctious young men could not resist the temptation to torment their new neighbors. Under the leadership of Link-River Jack, they ridiculed the Modocs unmercifully for giving up their free-roving life for the dull reservation routine. The Klamaths said that the only reason Modocs were able to exist was through the charity of the Klamaths, who furnished them with their land, their trees to cut for rails, and logs for houses. The Klamaths capped the climax when they demanded that the Modocs hand over some of their cut logs for rent on their part of the reservation.

Jack was a proud and willful Indian. He exercised commendable restraint, for a time, but did not propose to put up with ill treatment, taunts, or insults. To his credit, he seems to have made an effort to

[8] Bancroft, *Oregon*, II, 558–59; Meacham, *Wigwam and War-path*, 306–41; Nash, *Revivalism*, 398–99.

keep the peace; for a time he submitted to the heckling by the Klamaths with dignity. Finally, however, he exploded, and a tremendous row ensued. It was only with difficulty that trouble was avoided then and there.

The first time trouble broke out, Jack assumed that Agent Knapp would take care of the situation. Knapp had so far done his duty well, issuing rations and supervising the Indians, but he had very little interest in what was going on. Knapp was not at all happy about acting as overseer and chaperone for several hundred Indians. He had not asked for the job, and he wanted to be relieved of his responsibilities at the time of Jack's appeal. To him, the Indian Service was an assigned chore and nothing else.

Knapp was brusque with Jack. He met the Indian on the front porch, did not invite him into his office, told him to go back to work, and promised that the agency "would make it all right." Apparently Knapp hoped that the trouble would blow over without official action, because the Klamaths received neither reprimand nor punishment and continued to make life unpleasant for the Modocs. They hampered the Modocs while they were fishing, and they struck the Modoc women and drove them away when they tried to gather seeds in the lake.[9]

Again Jack appealed to Knapp, who told him that if he could not get along with the Klamaths, he should go where there were no Klamaths. Reluctantly, Jack's band gave up their work and moved north a few miles to the Williamson River Valley. Other Klamaths moved over to watch Jack's Modocs cut logs. It was the same story over again.

More quarrels developed, and once more Jack told Knapp about his relations with the Klamaths. Knapp was impatient this time, and Jack later complained that the officer cursed him roundly and accused him of being a chronic complainer. Jack left in a rage and refused to take further Klamath insults without action.

In April, Jack called a meeting of all Modocs, both his own band and Schonchin's. They met on the Williamson River and talked over the situation. Jack proposed that since they were not welcome

[9] Stephan Powers, "The California Indians: The Modocs," *Overland Monthly*, Vol. X, No. 6 (June, 1873), 543.

in Klamath territory and Knapp didn't want to interfere, the best thing to do was to return to the Lost River and demand a separate reservation north of Tule Lake. Old Schonchin himself was not present. He would have undoubtedly resisted, but Jack cut the ground from under any possible objection by accusing him of playing along with the whites only to make his old age secure. Old Schonchin's point of view was overruled. When Knapp stopped issuing rations to the Modocs the third week in April on the grounds that they could now support themselves by their usual methods of food gathering, the Modocs quietly made plans to leave.

On April 25 or 26, the Indians left the reservation. Jack had come with only forty-three people. He had so clearly convinced the Modocs that the white man's ways were not for them that he left with 371. This was the low point in the influence of Old Schonchin, who was so bereft of followers that he, too, had to go with Jack. Curley Headed Doctor and Jack seemed to have won a complete victory. Ivan Applegate tried to persuade Schonchin's followers to come back to the agency, but they would not listen to him.[10]

Captain Knapp, the agent, and Lieutenant G. A. Goodale, the commanding officer at the fort, each blamed the other for what had happened. Knapp accused Goodale of being inefficient in permitting the Modocs to get away. Goodale accused the agent of stupidity in needlessly antagonizing Jack. While they were blaming each other for the situation, nothing at all was done about the Modocs.

After a few weeks of living under Jack's control, Old Schonchin voluntarily returned to the reservation, where he felt that he counted for something. Little by little, other families drifted back, until a couple of years later, Schonchin was headman of 130 Modocs, who were separated from the Klamaths and put at Yainax, about thirty-five miles east of the agency. Many of them visited back and forth with Jack's band off the reservation any time they felt like it.

Jack was not interested in going to Yainax. After he returned to Lost River, he seemed to feel that none of his agreements with the whites were binding. His young men and young women began visiting the mining camps at Yreka again, and they were wel-

[10] From a "pass," Ivan D. Applegate, "To whom it may concern" (April 30, 1870), Applegate Collection.

comed. Meacham blamed the stories told to "dissolute" Yreka miners by the Modoc women for the bad reputation the agency and Knapp received.

In the camp of the Modocs, there was indecision about the next course of action. John Schonchin, the younger brother of the old leader, joined Curley Headed Doctor in advocating war. Jack was in favor of passive resistance. A third group of Modocs withdrew from the discussion completely and moved over to Lower Klamath Lake near the ranch of John A. Fairchild. They wanted to keep clear of the affair, but they made no move to return to the reservation.

As might be suspected, the white settlers who had moved into the Tule Lake basin were filled with consternation when Jack and the Modocs returned. They had thought that the Indian treaty was final and that the land was ready for homesteading. Now Jack had returned, and he demanded that the whites either get out or acknowledge his suzerainty over their holdings by paying him a "rent" in produce for their use of the land.

For the next two years, the Indians annoyed their white neighbors by taking hay from the fields[11] or turning their stock into the pasture land or hay fields and letting them graze without permission. They annoyed the women by walking uninvited into their kitchens and demanding free food. They sat around the house or lolled on the beds until the meals were ready. They snatched utensils out of cupboards. They whooped and yelled in the house. They threw water inside the cabins. No one was harmed by the Indians, but the settlers had no certain privacy and the manners of the Indians were unbearable. A few settlers forestalled Indian annoyance by giving up and entering into agreements with the Modocs to furnish them certain goods for the unhindered use of the land and for freedom from annoyance. Their sentiments, however, were about like those of any victim who had paid off to a petty racketeer for "protection." Jack was satisfied with the ones who paid off, for they indirectly acknowledged his title claims to the Lost River Valley and the Tule Lake Basin.

[11] *Oregon Superintendency, 1872*, Office of Indian Affairs, The National Archives; Powers, "California Indians," *Overland Monthly*, Vol. X, No. 6 (June, 1873).

One reason the settlers could not ask for military help was that in mid-August, 1870, all army posts of the West were depleted to furnish General Crook with troops to fight the Apaches. Crook's departure for Arizona meant that replacements had to be sent. Accordingly, General E. R. S. Canby was put in charge of the entire military Department of the Columbia, which included the Klamath-Modoc region in its District of the Lakes.

Canby was a distinguished veteran of the Civil War. Most of his fifty-three years had been spent in military service. He had fought in the Seminole War and also had taken part in the removal of the Cherokees and Seminoles to Indian Territory. He had served in the Mexican War and had come out of that conflict a lieutenant colonel. His first experience in the West came in 1858 when he was engaged in the "Mormon War," an affair which might have been tragic but happily was resolved without bloodshed. He was stationed at Fort Defiance in New Mexico, and he led the Union forces against Sibley's Confederates in the only battles of the Civil War that took place in the West. He was present during the draft riots in New York City in 1863. The next year he became a major general and was put in charge of operations in western Mississippi. He is credited with the capture of Mobile in 1865. In July, 1866, he became a brigadier general of the regular army and was assigned to occupation duty in the South. He reorganized the Confederate cavalry to rout out criminals skulking outside the pacified areas, and he was in charge of the military governments of North and South Carolina, Texas, and Virginia during the next three years. From Virginia, he was transferred directly to Fort Vancouver, Washington Territory.[12]

Canby did not have many troops to command because most of the regulars were in Arizona. Lieutenant Goodale and his command at Fort Klamath were reduced to one infantry company of seventy-two men.[13] The nearest relief forces in case of Indian trouble were stationed at Lakes District headquarters, at Camp Warner, in Paiute territory, almost one hundred miles away. Even here there were

[12] *Dictionary of American Biography*, III, 468–69.
[13] *Fort Klamath Letter Book*, VII, Office of the Adjutant General, The National Archives.

only two military units—one company of infantry and one troop of cavalry.

Since the army was so weakened, it was impossible to control Jack and his Modocs. The longer Jack stayed off the reservation, the more confident he became that nothing would be done to compel his return. The Indian superintendent made a half-hearted attempt in midsummer of 1870 to persuade Jack to return to the reservation. Jack knew that Paunina's Paiutes who were on the reservation were almost naked, living on crickets and some skimpy rations of flour given them by the army. Congress was slow in making its annual appropriations, and the Indian Service was even slower in bringing the supplies to the Indians. If this were the fate of the reservation Indians who trusted the treaties, Jack wanted no part of it. Although supplies arrived in August, the Modocs still considered the future too uncertain to trust the United States government.[14] Jack did visit Yainax from time to time, but flatly refused to live there. He was content to come and go freely to Yreka, on "passes" issued by the citizens of that community, to collect voluntary rent from the white settlers of his country, and to live as nearly in the traditional Modoc ways as possible.

In 1870, Jack made his first formal request for a reservation on the Lost River according to the general terms of the agreement he had worked out with Steele in 1864. Since there were no troops to compel Jack to live with the Klamaths, Meacham recommended that Jack's request be granted. The settlers heard of Meacham's recommendation and became alarmed that their uneasy association with Jack's band might be made a permanent arrangement. Jack also heard about the recommendation and was highly encouraged to believe that his resistance was at last paying off.[15]

In the late spring of 1871, Jack's niece became ill. The women decided that she must have dreamed of herself during her puberty dance, a very serious matter. A shaman had to be called at once. It happened that Curley Headed Doctor and some of the younger men were absent on a horse-stealing expedition.[16] Since the Modoc sha-

[14] *Annual Report of the Commissioner of Indian Affairs to the Secretary of the Interior,* 1870, 67–69.

[15] Bancroft, *Oregon,* II, 559–62.

[16] Nash, *Revivalism,* 393.

man was engaged in his private grand larceny, Jack felt he should call the nearest available healer, a shaman from Klamath. The Klamath medicine man was so confident of his success that he took a fee in advance, thus guaranteeing a cure.[17] The illness of the child seemed to be more serious than it was originally thought, however, and she died. In his annoyance, and in accordance with Indian custom, Jack promptly killed the Klamath shaman for inefficiency.

The Klamath friends of the unsuccessful healer informed Ivan Applegate, who asked the sheriff of Siskiyou County to arrest Jack the next time he came to Yreka.[18] The "Great Treaty" of 1864 provided that white man's laws applied to reservation Indians, and Jack's mark on the treaty bound him never to murder again. A warrant was issued for the arrest of Jack, and Major Jackson at Fort Klamath sent a small squad of army personnel under a Lieutenant Moss to make the arrest. Jack easily eluded the arresting force and promptly added Applegate to his list of bitter hates.

Although Jack realized that he had blundered in killing the Klamath medicine man, he did not propose to let the white men hang him for it. He made a trip to Yreka even before Applegate requested his arrest and asked Elisha Steele for advice. Steele wrote a note for him, advising against anyone's attempting to arrest Jack.

Yreka
January 28, 1871

Capt. Jack has been to Yreka to know what the whites are intending to do with him for killing the Doctor.

The white people should not meddle with them in their laws among themselves, further than to try to persuade them out of such foolish notions. White people here are not mad at them for executing their own laws, and should not be anywhere.

Let them settle all these matters among themselves and then our people will be in no danger from them.

E. STEELE[19]

---

[17] Meacham, *Wigwam and War-path,* 346–50; James McLaughlin, *My Friend the Indian,* 323.

[18] Letter, Ivan D. Applegate to the Sheriff of Siskiyou County, California, July 5, 1871, Applegate Collection.

[19] Pacific MSS, Palmer Statement, Bancroft Library.

Meacham, on the recommendation from Steele, suggested to Canby that the order for Jack's arrest be dropped. To this Canby agreed, but the settlers used the killing to discredit Jack as an "indicted murderer" when they wished to show the kind of person he was.[20]

During the summer of 1871, another cause for the Indian war appeared. About sixty miles south of Virginia City, Nevada, a man by the name of Ta-vibo was preaching an apocalyptic religion to the Paiute Indians. Believers in his doctrine were told that earthquakes were imminent which would destroy all human beings in the Western Hemisphere, whether they be white or red. The faithful would promptly rise from the dead, however, and the houses and lands and stock of the dead white men would then revert to the resurrected Indians.[21] Ta-vibo received visitors from many parts of Oregon and Idaho, as well as other bands in Nevada.

Whether his ideas were original, or whether he borrowed some of them from other Indians with similar ideas is not known for certain. In his report for 1870, Meacham ascribes the ideas of Ta-vibo to one Smohalla (Meacham called him "Smoheller"), a Columbia River Indian who lived near Priest Rapids. In the early 1860's he had had a bitter quarrel with another Indian named Moses who accused Smohalla of sorcery. Smohalla was driven from his home for a time, and traveled possibly as far south as Mexico. In his wanderings through the West, he went into Utah, where he was influenced somewhat by Mormon ideas. His subsequent religious teachings had Mormon overtones, as well as strong Christian ingredients which he had picked up from the priests at the Atahnum Mission in the Yakima country when he was a young boy.

Smohalla returned about two years later, announced that he had actually been dead for a time, and that the spirits had sent him back to earth. He would go into a trance and announce a direct revelation from the spirits. The general idea of his "dreams" was that the Indi-

[20] Meacham, *Wigwam and War-path*, 350.
[21] James Mooney, *The Ghost Dance Religion and the Sioux Outbreak of 1890, Fourteenth Annual Report* of the Bureau of Ethnology to the Smithsonian Institution, 1892–93, part 2, 701–702; Click Relander, *Drummers and Dreamers*, 60–79, 127; Leslie Spier, *The Prophet Dance of the North west and Its Derivatives: The Source of the Ghost Dance* (*General Studies in Anthropology*, No. 1), 21–22, 24.

ans should have no more to do with the whites. They should own no cattle, sheep, or hogs, nor should they cultivate the ground. Fish, roots, game, and berries were to be the only food for the Indians. No hay should be cut. Like Ta-vibo, Smohalla held to the idea that an earthquake would expose the bones of dead Indians, and they would join the living to drive out the whites.[22] Part of his ceremony included the hoisting of a flag before he delivered his talk. Music and dancing to drum accompaniment were a part of his ritual.[23] The teachings of Smohalla and Ta-vibo were so similar that it seems difficult not to believe that either they had some influence on each other or their ideas came from a common source. It is clear that both of them were part of the "nativistic" religious response that many American Indians made to the impact of white man's "manifest destiny." Even though these were antiwhite movements, the western European cultural influence is quite evident in such a concept as a resurrection, which was foreign to most Indian religions, but was an integral part of the "dreamer" or "ghost dance" religions.

The man who brought the new ideas to the Modocs was a Walker River Paiute named Frank Spencer. A great earthquake struck the trans-Sierra region in early 1871[24] and the Indians became excited, waiting for the prophecy to be fulfilled. In Nevada, the Indians began to dance in order to bring the dead back to life.

These rudimentary "ghost dances" were performed with the dancers holding hands in a circle. The participants painted their faces red and placed two horizontal black lines on each cheek. They built a fire in the center of the circle and erected a flag beside the fire. They sang a short song, lasting only a minute or less, over and over, while they performed a simple step of moving the left foot a pace to the side on one beat, and dragging the right foot even with the left on the second beat.[25] A long continuation of this monoto-

---

[22] Mooney, *Ghost Dance*, 717–18; Ruth Murray Underhill, *Red Man's America, A History of the Indians in the United States*, 314; Frederick Webb Hodge (ed.), *Handbook of American Indians North of Mexico*; A. J. Splawn, *Ka-mi-akin, Last Hero of the Yakimas*, 351–54.

[23] George W. Fuller, *A History of the Pacific Northwest, with Special Emphasis on the Inland Empire*, 262–64.

[24] Lt. Gen. John M. Schofield, *Forty-six Years in the Army*, 430.

[25] Nash, *Revivalism*, 414–16; Bruno Nettl, "North American Indian Musical

nous singing and dancing produced an emotional frenzy that would reach the point of complete collapse on the part of the participants. When one of the dancers would faint, two men were delegated to revive him by sprinkling water on him, praying or singing. If he failed to revive at once, they put him in a blanket and continued to carry him around the circle.

The Indians believed that the souls of the dancers left their bodies when they fainted and that their souls would go out to meet the spirits of the dead, whom they would try to entice back to earth to help drive out the whites. Skeptics, the Indians thought, would be turned to stone for failing to participate.

Spencer went first to Yainax, and then he visited the Klamath Indians. Before the next year had passed, four dances had been held at Yainax. Each dance lasted for five days and five nights without a let up, except that the participants bathed each morning before going on. They were under the sponsorship of the shamans, and they enhanced the prestige of the priest-doctors as nothing had done since the white men put them on reservations.

There was now a new agent on the Klamath reservation. Knapp had resigned from the army, retired from the Indian Service, and had returned to Ohio. Superintendent Meacham replaced him with his brother, John Meacham. John tried to stop the ghost dancing by issuing orders against it, but the Indians paid no attention. At about the same time, Goodale was relieved of his command at Fort Klamath.[26] No change in the *status quo* took place, however, for Jack did not come back to the reservation, and the dancing went on.

On the Fourth of July in 1871, fire broke out in Yreka and almost destroyed the little town. Jack and some of his Modocs were in Yreka for the holiday celebration, and they helped the volunteers put the fire out.[27] As an aftermath of the excitement, a group of white men who knew the Modoc problem met with Jack. They held an informal conference with him and another Modoc named Black Jim. At the conclusion of the meeting, they issued an informal statement:

Styles," *Journal of American Folklore*, Vol. LXVII, No. 265 (July-September, 1954), 297–99.
[26] Bancroft, *Oregon*, II, 563.
[27] McLaughlin, *My Friend the Indian*, 325.

We the undersigned have had an interview with the Modoc chief know [sic] as Capt. Jack. He wishes us to make know [sic] to whom it may concern that he will not resist the soldiers, nor in any way disturb the settlers in the Modoc country.

> A. M. ROSBOROUGH, Judge 8th Judicial District
> State of California
> JESSE APPLEGATE
> HENRY F. MILLER (of) Tule Lake
> JOHN S. MILLER of Jacksonville.[28]

About the first of August, Alfred Meacham wrote his brother at the Klamath Agency that Jesse Applegate had written of the Yreka meeting and felt that there was a good chance for peace if it were carefully negotiated. Meacham planned to secure a small reservation on the Lost River for the Modocs, but until they got it, they should go to the Klamath reservation. No one, including Jack, was to be arrested for anything he had done before. If Jack were tried for any offense, he should be guaranteed an Indian jury of his own band or of friendly white men. If the Lost River reservation did not materialize, Jack could take his men to the new reservation planned for the Paiutes in the Malheur Lake country.[29]

When John Meacham tried to work out a time and place for meeting Jack, the Modocs asserted their independence. Both Old Schonchin and John Fairchild went to Jack, but he refused to meet John Meacham. Instead, he paid a visit to Jesse Applegate and asked him for rent on Applegate's Clear Lake ranch. Applegate refused to pay. Jack then allowed one of his fighting men, Black Jim, to organize a raid on the stock belonging to a wagon train coming past the Applegate place across the emigrant road. After Black Jim's raid, Jack let it be known that he would welcome a new request for a parley. This would make it appear that the whites were negotiating from a position of weakness and that the Indians were willing to talk only on this basis.[30]

Jack agreed to a meeting at the Applegate ranch if only four

---

[28] Pacific MSS, Palmer Statement, Bancroft Library.

[29] Meacham, *Wigwam and War-path*, 351–54.

[30] Letter, Jesse Applegate to Meacham, July 27, 1872, Records of San Francisco Presidio, Department of the Columbia, 1873, #1836 (hereafter cited as: S.F.P., D.C.).

men came. He agreed to meet them with four Modocs. When John Meacham, Ivan Applegate, and the other two men arrived, they found not four, but twenty-nine, Modocs, armed to the teeth. John Schonchin, Hooker Jim, and Curley Headed Doctor urged that the four commissioners be assassinated, but Jack would not permit it. Black Jim then laid down the terms of agreement. The Modocs would not go to the Klamath reservation. He delivered a long tirade on Klamath faults and denied harming the settlers in any way.

When he was reminded that the wives of the settlers had been annoyed by Modocs, Jim did not deny it; he merely demanded to know who told. He was not given that particular bit of information. Jack then agreed that the Modocs should no longer annoy the settlers nor resist the military. He was then given permission to stay on Lost River until the superintendent could be brought down, which certainly was bound to be quite a time, for there was a council scheduled to be held with the Umatilla Indians.[31] John agreed to write his brother, the superintendent, telling him that there was no danger to be feared from Jack or the Modocs.[32]

Jack and his envoys had won a complete diplomatic triumph. They had made no concessions except a vague promise not to annoy the settlers, which they did not keep. In return, their right to Lost River was confirmed, and they were given possession of it until the grant could be legalized.

The Indians laid low for the next month. A military expedition through the Lakes country probably had something to do with their silence. Major Ludington, a military inspector who visited Forts Bidwell, Warner, and Harney reported no visible Indians and dismissed all threats of trouble as unfounded rumors. Jackson also reported no trouble in the Klamath area, but did say that the Indians were proving very insolent.[33]

In November, H. C. Tickner built a road from Yreka to the Modoc country. It was a difficult undertaking, but it did make travel between the two regions easier. The settlers of the Tule Lake Basin

[31] Meacham to Ivan Applegate, November 11, 1871, Applegate Collection.

[32] Bancroft, *Oregon*, II, 564-65; Letter, John Meacham to A. B. Meacham, August 21, 1871, S.F.P., D.C., 1873, #1811.

[33] Jackson to Assistant Adjutant General, Portland, August 29, 1871, S.F.P., D.C., 1873, #1811.

knew that this road would make their country much more attractive to settlers, but before many would come in, the Modoc question had to be settled. A petition was drawn up and forwarded to Meacham requesting him to have the Modocs sent back to the Klamath reservation. Since he had already recommended a Lost River reservation, Meacham delayed his answer for almost two months. In January he forwarded a second petition to General Canby with the advice that it would take at least fifty soldiers to make the Modocs move and that Yainax was the only possible place to send them.

Canby refused to take any action until the decision on the Lost River reservation was reached. He withdrew the army from the matter after instructing Jackson to protect the settlers.[34]

The settlers grew impatient waiting for some action by Meacham, and since they received none, sixty-five of them sent another petition to the governor of Oregon appealing to state authority to handle the dealings with the Indians. If Governor Grover would issue a call, they would form a volunteer company and take military action against the Modocs without waiting for the Indian superintendency or the army. Meacham also wrote Grover agreeing that matters were growing serious, but said he certainly did not advocate federal control of Indian matters. Grover was not quite ready to step into a traditionally federal concern. His urgent letter to General Canby made it clear that he expected action, but it resulted only in a reply that the army wanted nothing more than to keep things quiet. General Canby did issue an order to Major Otis and fifty officers and men of cavalry to establish a temporary camp on Lost River. Canby flatly refused to do anything more until the recommendation of the Indian superintendent to grant Jack's band the Lost River reservation was acted upon.[35]

Shortly after the arrival of Otis, "Doctor George," an advocate of the Paiute ghost dancing, appeared on the Klamath reservation. The Modocs there took word to the Lost River Modocs, and Curley Headed Doctor accepted the new teaching with enthusiasm. A dance ground was prepared along the river bank, a central fire was

[34] Canby to Meacham, February 5, 1872, S.F.P., D. C., 1872, #281.
[35] 43 Cong., 1 sess., *House Exec. Doc. No. 122*, Modoc Papers, 9.

built, a pole was set in place with a "medicine flag," and a circle dance was held, complete with face painting. A rope of tule fiber was braided, painted red, and laid around the camp to keep out unwelcome visitors. This was the only time the ghost dance was given on Lost River, but Curley Headed Doctor sponsored several during the fighting in Jack's encampment in the Lava Beds.[36] (Doctor George, curiously enough, was the last Paiute shaman to be executed by the Indians for losing a patient whom he had attempted to cure. This event occurred in 1906.)[37]

With the coming of spring, the pace of activity stepped up considerably. On the fifteenth of March, a reconnaissance ordered by Major Otis left Camp Warner, two days' ride east of Fort Klamath, for the Modoc country. With him were Lieutenant J. G. Kyle and a surgeon, plus the half-Indian scout Donald McKay, twenty-seven enlisted men, under the command of Captain David Perry, and guides, packers, interpreters, and mules. Marching and riding through deep mud and melting snow, they arrived on March 24.[38] There was little excitement, but McKay and four Indians were sent out to the Lost River "gap" about ten miles east of Linkville to try to arrange for a conference with Jack's band. Two days later, McKay returned with one Modoc. Later, another Indian visited the expedition. Both had the same story—Jack was not coming to talk to Otis; the officer had to go to the Indians.

When he received that message, Otis told Jack's messenger that if the Indians would not come in, the soldiers would go to him—in force. At that, Jack's man promised to bring Jack back by April 3, indicating that Jack had already given him word to yield if the whites proved obstinate. The Modoc insisted that the Indians feared the soldiers and asked that the conference should not be attended by the soldiers. Otis agreed to make this concession.

About noon, on the day appointed, Otis, J. N. High (who had replaced John Meacham as subagent), Ivan Applegate, McKay, and several Indian scouts arrived at the "gap." As usual, Jack had many

[36] Nash, *Revivalism*, 415–17.
[37] *Ibid.*, 417.
[38] Otis Report, *Oregon Superintendency, 1872*, Office of Indian Affairs.

times the Indians present that he had agreed to bring—there were almost forty with him.[39] Arms were stacked on opposite sides of the river but left within easy reach. While the talks were getting under way, some settlers came down to watch the proceedings, for they were eager to get the Modocs out of their neighborhood and back to the Klamath reservation.

Jack promised good behavior and denied ever having done anything wrong. He was told that he was illegally on land which had been ceded to the United States by the treaty of 1864 but that he would be left there until the President determined exactly where the Indians were to go. He was further informed that he had to control his men or he and they would be punished by the soldiers. Two of the citizens present at the council attested to Jack's good character. Jack asserted that he never started trouble, but when some of the other citizens present were queried on this subject, all cited specific instances of Modoc knavery. Jack ended the conference by repeating that he believed all Klamaths were thieves, but he made no promises about the future plans of his Indians.[40]

High reported later that the Indians had planned to kill all the whites at the conference, but his statement is contradicted by others who were present. Later in the summer, Jack furnished an escort for High's family when they were traveling through Modoc country; accordingly, High's charge probably was the result of an overactive imagination.[41]

Meanwhile, the War Department in Washington became increasingly disturbed over events in Oregon. On the nineteenth of March, the Secretary of War informed the Commissioner of Indian Affairs that the Modoc question could not remain unsettled forever. He enclosed a series of military reports describing the situation as seen through the eyes of the men on the ground who would have to fight a war if one developed.[42]

[39] Don C. Fisher, "Saving the Early History of Klamath County," *The Oregon Motorist*, Vol. XI, No. 9 (June, 1931).

[40] Otis Report, *Oregon Superintendency, 1872*, Office of Indian Affairs.

[41] F. A. Shaver, *An Illustrated History of Central Oregon, Embracing Wasco, Sherman, Gilliam, Wheeler, Crook, Lake, and Klamath Counties, State of Oregon*, 949.

[42] *Oregon Superintendency, 1872*, Office of Indian Affairs.

The most feasible suggestion was that the Paiutes should be moved to a new reservation north of Malheur Lake, and Jack's band of about sixty fighting men and their families should be moved to Yainax, whether they objected or not. The Indian Office, following this recommendation, turned down the idea Meacham had proposed earlier for the solution of the Modoc question and stated that there was to be no reservation for the Modocs on Lost River.

This decision, of course, did nothing to remove Jack's basic objection to leaving his old hunting grounds. At Yainax he would not be recognized as headman, he would be living on Klamath land, and he would have given up all traditional Modoc country. Jack's followers, like Curley Headed Doctor, who fiercely resisted the change to a new set of mores, would have objected to the point of offering violence to him if he had given in. No one in Washington, nor for that matter at the Klamath Agency, seems to have realized that Jack was not going to accept their fiat without argument. Jack turned once more to the invalid agreement that he had made with Steele in Yreka in the spring of 1864, and said that this was the agreement that he would live by.

The Interior Department decided to resolve the problem by changing superintendents. Meacham was removed, and T. B. Odeneal was appointed to the position in his place. Thus, at this critical point in the negotiations, a man who knew almost nothing of the background of the situation and had never met with Jack or the Modocs was placed in charge of the job of getting Jack to leave Lost River. It is to be granted that Meacham was not a strong agent and that he had shamefully neglected his duty and opportunity to pacify the Modocs by failing to visit them after Jack had asked for him. He did know Jack, however, and had succeeded in getting the astute Indian on the Klamath reservation in 1869.

Odeneal made matters worse by replacing High with another appointee who also did not know Jack. Mr. L. S. Dyar was assigned to Klamath, and he was an agent who knew little of the Modocs' plight. What he did know had been learned entirely from reading white men's reports. He was almost totally unaware of the conflicting cross-currents of opinion and prejudice in the Lost River country. He had to depend on information from the settlers who were almost unanimous in demanding that the Modocs be consolidated with Schonchin's band as soon as possible.

Early in May, Ivan Applegate cautioned Odeneal that to try to move the Indians during the summer would be difficult and probably disastrous. A troop of cavalry would only scatter the Indians and thus make it impossible for the settlers in the Tule Lake area to stay there. He blamed the Yreka citizenry for all the trouble and gave his opinion that these men would supply the Indians with arms and ammunition if it came to a conflict. An attempt to arrest Jack, Black Jim, Scarfaced Charley, Boston Charley, and Curley Headed Doctor might be successful, however, and, if so, the others probably would come peacefully enough. This would have to be done with great caution, for if the arrest were bungled, trouble would certainly follow. Applegate also suggested that the arrest be made in the early winter when the Indians were in permanent camp.[43]

Modocs from Schonchin's band were sent to Jack to ask him to meet Dyar and one of the Applegates at Juniper Springs on Lost River to see whether he had changed his mind in the month that had intervened since Otis had talked with him. Obviously, nothing had happened which would change Jack's mind, for the basic situation was exactly as it had been. New men meant new attempts to thresh the old straw, but Dyar, along with Ivan and his brother, Oliver Applegate, made the trip.

As might have been predicted, the results were highly unsatisfactory. The best that could be obtained from Jack was a promise to remain on his good behavior where he was until Odeneal or General Canby could make up his mind what to do. Since that was exactly what Jack had decided to do anyway, he readily agreed to the plan. The only change in the situation was that Jack now knew that his request for the Lost River reservation had been turned down. In a burst of generosity, Jack promised not to harm any of the settlers if they did not locate on the west side of Lost River where he had his winter camp. Although his promise did not bind any other Modoc whose winter quarters were on the opposite or settler side of the river, Jack did not bother to explain this point to Dyar or the Applegates.[44]

[43] *Ibid.*   [44] *Ibid.*

The settlers were furious. They were no better off after the series of conferences than if Jack had never signed a treaty. The settlers could easily set alight a brush fire of war, which might well bring on an Indian massacre of the settlers. Army leaders knew this and were inclined to blame the settlers for what did happen. In fact, several of the army leaders made specific statements blaming the settlers. Some years later, General John M. Schofield, commander of the Pacific area, claimed that the Lost River country was "rich grazing land and was much coveted by the ranchmen of that region."[45] Another officer said, "Were the snow-crowned summits of Mount Rainier set apart as an Indian reservation, white men would immediately commence jumping them."[46] The impatience of the settlers, therefore, received little encouragement from the army.

This being the case, Odeneal and his advisers conferred. The result was a recommendation to the Commissioner of Indian Affairs on June 17 that Jack should be arrested and exiled until he was willing to accept Schonchin's leadership and settle down peaceably at Yainax. Odeneal took the position that the Modocs were like wayward youths in a gang led by desperadoes. If the leaders were taken into custody, then civilization and "Christian virtues" would be the result as far as the rest of them were concerned. Major Otis agreed with Odeneal, but urged that the arrest be delayed until September because there were not enough soldiers available in case something went wrong.

A week before Odeneal made his recommendation, Lieutenant Colonel Frank Wheaton of the Twenty-first Infantry took up his newly assigned tasks as commander of the District of the Lakes, with headquarters at Camp Warner. To Odeneal's horror, one of Wheaton's first acts was to withdraw Otis and the cavalry from Fort Klamath. A letter of protest to General Canby brought the reply that the commander of Fort Klamath had "been instructed to keep a vigilant watch over the Modocs and to send an occasional scout through that country."[47]

When the troops were withdrawn, even Schonchin's Modocs

[45] Schofield, *Forty-six Years*, 435.
[46] Mooney, *Ghost Dance*, 711.
[47] Letter, Canby to Odeneal, June 20, 1872, S.F.P., D.C., 1872, #983.

began to wander over the countryside. The situation was understood by no white men except the settlers. They knew Jack, and they knew his men. They were afraid of the Modocs, but they were also grimly determined to get rid of them. Plans were started to organize a militia to control or drive out the Indians, since the army obviously did not intend to do so. This, of course, would have furnished the very spark that would have set off the war, and the army firmly told the settlers they could not form a militia.[48]

On June 27, Company F of the Twenty-first Infantry arrived at Fort Klamath from Crescent City. This was the army's response to the urgent pleas by the settlers for military force.

In mid-July, frost wiped out the crops at Yainax. The Modocs under Schonchin were reduced instantly to living on the meager bounty of the agent, while the wild Modocs under Jack continued to flourish like the proverbial green bay tree. The wild Modocs were more convinced than ever that the primitive way of gathering food was the only satisfactory way.

For several weeks nothing happened. Odeneal received approval from the Office of Indian Affairs late in July to take military forces and arrest the leaders of Jack's band and to take the rest to Yainax. This, according to his instructions, was to be carried out in September. Odeneal probably should have asked what military forces he was going to use, but he did not. Neither had he made any personal effort as yet to meet Jack, to ascertain Jack's objection to living under Schonchin or the temper of Jack's followers under the influence of Curley Headed Doctor. To Odeneal, force seemed to be the answer to the Modoc question, even though that force was woefully inadequate. Further, the troops available were only half-trained. Even the ammunition available for their rifles was defective.[49]

The rest of July and August went by with no action, and Jack remained triumphantly undisturbed. He did make a trip to Yreka to consult with lawyers Steele and Rosborough about finding a way for the Modocs to stay on Lost River. Their suggestion was for him to dissolve his tribal status, to take up claims like the settlers, pay

---

[48] Bancroft, *Oregon*, II, 570.
[49] Letter, J. McAllister to Lt. John A. Kress, August 22, 1872, S.F.P., D. C., 1873, #125.

taxes, and hold a plot of land for each Indian. There was no law at this time which authorized such action on the part of Indians, but Steele held the opinion that the Constitution implied that when Indians paid taxes, automatically they became citizens. He bolstered his arguments by a loose construction of the Fourteenth Amendment.

Early in September, Odeneal reminded Canby that this was the month of decision. Canby then sent word to Wheaton at Camp Warner that Odeneal might be planning to start something, and, if so, he announced (as though it had occurred to the military authorities for the first time) that "it is possible that they may resist and require a greater exhibition of force than can be furnished from [Fort Klamath]." If trouble came, Wheaton was to use what other resources he had in other posts. Canby went on to say that Odeneal had not yet given him any exact information about how and when he was going to have Jack arrested. He finished by saying that Major Green was being sent on a scouting sweep through the Modoc country, and maybe he could find out something.[50]

Obviously, communication between the Oregon superintendency and the army was poor. Yet success for the venture depended upon close co-operation between these two branches of government. Odeneal may have been only careless, or his failure to keep the army informed may have been a deliberate attempt to force Canby's hand. A good deal of the trouble that finally forced the open conflict between white and Indian was a result of this breakdown of communication.

In accordance with orders issued by Canby, Green left Fort Klamath on September 9 for his scouting expedition, and arrived at the mouth of Lost River on September 14. Jack apparently knew what was afoot and thought that the hour of reckoning had arrived. Horsemen rode furiously back and forth between Jack's village and that of Hooker Jim, a few hundred yards away, making plans for a course of action. Green sent in a Modoc-speaking interpreter to tell Jack he had not come to arrest him. Jack would not believe it until Green's men turned their horses out to graze. At this point, an

[50] Letter, Asst. Adj. Gen., Department of Columbia to Wheaton, September 10, 1872, S.F.P., D.C., 1873, #36.

English-speaking Modoc approached the military camp and asked whether Green wanted to see Jack. Since the white men had been coming regularly to see Jack and to ask him politely whether he wouldn't please go to the reservation, it seemed to the Indians that this must have been Green's purpose as well. To the surprise of the Indian, Green said he had nothing particular to say to Jack, but if he wanted anything, Jack could come to see the Major.

Jack sent word that his mother was dying and that he could not come. It is noticeable that in dealing with the white men, Jack always had a reason—valid or otherwise—why he could not just then meet with them at a time and place of their choosing. This strategy doubtless was part of his struggle for prestige and was designed to compel the whites to come to him for favors.

Green broke camp and proceeded along the old South Emigrant Road. He found it almost obliterated in places. He questioned the settlers, and although they said the Indians were making trouble continuously, "none could point out any especial depredations" or "any particular robbery they had committed."[51]

Odeneal did nothing until Green returned on October 1. More procrastination pushed the date of the projected arrest into an indefinite future. By mid-November no one yet knew what Odeneal planned to do. Wheaton commented that heavy snow was beginning to fall and hoped that nothing would require large troop movements at that time, but, if necessary, cavalry from Harney, Bidwell, Warner, and Klamath would be concentrated so that an overwhelming show of force would overawe Jack, and there would be no trouble.[52]

Again, lack of communication prevented Wheaton from knowing that already the wheels for action had been set in motion from Washington. In a letter of instructions to Odeneal, the Indian Office gave him explicit instructions to remove the Modocs to Yainax, "peaceably if you can, forcibly if you must." Promptly, Odeneal informed Canby that he was going to move some time during the month, and Canby informed Major Green that he might be called upon for troops. If more troops were needed, Green was to tell

[51] Green Report, October 5, 1873, S.F.P., D.C., 1873.
[52] Letter, Wheaton to Canby, November 14, 1872, S.F.P., D.C., 1872, #2118.

Canby, who would then provide the proper orders.[53] Odeneal next sent word to Wheaton on November 25 (which could not possibly have reached him for two days and would have taken another two to have received Wheaton's acknowledgment) that a messenger had been sent to Jack asking him to come in for a conference in Linkville on the twenty-eighth. Jack had never come to Linkville for any conference, and had Odeneal known the situation better, he would have realized that such a request was bound to be refused. In his note to Wheaton, Odeneal said that if Jack refused to move peaceably to the reservation—and the superintendent's hope that there was any possibility that the Modocs might agree, can be ascribed only to fatuous optimism—then Odeneal would inform Wheaton of Jack's decision, and he would request troops.

Wheaton logically could expect to hear about November 30, whether or not troops would be required; he should then get in touch with General Canby in Fort Vancouver to get the proper orders. It would have been about December 15, before troops would have been ready if the steps agreed upon had actually been taken, and Jack probably could have been arrested with safety if enough soldiers had appeared in front of his camp.

Ivan Applegate, whom Jack did not like, was sent to Jack's camp, and he brought back news which should have surprised no one. Jack not only would not meet Odeneal in Linkville; he would not meet him anywhere else, either. He did not want to talk, and certainly he had no intention of going to Yainax to live under Old Schonchin's control. This is what he had been saying for two years, and nothing had happened to cause him to change his mind.

Even more serious in Applegate's eyes was his unpleasant experience of listening to a brisk debate between Jack and some of the young hot-heads under the shaman's influence. The younger men enthusiastically urged the killing of Applegate and a companion named Brown in order to start a war, which, with the help of the spirits, they could win. Jack vetoed the suggestion but had to argue strenuously to make his veto stick.

When Applegate told his story to Odeneal, the superintendent was alarmed. He knew the Modocs were stubborn, but if they also

[53] Letter, Canby to Green, November 14, 1872, S.F.P., D.C., 1872, #2304.

planned to start a war, something had to be done. Instead of communicating with Wheaton, however, as planned, he consulted Applegate and Brown, who agreed they should act right away. After a consultation with Dyar, the local agent, Odeneal then sent Applegate directly to Major Green at Fort Klamath requesting him immediately to "furnish a sufficient force to compel said Indians to go to Camp Yainax, on said reservation, where I have made provision for their subsistence."[54] Although this message was forwarded promptly to Colonel Wheaton, he did not receive it at his headquarters until December 2, and no time was taken to wait for a reply.

About five in the morning of November 28, Applegate arrived at Fort Klamath. He was taken by the sergeant of the guard to Lieutenant F. A. Boutelle, the Officer of the Day. When Applegate explained his errand and asked whether Green would send troops, Boutelle told him that while he was certain the Major would not send troops, Applegate could make himself comfortable until the message could be delivered.

When he had taken the word to Green, Boutelle went back to duty. At eight o'clock Captain Jackson came to him and told him to be ready to leave for Lost River at once, and to prepare the official orders so that all available troopers could go with them. Boutelle did as he was ordered, but when he took the orders in for Green's signature, he could not help reminding his superior officer that Canby had asked to be told if troops were going to be used. Boutelle also said he believed that Jack would fight. Green's reply was that if he did not send troops, the citizens would think the army was afraid of the Modocs.

Without waiting to communicate either with Canby or Wheaton, Green then signed the order for Captain Jackson to take "all available men of his troop to Lost River and to arrest Jack, Black Jim and Scarfaced Charley by the next morning." He was to do this, ordered Green, without bloodshed if possible, but if he had to fight, the responsibility could be placed on the Indians.[55] His saying that the Indians were responsible did not make the statement true. The action of the Indian superintendent in demanding troops with-

[54] Letter, Odeneal to Green, November 27, 1872, S.F.P., D.C., 1872, #2304.
[55] S.F.P., D.C., 1872, #2304.

out consulting with Canby and of the army officer in granting this demand without consultation must be considered to make them at least as responsible as Jack for the immediate cause of the war.

Wheaton did not know what they were planning. The first battle of the Modoc War was fought and over with when he received Odeneal's first letter. His reply makes it plain that he knew nothing of what was afoot. He said that he was planning to concentrate all available forces and would be pleased to co-operate with the Indian Service whenever Odeneal's instructions provided for military action.[56] Wheaton was ill at the time he sent the letter, but knew that preparations had to be made if the Modoc leaders were to be arrested. Neither Odeneal nor Green seems to have had any realization of the consequences of what they were doing.

Assessment of blame for a disastrous war is never easy. Probably the over-all cause was the decentralization of authority so that no one knew what to expect—neither the army, the Indian Service, the agents, nor the Modocs knew who was in real authority. General Schofield, the Pacific Coast commanding officer, says that Odeneal took advantage of "an innocent old army regulation which directed department commanders to render such military assistance as might be necessary to enable the Indian superintendent to carry out their orders from Washington."[57] Neither the President of the United States nor the Secretary of War nor the General of the Army knew that the Indian Service had sent Odeneal the "peaceably if you can, forcibly if you must" order. Schofield declared that Canby assumed that the matter had been cleared with the War Department. Actually neither Canby nor Wheaton assumed any such thing. They did not have a chance. Odeneal went to a subordinate who exceeded his authority by issuing a military order that set off hostilities. The fact that President Grant promptly abolished the regulation cited, did no good. The war was on.

Green's action was incomprehensible. He did not know whether or not Jack would fight, and why he took orders from a civilian rather than waiting for his commander to issue them has never been explained. He was a brave man and received the Congressional

[56] Ibid.
[57] Schofield, Forty-six Years, 435.

Medal of Honor for his part in combat. He also deserved a reprimand for his part in making the combat an unhappy reality.

Jack cannot be absolved of all responsibility. He was no ignorant savage. He knew what was going on, and some concession on his part would have made peace possible; however, his followers might not have allowed him to make concessions. About the only valid argument that Jack made in his own defense at the trial after the war, was that the other members of his band would not let him compromise. In the final analysis, the basic cause of the war, on the Indian side, was the conflict between the new order, as exemplified by Old Schonchin, and the dependence on the old ways championed by Curley Headed Doctor. It may be that between these two conflicting positions there was no possibility of compromise.

The immediate responsibility must rest upon Odeneal. He had never actually met or talked with Jack, yet he presumed to know what the Modocs would do. He had promised to inform Canby and Wheaton before taking action, yet he not only did not, but made no effort to do so. He made no provision, either, for warning the settlers that they might be in danger after the troops met the Indians. He even went so far as to say that he did not know there were any settlers east of Tule Lake, although it was his job to know. When hostilities broke out as the result of his actions, he fled the country as fast as he could and let the dogs of war bark without having to listen to them. He was not very popular in the Klamath–Tule Lake area for a while with settlers, soldiers, or Indians. His actions were denounced on all sides, yet he never seems to have admitted that he made a mistake in going to Green. Rather, he blamed Green by saying Green told him that orders from Wheaton were unnecessary. He could issue the orders.[58]

Regardless of whose responsibility it was, when Captain Jackson and his men rode out of Fort Klamath in that stormy afternoon of November 28, the Modoc War began. It was the most costly Indian war in lives and money in United States military history if one considers the number of Indians involved. When the war was over, the ghost dancing had not stopped. The Indians were not all on reserva-

[58] 43 Cong., 1 sess., *House Exec. Doc. No. 29*, "Report of Governor Grover to General Schofield on the Modoc War."

tions. In fact, all Indian tribes in the West were encouraged to resist the army because Jack had been able to do so much with so little. The Indian Service seems to have learned nothing from the affair. And the army has a cairn of stones standing beside Tule Lake to mark the spot where its leader lost his life.

IV

THE FIRST BATTLE
FOR THE STRONGHOLD

THE ARMY'S ATTEMPTS to arrest Jack were badly planned and poorly executed. Interference by settlers not only did not help but led to a brutal massacre. Additional army units had to be brought from great distances to subdue the hostile Indians.

The war began when Jackson and his men left Fort Klamath about noon, Thursday, November 28, 1872. It was a wet and blustery afternoon, and the men were cold and miserable in the freezing rain. Captain Jackson, Lieutenant Boutelle, and Dr. McElderry, the surgeon, led the party of thirty-eight soldiers. Behind them came five packers and a small pack train. Ivan Applegate was the civilian guide.

The trip from Fort Klamath to Linkville passed without incident, and the expedition stopped at the little town to eat an evening meal and to feed their horses. Late in the evening Odeneal came down to the camp, met Jackson, and they talked for a long time, trying to decide the exact course of action they would take when the soldiers reached Jack's camp. They agreed that there should be no preliminary firing, that Jack was to be escorted to Yainax under arrest, and that the whole affair was to proceed as quietly as possible.

During the conference, Ivan Applegate's younger brother, Oliver, who was officially in charge of Schonchin's band at Yainax, rode into Linkville. He did not know that any military preparations were under way, and at once he pointed out to Superintendent Odeneal that he knew of at least two of Schonchin's Modocs who were at Lost River, gambling with Jack's people. He asked permission to take them out of the camp before any soldiers arrived to keep his Indians from harm in case of hostilities.

Odeneal replied that no shooting was expected, for it had been "generally agreed" that if the matter were handled carefully, Jack would go to Yainax peacefully. He assured the dubious Oliver that the thirty-eight soldiers were quite sufficient for any emergency, but he gave him permission to go down and rescue his Indians if it would make him feel any better.

Ivan talked briefly with his brother, telling him that the plan was for Jackson to ride down the west bank of the river and take about twenty-five men into Jack's camp, while Lieutenant Boutelle would take the other ten men, cross at the Stukel Ford, and ride into the camp of Curley Headed Doctor and his son-in-law, Hooker Jim, across and slightly downstream from Jack's camp.

By the time it had grown dark, Oliver noticed O. C. Brown and Dennis Crawley starting out for Linkville. Brown had been told by Odeneal that he should go out and warn the settlers that the soldiers were on the way, but since Jackson and Odeneal were sure there would be no shooting, no attempt was made to warn the settlers below Crawley's own cabin. Brown himself did not know that there were others living below Crawley's, and Crawley was concerned mainly with informing the people in the immediate vicinity of Jack's camp, which was only a little way from his holdings.

That very afternoon, Henry Miller, a settler on the northeastern corner of Tule Lake, had assured a delegation of Indians consisting of Hooker Jim, Bogus Charley, Scarfaced Charley, Shacknasty Jim, Steamboat Frank, Skookum Horse, and Curley Headed Jack, all of whom came from three different bands of Modocs, that he knew of no plans for soldiers to move into their country so late in the year, but if he heard, he would tell them at once. He did not tell them because he had not been informed of the plan. The first and last word he received came when the enraged Indians of Hooker Jim's band accosted him. Although they once considered Miller their friend, now they accused him of treachery and then filled him with bullets.

Oliver Applegate left Linkville about ten o'clock with Charlie

Monroe and Dave Hill, a Klamath Indian leader, ostensibly to get the Yainax Indians to go back to the reservation. Four other civilians from Linkville followed his trail shortly after he rode south to get his Yainax Modocs. Some probably went for the same reason that people follow fire trucks. Possibly they went because the word was out that Long Jim and another Modoc had been at Yainax that morning, and the two were probably even now riding furiously toward Lost River with the news that the soldiers were out. Applegate had a secondary purpose for going to Jack's camp—to intercept Long Jim and prevent him from warning Jack of the soldiers' coming. Ivan told Oliver that he would ride with the army, and that just before they reached Jack's camp, he would signal with a whistle so that they could meet to exchange information.

Long Jim had not yet passed Oliver when Ivan came to his brother about four o'clock in the morning to tell him that Jackson had changed his plans. Since the captain was not feeling well, he had directed Boutelle to stay with him instead of separating the two tiny forces. Jackson joined the Applegates and asked Oliver to cross the river, go to Crawley's, and wait until the arrests had been made. There would be no chance to get the two Schonchin Modocs out of Jack's camp before the soldiers arrived. Jackson ordered Oliver to listen and, if any firing should break out, to round up what settlers he could and come to the assistance of the army at once.

As Ivan and Jackson left, the four Linkville citizens, A. J. Burnett, W. J. Small, George Fiocke, and Henry Duncan joined the other three. The seven-man cavalcade then crossed the river and rode to Crawley's cabin, less than a mile from Hooker Jim's winter village. In the Crawley home were Crawley, Dan Colwell (Crawley's partner), a man named Bybee and his family, another citizen named Thurber, and three other men who were strangers to Applegate.

Leaving Bybee's wife and children in the cabin, in the early dawn the men moved quietly into a gully near the river to await developments across the river in the camp of Jack's sleeping Indians.

The officers had agreed to surprise Jack's camp while it was still dark, to get into the village, and to demand the arms of the Indians before they had recovered fully from their sleepiness and surprise.

The impatient civilians watched the sky growing gradually lighter and came to the conclusion that somehow Jackson was lost. The trouble, however, was that the weather had grown much worse. The sleet had turned to ice, and both men and animals were encrusted with it. The trail was deep in mud, and the men rode more and more slowly. By early morning they were numb with cold and the exhaustion of riding almost steadily for sixteen hours under such conditions.

About a mile from Jack's camp the troop halted, dismounted, and adjusted their saddles. Boutelle took off his overcoat and tied it to his saddle. The men followed suit. Although this deprived them even more of needed warmth, wearing their overcoats would have hampered their movements if trouble came. The little company was then divided into two platoons. When all preparations were made, the men stumbled forward through the freezing rain.

Scarfaced Charley of Jack's band (so named because as a child he had cut his face falling from the Yreka stage when he was trying to hitch a ride on the back axle) had not gone back to Jack's camp after the delegation returned from Henry Miller's. He had spent the night gambling in Hooker Jim's camp. About seven in the morning the game broke up, and Charley paddled a canoe across the river. Climbing the bank, he tripped and his gun discharged. No one was hurt, but to Applegate and the citizens waiting in their uncomfortable post, the sound was electrifying.

For a moment there was no further disturbance. The sleeping Indians seemed unperturbed. Charley reached the top of the bank and glanced out a few hundred yards to the south. His attention was arrested by a line of men moving toward the village through the storm. Immediately, all was confusion in the Indian camp. There was a great deal of loud talking in the Modoc language and considerable running between lodges.

When the soldiers reached the center of Jack's village of about fifteen dwellings, most of the women and children had gone inside the lodges again and were lying flat on the ground in the house pits to protect themselves against rifle shots. A few men stood watching the soldiers, but Jack did not appear. He said later that he went to his lodge and waited for the white officers to join him for the usual conference. All the talking, though, took place outside, with Jackson speaking and Ivan Applegate translating. Applegate used the Chinook jargon, which was at best a slow medium for conveying meaning. The whites and the Indians argued for almost forty-five minutes.

The impatient civilians across the river, who knew only that the soldiers were in the Modoc camp, found waiting unbearable. Unable to stand the strain, Brown mounted his horse, emerged from concealment, and rode down to the river opposite Jack's camp where he could see what was happening. When he came back, he said to the waiting men, "It's all right. Captain Jack's men are laying down their arms. Let's go down and drive these fellows in." Brown was as wrong about this matter as he had been about the number of settlers to be warned in the Tule Lake Basin. In the same blithe way that he left ten families unaware of pending disaster, he urged the citizens to enter Hooker Jim's camp. With his cheery assurance ringing in their ears, the men jumped up from their cramped positions and rushed into Hooker Jim's camp. When they arrived, they found that everything was definitely not all right.

Seventeen men of Hooker Jim's band, fully armed, were watching the drama in Jack's camp. They turned when they heard the settlers riding into their midst, not knowing quite how to react. Oliver Applegate quickly dismounted and thrust out his hand toward Curley Headed Doctor in the time honored greeting of Indian and white. After only a momentary hesitation, the shaman shook his hand. Applegate seized the initiative by announcing, "The soldiers have come—are on the other side." (This was certainly belaboring the obvious!) "I have come to save you and befriend you. You know I am chief at Yainax, and that I use your relatives well who are there. Come to me and lay down your arms, and I will see that the troops do not trouble you."

There was a long pause. Then, uncertainly, several Indians laid down their guns and bows in front of Applegate. Hooker Jim, however, turned and ran. He started to push a canoe into the river to cross to Jack's camp. Brown dashed after him and pulling a derringer, covered Jim, made him give up his gun, and grimly brought him back to the circle of civilians, which by now included all of the men on the north side of the river.

There was a period of tense waiting, broken only by the movement of two Indians sneaking out of Jack's camp, climbing into a canoe, and coming toward Jim's village. Applegate called on them to return to the whites and to be prepared to give up their arms. They proved to be his wandering Yainax Modocs, Little Jim and Billy. As soon as Applegate recognized them, he told them to start for the agency as quickly as their legs would carry them. Thankful to be out of the trouble, they started away on a dead run.

The diversion caused by their arrival gave one of Hooker Jim's band an opportunity to offer resistance. Miller's Charley seized Hooker Jim's gun from Brown, but Dave Hill, the Klamath who was in Applegate's party, grappled with him and took it back. The situation was rapidly reaching the breaking point. The whites tried to keep talking to the Modocs, but neither group was really listening. They were both trying to find out what was happening on the other side of the river during the long silence.

During the time that Ivan had been talking to a few of the Indians, others disappeared into their lodges. When they came out a few minutes later, they were prepared for trouble. Jackson said that they emerged painted, "stripped to the buff," and each carried one to three rifles. Scarfaced Charley dashed past Jackson and plunged into one of the lodges. Almost immediately he appeared with several rifles. He kept one in his arms, put two at his feet, and gave the rest to Black Jim.

Jackson asked Boutelle what he thought would happen. Boutelle's reply was, "There is going to be a fight, and the sooner you open it the better, before there are any more complete preparations."

There was no time to warn the civilians across the river. Indeed, it is probable that Jackson had completely forgotten their existence. He ordered Boutelle to get the rifles in Scarfaced Charley's possession. Scarface swung his rifle to a ready position. Boutelle drew a revolver and, trying to overawe Scarfaced Charley, suddenly moved toward him talking loudly, breathing curses and threats, anything to distract the Indians' attention momentarily until he was close enough to seize the weapons.

A sudden impulsive movement of Charley's, however, told Boutelle that the bluff was not going to work. In a flash he knew that in the next split second he was to be the target of a rifle bullet. Instantly, Boutelle fired an unaimed shot at the Indian.

This shot probably saved his life. Scarfaced Charley's aim was slightly off, and instead of killing Boutelle, the bullet grazed his left arm. As though this were a prearranged signal, Indians poured out of their lodges, shooting guns or discharging bows and arrows as they came. In Hooker Jim's camp the Modocs made a simultaneous movement, sweeping up any weapons they could grab; they opened fire on the civilians as soon as they could pull the triggers.

The civilians fled, though some of them fired at the Indians as they ran. One of them, Fiocke or Small, was carrying a double-barreled shotgun, and a charge from this gun killed a baby and wounded his mother, who was holding him. Otherwise, no one seems to have been hurt in the first exchange of shots. Two of the men, Thurber and Small, ran the wrong way in their mad flight, and Thurber was killed. Small joined the others, who ran to Crawley's cabin, and everyone prepared for a siege.

In Jack's camp, the firing immediately became general. An Indian known as The Watchman was killed at the first volley. Despite the close quarters, no other Indian was killed. Every soldier must have been in the last stages of buck fever.

At the sound of gunfire, the cavalry horses promptly stampeded. Soldiers ran about trying to catch and quiet the animals, while their comrades continued to fire blindly through the lodges behind which the Indians were hiding and shooting as fast as they could reload. Harris, an enlisted man, was killed, and seven others wounded by the more accurate fire of the Modocs. Boutelle managed to rally the men after the first few confused seconds. He ordered a charge, and the men made a shaky advance.

The whole affair on both sides of the river was over in less than five minutes. Both the Indians and the soldiers beat a hasty retreat. The Indians ran farther than the soldiers and kept running longer. Most of the Modocs fled into the sagebrush toward the low hills to the south, and as they ran, they fired an occasional shot to keep the soldiers busy. A few of the troopers returned to Jack's village and told the old men and women to leave the camp. The noncombatants promptly dragged several wounded Indians into canoes hidden in the tules of the river bank, put all the children in with them, and paddled furiously down the river toward Tule Lake. In the lake itself, the full force of the rain and wind struck the little flotilla, which came close to swamping, but they were able to reach the Lava Beds on the south shore of the lake with their mangled cargo. Miller's Charley, Black Jim, and Duffy were the most seriously hurt. In the next month, however, all recovered sufficiently to take an active part in a major battle.[1]

The soldiers were reluctant to pursue Jack's men far into the sage beyond the camp and returned to the village to wreak vengeance upon the property of the Indians. Jackson ordered the village burned, which was done. In the retreat, the Modocs had abandoned one very old woman, as was the Indian custom when the aged were known to be of no further use to the group. She was lying in one of the lodges and was burned to death in the fire. Subsequent atrocity stories circulated in the East reported this as a deliberate act of cruelty on the part of the soldiers. There were atrocities later, but this death was an accident. Another story charged that soldiers who burned the village raped a woman "before her husband's eyes" before they let her go. This is almost certainly untrue, for there were no men in the village, and if her husband had been there, the soldiers would have either run from him or killed him. Actually, while the village was being destroyed, the women were out on the lake, paddling frantically for the Lava Beds.

Hooker Jim's Modocs did not wish to attack the Crawley cabin, filled as it was with frightened but desperate and well-armed settlers. His band contented itself with yelling and firing an occasional shot at the defenders. Meanwhile, two settlers, Wendolen Nus and Joe Pennig, who had not received the warning, came down to find out what was going on. They rode directly into Hooker Jim's Indians and were immediately shot. Nus died instantly, but Pennig was fortunate enough to fall unconscious and the Indians did not finish him. He was rescued and, after a long convalescence, recovered.

[1] Ivan Applegate, "The Initial Shot"; Major F. A. Boutelle, "Boutelle and Scar-Faced Charley"; Colonel James Jackson, "The First Blow—Jackson's Expedition," in Cyprus Townsend Brady, *Northwestern Fights and Fighters;* Bancroft, *Oregon,* II 573–74; Meacham, *Wigwam and War-path,* 364–70; Interview, O. C. Applegate by Don C. Fisher, National Park Service files, Lava Beds National Monument, Tulelake, California.

Oliver Applegate, Dave Hill, and three settlers came out of the cabin after the Modocs had withdrawn a little way and found a Yainax Modoc, named Mooch, who was hiding until the fighting was over. Oliver sent him across the river to get Ivan and to ask for soldiers. He thought that if even a half-dozen soldiers crossed to the north bank, the settlers could attack from Crawley's and at least would hold as captives Hooker Jim's band as a result of the day's efforts.

Jackson overruled any further action that day. He was sick, eight of his thirty-eight men were dead or wounded, and the others, though exhausted, were busy around the Indian encampment, shooting at distant Modocs or burning the camp of Captain Jack. All Jackson wanted was a cease-fire which would permit him to escape. Hooker Jim's men quit firing, turned eastward, and rode away, a move which brought the soldiers tremendous relief.

Jackson then had Dave Hill ferry the wounded across the river in a canoe. The injured men, accompanied by a small guard and Dr. McElderry, were taken to Crawley's. About fifteen of the other men rounded up the horses and pack animals, moved up the river to the ford, and then rode south again to join the rest at Crawley's. Jack's men were free to join their women in the Lava Beds, and Hooker Jim's men were loose on the north shore of the lake. No effort was made to find out what either band of Indians was going to do, nor was any effort made to warn the settlers that the Modocs had not been captured and were probably moving across the country like a swarm of enraged wasps.

Lieutenant Boutelle and ten men were left to guard the Indian camps to prevent any Modocs from coming back. Hooker Jim was still in sight, for his men burned a few haystacks belonging to Charley Monroe before they rode away. Jackson's men just watched, since they had had all the Indian trouble they wanted for that day.

In Crawley's cabin, some of the settlers began to wonder why they had not heard anything from their neighbors living in the direction of Hooker Jim's withdrawal. It was not until several hours later that Brown admitted that he had not warned anyone beyond Crawley's. At once, Ivan Applegate, Brown, and Burnett rode away to try to salvage something from Brown's negligence. The first house they reached was empty, and repeated attempts to arouse anyone were unsuccessful. Concluding that the inhabitants had left and were safe, the party returned to Jackson's camp without riding any farther. Actually, while the women had gone and were safe enough, all the men of the house were dead.

Hooker Jim, Curley Headed Doctor, Long Jim, One-eyed Mose, Rock Dave, Humpy Jerry, Boston Charley, Slolux, Peter Schonchin, and five other Indians made a shambles of the northern and eastern shores of the lake. These Indians were known by sight and name to the settlers and were named by the survivors.

The first family the Indians met was a group of Australian immigrants. Of this household they killed four men—William Boddy; Nicholas Schira, his son-in-law; and two of Boddy's stepsons, William and Richard Cravigan. Mrs. Schira saw the horses coming in with no driver and knew that something was amiss. She ran out to the field and found the men dead, shot through the head, lying about half a mile from the house. Mrs. Schira and her mother started to run and met the Indians, who were searching for more white men to kill. Quite politely, the Modocs inquired whether there were any more men at their house. The women said there were not, and the Indians rode off, leaving the women unharmed. Meacham states that the Indians taunted the Boddy women with a speech to the effect that "This is Boddy's blood; but we are Modocs; we do not kill women and children. You will find Boddy in the woods. We will not hurt you."[2] The truth of the matter is that the Indians said nothing at all, but rode silently on to their next deed of violence.

A short distance to the north and east of Boddy's was the claim of William Brotherton. The Brothertons had built their cabin almost exactly on the boundary line between Oregon and California. Here the Indians waited until the morning of November 30, and seeing no sign of pursuit rode leisurely around the east shore of Tule Lake to join Jack in the Lava Beds.

Hooker Jim and his band met the Brotherton men in the junipers, cutting wood. Without ceremony, they killed William Brotherton and W. K. Brotherton. Then Jim rode south across the state line

[2] Alfred B. Meacham, *The Tragedy of the Lava Beds*, 14; Alfred B. Meacham, *Wi-ne-ma (The Woman-Chief) and Her People*; Riddle, *Indian History*, 47.

into California, where he and his Indians met Henry Miller, who had promised to warn them just as soon as he heard the soldiers might be coming. For his failure to warn them, even though no one had told him, he was murdered, as has been related. The Indians next rode to the place where a German sheepherder, Nicholas Shearer, was herding a band of sheep belonging to the Brothertons. With him was Joseph, the twelve-year-old son of William Brotherton. When the Indians broke from cover, Shearer jumped on his horse and started to run, but the racing Indians cut him off from escape, firing continuously. Eventually he was hit and fell from his horse. The boy started running for the house as fast as he could go, and when the Indians turned their attention to him, he had already covered half the distance. His mother, who had seen Shearer die, grabbed a Winchester rifle and revolver and ran toward her son. When the Indians began to overtake Joseph, Mrs. Brotherton fired the rifle at them, and handed her son the revolver as soon as they met. Neither hit any of the Indians, and while the Modocs went into a huddle to decide what to do, both mother and son reached the house in safety.

Mrs. Brotherton, her two sons, and an Indian woman known as Mrs. Swan, who had been living with Shearer, piled twenty sacks of flour around the floor as crude breastworks. They all lay down behind them while Mrs. Brotherton bored a number of auger holes through the walls of the house just above the flour-sack line. The Indians crept up behind Miller's house, only about fifty yards to the south, and fired from behind it, but after a while the fire by the woman and her son discouraged them. They mounted their ponies and rode away. For the next twenty-four hours the Brothertons dared not leave their cabin, for they thought the Indians were only a short distance away. They were still in the cabin when a rescue party arrived.

In addition to the Boddys, the Brothertons, Miller, and Shearer, the Modocs killed Christopher Erasmus, Robert Alexander, John Tober, Adam Shillingbow, and a man named Follins.[3] With Nus and Thurber, who were killed in the first fight, a total of fourteen settlers were dead as the result of the decision by Odeneal and Green to send troops to arrest Jack.

[3] Jackson Report, S.F.P., D. C., 1873, #2303.

While Hooker Jim's band was murdering settlers, in contrast, Scarfaced Charley met several white men who were unaware of the trouble. Pressly Dorris, A. W. Watson, and John Ballaout were searching for some stock that had strayed. Charley sent them home, telling them there was trouble between the whites and the Indians and that he did not want his friends to get hurt.[4]

The settlers between Lost River and Yainax had no idea of the Modocs' position. Jackson met his pack train at the ford on the evening of the thirtieth and remained with the men for the night. He returned to Crawley's and camped there December 1. He had still done nothing about the settlers, but he was probably waiting for orders from Green concerning the next course of action, since the original plans had gone completely awry. As soon as Ivan Applegate returned from the Boddy cabin, Jackson sent him back to Linkville so that he could warn the settlers north of Lost River that the Modocs were loose and that the army had failed to arrest Jack.

Applegate had no illusions about the aftermath of an unsuccessful attack on the Modocs. He left Crawley's in the early afternoon of the twenty-ninth, and about five miles from the cabin he met a settler named Donald McLeod. His words of warning are not immortal, but they are expressive: "Get the hell out of here, Mac, the Indians are on the warpath!" After bawling this greeting, Applegate, like a nineteenth-century Paul Revere, rode on to Linkville.

The McLeods did not stop to argue. They packed what household goods they could get into a wagon, rounded up their sheep and set the dogs to herd them, and started for Linkville and safety. McLeod dashed back to lock the door after they had gone a little way, much to his wife's consternation.[5]

Ivan Applegate rode into town, spread the news, and turned east into Langell's Valley, upper Lost River, and Clear Lake, to warn the settlers there that Jack and Hooker Jim were out. This time he did not go alone. At first, about twelve citizens agreed to go with him, but while they were arming themselves, five of them found excellent reasons for remaining in Linkville. Most of the rest, in order to fortify their courage, had been absorbing whiskey as rapid-

[4] Meacham, *Wi-ne-ma*, 82.

[5] Ken McLeod, "Along Nature's Trail," Klamath Falls *Herald-News* (May 26, 1954).

ly as they could. Some found it extremely difficult to get on their horses; others found that even the booze did not provide the proper amount of courage.

Applegate actually left town with seven men, including Charles Monroe, whose hay had been burned by Hooker. O. A. Stearns gave the report of the trip. This Saturday night was cold, and the fog hung freezingly over the valley. The strong wind chilled the riders to the bone. When the men reached the Lost River gap where the April conference had been held, they came to the Galbraith cabin and found Mrs. Boddy and Mrs. Schira there. The women had hiked along the ridge and over Stukel Mountain in their flight from the Indians. While they were exhausted, hungry, and in a state of semi-shock, they were safe enough. The men went on warning other settlers as fast as they reached their homes. They had breakfast on the Vincent farm, rested briefly while their horses fed, and then re-mounted. They rode all that day and reached Clear Lake about sundown on November 30. Here they found Jesse Applegate, who knew that something was wrong because the evening before he had seen many Modoc signal fires burning in the direction of Tule Lake.

Ivan had not been to bed for almost sixty hours, and the men with him were very tired. They slept at Jesse's house while he and his neighbor, Richard Hutchinson, prepared to build a stockade the next morning.

During the day of December 1, two men rode into Jackson's camp at Crawley's and told him of the murder of the Boddy men. Lieutenant Boutelle was sent on the morning of the second with a detachment of cavalry to do what he could for the settlers. The party found the bodies of some of the slain men and buried them. As they were riding east, they met Ivan Applegate and his party on their return from Clear Lake, who reported the death of the Brother-tons and their neighbors and the rescue of the women and children from the Brotherton cabin. The women were with them, and Bou-telle and Applegate brought them into Jackson's camp. There they found a large group of civilians who had come down from Link-ville to help if they were needed.

On Monday morning, the second, a force was sent out along the lake shore to find the bodies of the dead and ascertain the whereabouts of the Indians. Part of Jackson's troop was sent to Clear Lake to reinforce the settlers there, and Jackson sent Green an urgent request to divide the infantry between Langell Valley and Clear Lake.

Alfred Meacham's brother-in-law, Captain Ferree, who was living on the Klamath Agency, sent down thirty-six Klamath Indians to track the Modocs and to try to prevent their raiding other settlements. Beyond this, the military could do nothing except to report to their superior officers that the expedition of the twenty-ninth had ended in disaster.

Almost simultaneously Canby received the word of the fight and a message from Governor Grover of Oregon wanting to know what the state could do to help the army. As soon as Oliver Applegate and A. J. Burnett got back to Linkville, Burnett sent Grover a telegram informing him of what had occurred and stating that the military forces were not strong enough to cope with the situation. This was certainly true, but Canby was not ready to admit it. Further, he was mildly annoyed at the general tone of the Governor's memorandum, for he felt that the settlers had started the trouble and that the Governor was exerting undue pressure on him. The Governor informed Canby that the state had assumed the authority to raise a force of volunteers "to co-operate with the regular troops, sufficient to quell disturbances, and to protect the settlements."[6]

Accordingly, Canby wrote a courteous letter to Grover telling him in veiled language that he did not have the slightest notion what was going on, but, "I have no reason to doubt that, if not already in the Modoc country when the hostilities commenced, a sufficient force to suppress them and give protection to the frontier was close at hand."[7] This optimism was belied by the fact that Canby wired everybody he could reach in the Klamath country asking what the situation actually was. John Ross, of Jacksonville, said that five men had been killed. John Fairchild, living twenty-five miles west of the fighting, went on a trip with one of his hired hands to see what he could find; he met several Modocs who told him that while they had nothing against him, he had better leave, for they could not guarantee his safety.

[6] Letter, Grover to Canby, December 2, 1872, S.F.P., D. C., 1872, #2152.
[7] Canby to Grover, December 3, 1872, S.F.P., D.C., 1872, #2152.

These people could not tell Canby what had gone wrong, and in a burst of annoyance the General sent a grumbling wire to headquarters in San Francisco wondering what had been wrong with Wheaton's brains, for all "Troops at Bidwell and the District of the Lakes . . . ought to have been in the Modoc country before the attempt to remove the Indians by force was commenced." Even in his ignorance of the state of affairs, however, he took action, for before he received official reports, he ordered Major Mason and two companies of the Twenty-first Infantry Regiment to move from Fort Vancouver to Fort Klamath, with the promise that they would be joined by a third company and all should march against the Modocs.

Grover politely acknowledged Canby's letter, but called out the volunteers just the same. He gave orders that the volunteers were to remain in the field only until "the regular troops take the field in force sufficient to protect the settlements."[8] Who would decide when this point had been reached, he did not say.

While Canby was vainly trying to get information, Wheaton was trying to rectify Green's error as well as he could. When Wheaton heard what Odeneal had done, he probably flew into a rage; in any event, he ordered Captain R. F. Bernard, an old soldier possessing considerable judgment and experience (which varied from an enlisted man serving as a blacksmith to a commissioned officer in the cavalry), to take everyone he could spare and move to Crawley's, "where Captain Jackson is now supposed to be."[9] Wheaton did not know where Jackson was or what he was planning.

Similar orders were sent to Captain David Perry at Camp Warner, to take all the available cavalry "by forced marches via Yainax to Crawley's ranch." Since Wheaton did not know where Green was either, he had to make his orders flexible: "If Major Green is with either command, report to him for further instructions; if he is not, co-operate with either of the two troops until you receive orders from Colonel Green." Why Wheaton promoted Green in a single sentence, he did not explain.

While the army and the settlers were scurrying about after the

[8] Grover to Canby, December 4, 1872, S.F.P., D.C., 1872, #2195.
[9] Wheaton to Bernard, December 3, 1872, S.F.P., D.C., 1872 #2304.

fight on Lost River, the Indians were roaming in and out of the Lava Beds at will, watching to see what action the soldiers and the settlers would take. Oliver Applegate raised a force of fifteen of Schonchin's Modocs to guard the Yainax station, then took nine Klamaths to Clear Lake to find out how brother Jesse was making out. Ivan, six citizens, and five cavalrymen were already there. Since things seemed quiet, a number of them ventured down on the Tule Lake flat and buried the bodies of the last of the murdered settlers.

In the Hot Creek region, a small band of Modocs under the leadership of Shacknasty Jim came over to Fairchild's ranch to ask him what they should do. They said they did not want to join Jack, for they felt that to do so would be to sign their own death warrants. They could not see how his tiny band of Indians could hold out against the forces they knew were converging from all directions.

Not all whites were troubled by the Indians. John Fairchild, for example, was liked by both whites and Indians. He was a Southerner who had come to the mines during the gold-prospecting days while he was just a boy. Now he was thirty-eight years old and a respected stockman. He had made a personal "treaty" with the Indians and paid them a small rent for his magnificent ranch, and the Indians were satisfied. They never complained of mistreatment in their dealings with him. His neighbor, "Press" Dorris, got along with the Modocs almost as well.

Together, Dorris and Fairchild persuaded the Indians to go to the Klamath reservation and promised to help them get there without harm from either the army or volunteer soldiers. Modocs destined to play an important and tragic part in the drama unfolding in the Lava Beds were thus almost removed from the war during the first week. The Hot Creeks included Shacknasty Jim, their leader, and his brother Shacknasty Jake. (Their mother had been a sloppy housekeeper, and the whites had named both boys after the state of their home.) Bogus Charley was there (he was named because his cabin was on Bogus Creek). There was Steamboat Frank (whose corpulent mother huffed and puffed when she walked), Ellen's Man George, was one of the Hot Creeks. He was a moon-faced young

Indian, perhaps the best strategist of all the Modocs, who had been first adopted, then married by "Ellen," a woman several years older than he. There were nine others in the band.

These Indians, like Scarfaced Charley, were more eager to avoid killing than to start trouble. Not long after the Lost River fight, a white man named Sam Watson was riding toward the Lava Beds when some of the Hot Creek Indians stopped him. Bogus Charley seized the bridle of his horse and told Watson there was fighting ahead, and he had better turn back.[10]

Fairchild sent word to L. S. Dyar at the Klamath Agency that Dorris, Samuel Culver, and he were bringing the Indians in, and that preparations should be made. Somebody along the line of communication talked too much, and the word was spread through Linkville that a band of Modocs was on the way to the agency.

The saloons were full of loud-mouthed men who hated Indians on general principles. Agitators were also hard at work in the little Linkville hotel. "They" said that over two hundred soldiers were on the way. Why, there would not even be a grease spot left when they got done with the Modocs in the Lava Beds! Although some skeptics asked the positive souls whether they had ever seen Captain Jack's Stronghold, they continued to assert that Jack could not possibly win. There were a few realistic people who said no one could break into Jack's home ground when he had his men properly placed.

From argument and speculation, the conversation turned to grim fact. Some of the murdered settlers had been brought in to Linkville for burial. Those who saw the bodies found in their fields told others what the Indians had done, and the stories grew with each telling. Probably the bodies had been mutilated, for the Indians were often brutal. "They" also said that another murdered settler had been disemboweled and his heart removed. Another man's body was said to have been completely hacked to pieces by Hooker Jim.

Conversation in the saloons next turned to the Hot Creek band, which was on its way to the reservation by way of Linkville. Some intrepid person proposed a lynching bee. It was immaterial to him that not one of these Modocs had been either in Jack's camp or in

10 Yreka *Union* (December 7, 1872).

Hooker Jim's raiding party. It was equally immaterial that they were giving up to avoid trouble. They were Indians and that was enough. Well fortified with whiskey, eight or ten of the lynching party, led by a German known to history as "Fritz," rode hilariously out of town headed for Whittle's Ferry to seize the Indians and take them back to town for hanging. William Small, who was visiting at Whittle's, overheard their unguarded talk. Two other settlers, named Harris and Howard, also overheard them and warned Dorris and Fairchild. The two Californians armed themselves and rode to the Linkville party to try to get them to leave the river crossing without making trouble. Although the men made threats against the Indians, the cold and chilly night was cooling the ardent spirits within the fire-eating citizens, and they began to talk more calmly. Finally Fairchild, Dorris, Culver, Ball, Harris, and Howard, all settlers interested in getting this potential reinforcement for Jack safely on the reservation, were able to talk the would-be lynchers into returning to Linkville.

"Fritz" hung back and was able to talk to some of the Indians before he followed the others back to town. When Dyar reached Whittle's about seven in the evening, the damage had already been done. The Modocs were seething with near panic. Dorris and Dyar tried to explain to them that, although there might be trouble in Linkville, if they would wait until early the next morning, the escort could probably move them through town under cover of darkness, and they would be safe.[11]

Many of the Indians knew English, and they didn't trust Dyar, whom they did not know, to protect them. They believed that Fritz's threats were not empty ones and that their lives would be taken if they went any farther. While the white leaders were making plans in Whittle's cabins, the Modocs outside quietly sneaked out of camp and fled to the hills south of the Lava Beds, taking all the horses they could round up, including Fairchild's own mount. Forty-five Indians, of whom at least fourteen were warriors, thus joined Jack and became part of the most eager supporters of Curley Headed Doctor and a war policy.[12]

[11] Bancroft, *Oregon*, II, 578–79.
[12] Meacham, *Wigwam and War-path*, 371.

A few people surmised where the Hot Creeks had gone, but no one knew exactly. Dorris went to an Indian woman who had connections with the Hot Creeks, and said, "You know I am your friend. Now I want you to tell me straight where those Indians are."

She answered, "They have run off."

Dorris asked, "What have they run off for?"

"That Dutchman told them if they go with Mr. Dyar they will all be killed. They never get to the reservation."[13]

The woman also told him that Black Jim, Scarfaced Charley, Jack, and Curley Headed Doctor had all been killed in the Lost River fight.[14] Dorris knew better than that, for he had seen Charley alive since the fight. Time and again, it might be noted, the Indians sent word of this kind, and the whites usually believed it, although within a few days the "deceased" always turned up healthy and full of fight.

Since they got little information from the woman, Fairchild and Dorris went to Yreka to talk with Elisha Steele. They asked him, if the Indians came there, to use his influence to get them to go to the reservation.[15] Jackson even sent wagons and an escort to convince the Hot Creeks that they could get through to the Klamath Agency safely, but no Indians were to be seen.

Finally it was definitely established that Shacknasty Jim and his band had joined Jack. Fairchild was enraged at the stupidity of the Linkville settlers. His remarks did nothing to bridge the gap that already existed between the settlers of northern California and those of southern Oregon.

While the soldiers scattered their forces to protect as many ranches as they could, Fairchild, Dorris, Ball, and Nate Berwick, a Californian, found the Indians in the Lava Beds.[16] Jack met them on the bluff to the west of the lake and had a long talk with them. He denied any responsibility for the fighting on November 29, and

[13] Letter, L. S. Dyar to Oliver Applegate, December 20, 1872, *Records of Modoc War*, on file at Lava Beds National Monument, Tulelake, California.

[14] Yreka *Union* (December 7, 1872).

[15] Telegram, McConnell and McManus to Headquarters District of the Columbia, December 5, 1872, S.F.P., D.C., 1872, #2205.

[16] Green to Jackson, December 1, 1872, *Ft. Klamath Letter Book*, National Archives.

blamed Long Jim, Scarfaced Charley, and Hooker Jim for all the trouble.[17] He told the Californians that he liked them, and they might use the Tickner Road any time they wished, but the South Emigrant Road, around the north end of Tule Lake, was closed as far as the Modocs were concerned. Any white man using it was liable to be shot. While they talked, two of Fairchild's horses strayed away, and Jack lent him two others to help make the return trip.[18]

After a few days, the Modocs sent out scouting parties. On December 5, George Fiocke and Charles Monroe had the misfortune to run into a band of scouting Indians. They were not liked by the Indians and barely escaped with their lives. For a while they were reported dead, for they had to make a long detour to get back to safety.[19]

Bernard's cavalry sent by Wheaton to the Modoc country approached the Lava Beds, during this first week, by forced marches over the Old Emigrant Road. Captain Perry was at Camp Warner when he received orders to get to the Lava Beds as quickly as he could and to leave his wagons behind. He started immediately and stopped only long enough to join Lieutenant Kyle at the north end of Goose Lake, so that the combined troops could go to Crawley's and join Jackson's command.

These soldiers needed more than a week to arrive at the Lava Beds. Perry actually was not ready for action until December 13. The roads were very bad and the men had trouble making progress.

When all had arrived, however, Colonel Wheaton (sometimes called "General" Wheaton because he had been a divisional commander in the Civil War) came down from Camp Warner and took personal command of all two hundred of the troops. Bernard was stationed at Louis Land's ranch on the east shore of Tule Lake opposite the "Peninsula" and about seven miles south of Bloody Point on the old road. With Bernard was Kyle's troop of First Cavalry. Both had been at Bidwell together and knew each other. Their camp was about thirteen miles from Jack's Stronghold and two miles west of the flows that marked the boundary of the Lava Beds.

[17] Bancroft, *Oregon*, II, 580.
[18] Yreka *Union* (December 14, 1872).
[19] Telegram, Turner to Headquarters, December 6, 1872, S.F.P., D.C., 1872, #2221.

Jackson and Green were left at Crawley's on the Lost River, which was used as the depot for stores. Perry was sent to Van Bremer's ranch, south of Lower Klamath Lake and about ten miles southeast of Crawley's.[20]

On the evening of December 3, Major E. C. Mason and Companies B and C of the Twenty-first Infantry Regiment started for the Lava Beds from Fort Vancouver. They boarded a steamboat at seven o'clock for Portland, where they met Canby and his staff a few hours later. They spent the night on the train and arrived in Roseburg the next morning. All of Wednesday, December 4, was needed for arranging transportation for their baggage to Jacksonville. It rained the entire day, and the men who had to stay in the open were soaked to the skin.

In Roseburg, they found a deserter from their outfit who voluntarily turned himself in for punishment. He was completely worn out from the miserable life he led outside the army. The captain of his company went to Mason with the problem: he could not take a deserter on the march, and there was neither time nor opportunity for a suitable court to be held to try him and punish him for his offense. Mason shrugged it off, and Captain Burton turned the problem over to a sergeant who took charge of the trembling deserter.

After some suitable remarks the sergeant left with threats of punishment which would be meted out when they returned. As it happened, Mason's force did not come back through Roseburg, for when the war was over the following summer, they marched back to the Columbia River by way of Camp Harney and Walla Walla. Doubtless the deserter was vastly relieved at the turn of fate when he heard of the sufferings and troubles his old outfit had during the next few months in the Lava Beds.

On December 5, Mason's little army marched up the Umpqua through the rain and mud. Their wagons promptly mired down, and the men marched by, unsympathetically jeering at the quartermasters who were up to their waists in mud trying to move the wagons. When the infantry camped for the night, however, they realized that their food supplies were in those wagons, now several miles back. The supplies had moved less than two miles during the

[20] Bancroft, *Oregon*, II, 582–83.

day, and some of the hungry soldiers hiked back to bring in enough food for a meal after dark.

It took seven days to reach Jacksonville, where the Twenty-first Infantry camped Thursday, December 12. During these seven days, the rain had not stopped once. The teams were doubled, and men were detailed to help the wagons up the steep slopes. On Friday, the thirteenth, the rain turned to snow, and the men camped in a foot of it. On this day the men heard that there would be no advance against the Modocs until their units arrived. They cheered valiantly, for they were afraid the trip was to be wasted and the fighting would be over before they got to Tule Lake. With that, they returned to pushing wagons uphill.

On Sunday they did not march, but rested at the summit of the divide between Jacksonville and Linkville. During this day, Captain Silva collapsed from exhaustion caused by his efforts to move supplies over the almost impassable road. His place was taken by a Lieutenant Moore, normally a signal officer, and Silva went back to Portland.

For another week the two companies struggled through the mountains with their supplies and finally arrived at Linkville three days before Christmas. There they met Colonel Wheaton and Captain Ross of the Oregon Volunteers.[21]

These volunteers had enlisted on December 2, as soon as Governor Grover sent out a call for their services. They had reached the rendezvous more quickly than the regulars since they were mounted and not burdened with supplies. In fact, what supplies they had were furnished by the army after they arrived. The first arrivals reached the Klamath Basin on December 7, and came on to Linkville on December 9. A small detachment of sixty-five men under Captain Kelly arrived from Jacksonville and made camp about ten miles from the mouth of Lost River and a few miles from Jackson's camp at Crawley's. Shortly after Kelly came in, Captain Ross, an old Indian fighter who had been with Ben Wright twenty years earlier, took over the command. A second Oregon volunteer company was raised in the immediate vicinity of Klamath Lake by Oliver Apple-

[21] Lt. W. H. Boyle, "Personal Observations on the Conduct of the Modoc War," (handwritten MS) Pacific MSS #A96, Bancroft Library.

gate. His sixty-eight men were mainly reservation Indians, plus some whites from Linkville and a few from Jacksonville who had not been able to join Kelly's company. The men of Applegate's company camped with Kelly and also assumed the duty of guarding the settlements to the north and east of the Stronghold.[22]

On the day that Mason's infantry reached Jacksonville, the volunteers moved to Van Bremer's ranch at the western base of what is now known as Dome Mountain. Perry reached there, also, the next day and camped with the volunteers. As there were more volunteers than cavalry, Perry asked them to help guard the country against a surprise raid by the Modocs.[23]

Since neither volunteers nor regulars knew the country, a request was sent to Fairchild and Dorris to form a company of California volunteers who could act as guides and also add man power to the gathering forces. The two Californians agreed, and a small group of twenty-nine men—mostly employees of the two ranchers—took the field intermittently. Sometimes they scouted, sometimes they fought, but most of the time they tended cattle and sheep as they had done before the war. The men received their usual wages from Fairchild, along with fifty-five cents a day from the government plus clothing allowances.

While the troops were resting and waiting for Mason to arrive, Ross, Kelly, and Perry made a short reconnaissance of the Lava Beds, but stayed a respectful distance from the Stronghold itself. They found no Indians, but this did not mean that all of the Modocs were holed up in shivering terror in the Stronghold. They reported that, as they rode through the lava fields, they could see a lone white horse, which was not theirs, wandering about at some distance from them. They started to go after it, but decided that this action might not be wise. As they turned away, they heard the voice of an exasperated Indian crying in quite understandable English, "Come on! Come on!"[24] They were sure that this indicated the Indians were ready with an ambush. Undoubtedly, if the scouting party had gone

[22] 43 Cong., 2 sess., *House Exec. Doc. No. 45.*

[23] L. F. Grover, *Report of Governor Grover to General Schofield on the Modoc War and Reports of Major John F. Miller and General John E. Ross to the Governor,* Salem (Oregon).

[24] Yreka *Union* (December 21, 1872).

much farther after the white-horse bait, some of them would have been dead. In their report, they concluded it with a terse five-word statement: "A Hell of a place."[25]

To show their eagerness to fight, a band of six Modocs the following Monday morning appeared in plain sight opposite the camp at Crawley's and fired into the camp. They dared the white soldiers to cross the river and fight them. Their bravado did not deceive the soldiers, who had orders not to attack until all forces had been concentrated. The Indians became downright cocky, however, as their repeated challenges went unanswered.

While Kelly's party was out, things were uneasy. No one could be certain whether there was to be a fight soon or not. As the Indians grew bolder, they were seen far to the west of their Stronghold, on the slopes of Dome Mountain (then called Van Bremer's Peak). This was less than half a mile from Perry's and the volunteers' camps, and their activity showed that the Indians were more conscientious than the army in making observations on the enemy. Kelly had probably been no closer than five miles from the Indian encampment.

During the lull between the arrival of troops and a battle Canby had time to collect all the reports and try to make some sense out of affairs in the Modoc country. He came to the cheerful conclusion, "I do not think the operations will be protracted. The snow will drive the Indians out of the mountains and they cannot move without leaving trails that can be followed. It will involve some hardships upon the troops; but they are better provided and can endure it better than the Indians. In that respect, the season is in our favor."[26]

On Thursday, December 19, Ross moved the volunteers to Small's ranch, near Whittle's ferry on the Klamath River near Linkville, because he did not like the Indians' peering down his neck at Van Bremer's. In the new location no supplies came to the military forces, and the Linkville merchants discovered a bonanza in selling supplies to the poorly equipped army. The Van Bremer family was not set up to supply an army, even a small army of 150 men, but what they had they sold at extravagant prices. It was seen that Indian wars were not all blood, mud, sweat, and tears, but profits as well.

[25] Portland *Oregonian* (December 24, 1872).
[26] Canby report to Headquarters, December 10, 1872, S.F.P., D.C., 1872, #2228.

Saddles previously sold in Linkville for twenty dollars suddenly were marked up to forty dollars.[27]

The army purchased every pound of grain and hay in the Klamath region and requisitioned all of the spare horses and mules for the use of the pack trains. It was found necessary to bring all goods by pack train from Jacksonville, for wagons just could not be taken through the mountains. The cost of this operation during the winter months was almost prohibitive, but the alternative was to break off the action and leave the Modocs in triumph on the field, an unthinkable outcome. Costs, accordingly, began to mount at a frightful rate, particularly in relation to the small number of troops in the area and the small number of Indians engaged.

Even high prices did not always produce the supplies needed by the army. Through inefficient purchasing, ammunition might arrive that did not fit the guns.[28] Even when the supplies were satisfactory, they had to be brought in by pack mule. Major Green ordered two mountain howitzers and three hundred rounds of ammunition from Fort Vancouver, which meant additional costs and additional effort, yet Green said that he could not fight without "howitzers and one snow storm."[29]

Waiting for military supplies and reinforcements meant a period of tense inactivity at Yainax. The Modocs of Schonchin's band were deathly afraid that Jack would raid them on the reservation. Jack sent word out that if Schonchin's band did not join him, he would burn Yainax to the ground. Oliver Applegate felt it necessary to move most of his volunteer company back to the reservation for defense, and also to prevent any wavering member of Schonchin's followers from sneaking off the reservation to join Jack.[30] Jack's threat tied up man power thirty miles from the scene of hostilities.

Waiting for more men and artillery was hard on the morale of the soldiers, and they began to grumble. Mason's battalion had served in Arizona against the Apaches, and their confidence in their own ability was high. They could not understand the need to wait

[27] Portland *Oregonian* (January 9, 1873).
[28] Portland *Oregonian* (December 24, 1872).
[29] Bancroft, *Oregon*, II, 584.
[30] Letter, Applegate to Hyzer, December 17, 1872.

for more equipment and man power in order to rout out a few dozen miserable savages like the Modocs.

Finally the supplies were assembled and the period of waiting came to an end. Green was given orders on the twentieth of December that he could attack any time he felt he had a chance for success. Ammunition was still in short supply, because many of the rifles and almost all the cartridges had been issued to settlers for their self-defense. Green ordered additional supplies from Fort Bidwell, and he did not plan to attack until the supply train arrived.

The plan for the proposed operation was that Companies B and C, Twenty-first Infantry under Mason, Perry's Troop F, and Jackson's Troop B of the First Cavalry with Ross's volunteers, should attack from the west, while Bernard with Troop G, First Cavalry, should move up with Klamath Indian scouts and attack from the east side by way of Land's ranch. The leaders also discussed the best means of a rapid and effective pursuit of any Modocs who had not surrendered after the action was completed.[31]

Alas, for their plans and their orders! They had forgotten to anticipate the strategy of the Indians.

The howitzers and the mortar shells were sent from Vancouver on the twenty-first. But they did not relieve the ammunition shortage for ordinary rifles. A near disaster occurred, therefore, when the ammunition train from Fort Bidwell arrived and was attacked by the Modocs before its supplies had been unloaded. The escort was much too small for such an important train, but the weakness of the escort was only another example of the overconfidence of the army. Only five men were sent to bring in the wagons, and all the way through the Hot Spring Valley near present Canby, California, until they reached the lava flow north of Casuse Mountain, they were under observation by Modoc or Pit River Indians. They were less than a mile from Bernard's camp at Land's ranch when the Indians felt the situation advantageous for an attack.

At the first volley two men and five of the horses were killed. After the engagement one of the drivers, Private Sidney Smith, was found by the roadside entirely naked, scalped, with both ears cut

[31] General Orders, December 20, 1872, S.F.P., D.C., 1872, #2427.

off, and with bullets in his head, leg, and abdomen. Not too surprisingly, he died quickly.[32]

The only thing that saved the ammunition, which the Indians were after, was the fast action of Lieutenant Kyle. Only ten of the cavalry had their horses ready to mount, but Kyle told the others to leave their animals and march out to the scene of the firing as quickly as possible. The horsemen arrived within a few minutes, and the running soldiers were able to get there before the Indians could unload the wagons. The Modocs left when they saw the cavalry approaching, but kept up a steady fire at long range until after dark, when they retreated into the Lava Beds. Bernard's men began to follow them for a short distance, then stopped. It is probably fortunate that they did, or casualties would have been considerably higher. The Indians were apparently trying to entice the whites into an ambush.[33]

Bernard sent a bugler to Jackson to tell him that Land's ranch was under attack and to ask for support. The Indians saw the messenger after he had gone only a little way, and several of them started after him. Fortunately he was able to outdistance them. As soon as he heard the news, Jackson broke camp and marched some of his men around the north end of the lake to join Bernard. He did not arrive until eleven o'clock that night, and by that time the fighting was over.

Even after the imperiled train came in, ammunition remained in short supply. Some of the men were down to five or ten rounds apiece. Gunnery practice under such shortages was impossible, and many of the soldiers were very poor marksmen at best. A second train was sent to Fort Bidwell for additional supplies, but it could not possibly make the round trip before the beginning of the New Year. A sizable escort was sent to bring in that train.

While the army marked time waiting for additional supplies, Wheaton held an informal inquiry into Green's reasons for sending Jackson to Lost River on November 29 without consulting his superior. The results were summarized in a series of alibis. Green said that Odeneal insisted on an immediate movement of Jackson's

[32] John R. White, Report of Casualties, S.F.P., D.C., 1872, 1/D.C.
[33] Wheaton report to Canby, December 26, 1872, S.F.P., D.C., 1872, #2427.

troop. One may ask, "What if he did? Why did Green issue the orders?" Odeneal could not have taken soldiers to Jack's camp without Green's approval.[34] Odeneal himself wrote that he told Green to send troops if he had the authority and sufficient force. If not, Green should have sent word to Wheaton. The fact that Green did approve of the troops caused Odeneal to feel that the entire responsibility rested with the army, and he did not consider himself in any way to blame for the death of the settlers that followed the failure to arrest Jack.[35]

On Christmas Day, 1872, Wheaton arrived at Crawley's ranch on the Lost River to set up his personal headquarters. He was shocked and disgruntled to discover that the only building available was "a miserable shanty on Lost River north of Tule Lake."[36] The men camped in the open, and were uncomfortable in the cold wind, snow, and rain. Mason's sixty-four-man "battalion" was camped there. Perry was at Van Bremer's, the volunteers on the Klamath River, and Bernard and Jackson were at Land's ranch.

Since Wheaton had decided on an early January date for his attack, he sent word to the settlers in the Langell Valley to fortify, because trouble was coming. Instead of following his advice, they put their movable goods into wagons, and fled into Linkville. Their Christmas was almost as miserable as that of the soldiers, for the little town had scarcely a dozen buildings in it and there were not accommodations enough for the sudden influx. The equilibrium of the Linkville citizen was further upset when some of the refugees reported that they had been fired on as they drove toward town.[37] The Modocs, returning to their Stronghold, also fired on a wagon train coming south from Fort Klamath to Crawley's.

At Camp Harney, far to the north, Christmas was also a dismal day. Wheaton's orders arrived, and the troops there had to leave at once for Tule Lake. They had to cover a distance of three hundred miles through deep snow, and the orders specified that they were to go in "light marching order." That meant no wagons and camping

34 *Ibid.*
35 Odeneal Report, *Oregon Superintendency, 1873*, Office of Indian Affairs, The National Archives.
36 Wheaton Report, S.F.P., D.C., 1872, #2427.
37 Bancroft, *Oregon*, II, 585.

in the open. The country was covered with deep drifts, and the pack mules moved very slowly. In order to make any time at all, the soldiers had to break trail through the drifts and the mules followed.

The Harney detachment did not arrive until the second week in January. For the first 150 miles they moved across the open sagebrush plain, sleeping in hollows scooped out of the snow, and keeping warm by aromatic sagebrush fires, which would burn even with wet wood. After they reached Camp Warner, the men traveled through pine and juniper woods. Since there was no forage for the animals under the deep snow, they had to be fed entirely from nose bags. There were no tents for the men. A sort of shelter could be made from boughs spread over the blankets. One soldier reports that the "wash-up" each morning was a "superficial" affair. In the open spaces between trees, the men floundered through drifts to their armpits. At Goose Lake they found the water frozen, and crossed on the ice, then marched over the ridges and hills to Linkville, and on to the Modoc country. One of the officers later wrote:

> And for what? To drive a couple of hundred miserable aborigines from a desolate natural shelter in the wilderness, that a few thriving cattlemen might ranch their wild steers in a scope of isolated country, the dimensions of some several reasonable sized counties.[38]

While the soldiers were marching from Harney, the men around Tule Lake did nothing but wait, shiver, and complain. A sarcastic citizen, writing to a Portland newspaper, said the battle was being held up until the contractors could decide how large a percentage to take from the expenses.[39]

Complaints were heard about the food. It was poor. The volunteers got only what the army left, and that was issued just to keep them around.[40] Perhaps the hardest blow that fate dealt the soldiers was that their whiskey supply, brought with extreme difficulty over the mountains from Jacksonville for the New Year's Day celebra-

[38] Major J. G. Trimble, "Reminiscences," from Brady's *Northwestern Fights and Fighters*, 280.
[39] Portland *Oregonian* (January 14, 1873).
[40] Boyle, "Personal Observations," 6–7.

tion, arrived in deplorable condition. Much of it had "leaked out," the packers reported. What they had not stolen was ruined. The whiskey was so bad, in fact, that the Oregon volunteers gave their supply to the regulars. If that were the case, it must have been very bad indeed! Even General Ross was unhappy over the state of affairs. "The Gen'l said Dam it," reported the volunteer adjutant when the dismal news of the ruined whiskey reached him.[41]

A few days before New Year, a number of mules were delivered, ostensibly as pack animals. To the consternation of the packers, they were found to be unbroken, so the men had to take time to condition them to carry packs.[42]

After the first of the year, the threat at Yainax was not considered serious any longer, but it was with difficulty that Oliver Applegate got his Indians (including some of Schonchin's band) to move to Tule Lake. Schonchin was opposed to their going, for he wanted none of his Modocs fighting Jack. He told the whites that while he thought Jack was bad, so were the soldiers, and that Jack and the army should fight it out between them.[43] It finally took a direct order to get Applegate to bring Company B, Oregon Volunteers, down to the fighting zone.[44] When they arrived, Oliver informed Wheaton that things were under control at the agency. He had left ten men of the volunteers to act as leaders for 150 Modoc and Klamath Indians in the unlikely chance that Jack might stage a raid. Wheaton concluded that in case Jack should attack, that Yainax was better prepared than Camp Warner, Bidwell, or even Fort Klamath.[45]

This first week in January was a quiet one for the most part. The troops rested in their camps and waited for their howitzers or the troops from Camp Harney. On January 5, however, about fourteen of Kelly's volunteers had a skirmish with "eighteen or twenty Modocs" while on reconnaissance. No damage seems to have been done to either group. This same week, Canby received orders from Gen-

---

[41] E. D. Foudray to W. A. Owen, January 1, 1873, Applegate Collection.
[42] Pollock to Green, December 29, 1872, *Fort Klamath Letter Book*, VIII, National Archives.
[43] S. Grubb to O. C. Applegate, January 4, 1873, Applegate Collection.
[44] J. E. Ross to O. C. Applegate, December 29, 1872, Applegate Collection.
[45] Wheaton Report to Headquarters, January 9, 1873, S.F.P., D.C., 1873, #77.

eral Sherman to take command of the entire Pacific Division of the army while General Schofield was in Hawaii.

At the end of the week, Governor Grover issued orders mustering the volunteers out of service since they had enlisted for only a thirty-day period and no battles had been fought. Undoubtedly this was his way of putting pressure on the army. Wheaton was horrified at the prospect of losing a quarter of his potential strength before the battle began, and he requested the volunteers to stay on. This immediately made the federal government responsible for the expenses of the volunteer forces.

The volunteers remained, but they wanted another point to be settled. Since they had enlisted for service in their home state and since Jack was over the line in California, could they legally fight Jack? Wheaton, Green, and Ross worked out an agreement whereby the volunteers would serve under Wheaton's orders and could also serve in California.[46]

All was therefore in readiness for the capture of the Indians. Orders were issued on Sunday night, January 12, giving each outfit its station for the forthcoming attack. Perry and Troop F were to clear the bluff southwest of Tule Lake, and prepare a campground for the bulk of the soldiers who would camp at the top of the bluff Thursday night. Mason's battalion, by now enlarged to three companies totaling about eighty-five men, Ross's two companies of volunteers, and the long-awaited howitzers were to march from Van Bremer's and camp on the bluff which Perry's men would get ready. Bernard's two troops of cavalry were to fight dismounted as infantry and with the Klamath scouts, under Dave Hill, were to attack from the east side of the Stronghold. Wheaton's orders provided for rations and water supplies because the men would have to make a dry camp on the top of the bluff. Green was to have command in the field.[47]

On Monday afternoon, Perry and Applegate with a force of fifty-four men made a reconnaissance in force to the top of the bluff to look over the Lava Beds. As they rode to the edge of the bluff that they were to descend in three days in order to capture the Indians,

46 Portland *Oregonian* (December 24, 1872).
47 General Field Order No. 3, January 12, 1873, Applegate Collection.

they were fired upon by a number of Modocs hidden among the rocks at the edge of the bluff. Again, no one was hurt. Many of the soldiers claimed to have shot an Indian, but later investigation showed that their imagination was much better than their marksmanship. The shooting slowed them down considerably, and their approach to the edge of the bluff was extremely cautious. About all that they could show for their afternoon's ride from Van Bremer's was the capture of one rifle used by a Modoc.

The most disturbing feature of the adventure was that the Modocs had called to those Klamaths in the scouting party inviting them to desert the whites and to come over to them. The Klamaths answered them, and some whites who claimed to understand the Indian language said that the Klamaths promised to help Jack. Their officers were afraid to let them talk any more, and the scouts were sent beyond the ridge about a mile distant from the bluff. The Modocs then switched to English and invited the soldiers to come and fight, but the force refused either to fight or to answer.[48]

Tuesday and Wednesday were spent in the preparations, with the men vastly relieved to be getting into action at last. They had come so far and then had waited so long, camping out of doors in the middle of a severe winter, that the end of their misery and boredom was welcome. The usual boasting talk went around the camp as last-minute preparations were made. There was the soldier who was going to ride Jack's horse back from the battle. Another laid plans to eat Modoc steak when he returned. A third decided to bring a young Modoc woman back to wash his dishes.

After the chattering stopped, they laid down in their cold bivouac to sleep. The next day they would move into position for the attack on Friday.[49]

[48] Bancroft, *Oregon*, II, 587.
[49] Meacham, *Wigwam and War-path*, 386–87.

V

FIGHTING PHANTOMS

AFTER A NIGHT'S REST, the army moved toward the battle that was expected to wipe out Modoc resistance. Promptly at four o'clock on the morning of January 16, Perry's troop rode out of their Van Bremer ranch camp toward Lower Klamath Lake and Lost River, where they would ride to the bluff which formed the southwest shore of Tule Lake. Their job was to clear this bluff of any Modocs by three that afternoon, so that the main body of soldiers could camp there in safety the night before the grand assault.

Between Van Bremer's and the lake is a series of bluffs raised by fault action in the distant geological past. At the base of each bluff, there is a sloping plateau across a two- or three-mile expanse rising to the summit of the next ridge. All of these plateaus run parallel to each other in a north to south direction, with the faces of the bluffs turned toward the east. It was necessary for the soldiers to ride north, almost to Lost River, then to turn south again and ride up the plateau just west of Tule Lake, until they reached a point where they could descend the rocky face of the ridge.

By the time Perry's men had reached the plateau, their objective, they found that a heavy fog limited visibility to only a few yards. The officers professed satisfaction, saying that it would help them to surprise the Indians. Inasmuch as the soldiers were unfamiliar with the terrain and the Indians knew every inch of it, their optimism was considerably misplaced. Any surprise would not be their work.

When Modoc sentries on the bluff heard the soldiers coming, they fired at the ghostly figures moving through the mist. At once, Perry's men prepared to attack, but while they were dismounting, the Indians scrambled down the bluff, and the soldiers captured nothing but empty picket posts. By noon, Thursday, every Modoc in the Lava Beds knew that the United States Cavalry was moving in from the west.

The fog lay across the entire lava flat and lake. Bernard was ordered to move his men from Land's ranch to a prominent rocky point situated a few feet above the lake shore and about two miles east of the Stronghold which was Jack's main area of defense. There he was to send out patrols during the night of the sixteenth to capture any concealed Modoc canoes on the lake shore so that by the morning of the seventeenth when the main attack took place, the Indians would be prevented from escaping by water in the mad flight they were expected to make.

In the fog, Bernard's officers missed their objective altogether, and Jackson's troop advanced much closer to the Stronghold than he had planned. About a mile from the Modoc outer line of defense, the watchful Indians opened fire while the soldiers were in the rough ground between the point of rock and their inner fortress. The fire wounded one of the men. The cavalry retreated as quickly as it could, but three more men were wounded before the soldiers could scramble back to the others. The soldiers had succeeded only in informing the Indians that the attack would come from the east as well as from the bluff. When the army let the Indians know this, all possibility of surprising them was gone.

When Mason's battalion with the volunteers and the two howitzers left Van Bremer's, a little later in the morning than Perry, the men could hardly be kept in line. The sardonic Fairchild commented, "Don't fret. They won't be hard to keep back when the Modocs open fire."[1] Wheaton, too, tried to calm his men by telling them that scouts and friendly Indians insisted that the Modocs would fight desperately. The men blithely shrugged off his words of caution as if they were hearing a routine pre-game pep talk by a paid coach.

[1] Meacham, *Wigwam and War-path*, 382.

For that matter, probably, Wheaton himself did not believe the fight would be long or difficult. His letter to the War Department a few days earlier had been full of glowing optimism.

"I am happy to announce that after all our annoying delays, we are now in better condition than I ever saw troops for a movement against hostile Indians. . . . Now our artillery pack train and Howitzer details are admirably drilled: We leave for Capt. Jack's Gibraltar tomorrow morning and a more enthusiastic jolly set of Regulars and Volunteers I never had the pleasure to command.

If the Modocs will only try to make good their boast to whip a thousand soldiers, all will be satisfied. . . . I don't understand how they can think of any serious resistance tho' of course we are prepared for their fight or flight.

All works well, the Regulars and Volunteers harmonize wonderfully.[2]

Wheaton had no idea of the number of Modocs in the Stronghold, but estimates put the total at less than one hundred. Actually, there were nearer 50. The army forces included 225 regulars, and 104 volunteers, which gave Wheaton a clear superiority in numbers, and no one questioned the superiority in discipline of the troops over a bedraggled, rag-tag and bobtailed force of ill-equipped and miserably led Indians.

Seldom had a military leader so underestimated his opponents.

By three o'clock, Thursday afternoon, Perry had secured the bluff, and the infantry took its position at the edge of the bluff. A few curious individuals peered over to see where they were to fight the next day. The fog was still close to the ground at the foot of the hill, and they could not see much. What they could observe looked satisfactory enough. As far as the soldiers could see, they had only to fight across a stretch of almost perfectly flat country between the base of the cliff they were on, and Land's ranch, twelve miles away where Bernard's men had been camping. The ground mist

[2] Wheaton report to Canby (forwarded to Military Division of Pacific), January 15, 1873, *Oregon Superintendency, 1873*, Office of Indian Affairs, The National Archives.

covered all irregularities, and the unfrozen lake was a placid gray in the misty January afternoon. There were hills and mountains toward the south, but the Indians were not there, and their Stronghold looked as though it could easily be reached.

The ground was frozen at the top of the bluff, and as the weather grew colder, the men gathered sagebrush and built fires to keep themselves warm during the night. Some slept, but most stood around the fire. As the night hours dragged by, the cold and weariness of the men began to sap their enthusiasm. What had started out to be a lark, grew increasingly sinister as the time for attack drew closer. In the early morning darkness a shot suddenly broke the silence, and the men rushed to see what had happened. They discovered a groaning soldier who, deciding he was not brave after all, had shot a toe off to save himself from marching down the bluff the next morning.[3]

In the Indian camp, the night was also spent in preparation for the next day's fighting. Curley Headed Doctor knew that he faced an all-out test. He had been promising the Modocs of Jack's band for months that if they would believe his teaching, no harm could come from any soldiers. If he failed and Modocs were killed, he would in turn probably be killed by the Indians; his fate would be that of a medicine man whose magic had failed.

When Jack first heard that the soldiers were marching toward him, he suddenly lost his nerve and wanted to call the whole affair off and surrender. Scarfaced Charley was almost persuaded to agree with him. Naturally the Indians who had murdered the settlers were opposed to surrender, for they were certain that they would be handed over to civil authorities and would be hanged. A bitter debate took place, and finally the Indians voted on the question. Fourteen sided with Jack and surrender. Thirty-seven agreed to go along with the shaman and let him try to turn the bullets of the white men.

The medicine man ordered a rope of tule fiber, which he had been braiding for such an occasion, to be laid entirely around the Stronghold. Many hundred feet of rope were required before the job was done. No one now knows exactly the area that it surrounded.

[3] Thompson, *Reminiscences*, 95.

The rope had been painted red to avoid the possibility of mistake that this was the magic circle into which no white soldier should come the next day.[4] Then Curley Headed Doctor had a medicine pole erected, according to the method decreed by the ghost-dancers. It was a crooked limb chopped from a convenient juniper tree. Upon it were hung several white-haired dog skins, the tail feathers of a great hawk, an otter skin, and the skin of a white weasel.[5] The magic fire was built on the dance ground, and the musicians began their drumbeat. The women chanted in cadence, and the shaman began to dance. He was followed by others in the one-step-drag, one-step-drag which characterized the ghost dance. Into the medicine fire the Indians threw sacrifices of roots and meat. Curley Headed Doctor inhaled the smoke, and is then reported to have fallen down and staged a highly satisfactory fit, jerking and twitching as he lay there. It was impressive medicine, and calculated to render any Modoc impervious to bullets.[6] The Indians were properly stimulated, therefore, for their ordeal in the morning.

There is no record as to whether army chaplains performed appropriate religious services for the soldiers waiting on the bluff above the Lava Beds. Apparently not, however. Perhaps the white soldiers did not feel they needed supernatural aid as badly as the Indians needed the professional services of Curley Headed Doctor.

Very early on Friday morning, the soldiers were awakened when, about four o'clock, the bugler blew reveille. This also served to inform the Indians that it was time to move into their prepared positions. In the cold January air along Tule Lake, a bugle call could easily be heard three miles away.

Now that the army had succeeded in alerting both friend and foe, a tattoo was blown, which signaled the men to move out. It took nearly two hours for the chilled and frightened men to get to the bottom of the bluff and line up in the order specified by Wheaton.

On the extreme left, touching on the shore of the lake was Fairchild with his twenty-four Californians—mostly his and Dorris' employees. These volunteers, like the Oregonians, were armed for the

4 Nash, *Revivalism.*
5 Meacham, *Wi-ne-ma*, 130.
6 Meacham, *Wigwam and War-path*, 399; *Wi-ne-ma*, 129.

most part with Springfield rifles. Mason's battalion of infantry, armed with Springfields, with a few Sharps rifles, was on Fairchild's right toward the south, and it was assumed that his infantry companies would bear the brunt of the attack. To Mason's right were the Oregon volunteers, numbering about eighty, and on their right was Perry's cavalry troop, armed with lever-action Spencer carbines. Wheaton ordered Fairchild and the infantry to advance until they came into contact with the Indians, and then the volunteers and Perry's cavalry would pivot, using the infantry for an anchor, meeting Bernard's and Jackson's men who would be attacking at the same time from the east. They had been given orders to swing to the south until they met Perry. All would then advance triumphantly northward and force the Indians into the lake.

At about six-thirty, the howitzers fired three shots, which was the signal agreed upon for starting the battle. There was then a lull of about fifteen minutes until a Modoc-speaking Indian could go out into the Lava Beds and announce in as loud a voice as he could muster that the Indians in the Stronghold had ten minutes to surrender or should be prepared to face the consequences. Only silence greeted his ultimatum.

Within minutes the first shots were fired. It was almost pitch black, and a chilly wind was blowing. Soldiers were certain they saw Modocs, however, and shot at phantoms in the fog. The Modocs were almost a mile distant when the soldiers began to shoot, but were well beyond their Stronghold. They did not fire on the troops until the advance had progressed the mile toward the center of the Indian position.

When dawn began to break dimly, visibility improved very little. Instead of foggy blackness, the men advanced in foggy whiteness. The Indians had tied sagebrush around their heads, and crouched behind rocks where they fired at the troops, which were conveniently lined up as targets in the approved "skirmish line" used in post-Civil War infantry advances. The Indians, of course, could see no better than the soldiers, but they knew the country better, and soon had reduced the morale of the numerically superior army troops almost to zero.

Practically no one was hurt during the morning, but the soldiers advanced with increasing reluctance as the time went by. The distance from the bluff to the Stronghold is less than three miles and a half. They marched almost a mile before they came under fire. While the remaining two and a half miles is rough terrain, it is not impassable. A hundred of Pickett's Gettysburg veterans would probably have been in the Stronghold in two hours. To the men attacking from the west, however, every rock began to take on the appearance of a mountain. Reports after the battle indicated that the Indians were firing from cliffs a hundred feet above the advancing line. Actually, there is probably not a single spot where the elevation is more than twenty feet above the average of the plateau, and at most, the depressions in the lava flows, instead of being "chasms" as the soldiers called them, are less than another twenty feet deep.

Six hours after the first Modoc rifle sounded, the soldiers on the west had advanced barely more than another mile. Reports of men advancing "smartly" at "double time" cannot possibly be true. If they had crawled steadily on their hands and knees they would have gone at a faster rate than they actually advanced. Losses were extremely light, and the failure to move forward comes close to being inexcusable. Part of the trouble may have been the lack of a protecting howitzer fire which the men had been counting on. In the fog, Wheaton had to order the guns to stop firing, for not only did the artillerymen not know where their targets were, they did not even have any idea where their own men were.

Inefficient as the soldiers on the west were, Bernard's men on the east were even worse. After their withdrawal, the previous afternoon, these soldiers bivouacked in the rocks for the night. When they began to move forward in the morning, they reached a collapsed lava tube that they labeled a "chasm," stopped, and refused to budge for the rest of the day. From about ten o'clock in the morning until dark, they contented themselves with firing random rifle shots in the general direction of the Indians. Many of the bullets went clear across the Stronghold and landed in the ranks of their comrades-at-arms. It is doubtful whether anyone was hurt from the east side, for the Indians kept under cover, and the white soldiers were also well protected.

The reports of the battle add to the confusion of one trying to understand the affair. All reports agreed that visibility in the fog was less than fifty yards, yet the soldiers fired at distant Modocs who, they claimed, were in plain sight. The Oregonians asserted in their official reports to have killed four Modocs at a distance of a quarter of a mile, although they admitted that when they reached the scene of the killing, the bodies had mysteriously disappeared.

A little before one o'clock, the regulars in the west were able to advance three hundred yards ahead of the volunteers, leaving a gap between Mason's infantry and the Oregonians. Green sent a message by Donald McKay ordering the gap closed. The Oregonians passed on the order to Perry, who was on their right, and then promptly retreated, carrying the body of one young man, their only casualty. In their withdrawal, volunteers made a "slight detour" around any Indian positions they thought they saw through the fog, and they found themselves at the end of the maneuver on Perry's right rather than on his left where they had started. When the volunteers found that by their own actions they were on the exposed left flank, "they were not so anxious to shoot Indians as they were in the morning." Since the Oregonians refused to go back into line, and since Bernard's regulars had not moved for hours, there was no chance to carry out the original battle plans to join forces on the south and drive the Indians into ignominious surrender by one glorious charge.

At one fifteen, Green, the field commander on the west side, saw that something else would have to be done. He sent word to Wheaton that his right was pinned down, and that, while bullets from Bernard's men were striking his positions, no advance was apparent or audible from that direction. Wheaton agreed with him that Perry's men and Mason's infantry should be moved down to the lake, if possible, and a junction should be made with Bernard along the shore. Just what good this would have done, neither seems to have spelled out. If the military had successfully completed the maneuver, the Indians might easily have escaped to the south.

When Perry received orders to move, he objected. His men would have to cross a depression which was under fire from the Modocs. He sent word to Wheaton that he was held up by the "chasm." Wheaton replied with some asperity, "By Gad, Colonel Perry, you must cross it." Perry then sent the response, "I can cross it, General, but it will cost me half my command." Actually, Perry lost almost no one when he advanced.

The whole area immediately west of the Stronghold and about half a mile south of the lake, is broken into a series of roughly parallel gullies about a quarter of a mile long, possibly a hundred feet wide, and averaging about twenty feet deep. In some places, jagged rock outcroppings make the depth as much as thirty feet. The slopes up either side vary from gradual to precipitous.

Perry's greatest difficulty was large cracks in the lava on the low ridges between the gullies; here the Indians could lie down, fire, and then retreat into the fog before the terrified army knew the enemy's position. The Modocs knew these spots, and took full advantage of them.

It should be emphasized that the Indians had only fifty men to fight over three hundred, and they had to operate across three miles of lava. When the chips were down they still had to defend a perimeter of over a mile of trenches and outpost positions. The only way they could do this was to shuttle men rapidly back and forth between threatened spots. Two or three riflemen could and did pin down a company of soldiers until the Modoc "fire department" could suppress an attack on another point and return to fire a few shots at the creeping advance.

Every army unit was convinced it had equal or superior numbers of Modocs directly opposite them, and at the end of the battle, many soldiers asserted that there were as many Modocs present as there had been troops. When the officers thought they were outnumbered and that the Modocs were firing from superior positions, they ordered the advance to stop.

By two in the afternoon, a few soldiers along the lake shore were within one hundred fifty yards of the Stronghold itself. This is a roughly rectangular area about three hundred yards in width, and perhaps half a mile long. There are several large pitlike depressions characteristic of the whole region; here the Modocs had their dwellings. In a few cases the Modocs used the natural rock shelters around the edge of the pits and hung a few skins or blankets in front of the overhanging rocks for shelter. There are about a dozen caves in the area. The rest is a series of rough lava fields and natural cracks in the lava rock; these cracks run around the entire perimeter and vary in depth from two to ten or twelve feet. There are also at least three or four lateral cracks in the lava which served as communication trenches. Through the gaps in the rock, the Indians piled stones which gave them natural loopholes from which to shoot. Along the lake shore, where Perry's men were attacking, there were several mounds of rock which gave the Indians about a twenty foot altitude advantage over the soldiers. They had fortified these strongpoints, and an Indian or two was stationed in each. (Ignorant savages, indeed!)

The Indians in these lakeside fortifications shouted derisive epithets in poor, but understandable English; they tried to get the soldiers to stand up so that they could get a better shot at them. They were particularly delighted to see Fairchild's Californians, for they knew many of them by sight and name. Steamboat Frank was in one position, and Scarfaced Charley was in another near by. A reporter gave an account of a typical bit of Indian humor:

> Said Steamboat Frank, "Hello! Charley, here is some Yreka boys, don't you see them?"
> "Yes."
> "Boys, what do you want? What makes you come here to fight us? Charley, there is old Dorris! Dorris, what do you want here? Say, Dorris, how long are you going to fight us?" Steamboat punctuated each question with a rifle shot, then continued. "What's the matter with you Dorris? Can't you hear?" (Bang!) "Ain't you got ears?" (Bang!) "Can't you talk?" (Bang!) "Ain't you got a mouth?"[7]

Dorris refused to say anything. All of the Californians were in an awkward spot and far too busy avoiding casualties to joke with the Modocs. Most of the casualties suffered in this fight were received by the men who tried to crawl next to the water over the huge boulders along the lake shore; there was no protection from the Indians stationed in the outposts above them.

About four o'clock Perry himself was shot through the upper arm as he raised himself on one elbow to look at a man who had just

[7] Yreka *Union* (February 15, 1873).

been hit. He uttered an involuntary cry of pain, and was immediately the target for jeers from the Indians. Falsetto cries of "I'm shot!" came from the rocks. A woman yelled at him, "You come here to fight Indians, and you make a noise like that. You no man, you squaw."[8] Derision or not, Perry was out of the fight. Lieutenant Kyle was also hit, though not seriously hurt. A number of men were killed, and few more were wounded when they crawled past this particular spot, which is not more than one hundred yards west of the present trail into the stronghold area.

The firing was so heavy and the men so reluctant to move that Green came to the spot to persuade them to advance. Most of his men either refused to leave what shelter they had, or else ignored him completely. He grew so angry that, disregarding his own safety, he leaped on a rock in plain view of both Indians and soldiers and delivered an impromptu, but profane, tirade about the character, ancestry, and probable eternal future of the soldiers under his command. The Modocs took a few tentative shots at him, but missed. He snatched a glove off his hand and kept striking it against his other arm and hand. The Indians later spread the word that Green's glove had magical properties and he could not be killed as long as he held it.[9] For this bit of personal leadership, Green was later given the Congressional Medal of Honor.

Green obtained his desired end, however, for part of his men began moving past the deadly spot. They did not try to hold the lake shore when they reached it, but passed as rapidly along as they could, joined Bernard, and thankfully sank beneath the protection of his snugly concealed riflemen.

It was now after five o'clock and growing dark. When Wheaton came up, he found a few anxious volunteers and fifteen demoralized infantrymen still in position between the Modocs and the bluff. There were also a few men guarding the inactive howitzers. On both sides of the Stronghold, there were probably not more than a hundred soldiers still in action. In the hazy evening, signal fires began to spring up all around them, and several were lit between the soldiers and the bluff. Hooker Jim, the Indians said later, realized

[8] *Ibid.*
[9] Yreka *Union* (March 22, 1873).

that complete victory was within the Modoc's grasp. He ordered an attack on the bluff to cut the soldiers off so that they could be annihilated, but, since he did not have the authority to command, the individualistic Indians muffed their golden opportunity.

Wheaton knew that things were growing serious. He turned to the leader of the volunteers and asked him, "General, what had we better do?"

The old Indian fighter's reply was simple: "We'd better get out of here, by God!"

Wheaton looked at him and after a moment's pause blurted, "General Ross, I leave this matter in your hands," and strode away into the gathering darkness.

Only about seventy-five men went back with the leaders. The rest had been hurt or had already fled. They were so panic-stricken by the time they reached the base of the bluff that someone spread the rumor among the others that the Modocs held the top of the ridge. The men refused to climb it to see, but, rather, huddled at the base of the hill in terrified misery. It was two in the morning before anyone could be induced to see what lay at the top, and, when this courageous soul called down that all was clear, there was a mad scramble up the hill to safety. General Ross himself was helped up the hill by hanging on to the tail of a mule after he had put the beast in motion with a blow. No one helped anyone else, and the walking wounded were left to climb the hill as best they could.

For almost forty-eight hours these men had been without sleep. They were hungry, for most had lost or thrown away their rations. They were cold, terrified, and badly whipped. Many were weaponless, having thrown away their guns in panic. From contempt of the Modocs, their feelings had taken a pendulum swing, until they decided that all of their enemies must stand nine feet high.

They remained on the bluff until eleven thirty the next morning, when it was evident to Wheaton that there was no point in ordering another attack. His men were worn out, and demoralized. He then ordered them to take their wounded and return to Van Bremer's.

On the east side of the Stronghold, Bernard's men were also returning from the wars, if their activities could be called fighting. The total loss of Bernard's cavalry was one man killed and eight wounded. Perry's men, who were with him, had one killed and five wounded, but almost all of these were hit before they crossed to join Bernard. By ten thirty that night it was clear that there was no fight in the men on the east side, and Green gave orders to retreat to Land's ranch. The wildly joyful Indians permitted them to withdraw without further attack.[10]

There was no order to the retreat. The wounded were put in blankets with four men carrying each victim. (It had never occurred to anyone to have stretchers brought to the area.) In the plunging retreat the frightened and weary men bumped their injured comrades carelessly against rocks and trees as they blundered through the darkness. The wounded men were in great pain, and groaned horribly. Their pain, however, was not severe enough for them to want to be abandoned for the Modocs to find, and they were taken back to camp.

The volunteers had no medical corps. One Californian named Crook had been hit in the leg and was suffering from a broken bone. A horse was provided for him, and he was helped on the animal, then left to his own devices. His dangling leg kept hitting on the rocks, and it hurt so badly that he finally rigged up a rope, tied it around his knee, and lifted the injured leg whenever he saw he was going to bump something.

At one o'clock in the morning of the eighteenth, the last weary soldier had made his way to Land's ranch. The men were so tired that there were tales told of men who went sound asleep while they were walking. Almost all those who were riding fell asleep in spite of the rough ground. When halts were allowed so the men could rest, the exhausted soldiers fell asleep instantly, and it took longer and longer after each rest to get them moving again.

It is not clear whether any of the wounded had been abandoned on the field or not. The casualty report following this encounter stated that the nature of the wounds had not been determined, since the bodies had been left on the field. At any rate it is certain that if they were not dead, any of the nine listed would have been killed in the morning when the Modocs found them.[11]

[10] The foregoing account of the battle is a composite taken from the official reports of Maj. E. C. Mason, Bvt. Col. and Maj. John Green, Lt. Col. Frank Wheaton, Applegate Collection.

The reluctance of the Klamaths to fight during the battle disturbed the officers. When the Indian scouts saw how the regular troops clung to the protecting rocks and refused to leave them, the Klamaths could see little point in fighting all by themselves. The Modocs found out where they were and began to talk to them. Before long the Klamaths were answering freely and trading began to take place right on the battlefield. Scarfaced Charley told a Klamath that if they liked the Modocs so well, they could prove it by leaving ammunition under a rock for the Modocs to pick up. The next day, Charley went to the spot he had designated, and picked up almost half a flour sack full of ammunition.[12] None of the Klamaths actually joined the Modocs, but the army sent their erstwhile allies home almost immediately after the fighting was over, never recalling any great number of them for further military service. Wheaton stated simply, "Our enlisted Klamath scouts have proved to be utter failures. We want Warm Springs Indians. Donald McKay, my district guide, will take charge of them."[13]

This type of trading, of course, was not the only source of Modoc supplies. The panic-stricken soldiers and volunteers threw away so much of their equipment when they ran from the battlefield that the Indians had much better rifles at the end of the battle than they had at the beginning. Bernard said, "A few days like this would be all the Modocs would want to supply every man they have with the most improved arms and a hundred rounds of ammunition for each." He admitted ruefully in his report that "all they did was to take about eighty" ponies from the Indians. The men were so demoralized that "they could hear the whizzing of the balls, and the War-whoop of the Indian, for the next twenty-four hours; besides, two-thirds of the command was so badly bruised and used up that they are limping about yet."[14]

On Sunday morning, the nineteenth, Green and Mason, Fairchild's Californians, and ten Klamath Indians, along with any of the

[11] Bancroft, *Oregon*, II, 592.

[12] 43 Cong., 1 sess., *House Exec. Doc. No. 122*, Trial of the Modoc Prisoners. Scarfaced Charley's testimony.

[13] Telegram, Wheaton to Canby, January 25, 1873, S.F.P., D.C., 1873, #131.

[14] Bernard report to Headquarters, Department of the Columbia, January 26, 1873, S.F.P., D.C., 1873, #724.

infantry that could march, made the long detour around the north end of the lake to return to their command headquarters at the Van Bremer ranch. They arrived on the twentieth, and found those who had fled from the field with Wheaton already there, along with the wounded from the west side.

Jackson was detailed by Green to take the wounded from Land's ranch to Fort Klamath for treatment. There were no ambulances available, so the dozen wounded were laid on the beds of several freight wagons and started on the seventy-mile jaunt to the post hospital. There was almost no road, and the wagons had few springs. The wheels would mount a rock in the tracks, and then descend with a lurching jolt, which hurt the injured men severely. The ordeal lasted three days. Captain Jackson and twenty of the more or less able-bodied men rode along as an escort. Bernard's force was stripped to a skeleton.

The Oregon volunteers were very eager to get home. Some of the scornful army personnel gave its opinion that they were just wanting "to place the Cascade Mountains between them and the Modocs," but the army was in no position to be supercilious. The regulars had not given a very creditable account of themselves either. Wheaton was so out of sorts with them that he ordered the military personnel to drill every possible moment of every good day.

He then sat down to write his report. In it he made no reference to his bombastic hope that the Modocs would fight, or to his optimistic assessment of his army's hopes for victory. In his first official information to Canby he stressed the difficulties of the battle:

> ... We fought the Indians through the lava-beds to their stronghold, which is in the center of miles of rocky fissures, caves, crevices, gorges and ravines, some of them one hundred (100) feet deep.
> In the opinion of any experienced officer of regulars or volunteers, one thousand men would be required to dislodge them from their almost impregnable position, and it must be done deliberately with a free use of mortar batteries. The Modocs were scarcely exposed at all to our persistent attacks. They left one ledge to gain another equally secure. One of our men was wounded twice during the day, but he did not see an Indian at all, tho' we were under fire from eight A. M. until dark. No troops could have fought better than

all did, in the attack advancing promptly and cheerfully against an unseen enemy over the roughest rock country imaginable. It was utterly impossible to accomplish more than to make a forced reconnaissance, developing the Modoc strength and position. It is estimated that (150) one hundred and fifty Indians opposed us. The Pit-River Indians are believed to be with them.

. . . Please send me three hundred (300) foot troops at the earliest date. . . . Can the Governor of California send volunteers to protect this threatened portion of his state, which is open to Modoc raids?[15]

Wheaton called a council of his officers as soon as Mason and Green arrived from Land's ranch. He asked them to write out their suggested plans for attack. They also discussed their plans informally and it was decided that two barges should be built for use as "mortar boats" to bombard the Stronghold by mobile artillery. The camp should be moved back to Crawley's to be closer to the scene of operations, and the next attack should come from the lake in order to avoid the rough country that had stopped them on Friday.

Canby was deeply disturbed by the defeat suffered by the army. He had been led to expect victory, and now he was informed that it had only been a "forced reconnaissance." He could not understand what had happened. In other Indian wars, the army had usually been numerically inferior to the Indians, and almost always when it came to an open fight the army won. Yet here in northern California, though the army had a superiority in number and equipment it had failed utterly. To Canby the only solution lay in change of leadership. He began looking around for someone to replace Wheaton.

Wheaton did not know that he was to be removed. He went ahead with plans for the next attack and, on January 21, moved the camp away from Van Bremer's according to the agreement between him and his officers. He began with commendable energy to have the boats built to float the cannon close to the Modoc encampment.

When the military forces pulled out of Van Bremer's, that family was filled with consternation. They did not want to be left without some protection against the Indians, but they had not welcomed the soldiers. Since they made their dislike known, relations between the troops and their hosts were not friendly. When the Van Bremers

[15] Telegram, Wheaton to Canby, January 19, 1873.

announced they were leaving with the army, no one stopped them, but neither did anyone help them. A few miles from the Crawley place, Van Bremer's wagon became mired in the muddy ground, and the soldiers marching by ignored their pleas for help; they offered gratuitous and grinning advice, or made nasty comments, but no one lent a hand.[16]

In the Indian camp, all was jubilation. Curley Headed Doctor claimed the credit for the victory. His medicine was obviously potent. No one would argue with him. Although the Modocs had been outnumbered six to one, they had not suffered a single casualty. They had inflicted almost as many casualties on their attackers as their own total effective manpower. No soldier had crossed the red tule rope. They had acquired a score of government issue rifles, and plenty of ammunition to fire from them. They had even picked up a pair of field glasses. The uniforms taken from the bodies of the dead soldiers served to clothe some of them during the rest of the winter. The army was as far away from the Stronghold on January 20, as it had been on the fifteenth. What army was opposed to them was not at all eager to fight. Meacham claims that at the very moment the weary and frightened soldiers were retreating, the Indians were holding a scalp dance to celebrate.[17] Rumor had it that Jack offered a reward of one hundred fifty dollars for the scalps of Oliver and Ivan Applegate and Dennis Crawley.

On the twenty-second, Bernard was ordered to abandon Land's ranch. He was to take the few men remaining on the east side and ride to Applegate's ranch on Clear Lake. He left that very afternoon, taking all of his supplies except three tons of grain. Two wagons and an escort of twenty-two men were sent back for it the next morning. As the supplies were moving around the base of Scorpion Point to take the road east of Casuse Mountain, the Indians, who had watched the activities of the wagon train and its escort, opened fire. The men promptly fled, abandoning their wagons. The escort stopped running and rallied to try to recapture the wagons, while others sent word to Bernard. In time, help came from Bernard, and the Indians were driven away from the wagons. The Modocs had burned the

16 Thompson, *Reminiscences*, 108.
17 Meacham, *Wigwam and War-path*, 409.

grain and destroyed the wagons, but the army horses were recaptured.[18] No Indian was hurt, however, and they felt even more confident of their ability to attack and defeat the soldiers wherever and whenever they chose.

On a routine investigation of the camp at Van Bremer's, the Indians fired a few shots from the mountain and created a near panic in camp. Delighted by the confusion they had created, the scouting party paid their respects to the Dorris place and fired at some Indians who had not joined them. Others attacked a group of twenty-five volunteers moving horses along the north shore of Tule Lake.

The result was that the volunteers began deserting with increasing frequency. Ross's Company A was pretty well depleted by Wednesday after the Stronghold fight. Since they were not officially discharged for three more days, they put in claims for pay until February 2. Applegate's Company B watched the departure of the Rogue River detachment with deep disgust. Oliver himself had fallen and injured both knees in the Friday battle and was at Yainax recovering. His lieutenant wrote him that "Co. A. Vol. have gone to the four winds, disbanded, they are even now scattering over the country, some enroute for Rogue River Valley. What think you! of this state of affairs . . . things look more demoralized every day, surely it is very discouraging, there seems to be a morbid fear or panic holding upon the regulars."[19]

The day after the Indians attacked the wagon train at Scorpion Point, orders went out from San Francisco to Colonel Alvan C. Gillem of the First Cavalry, assigning him to command the troops in the Modoc country, effective as soon as he could get there. Word of the change in command was also sent to Wheaton, who was left in command of the District of the Lakes, but relieved as far as the active theater of operations was concerned.

When Wheaton heard that he had been relieved, he protested to his superior officer. "I am greatly disappointed and pained at not being permitted to retain this command in the field—I am perfectly familiar with the situation and confident that we can easily kill or

[18] Wheaton to Headquarters, January 27, 1873, S.F.P., D.C., 1873, #754.
[19] Letter, J. Henry Hyzer to Oliver Applegate, January 22, 1873, Applegate Collection.

capture every hostile Indian in arms with the force now enroute as this outbreak is in my district. I hope to be permitted to retain the immediate command of the troops, even if I am not allowed to operate under your direct orders."[20] Canby ignored the request, and Gillem left San Francisco to take command.

Colonel Gillem was a Tennessee mountain man and a personal friend of former President Andrew Johnson. Johnson had been responsible to a considerable extent for Gillem's rise in the army and when Johnson went out of office, Gillem was neglected. He had been a regular "West Point" man, but had received his promotions largely on political grounds since the Union needed loyal southern volunteers badly in order to show that not all men south of the Mason and Dixon line favored the Confederacy. For a time, Gillem was acting as general to a division of Tennessee volunteers. He had been attached for a time to the Marine Corps, and had gained some military experience through that branch of the service. Politically, he was highly successful. He had helped restore Tennessee to the Union, and served as vice-president of the convention that rewrote the Constitution of Tennessee in line with the demands of Congress. After the war, he elected to remain in the regular army, and served as commander of the military occupation of Mississippi. When Grant became President, Gillem was transferred to California.

He was not a popular officer. The career officers, who had to wait a long time after the Civil War for promotion through seniority, resented Gillem's easy rise to a colonelcy. He was also disliked by some because he had been a marine. Gillem did not help the situation by his own personality; at times he was capricious and unfair in dealing with subordinates. When the officers at Lost River heard that Wheaton had been relieved by Gillem, they were deeply disturbed. Gillem's unpopularity with the officers was quickly observed by the enlisted men, and their attitude was affected by what they saw. His orders were usually obeyed, but without enthusiasm, and no extra effort was made to help him win. On at least one occasion his orders were deliberately disobeyed to make him look foolish. Naturally, the attitude of these subordinates did nothing to beat the Indians.

[20] Wheaton to Canby, S.F.P., D.C., 1873, #187.

While the unhappy Wheaton was waiting for his successor to arrive, the written suggestions for the best way to beat the Modocs began coming in from the officers. There was no major change from the agreement in their discussion. All three thought that the attack across the Lava Beds had been a mistake. Next time there should be an attack over the water, supported by gunboats firing cannon. Mason suggested that other Indians be recruited as shock troops in order to spare the lives of the soldiers. He felt that attrition was the only way to win. Kill one Modoc at a time until there were no more left. Bernard also agreed to an over-water attack, but could not help adding a dig at the Oregonians. His plan was for attacks to be made from west, east and south, then, with the slowly closing ring to invite all Indians not implicated in the murder of the settlers to go to the reservation. The murderers, he predicted, probably would not come out, but they could be left there, and the Oregonians could go in to get them if they wanted them badly enough. Green agreed to the plans of the others, except that he proposed a third attack by way of the Tickner road across the lava to the south of the Stronghold.[21]

They agreed that they should suspend the building of the "mortar boats" until Gillem arrived. They believed that troops were coming from all directions to take their place beside the defeated veterans of the January fight and they should wait to attack again until the reinforcements were there.

On January 30, Gillem reached Yreka, and found the whole of northern California enveloped in a blinding snowstorm. Nothing could move, all supply trains were immobilized, and he did not try to approach his new command until the storm stopped. Only the Indians moved about.

Under cover of the storm, Jack sent in one of his women to the military camp to say that he was tired of fighting and would welcome Fairchild in the Stronghold to discuss a settlement. The woman was sent back, and told to say to Jack that when the storm let up, a guide could be sent, and both Fairchild and Dorris would go down the bluff from the point the ill-fated attack had started on the seventeenth. Jack could then make his proposition. At the beginning of February, therefore, the situation was stabilized. Some

[21] Bernard's report to Headquarters, January 26, 1873, S.F.P., D.C., 1873, #724.

of the Modocs were tired of fighting, but most were jubilantly awaiting the next test of Curley Headed Doctor's medicine against the soldiers.

The little army was awaiting its new commander with sour pessimism. Several hundred new troops would arrive as soon as the weather made it possible. The volunteers were all gone, and the regulars, now numbering less than two hundred, were divided into two camps, thirty miles apart. The Modocs were free to go and come as they pleased, and other Indians in the vicinity were cautiously exploring the possibilities of joining the Modocs, either as individuals or as groups.

It was not a pleasant situation.

Schonchin (Courtesy Western History Collections, University of Oklahoma).

Hooker (or Hooka) Jim (Courtesy Western History Collections, University of Oklahoma).

Scarfaced Charley (Courtesy Western History Collections, University of Oklahoma).

Bogus Charley (Courtesy Western History Collections, University of Oklahoma).

VI

PROTRACTED NEGOTIATIONS

ALMOST AT THE SAME TIME that Jack's Modocs were driving the soldiers from the Lava Beds, the Electoral College met in Washington, D. C., to cast the formal ballot making U. S. Grant President of the United States for a second term. Most of the electors were not concerned with events in California, but one of them played an important part in the negotiations which filled the time between the battle of January 17, and the tragedy in the Lava Beds on Good Friday. This elector from the State of Oregon was A. B. Meacham, formerly Indian superintendent for Oregon, and a strong Republican party worker.

While Jack was beating the army in the Stronghold and while the Electoral College met, there were, almost at the same time, several other Oregonians in the capital. These included Lindsay Applegate, the Portland newspaperman S. A. Clarke, D. P. Thompson, M. P. Berry, R. H. Kincaid, Daniel Chaplin, and Jacob Stitzel. These men visited each other several times to talk over home news and mutual acquaintances.

When they heard that Jack's Modocs had defeated the army and volunteers, the Modoc situation became the prime topic of conversation. The Oregonians analyzed the reasons for the failure of the army, and proposed various solutions. Lindsay Applegate blamed the system of Indian administration. A commission to talk to the Modocs, he said, was better than any army to fight them, especially when it allowed itself to get beaten. "Jawbone is cheaper than ammunition," he said.

On January 25, the Oregonians approached the Attorney General with a plan for a peace commission to persuade the Modocs to leave their Stronghold. Attorney General Williams sent them to the Secretary of the Interior, Columbus Delano, who agreed that they had a good idea, but that they should reduce their ideas to writing and submit them formally.

On Monday, January 27, while Wheaton was glumly awaiting the arrival of his successor at the fighting front, a group of men he did not know were working out the next moves in the war from a distance of three thousand miles. They presented their petition to Secretary Delano as he requested. In it the Oregonians pointed out the demoralizing effects of keeping soldiers on the reservation, mentioned the hostility of the Modocs and Klamaths toward each other for two or three generations and especially for the past five years, and drew attention to the fact that Jack's men were desperate and would stop at nothing. They felt that some of the discontented Indians from one of the surrounding tribes might join Jack and add to his strength, or else attack the settlers in areas depleted of soldiers by the need for troops in the Tule Lake Basin. Finally, they suggested that all of Jack's band should be moved completely out of the Klamath country to the coast; somewhere between Siletz and Tillamook. This was a land empty of people, and "abounding in fish." Meacham was suggested as the logical man for the job of "belling the cat"—Jack.[1]

Since Meacham was a party "stalwart" (and a presidential elector), and since he had once enjoyed the modest victory of inducing Jack to give up his Lost River home, Delano was willing to accept the suggestion. The next day the Secretary invited Meacham to return for a formal conference, and Meacham went, talked to Delano, and finally accepted the appointment to try to talk Jack into peace. "I did not believe that doubling the number of widows and orphans would make the griefs of the mourners less or lighter to be borne," he said afterward.[2]

Formal instructions were drawn up, defining the position and duties of the Peace Commission. It was to consist of three men who

[1] Bancroft, *Oregon*, II, 595; Meacham, *Wigwam and War-path*, 414ff.
[2] Meacham, *Wigwam and War-path*, 415.

were to proceed to the Modoc country, to talk to General Canby, and to take advice "freely" from him. The commissioners were to find the causes of the war and stop its spread. The Department of the Interior ordered the commission to try to find a spot along the coast where the Modocs would consent to go, but if they would not go to the coast, then they should try to find another place the Indians would accept as a reservation. They were not to give orders to the field officers, but on the other hand, they were expected to remind the soldiers on the battlefield that violence was to be used only as a last resort. Finally, they were to make almost daily reports of their progress to the Secretary.[3]

Grant was informed of Delano's action, and he approved. The unhappy President was apparently willing to try any alternative that might bring peace rather than face the criticism that was being heaped on his Indian policy—or lack of it—as the result of the fighting in California. He gave instructions through General Sherman, the head of the army, to telegraph Canby about the decision to try for peace by negotiation. Troops in the Modoc country were to be used only to protect settlers, and they were to avoid battle.[4] Canby received the orders from Sherman on the thirtieth of January.

Delano proposed three names for the commission members. Meacham would be chairman. T. B. Odeneal, who had ordered the arrest of Jack and was still superintendent for Oregon and Agent J. H. Wilbur of the Yakima Agency would be the other members. Meacham was to be paid ten dollars a day, (a remarkably high wage for those days) plus his expenses. The other two men, already in the employ of the government, were to receive expense money in addition to their ordinary salaries.[5]

The first hitch developed when Meacham refused to have anything to do with the commission if either Odeneal or Wilbur were on it. Meacham did not like Odeneal because he had been fired from the Oregon superintendency to make room for Odeneal, and he also disapproved of the way Odeneal had handled Modoc problems. He did not like Wilbur because he had assumed a paternalistic juris-

[3] Orders to Commission, *Oregon Superintendency, 1873,* Office of Indian Affairs, The National Archives.

[4] Telegram, Sherman to Canby, S.F.P., D.C., 1873, #212.

[5] *Oregon Superintendency, 1873,* Office of Indian Affairs.

diction over all the Yakimas, whether they were under the Yakima Agency or not. Since sometimes there were Yakimas in Oregon, Wilbur's interference in Oregon affairs had irritated Meacham considerably.[6] Apparently neither Odeneal nor Wilbur wanted to work on the commission, for both of them gave excellent reasons for not wanting to serve.[7] These personality conflicts meant a delay of several days until men, acceptable to Meacham, were chosen.

Canby did not know why the organization of the Peace Commission was delayed, but he wired Gillem that he was to assume command as quickly as possible and keep the soldiers quiet. Why they were to be quiet, Canby did not know, but he had his orders and he would carry them out.[8] The instructions to Gillem necessitated holding up all plans for aggressive action. A company of Warm Springs Indians had been recruited to take the place of the discarded Klamath Scouts. If there was to be no more fighting, they would not be needed.[9] Soldiers were coming from distant states to join the fighting, and they would have to be shifted quickly to a standby capacity. The construction of the boats being built to float the cannon into position was permanently stopped. Fairchild's projected parley with Jack could proceed, but no definite arrangements could be made until the official commission assumed its duties.

By February 5, Meacham left Washington. He had approved Jesse Applegate as an acceptable commissioner, and Samuel Case, acting agent at Siletz was selected to represent the Indian Service in place of Odeneal. Meacham told Canby that the commission wanted a conference with him; accordingly Canby made plans to meet them at Yreka when they arrived there.[10] Delano arbitrarily ordered them to meet Canby at Linkville on the fifteenth of the month, since this would be easier for all concerned. He also put $1,000 at Meacham's disposal for expenses.[11]

By the time these plans were worked out, it had been three weeks since the army's defeat in the First Stronghold Battle, and the In-

---

[6] Portland *Oregonian* (February 28, 1873).
[7] 43 Cong., 1 sess., *House Exec. Doc. No. 122.*
[8] Canby to Gillem, S.F.P., D.C., 1873, #210.
[9] S.F.P., D.C., 1873, Vol. I, 87–88, #114; 106, #147.
[10] S.F.P., D.C., 1873, Vol. I, 100, #137.
[11] 43 Cong., 1 sess., *House Exec. Doc. No. 122.*

dians were still untouched. Gillem had not yet arrived from Yreka, for the snow was much too deep for travel. Wheaton was still marking time. Gillem did try to discover the state of affairs in Jack's camp; his messenger went to Fairchild's ranch and learned a great deal about the disposition of the Indians.

On his return, the messenger told Gillem that there were always at least three factions in Jack's camp, and sometimes a fourth developed among the few Modocs in the Lava Beds. Jack had his own followers, Hooker Jim and Curley Headed Doctor had theirs, the Hot Creeks under Shacknasty Jim stuck together, and sometimes, in case of argument, John Schonchin was able to muster a following. All except Jack's friends did pretty much as Curley Headed Doctor directed.

Jack sent word out to Fairchild that he would like to call off the war, but he did so without consulting the leaders of the opposition within his own ranks. They had won, they thought, a smashing victory with the help of the medicine man, so they could see no point in surrendering. Jack, somewhat more realistically, realized that he could not hope to beat the army every time. If his victory over Jackson was good fortune, his victory over Wheaton was too good to be true. He felt there was no use in pushing his luck forever.

On February 2, accordingly, Jack and Scarfaced Charley borrowed horses and started to leave camp to meet Fairchild as they had promised. Curley Headed Doctor and Shacknasty Jim of the Hot Creeks rushed out when they saw them leaving, and a frightful quarrel took place. Finally Curley Headed Doctor told Jack that he might go if he would leave his arms at the Stronghold and that he had better stay if he left once, for, if he came back, they would kill him. Under these circumstances, if Jack left, he would be abdicating his leadership to Curley Headed Doctor, and this was something he was unwilling to do. After an interval, he dismounted, but the argument went on all night.

On the morning of February 3, the "hold-out" faction convinced Jack that the invitation to visit with Fairchild (even though Jack had himself initiated the idea) was only a trick by the white men to get him into their power so they could kill him. They seemed not only to have convinced Jack, but also Scarfaced Charley, Black

Jim, Big Dick, and eight other of his chief supporters that their only salvation lay in a last-ditch defense of the Stronghold. Since this was protected by the medicine man's magic, their defenses were good enough. Curley Headed Doctor was backed by Shacknasty Jim, Bogus Charley, Ellen's Man, and Hooker Jim. The rest of the Indians followed their own best interests and this time took the advice of the jealous John Schonchin. He was jealous of Jack, but had nothing to gain personally by supporting the murderers of the settlers.

Jack was not convinced that Curley Headed Doctor was right. As soon as the quarrel ended he sent word quietly to Fairchild's ranch that if no troops were sent, Jack would come alone to talk to Lieutenant Adams, in the presence of Fairchild and the Californians Jack knew, Dorris, Dan Van Bremer, "Doc" Skeen, and Donald McKay, the scout. The conference took place as planned. After smoking together for a while, Jack invited the whites to go back with him to the Stronghold for a conference.[12] He was then told that a commission was on its way to talk to him, so there would be no conferences until the new commanding officer arrived and the Peace Commission could take over at the diplomatic level.[13]

For several days there was a lull in activities at the army camps. Some of the individual soldiers went out from camp to explore the country. On one such foray, a Portland lawyer, named "Colonel" Bellingar, and William Thompson, an officer of those Oregon volunteers who were still in camp, went to look along Willow Creek for the remains of a wagon train allegedly attacked, captured and destroyed there twenty years before. They also wanted to find what had become of the two white girls whom Ben Wright had tried to rescue and the Modocs later killed.

Scarfaced Charley told Thompson before the war where he could find the wagons and the remains of the older girl. The two white men found the burned wreckage of the wagons where Charley said they would be and were encouraged to look for the bones of the unknown captive. On a ledge of rock not far from Van Bremer's, they found what they were looking for. A skull, a rib,

[12] Yreka *Union* (February 8, 1873).
[13] Wheaton to Canby, S.F.P., D.C., 1873, #280.

and one arm bone were all that remained of the wretched girl. They were unable to find where her sister had been murdered.

When the bones were brought into the camp, the old Modoc atrocity stories were trotted out and retold with embellishments, especially in the description of the treatment accorded women captives. Further, to inflame public opinion against the Indians, Bellingar took the skull to Portland and exhibited it there as an example of the work of the present enemies of Oregon.[14]

At last the waiting period came to an end, the weather eased, and Gillem left Yreka. On February 7, Gillem arrived at his headquarters camp on Lost River. Wheaton at once packed to go back to his former location at Camp Warner. As he was preparing to leave, Gillem said to him, "Frank, should a fight occur, I will send for you and you can have your half the chicken pie."[15] He had no intention of calling Wheaton, and when the fighting did come, Wheaton did not hear about it until it was over. Gillem seemed to have unbounded confidence in his own ability. To the disgruntled officers to whom he talked, his words of confidence, which he thought would restore the shaken morale of the troops, were shrugged off as sheer bluster.

Gillem's way was not made easy at any time while he was in the Modoc country. The behavior of his officers and men was usually correct, but his associates were neither warm nor enthusiastic. In addition, shortly after he arrived, his health failed him and he never did feel well during the months he spent in the field. He died only a little over two years after the war ended, apparently never having completely recovered. Probably he was secretly uncertain of his own ability, and as discouragement, coldness on the part of his subordinate officers, and sickness took their toll, he became more and more uncertain in his decisions until in chill contempt, his officers openly described him as incompetent. Eventually, their dislike found its reflection in his feelings toward them. He particularly detested Mason. His relations with the volunteers were even worse than with the regular army officers. Military efficiency suffered severely as the officers sniped at each other.

[14] Portland *Oregonian* (February 5, 1873).
[15] Boyle, "Personal Observations," 48.

The day after Gillem arrived, he asked to be shown the usual papers which recorded what had been going on before. His analysis of the situation, made to Canby the day after he assumed command, showed that he had a sound grasp of the situation. He estimated that there were between 55 and 75 Modocs. Jack said at the trial that he had never had more than fifty-one, but Judge Steele on his second visit to the Stronghold claimed to have counted sixty-nine men at the height of the Modoc strength. Gillem reported no Indians of other tribes with the Modocs, and that was the case except for two Pit River Indians; many settlers, however, were firmly convinced that the Pit Rivers, Paiutes, Klamaths, and Rogues were trembling on the verge of joining Jack. Gillem planned to call no more volunteers unless he was convinced of the absolute necessity for them.

The thing that shocked Gillem most were the records of payments made to teamsters in hauling supplies. Freight rates from Jacksonville and Roseburg were exceptionally high. The roads were frightful, and the rates matched them. Freighters charged from thirty to thirty-two cents a pound to bring supplies over the mountains, and tons of freight were required. When he discovered that rates from Redding were only half as much, he promptly cut off the freight business from Oregon in order to save the government money, and his action did not endear him to the Oregonians.

Gillem had much more man power than did Wheaton. By the time Gillem took command, even though the volunteers had all gone home, he had almost seven hundred troops at Lost River, Van Bremer's, Dorris', or Applegate's ranches in the Tule Lake country, with another 140 in reserve at Camp Warner and Camp Harney a hundred miles away. By now he had five troops of the First Cavalry, three batteries of artillery, and elements of the Twelfth and Twenty-first Infantry Regiments.[16] This was designed to help the army and the commission to have a position of strength from which to negotiate. Unfortunately, the Indians paid no attention to numbers; they had Curley Headed Doctor and his magic, and they had had victory thus far. Any negotiations the United States government carried on seemed to these Modocs an attempt by a beaten army to salvage something from their January 17 defeat. Each side felt itself stronger

[16] Gillem to Canby, S.F.P., D.C., 1873, #908.

than the other, and no compromise was possible. If someone had recognized this deadlock at the time, it would have been seen at the outset that to try to work out a negotiated peace was almost hopeless. No one in a responsible position understood the actual situation, and the talks dragged drearily on for over two months without solving the basic problems.

On February 15, Canby came through a driving rain to Linkville to meet with the Commissioners. Because Meacham was not yet there, Canby met informally with Applegate and Case. The next day the two men there agreed with Canby that the little frame hotel furnished too much opportunity for eavesdroppers. They moved to Fairchild's ranch and set up their headquarters in army tents. They left word for Meacham that when he arrived, he could find them in California.

The newspapers and government of Oregon did not know exactly what was afoot, but they were suspicious. The grand jury at Jacksonville met and indicted Scarfaced Charley, Hooker Jim, Long Jim, One-eyed Mose, Curley Headed Doctor, Little Jim, Boston Charley, and Dave for the murder of Oregon citizens on November 30, after the Lost River fight. Some of these Indians were guilty, and some were just names the Oregonians picked at random. Scarfaced Charley was certainly not involved. Probably he was unfortunate enough to have his name known in Jacksonville.[17]

After the indictment of the Indians, Grover wrote to both Canby and Meacham, told them what the grand jury had done, and informed them further that this placed these particular Indians under the jurisdiction of the state government, and that a civil court was the only competent and final tribunal to judge their guilt or innocence. If the commission wished, it could make peace with the rest of the Modocs, but a reservation on Lost River was out of the question. The Lost River Valley was in Oregon, and only the state government could make any disposition of these lands other than to Oregon settlers.[18]

Grover's letter was referred to Delano. The Secretary of the

[17] Sacramento *Union* (February 15, 1873).
[18] Letter, Grover to Canby, February 10, 1873, *Oregon Superintendency, 1873,* Office of Indian Affairs.

Interior responded by reminding Grover with some asperity that this was a federal matter, and that federal authority was superior to that of a state. Delano wrote Meacham to proceed as he had been instructed without consideration for Grover's protest. This meant that Meacham felt himself bound to run counter to the feelings of the Applegates, and all the rest of the inhabitants of Oregon.

On Tuesday, February 18, the full commission met with General Canby at Fairchild's. Oliver Applegate was invited down from Yainax to act as secretary to the commission, and he accepted the post. The meeting quickly showed a strong difference of opinion. Jesse Applegate and Samuel Case stood for the "Oregon Platform": unconditional surrender of Jack and his people, execution of the murderers, transportation of the remainder to a distant reservation. Meacham and Canby stood for a different settlement, for they knew the Modocs would never surrender while they were winning.

Various newspapers sent reporters to cover the commission meetings. Some of these reporters reflected the same differences of opinion existing between the Governor of Oregon and the federal government or the Applegates and Meacham. The San Francisco *Chronicle* reporter opposed the Oregon point of view, and the Applegate family in particular, while the San Francisco *Bulletin* favored the Oregon position.

On the twentieth, the commission tried for the first time to communicate with Jack. It will be remembered that he was ready to negotiate as early as the thirty-first of January, but had been talked out of it, and now three weeks had passed, further convincing the belligerent Indians that the white men were uncertain of their power. The Modocs were willing to listen to the officers of the army or commissioners, but they did not intend to surrender.

Robert Whittle's Indian wife, Matilda, and a Modoc girl called Artina Choaks, usually called One-eyed Dixie, were selected to leave Fairchild's and go to the Lava Beds to tell Jack that the commissioners wanted to talk to him. Whittle, who ran the ferry on the Klamath River, was asked to serve as interpreter for the commission when the expected Modoc delegation arrived.

The women came back and reported that the Modocs wanted to know more, and wanted to talk to a man. The next day, therefore,

Whittle went to the Lava Beds, met the Modoc leaders, and talked to them. He was instructed by the commission to suggest no terms for a peace settlement, but just to listen to them while they talked. While he was in the Stronghold, Whittle looked around and took mental notes. He reported less than sixty men in evidence, but noticed that they were armed with excellent rifles and seemed to have an abundance of ammunition. The Indians laughed at him when he asked how many had been killed in the fight on January 17. They denied losing any and were probably truthful. They told Whittle that they had been expecting someone to come and talk to them, that they were tired of war, tired of living in the Stronghold, and wanted to hear good words from Washington. They recalled Ben Wright's treachery, but said they would talk to the commission if Meacham and Case themselves would come to see them.

They also told Whittle that before they would talk to the commission, they had to have friendly witnesses present. Specifically, they said they would talk only if Steele and Rosborough from Yreka were put on the commission, for they could trust them. The Modocs would accept Fairchild but not the commission of Oregonians.

These demands were another way of Jack's to gain prestige in the negotiations. If he could designate the commission, naturally he would feel superior to the United States. Jack gained his point, in spite of the fact that the commissioners saw through his demands. President Grant appointed Rosborough to the commission, and Steele was invited to Fairchild's to try to conciliate Jack.[19]

On February 23, Whittle went back to the Stronghold, and came back about eleven at night with "Dave", one of the Rock Indians. Dave had been chosen to act as messenger, and he was rushed to the commission tent to be told of the appointment of Rosborough. The lateness of the hour aroused the curiosity of the reporters, and they crowded to the tent to find out what was going on. Bustling with importance, Meacham told them the meeting was closed to reporters. He was then asked whether one of their number might be allowed in the tent to represent the group. The chairman was brusque this time and refused to give them any information. From

[19] Letter, Meacham to Clum, February 22, 1873, *Special File Modocs, 1873,* Office of Indian Affairs.

that time on, Meacham's relations with the press were strained and newspaper treatment of him was extremely severe. He was criticized for almost anything he did.[20]

Reporter Fox, of the New York *Herald*, was so angry with Meacham that he decided to take matters into his own hands by going directly to the Stronghold for his story. He asked Meacham to be permitted to go with Whittle, but once again Meacham refused. Fox borrowed a horse, left camp, and rode into the Lava Beds. He was surrounded almost at once and taken to Jack.

An argument took place in the council ground with Miller's Charley demanding that Fox be killed as a spy, while Dave, Bogus Charley and Scarfaced Charley were loud in favor of treating him well. Jack also said that the reporter was not to be harmed, that he might look around, and that he could leave in safety. When he returned, Fox wrote a story of Modoc wickiups built in the cracks and pits of the Stronghold, of the paint on the faces of the Indians, of a council in Jack's cave where the Indians sat around the walls in four or five semicircles, and of his own thankfulness to escape alive.[21]

The newspaper feud between the Oregonians and Californians took a personal turn during the third week of February. Since the Applegate family had played such a vital part in the settlement of the Klamath Basin, and were closely involved in every phase of the Modoc trouble, they were charged by the *Chronicle* reporter with having cheated the Indians at the agency and also with having a financial interest in ordering the Modocs to the Yainax Agency where Oliver ran the commissary. This story, published in the San Francisco press, created a sensation up and down the coast.[22] The commission, therefore, said that the first order of business had to be to clear the Applegates' name, or to establish the truth of the charge. When Jesse Applegate learned that Meacham and Case were going to investigate Oliver and Ivan, he promptly resigned from the commission on the ground that it would be impossible for him to be impartial.[23]

20 Yreka *Union* (March 1, 1873).
21 Yreka *Union* (March 15, 1873).
22 Yreka *Union* (February 22, 1873).
23 Letter, Jesse Applegate to Clum, February 26, 1873, *Oregon Superintendency, 1873*, Office of Indian Affairs.

Ivan and Oliver had gone to Klamath as young men to help their father establish the agency. After Lindsay retired, the two sons were kept on by other agents, and they issued what supplies came through for the Indians. These supplies were meager at times, and it was only natural that the Modocs would blame the men directly representative of the government for whatever ills they suffered. These normal complaints were magnified by unsympathetic Californians into the charge which the *Chronicle* reported.

Meanwhile, the negotiations between the commission and Jack had barely gotten started. On the twenty-fifth, Whittle went back to the Stronghold for the third time, accompanied by Fairchild. While they were still a mile and a half from Jack's headquarters, they met about twenty Indians, who, when they saw them, laid down their guns and shook hands. Shortly afterward, Jack and John Schonchin arrived with seventeen mounted Modocs. They, too, shook hands, and negotiations got under way. Jack said he did not want to negotiate at Canby's camp at Fairchild's, risking the possibility of arrest, and that he did not want to deal with Oregon commissioners. He repeated his request for a Lost River reservation. His strategy was probably to gain time until summer. If things became impossible then, the Modocs could scatter into the mountains, and all the soldiers in the army could not capture them. Thanks to the slowness of the Peace Commission to begin work, he was already a valuable month closer to mid-May, when he could safely leave the Stronghold.

When Whittle and Fairchild went back, Jack sent two Modocs, Boston Charley and Bogus Charley with them. Both these young men spoke English, and it was their job to see what the commission had to offer. Their appearance must have been something of a shock to the soldiers and the commission members. The battle of January 17 had led them to believe the Modocs were a very tough lot. These two representatives were young, Bogus was about twenty-one, and Boston not more than nineteen. They were certainly not a handsome pair, yet these short, unprepossessing individuals made up four per cent of the Modoc force that had sent the volunteers and regulars into headlong flight up the bluff only a month before. Perhaps both had killed some of the soldiers. They were dressed in the clothes of a white working man of that day—calico shirt, ragged trousers, and work shoes.

They told Canby that they would negotiate only at the Lava Beds. Certainly, Jack was not coming in to Fairchild's. They firmly believed that if the United States government ever had all of them at one time in their hands, they would be arrested and hanged. The news of the indictment of their leaders by the Jackson County grand jury did nothing to allay their fears. Canby talked to them, but told them to inform Jack that the commission would not negotiate in the Lava Beds without a military escort. The general then sent Fairchild back with Bogus and Boston to emphasize the message to Jack himself.

On Thursday, the twenty-seventh, Steele and Rosborough arrived at Fairchild's ranch. The Applegates and their friends viewed their arrival with a jaundiced eye, for, to the Oregonians, these two men represented the California influences that were blamed for Jack's defiance of the orders to move to the reservation. The Applegates were probably somewhat unfair to Steele, though he is not without responsibility, but emotions were high in the winter of 1873, and the men involved could hardly be blamed for yielding to bad temper under the pressures to which they were subjected.

Sometime during the last week in February, the Whittles were sent home, and Meacham again secured the services of Frank Riddle and his wife, Toby. Meacham felt he could work with the Riddles, for they had been in his party as interpreters when Jack went to the reservation the first time. They were in camp when Fairchild returned from telling Jack the conditions under which the commission would talk to him.

This return trip must have been something of a mild success. When Fairchild came back, he brought with him the leaders of the shamanistic faction in the Modoc camp. Hooker Jim, leader of the murder raid on November 30, was with him, and so was Curley Headed Doctor himself. Shacknasty Jim rode behind. Jim was only a youth, like Boston Charley or Bogus Charley, but he was the leader of the Hot Creek band who had fled the lynching party at Whittles in December and had taken his followers to Captain Jack. The three came probably out of curiosity to size up Fairchild's establishment now that a real general had come down from Portland to talk to them, and also to try to negotiate with the Klamaths for the return of the forty horses, captured in the preliminary skirmish before the January fight. The horses were not returned. The Klamaths gave them a feeble promise to take care of the horses until the war was over.[24]

While the three Modocs and the Klamaths were dickering over the horses, Steele and Rosborough were meeting with the commission and Canby. They knew that Jack would not surrender so long as the Oregon indictment hung over the heads of Hooker Jim's band of killers. To end this difficulty, the commission decided to authorize Steele to tell the Indians that, if they surrendered as prisoners of war to the army, they would not be turned over to the wrathful Oregonians, but would be taken to some warmer climate—probably Arizona—and put on a reservation under army protection. After a cooling off period, the government could then negotiate for a final and permanent reservation. The authorities in Washington were notified of this decision, and they approved with the exception that the Modocs were to be shipped to Indian Territory rather than Arizona.

On the last day of February, Steele and Fairchild, the Riddles, and R. H. Atwell, a newspaper reporter from Sacramento, went back into the Lava Beds with the three Modocs to explain the sense of this decision to Captain Jack. Until they returned, the commission spent its time investigating the causes of the war. Meacham, to his embarrassment, found himself under investigation for the Modocs had claimed that he was responsible for their mistreatment under Knapp's jurisdiction. As Jesse Applegate had already resigned from the commission because the investigation came too close to home, Meacham decided that although he considered himself blameless, "any investigation as to the Cause of War would embarrass and possibly frustrate and defeat the main objective which was to obtain a peace with the Indians,"[25] so he called off the inquiry.

On March 1, Canby learned his first lesson about Jack's tactic of

[24] Sacramento *Union* (March 1, 1873).
[25] Letter, Meacham to Clum, March 3, 1873, *Oregon Superintendency, 1873,* Office of Indian Affairs.

procrastination. Even before Steele and Fairchild came back, Boston Charley, Bogus Charley, Hooker Jim, Long Jim, Shacknasty Jim, Duffy, William "Faithful," and Curley Headed Jack, along with "Queen" Mary came into camp to announce that they accepted the terms of surrender. Then the small delegation scattered through the army camp to look things over. Canby took their message at face value and was delighted. He sent an enthusiastic telegram to General Sherman, telling him everything was over except the approval by the War Department to send the Modocs outside of California and Oregon under army protection.[26]

The Indians did not mean a word of what they said. When Steele and Fairchild returned, Canby repeated Bogus' remarks, and Steele said he thought his impression was right. Fairchild, on the other hand, did not believe that Canby understood them. Steele reported that when he explained his terms for peace to the Modocs, the non-English speaking ones demanded a long period of discussion and clarification in the Modoc language before resuming negotiations. He stated that Jack had been sick in bed, but admitted that the Indian leader was well enough to climb on the "rostrum," a lava outcropping just outside his cave in the council ground, and make a long speech. In his harangue, Jack attacked Meacham, the Applegates, and all Oregonians in general, saying that his true friends all lived in California,[27] and finally accepted the terms Canby offered, though he said there were protests on the part of the "war party" in his camp. Steele's verdict was, "Peace is made, they accept." Fairchild, on the other hand, said "There is some mistake, the Modocs have not agreed to surrender and removal."[28]

Canby did not know which man was giving the true picture, but he wanted to believe Steele and the evidence of the Modocs who had been in the army camp. Since both Steele and Fairchild insisted that the other was wrong, the Modocs still in camp were called in to give their account of the meeting in the Stronghold. When

[26] Telegram, Canby to Sherman, March 2, 1873, S.F.P., D.C., 1873, Vol. III, 10.

[27] Yreka *Union* (March 8, 1873).

[28] *Report of the Commissioner of Indian Affairs, 1873;* Meacham Report, 2; 45 Cong., special sess., March 5, 1877, *Senate Exec. Doc. No. 1,* Gillem Report, 2 (hereafter cited as *Gillem Report*).

pressed, the Modocs no longer said Jack had agreed to surrender. They began to argue among themselves about the Indians' intentions. Obviously Steele's and Fairchild's visit to the Stronghold had gained exactly nothing, but Jack had gained another week.

During the two days the Modocs were in the army camp, they circulated freely among the soldiers and the many hangers-on. One Sam Blair of Linkville was angry at the liberty granted the Indians because he felt that most of them ought properly to be hanged. So much was being made over them that when he met several alone, he patted his empty pocket and sourly informed them that he was carrying an order from the Governor of Oregon, authorizing him to seize and hang nine Indians of Hooker Jim's band as soon as he could get his hands on them. He had no such warrant, but when the Modocs left the camp, they were alarmed, and told all the Modocs in the Stronghold that it would be unsafe to go back to Fairchild's, for any negotiations were just tricks to place the indicted Indians at the mercy of the Oregonians.

Steele was so firm in his opinion that Jack was planning to surrender, that he offered to go back to the Modoc camp alone and settle the matter beyond any doubt. Fairchild told him that if he went he would certainly go alone, because to go back without an invitation would be to place their lives in real danger. Therefore, Atwell, the reporter, offered to accompany him.

Atwell and Steele left camp Monday afternoon and went into the Lava Beds before night. When they arrived, they were permitted to enter the Stronghold once more, but the Modocs were rude. Obviously, the other Indians had told everything they had seen and heard at Fairchild's. When Steele was accused of reporting the proceedings of the previous meeting incorrectly and working against their interests, he denied it. He was accused of trying to get them to go to Fairchild's so that they could be arrested and hanged. He protested against this charge, but in vain. John Schonchin openly threatened him. To his consternation, he heard the wrathful followers of Curley Headed Doctor and Hooker Jim propose that they stop talking and proceed with the killing so that everything would be finished.

Steele and Atwell were terribly frightened. The hostile looks and threatening actions of their hosts convinced them that there would be no more reports from the Lava Beds. Atwell, an enterprising reporter, thought he would never get this interview to his paper. Nevertheless, he instinctively counted the Indians who were debating his fate, and he and Steele came up with a total of sixty-nine, many of whom were strangers to Steele.

Their lives were saved when Jack and Scarfaced Charley opposed the murder of the whites. Jack had been a friend of Steele for a long time, and although he did not know Atwell, he accepted him because he came with Steele. Jack and Scarfaced Charley took the two men into Jack's own cave, told them to make themselves comfortable, and the two Indians took turns standing at the entrance of the cave with loaded rifles to make sure that Hooker Jim's followers did not try any free-lance killing during the night. Toward morning, two other Modocs joined Jack and helped guard the whites.

Steele and Atwell did not sleep soundly that night. When morning came, their one wish was to get out of camp as quickly as possible. They were afraid that when they left the Stronghold, one of their enemies would kill them when they were beyond Jack's protection. Steele proposed, therefore, that if they let him go peacefully, he would try to come back and bring the whole commission with him. To the murder-happy followers of the shaman, this sounded like a good opportunity, and they asked particularly that their pet hates, Meacham and Applegate, be included and said that Rosborough and Case could come if they liked. Steele and his thankful companion ran from the Stronghold as fast as they could go. When they returned to Fairchild's, Steele said that no amount of money would ever induce him to go back to the Stronghold again. He advised anyone who had any further dealings with the Modocs to be well armed.

When Canby asked Steele what the result of his second visit had been, the Yreka lawyer admitted that he had been mistaken, and also that the Modocs had had a reinforcement of twenty additional fighting men. He cautioned all commissioners against ever meeting the Modocs except on equal terms and in neutral territory. Finally, he gave his opinion that peace was impossible. Badly shaken, Steele went back to Yreka.[29]

Rosborough, who had been appointed to take the place of Jesse Applegate was now ready to assume his duties. On March 2, Case also resigned, and once more the commission was down to two members. More and more Canby assumed the role of a commissioner, and he dominated the proceedings most of the time.

Canby wired headquarters in San Francisco after Steele's narrow escape in the Stronghold only that "The News from the Modocs this evening indicates a renewal of hostilities, and that they have received an accession of numbers."[30]

Meacham's report to Delano predicted that any meeting of an unarmed commission with the Modocs in the Lava Beds would result in the death of the commissioners. Bluntly he gave his opinion, "The mission is a failure."[31]

Safe at his desk three thousand miles away, Delano second-guessed Meacham with a considerable amount of wishful thinking. He promptly replied to Meacham's report, "I do not believe Modocs mean treachery. The Mission should not be a failure. Think I understand now their unwillingness to confide in you. Continue negotiations. Will consult President and War Dept., Confer with Gen. Canby tomorrow."[32]

"Tomorrow" was March 6, the day the commissioners were supposed to have gone out to meet with Jack. Following Steele's advice, however, they did not go. In Oregon, the Peace Commission was being attacked violently. In a burst of vitriolic journalism, the *Daily Oregon Herald* regretted that Meacham had seen fit to reject Jack's "kind invitation" to an interview. Since this would have led to the murder of the commissioners, the paper pointed out, "such an event would have thrown the citizens of Oregon into deep mourning, and we are glad they did not go—on Jack's account. His conduct might have been misrepresented." The paper concluded with the hope that "the arrangements will be hastened for transferring [the Modocs] to

[29] Bancroft, *Oregon*, II, 600–601; Meacham, *Wigwam and War-path*, 431–32; Portland *Oregonian* (March 6, 1873); Yreka *Union* (March 8, 1873).

[30] Canby to Headquarters, S.F.P., D.C., 1873, Vol. III, 13.

[31] Meacham to Delano, March 4, 1873, *Oregon Superintendency, 1873*, Office of Indian Affairs.

[32] Delano to Meacham, March 5, 1873, *Oregon Superintendency, 1873*, Office of Indian Affairs.

a 'warmer climate'—warmer than Arizona, and more suitable to their devilish natures."[33]

The Army Chief, General Sherman, wired Canby the same day, advising him to take over most of the direction of the Peace Commission. The difficulty of keeping the full membership, and the attacks on Meacham, plus his reports, which seem to have irritated the officials of the Interior Department, had caused the War Department to lose confidence in Meacham's ability to end the war. Sherman noted that all parties mistrusted the commission and advised Canby to find two others whom he could trust, and try to work out a surrender with the Indians outside of the commission activities. This suggestion, of course, had the effect of transferring the negotiations from the Department of the Interior to the War Department. It is doubtful whether Sherman had Delano's agreement, and certainly no one told Meacham, but to all intents and purposes, the duties of the commission were at an end. This is only another example of the fumbling Indian policy of the Grant Administration in 1873.

Jack waited as long as he thought the commissioners would be patient with him and then sent in his sister Mary with several warriors. She asked to see Canby, and when he granted her an audience, she gave him the message entrusted to her by the Indians in the Stronghold. She quoted John Schonchin as saying that he was not "mad" any longer, that he had thrown away his country, and was willing to look for a warmer one. Jack sent word that he wanted to make peace quickly, that he was also willing to go to a warmer country, and that he had quit fighting for good. He had thrown his gun away. The Klamaths had stolen his best horse. He was sorry that Steele did not trust them any longer, but he could not give up the murderers to be hanged. He asked permission only to be allowed to go to Yainax and see his relatives before he left the country. He invited Riddle and Fairchild to come to the Lava Beds and talk with him so he could prove his sincerity.[34]

When Mary had finished talking, Canby replied that this was

---

[33] *Oregon Superintendency, 1873.*

[34] Report of Mary's message, *Oregon Superintendency, 1873.* Office of Indian Affairs.

certainly good news, but that Jack himself had never come into camp at any time during the six weeks of negotiations. He went on to tell her that unless Jack or some of his principal men came in by the evening of March 8 and actually surrendered—not just parlayed, then all talks were off. To show his good will, he sent a horse back for Jack to ride, and promised to send wagons to bring in any sick or wounded Modocs.

The Modocs asked to be allowed to talk together. After a brief consultation, they gave Canby their word that the terms would be met. They asked only that when they left the country that any of the Yainax Modocs might be permitted to go with them. Canby promised them that this would be granted, and the Indians left. The more he thought about it, the more suspicious Canby became that this was only a device to gain time; he reported his suspicions to Sherman.[35] Meacham agreed with him in his report to the Commissioner of Indian Affairs.[36]

Nevertheless, in the possibility that Jack's band might come out, teams and wagons were sent to the place promised on March 8. As Canby suspected, no Indians appeared. After a time, a couple of messengers came to the camp and said the Modocs had to burn their dead and it would take two more days. Canby patiently agreed to wait until the tenth. Jack had won another victory in the battle for prestige. His broken promises and delays were making a fool of the government representative; the Indians were delighted.

During the two days the commission waited for the final surrender of the Modocs, the members finished their report on the causes of the war. The conclusions reached were hardly earthshaking. They agreed that the dissatisfaction in Jack's mind over the treaty of October, 1864, was the indirect cause of the war, and that the immediate cause was the attempt to use military coercion. The commission further agreed that the unconditional surrender of the Indians and the hanging of Hooker Jim's band would be better, from the settler's point of view, than exile to Indian Territory. They recommended that any further investigation of the causes of the war be carried out by an independent agency whose members were en-

[35] Canby to Sherman, S.F.P., D.C., 1873, Vol. III, 15.
[36] *Special File Modocs, 1873,* Office of Indian Affairs.

tirely disinterested in the outcome. With that pronouncement, the members of the Commission prepared to wind up their affairs and to go home. They assumed that by March 10 the Modoc War would be over.[37]

Alas for their hopes. Although they asked Odeneal to come down in order that supplies could be obtained for the expected band of destitute Modocs, his services were not required. On the tenth no more Modocs came than had come on the eighth. Riddle and his wife had freely predicted that either the Modocs would not appear, at all, or if they did it would only be to capture the teams and wagons. Gillem talked with the Riddles, then sent them to Canby who reprimanded them for their attitude, saying that since they were not for peace, he would send Steele out with the wagons. New hay was placed on the ground for the Modocs to sleep on, new blankets, firewood, food and presents for the headmen were made ready. Tents were pitched for their shelter.

Canby hoped that this time Jack would surrender. Once again, however, Jack did not put in an appearance, and at five o'clock in the evening Steele ordered the wagons packed and the cavalcade returned empty-handed. Steele went back to Yreka once more.

Although the commission had expected to go home, it was evident that their services would still be needed if negotiations were to be continued. The members were not in any agreement upon what the next move should be. Each member wanted to submit a minority report to the Commissioner of Indian Affairs. The only thing they could agree on was that any further negotiations with Jack would be fruitless. Meacham asked for permission to visit Salem before resuming his work.[38] Odeneal asked that he be relieved of his duties. He did suggest that since his subagent at Klamath, L. S. Dyar, was so close, that perhaps Dyar would make a good substitute.[39]

Gruff old General Sherman was as exasperated as the men at Fairchild's ranch. He wrote Canby to be patient, but if the Indians were just giving him the run-around, "I trust you will make use of

[37] Jesse Applegate to H. R. Clum, *Oregon Superintendency, 1873*, Office of Indian Affairs.

[38] Bancroft, *Oregon*, II, 604; *Gillem Report*.

[39] Odeneal telegram, March 12, 1873, *Oregon Superintendency, 1873*, Office of Indian Affairs.

the Military force that no other Indian tribe will imitate their example and that no other reservation for them will be necessary except graves among their chosen Lava Beds."[40]

To put some pressure on the Modocs and let them know the army did not take kindly to their ignoring its invitations and its ultimatums to surrender by the tenth "or else," Major Mason was ordered to make a sweep around the north and east sides of Tule Lake and return to his camp by way of the Tickner Road on the south end of the Lava Beds. He detailed Captain Biddle and a troop of the First Cavalry from Clear Lake to do the job. For three days, Biddle and his men looked for Modocs while the army prepared to move its camps closer to the Stronghold in order to worry the Indians.

Two days away from Clear Lake, on Wednesday the twelfth, Biddle encountered a group of Indian women with their children, herding a small band of horses grazing in the early spring grass between five and ten miles south of the Stronghold. He chased the women away and rounded up thirty-three horses. Since horses were the wealth of the Modocs, this loss was not only a blow to their pride but also to their pocketbook, which they could not afford to ignore. On Thursday, Biddle rode in to Van Bremer's and turned the horses over to the troops stationed there.

When the Indians heard what had happened, they stopped laughing at Canby and the commissioners. On Friday, a group of women came to Van Bremer's very much upset over the loss of their horses. They claimed, in addition, that after the soldiers had left with the horses, three of the children were missing, and they angrily accused Biddle of kidnaping them. Biddle indignantly denied this charge, but the dispute grew louder and louder. In his report, Gillem said that he thought this was preliminary to reopening hostilities, and expected the Modocs to attack the camp. After a time, the tempers of the women cooled, and they were allowed to see the horses to prove that they were being well cared for. No Modoc fire materialized from the nearby ridge. The women were promised that, as soon as the Modocs surrendered, they could have their animals back, but not before.

In the continuous struggle for prestige, the army was now ahead

[40] Sherman to Canby, March 12, 1873, S.F.P., D.C., 1873, #932.

of the Modocs. Time was going by, however, and the Indians were still in their Stronghold, while an army of fifteen times their number fumed outside in impotent rage.

There was another lull but the Modocs continued their defiance.

Canby was reluctant to order another attack on the Stronghold as long as there was even a shred of hope that peace could be gained through negotiation. He knew he would be under bitter denunciation from pacifist groups in the East if he were to break the truce, but he did not know how to cajole the Indians into giving up their fortress.

Canby then decided to try a different tactic. Old Schonchin was asked to come down from Yainax to see whether he could talk his recalcitrant kinsmen into going to Oklahoma. Schonchin did not think he could, and was extremely reluctant to go to the Stronghold, but he finally consented. When the old leader came down to the army camp, he entered the Lava Beds, but soon returned and reported that as predicted, Jack met him with an outright refusal to alter the *status quo*.

During the third week in March the army spent most of its time moving closer to the Lava Beds. If fighting came, the officers wanted to be close to hostilities. If Jack tried to break into the hill country to the south, they wanted to be near enough to pursue. The main motive, however, was to let the ever watchful Modoc scouts know that the army was on the move and the Indians could expect trouble unless they made some concessions.

Canby had another motive for moving. He wanted to remove his men as far as possible from the hordes of camp followers who were making a shambles of military discipline.

Every payday was the occasion for a gambling and drinking spree. Although these diversions are common to military encampments, the lack of combat and drill for two months intensified the men's enthusiasm for cards and liquor. For two days after payday, games of Monte, Chuck-a-luck, "Honest John," and Twenty-one were played furiously. Blankets spread on the ground made gaming tables, and high stakes were the rule. There was no limit to what a man might bet, save only that he was not permitted by the mores of the camp to wager more than his bankroll. Usually, by the time forty-eight hours had gone by, the professional gamblers had cornered most of the money. Drinking was so excessive that an official order was issued allowing only two drinks of hard liquor a day to each man and there had to be an hour interval between drinks.[41]

The civilians, however, caused the most trouble. There were at least two hundred teamsters, packers, scouts, stockmen, "sutlers" (the private-enterprise post exchange of the nineteenth century), squawmen, settlers looking things over, newspaper men, world travelers, and "laundresses." Though there are no official records of the civilians' activities around the camp, there are plenty of unofficial comments. The civilians were always underfoot. They interfered in the normal routine of camp life. They stole supplies. They listened to rumors, improved on the stories, and promptly recirculated them. Civilians frightened the Indians that came in to talk to Canby about ending the war. One group of playful civilians, as a joke, helped Bogus Charley steal a can of gunpowder from the middle of the camp almost under the noses of the soldiers.[42] Civilians told some of the Modoc women who were in camp at the early part of the month that the large piles of wood Gillem had ordered the men to cut at the Van Bremer camp—mainly to give them something to do—were for the purpose of burning Jack alive. Jack later gave this as his reason for not coming to meet Steele and the wagons on March 10. The presence of so many camp followers also gave the Indians much freedom to run and prowl through the camp, for it was almost impossible to keep track of them. There is no documentary evidence, but local legend had it that when the Modoc women came into camp they would first deliver any message they had, then would look up some soldiers and become their temporary bed partners for a fee of sixty rounds of ammunition. The "laundresses," of course, were not for men who had gambled away all their money but ammunition was practically free, and when it was gone, the soldiers could ask for more. It is no wonder that Canby wanted to break up this situation if he could.

The politicians were active while the Indians stalled for time. Senator A. A. Sargent of California talked to Secretary Delano and

---

[41] Pollock to Post Trader, February 21, 1873, *Fort Klamath Letter Book*, VIII.
[42] Portland *Oregonian* (March 12, 1873).

convinced him that another Californian should be on the Peace Commission, since Rosborough resigned. He further suggested that it might be well to placate the militant humanitarians in Philadelphia who kept Grant deluged with petitions and letters demanding that he call off the Modoc War. Sargent submitted the name of a Methodist clergyman from Petaluma, a man active in Methodist publications in California. Delano accepted the suggestion and notified the Reverend Eleaser Thomas that if he would accept, he was now a member of the commission. The fifty-nine year old minister said he would be delighted to serve and at once left for the Lava Beds.[43]

Neither Meacham nor Dyar had heard of Thomas before except in the vaguest way. Canby did not know him. Delano did not ask them their opinion, and since Canby by this time was practically running the commission, perhaps Delano did not think it would make much difference as long as another political fence could be mended. Delano was expert at mending fences.

By the middle of the week, the headquarters of the commission had been moved along with the army at Fairchild's to the Van Bremer ranch, about ten miles to the southeast. Meacham was alone, for Case and Rosborough had gone, and Thomas had not put in an appearance. Dyar was at the Klamath Agency. Meacham tried to convince Canby to go personally to the Stronghold, but Canby could not see putting himself at Jack's mercy, and he also knew that if he were to seek Jack, he would lower himself in the eyes of the Indians.

In spite of the fact that only two weeks before Meacham had indicated that he thought the mission was a failure and that he agreed with Steele that further negotiations would be futile, he now changed to complaining about Canby. "Left to my own judgment, I should have visited Captain Jack in the Lava Beds—meet him on his own terms: would now, however dangerous it might be."[44] Canby simply ignored him. He sent Donald McKay to the Warm Springs Agency to pick up the scouts that had been enlisted before the Peace Commission was established. Then he sent a Modoc

43 A. A. Sargent to Delano, March 18, 1873; Thomas to Delano, March 19, 1873, *Special File Modocs, 1873,* Office of Indian Affairs.
44 Meacham to Clum, March 17, 1873, *Oregon Superintendency, 1873,* Office of Indian Affairs.

woman into the Lava Beds to ask Jack why the Modocs had not kept their appointment ten days before.

The Indians told her that at the last moment they could not bring themselves to part with their home. When she reported their answer to Canby, he knew that this was not the real answer, but he did not know the story of the civilians telling the Modocs they would be burned alive if they did surrender. He felt that the peace party in the Modoc camp was not strong enough, and the only way he could get results was to put pressure on the Modocs by moving the army closer and closer until the Indians were convinced that they were hopelessly surrounded and outnumbered.

On Saturday, the twenty-first, Gillem and Canby made a short, personal reconnaissance of the Lava Beds from the summit of the ridge used in the January attack. They arrived a little after mid-day. When the Modocs saw the party with its escort, they became extremely agitated. The men saw so much scurrying around in the Stronghold it reminded them of an anthill that had suddenly been disturbed. As the whites stood looking over the desolate stretch of lava country and talked over the best course of action, two Indians could be seen making their way in some haste along the trail from the Stronghold to the foot of the bluff. The officers waited, for it was evident the Modocs had something to say to them. When the men were within calling distance, they stopped, and a long-range conversation took place. The agitated Indians tried to find exactly why Gillem and Canby had come that far east. The general and his colonel gave a non-committal answer, and the Indians then volunteered the information that they did not want to fight any more. They were quite satisfied to go on talking.

Dr. Cabaniss, the acting assistant surgeon, volunteered to go down the bluff in order to carry on the conversation a little more directly. When he had gone down the trail, he found that Scarfaced Charley had been doing most of the talking, and a little distance back was Jack himself with several other Modocs, concealed but watchfully waiting. Cabaniss called Jack over, and speaking through one of the Indians who knew English, told him that both Gillem and Canby were there. Jack immediately proposed that the two leaders come down unarmed and talk to the Indians. He promised that John

Schonchin would come out of the rocks, and thus the three white men could talk directly to the three Indians without anyone being afraid. Cabaniss returned, told Canby of Jack's proposal, and the three men agreed to accept.

As they descended the bluff to where Jack and Scarfaced Charley were standing, a third figure joined the Indians. They assumed that it was John Schonchin, but when they got close enough to distinguish the man, they saw Curley Headed Doctor. Both Scarfaced Charley and the shaman were wearing shot pouches covered with human hair, a subtle reminder of events in January.[45] Curley Headed Doctor was afraid, possibly, that Schonchin might sell the war party out, and he wanted to watch Jack and Charley to make sure they didn't jeopardize the murderers of Hooker Jim's band.

The talk had scarcely started when three more Indians joined the group, and all three of these were armed with revolvers. Curley Headed Doctor let it be known that he was armed as well. If the Modocs had wanted to murder the two army leaders then, they had a golden opportunity. But the visit had caught the Indians so unprepared that they had not agreed among themselves what they would do, so they did nothing but talk aimlessly about their desires.

Deciding to make the best of an awkward situation, Canby asked Jack what he had in mind by inviting them down the bluff. The Modoc leader actually had nothing new to offer. Through his English-speaking companions, Jack delivered a rambling oration in which he claimed that he was a good man, that he was tired of being chased, and that he wanted to be left alone. He asked Canby why he did not take the soldiers away. Jack wanted to have a reservation on Lost River. If anyone wanted to talk to him, he would have to come to the Lava Beds.[46]

Canby had never met any of the Modoc leaders face to face before, and it must have seemed to him a dramatic moment. Here was a chance to split Jack and Curley Headed Doctor while they were both facing him. For once he would not have to depend on intermediaries. Canby had established a reputation for getting along

[45] Sacramento *Union* (March 25, 1873).
[46] Canby report to the Adjutant General, March 24, 1873, *Oregon Superintendency, 1873,* Office of Indian Affairs.

with Indians, and he probably thought that it would be a crowning achievement if he could persuade Jack to surrender on their first face-to-face meeting.

Canby gave a short talk, telling Jack that if the Modocs came out of the Stronghold, they would be handsomely treated. He dwelt on the gifts that were waiting at headquarters for the Modocs as soon as they came in and gave up. Food and clothing would be plentiful. Jack waited until Canby had finished, then said he did not want to go anywhere, and if Canby had so much to give away, why had he not brought some of it with him.

The two groups then separated. The Modocs let the officers climb back up to their escort without trying to prevent them. Gillem had remained silent during most of the talks, but when they reached the top, he offered his opinion that Jack had no idea of leaving the Stronghold. The only thing that would make him quit was force.

Over Saturday and Sunday nothing happened in either camp to change the status of things. On Sunday afternoon, Canby tightened the screws a little harder on Jack by ordering Mason to shift his camp from Lost River around the north end of Tule Lake, and take up a position very near to Jack, a little over six miles east of the inner defenses of the Modocs. The camp was set up Monday on Scorpion Point on a small plateau that would make a successful Indian attack almost as difficult as the military assault on the Stronghold had been. The Indians did nothing to prevent Mason from moving, although they watched him with growing uneasiness.

The most important thing the pressure might do was to induce the Indians to give up before summer came.[47] Already the Indians were moving through the lava country outside of the Stronghold. On March 4, Hooker Jim and four others left the Stronghold and rode to Yainax undetected, for what purpose no one knew. If he could ride by the army scouts that easily, though, it was clear that the army was not alert enough, and in another six weeks the whole band could leave the Stronghold if they wanted to.

Delano moved to turn all control over to the army on March 22. Without telling Meacham, Delano cut the ground from under him

<hr/>

[47] Canby to Sherman, March 22, 1873, *Oregon Superintendency, 1873,* Office of Indian Affairs.

almost entirely when he gave Canby the authority to remove any of the commissioners and to appoint anyone he wished.[48] In effect Canby now *was* the commission,[49] though no one told this to Meacham. With his authority in mind, Canby sent a memorandum to Gillem informing him that the sentries should be instructed to bring anyone coming from the Modoc camp under a flag of truce directly to the headquarters tent. If any Modoc came in without a flag just to prowl around the camp, he was to be considered a prisoner of war and treated as such.[50]

The same day, Dr. Thomas put in his appearance, coming to Van Bremer's from Yreka with an army ambulance that had been driven back from the Shasta country. Dyar arrived on Monday, and once again the powerless Peace Commission had three members. They held a brief "get-acquainted meeting," but transacted no business.

It was evident from the rapid approach of better weather and from Hooker Jim's visit to Yainax that it was only a matter of time until either the Indians surrendered, were captured after a fight, or escaped to strike at settlers and run from the army. Modocs and soldiers both sensed that the two months of waiting amid futile negotiations had come to an end.

On Wednesday, Gillem decided to have another look at the route between Van Bremer's and the Lava Beds. The road that the soldiers had traveled in January was hard and snow-covered. Now in late March, the rain and melting snow had made it almost impassable even for a horse. Gillem took the Reverend Mr. Thomas with him to look over the countryside, and also to let the commissioner see what the troops might face.

When the two men and their escort arrived at the edge of the bluff, which was coming to be known as Gillem's Bluff, they flushed out two Indians who had been watching their approach from the rocks. One was Bogus Charley, who spoke fairly good English. The other was Boston Charley. Later, they were joined by Jack's two sisters, Mary and "Wild Gal." They were invited to come and talk

[48] Delano to Secretary of War Belknap, March 22, 1873, S.F.P., D.C., 1873, #572.
[49] Sherman to Canby, March 24, 1873, S.F.P., D.C., 1873, #571.
[50] Canby to Gillem, S.F.P., D.C., 1873, Vol. III, 28–29.

to Gillem. He was impressed by the apparently sincere manner in which they expressed their desire to quit fighting. The obvious difference between their talk and the one that Gillem had had with Jack was that Curley Headed Doctor was not present to check on what happened at this interview.[51] Gillem was so impressed by Bogus Charley's manner that he subsequently used him as an interpreter whenever he could. When Bogus asked for the horses Biddle had captured, however, Gillem refused him.[52]

When they returned to Van Bremer's, Gillem announced that his plans were to move his camp that Saturday to the foot of Gillem's Bluff at the very fringe of the Lava Beds. Events on the east side of the beds, however, forced the hand of the Modocs before Saturday arrived.

While Gillem was scouting for the best approaches to the Lava Beds from the west, Bernard had moved back from Clear Lake to Mason's camp at Scorpion Point. The trip of the cavalry from the Applegate ranch was made without incident, but the ever watchful Indians could see that Canby's plan to constrict them into an untenable position were almost completed.

Earlier in the month, the "war party" in the Modoc camp decided it would be better if the white men attacked first to provoke Jack to commit acts of violence in defense from which he could not retreat. Early Wednesday morning, March 26, smoke could be seen in Jack's camp, and Mason considered this to be some kind of signal. He ordered signal fires prepared for an answer. Around noon, Indians appeared about a mile and a half from Mason's camp and fired the grass and tules along the lake shore with the obvious intent of burning the soldiers out.

The grass was too wet to burn, although the heavy smoke obscured everything. The army remained watchful, but was not stampeded, and the men had orders to hold their fire. The disappointed war party fired three shots from the midst of the smoke, but no one in the army camp was hurt, and no one fired back. The troops were bewildered, since they did not know the plans of the Indians.

Back in the Indian camp, the war party told Jack they had been

[51] Canby to Sherman, March 27, 1873, S.F.P., D.C., 1873, Vol. III, 34.
[52] Yreka *Union* (March 27, 1873).

fired on and he had better attack. Jack ignored them. Instead, on Friday, he sent two of his men into Gillem's camp and asked the commission to meet with him on April 1. The next day, Jack modified his request to peremptory orders that they were to meet him in the Lava Beds, that he would talk only to the three commission members, Canby, or Gillem, and that they could not bring more than ten soldiers for an escort. Jack again gave orders to enhance his own prestige.

The reply was sent to Jack that all of his conditions would be met, except that there would be more than ten soldiers in the escort. Canby and Gillem had to do something to prove that they were not jumping while Jack called the tune.

In order to show Jack that he was trying to negotiate from weakness rather than strength, Gillem had his camp moved as he had planned. On Monday the thirty-first, the men left Van Bremer's, and spent the night on the top of the bluff. On Tuesday morning the entire force marched down the face of the hill into permanent quarters. The number of soldiers involved was considerably more than ten. Two Indians who watched the military force move into position came into camp at the invitation of the officers, and when Gillem asked them whether Jack still wanted to meet him, since this was April 1, they said he was not coming to talk in the face of a force like that. A little later they brought word that the next day Jack would talk to the commissioners; then they scurried back to the agitated Stronghold.

Canby felt that by these moves he could force Jack to make some concessions. What he did was to force Jack into acts of desperation.

On Wednesday, April 2, Jack sent word that he would meet the commissioners at a point half way between the Stronghold and Gillem's camp. General Canby, Meacham, Dyar, and Thomas went out to meet them, using Frank Riddle and Toby as their interpreters. The conference took place peacefully enough, but there was nothing remotely approaching agreement. Greetings were exchanged, and a pipe was passed around. The whites explained why they had moved the army camps and assured the Indians there was no hostile intent. The Modocs probably were hard to convince on this point.

166

When Jack talked, he said nothing different from what he had been saying. He wanted the soldiers taken out of the Lava Beds. He wanted them sent home. He wanted a reservation on Lost River. He wanted a general amnesty for the murderers of Hooker Jim's band. Canby would promise none of these things. All he was authorized to say was that if the Modocs would surrender as prisoners of war, the army would decide what would be done with them and where they should go.

They did agree on one small point. A bitter wind and rainstorm came up while the talks were taking place, and Canby asked Jack if he would be willing to have a tent erected at the meeting place so that discussions in the future could go on in spite of the weather. Jack at first jeered at Canby's request, asking the general whether he would melt like snow in the spring thaw. He boasted that Indians did not mind bad weather. As the storm increased in violence, both parties broke and ran for the shelter of their respective encampments. As he left, Jack told Canby to put up the tent.

When they returned to camp, Toby (Winema) Riddle told Meacham that she did not trust her kinsfolk. She reported that at one point in the talks, Hooker Jim had ordered her to "get out of the way." What he proposed to do, she could only guess. In some annoyance, she told Hooker to behave himself, and he made no more hostile moves.[53] She thought that Jack's reiteration of the old demands in the face of Canby's moves to tighten the encirclement of his camp was a further play for time until the Indians could decide what they were going to do. She advised the white men to look for treachery.

Meacham passed on the Indian girl's hunch to Canby, who dismissed it with a shrug. Rumors were always floating around the army camp. The night before, word came to Meacham, partly as a practical joke, that there was to be an attack on Gillem's camp, and the Indians were going to rush the tents of the commissioners, of Gillem and of Canby, and then run back to the Stronghold after assassinating all five men. Meacham took the word to Canby, who posted special sentries all around the camp. During the night, not an Indian was seen or heard. Gillem conducted a brief investigation the

[53] Meacham, *Wigwam and War-path*, 438.

next morning, and the man who brought the story to Meacham denied with a straight face having said a word. This made Meacham look foolish, and it is no wonder that Canby dismissed this second warning by Meacham as a figment of his imagination.

On April 3, the commissioners went out with the soldiers, erected the tent and waited for the Modocs to appear. None came. None came on Friday. Later Friday, Boston Charley came into camp to ask whether Meacham and Fairchild would talk with him in the tent. He and Hooker Jim thought they might be able to work something out. Both Canby and Dr. Thomas advised against it, but Meacham said he was willing to take the chance, and said that he would be out with the Riddles the next day to meet Jack. During the night, Judge Rosborough came back from Yreka to see how things were coming along, and Meacham invited him to go along.

Boston Charley and Hooker Jim did not go directly back to Jack. Instead, Canby allowed them to roam freely over the camp. The officers thought that when the Indians saw the gun emplacements, the sentry posts, and the numbers of men, they would become discouraged and advise the Modocs to surrender. The two Indians were particularly fascinated with the men sending messages from Gillem's camp from Signal Rock above the camp to Mason's camp at the east end of the lake nine miles farther east. They asked what was going on, and when they were told that this was a form of talking, they protesed to Gillem and Fairchild that it was unsportsmanlike to talk over the heads of the Modocs in the Stronghold. When they were told that Canby had sent Donald McKay for one hundred Warm Springs Indians, their complaints grew violent. Finally, in glum silence, they watched boats ferrying supplies and messages back and forth between Gillem and Mason.[54]

On Saturday the five white men were at the tent when Jack and his delegation arrived. Seven Modoc men and a number of women came out of the rocks along the trail, and the customary hand-shaking and tobacco smoking took place. This time Jack was much more conciliatory than he had been before. He started his talk by saying that he was afraid of Canby because he was in charge of powerful army forces which were visible on all sides of the Strong-

[54] *Ibid.*, 440.

hold. He was afraid of Thomas because he was a religious leader. Although Jack was tentatively following Curley Headed Doctor, there was a lingering fear that maybe Thomas' religion might be stronger than that of the shaman, and if so, Jack did not want to be in the middle of a struggle between two sets of magic. He then claimed that he knew and trusted all of the others—a different attitude from that shown in previous remarks about the Oregonians. He blamed Odeneal for the whole trouble and said that if the soldiers would leave and give him Lost River, the Modocs would settle down and make no more trouble. Jack's continuous insistence upon Lost River was only a "horse trading" move as was shown when he almost immediately afterward proposed a new solution. When Meacham told him that the murder of the settlers by Hooker Jim and Curley Headed Doctor made the granting of a Lost River reserve out of the question, Jack immediately countered by asking to be left indefinitely in the Lava Beds where he could be independent. "Nobody will ever want these rocks," he said.

Meacham sat up suddenly. Here was the first break in the negotiations in weeks. He quickly pursued the point. If the murderers would surrender to the army as prisoners of war, he promised, he would try to get the Stronghold and the cinder buttes to the south reserved for the Modocs in perpetuity.

Jack then asked who would try the murderers, Indians or white men. Meacham quite honestly answered, "White men, of course." Jack then asked in all seriousness whether the citizens who had been at the Lost River fight on November 29 could be turned over to the Modocs to be tried for the killing of the Modoc baby. Meacham said that Modoc law was dead and their courts were not binding upon white men. Then Jack really pinned him down.

"All right," said Jack, "will you try the white men." Meacham was forced to say "No," for he knew there was not a civil court in Oregon that would convict a white man for killing an Indian. Local prejudice was much too strong for that in 1873.

Meacham's admission practically ended the parley. Jack refused to give an inch until he had some assurance of equal justice. While he conceded that Hooker Jim's band had been wrong, he said that white men had started all the trouble and they had to share the blame. Jack seems to have been more honest in this conference than at any other time. Almost pathetically he laid his hand on Meacham's arm. "Tell me, my friend," he pleaded, "what am I to do—I do not want to fight." Meacham could only give him the stock answer. "Come out of the rocks, we will find you a new home when the President decides where you shall go. There can be no peace while you stay in the Stronghold." Jack then said he had been born in Modoc land, he knew no other country, his father was buried there, and he would not leave. He complained about the broken promises that marked the course of relations between Indians and whites. He talked of his time on the reservation, mentioning Klamath insults, Knapp's neglect, and the fact that Odeneal had broken his promise by sending troops instead of negotiating person to person. Jack complained about Biddle seizing the Modoc ponies two weeks earlier during a period of a truce. Finally he denounced Ben Wright and his sudden attack on the Modocs twenty years earlier. Two men in the Stronghold had escaped from that attack—John Schonchin and Tee-He Jack.

Meacham countered by reminding Jack that Bloody Point had in the old days been a hunting ground for the Modocs who took scalps of white men and women. With a bit of peculiar Indian logic, Jack shrugged off the Indian attacks as skirmishes during a war, while Wright had attacked when there was no war going on. This argument, of course, would depend on the definition of a war.

Meacham conceded that Wright did wrong, and Jack came back by pointing out that instead of reprimanding him, the United States government had put its stamp of approval on his work by making him Indian agent. He then ended the interview with an oratorical boast that while he expected to be killed, his body would not fall on the bare rocks, but on the broken corpses of his enemies whom he would slay before he died.

Meacham warned Jack to leave the Stronghold because the government was very powerful. Then the men separated. The conference had lasted for seven hours. Although it did not produce any lasting results, it did reveal an effort on Jack's part to make a real peace. This was about the last evidence of sincerity Jack made in his talks with the whites.

When the conferees reported the conversation to Canby, however, he was greatly encouraged. Jack's willingness to concede the Lost River reservation in favor of a permanent encampment in the Stronghold was recognized by Canby as the break he had been waiting for. In talking the matter over with Meacham, Fairchild, and Rosborough, Canby came to the conclusion that Jack really wanted peace and was willing to accept terms, though many of his followers were not ready to quit. Canby thought Jack could be induced to give up the Stronghold idea as well, but to this, Meacham disagreed.

In order to clarify the situation, it was decided that Winema should go out to the Stronghold by herself and give Jack a message that anyone who wanted to surrender would be protected by the army from those who wanted to remain. She went into the Stronghold on Monday, and spent the day there. Upon her return, she reported that the usual quarrel between Jack's followers and those of Curley Headed Doctor started as soon as she gave the message. Jack and eleven of his followers were willing to take Canby's offer, but the war party, consisting of Hooker Jim's murderers and the Hot Creeks under Shacknasty Jim, not only refused to go with him but said they would kill anyone who tried to quit.

When she left, Winema was met by one of Jack's followers, called William, who told her that he would advise her not to go to the tent again, and to tell her friends not to go. A great deal of talk had gone around the Modoc camp in the past several days, and he thought from the tone of it that there would soon be some bloodshed. She was badly upset at this news, and when she came back to Gillem's camp, she sat on her horse for a long time before she would dismount. When she was asked what Jack and his men thought of her offer, she refused to talk to anyone except her husband.

As soon as Frank Riddle heard of William's warning, however, he took the message to Gillem and Canby. They discussed it with the commission members. Gillem refused to believe it. Canby said it might be true, but it was his opinion that the Indians preferred talk to action. Thomas said he considered it only a sensational story, for this good-hearted man could not bring himself to believe that anyone would want to murder him. Dyar and Meacham, who had learned a few things about Modocs, said that they did believe the story. Gillem suggested that the release of a few Modoc ponies captured on April 7 by Mason's infantry might allay the Indian's suspicion. He gave orders to do this, but otherwise, nothing was done.[55]

The capture of the horses had been a shock to the Indians. They were captured when Mason moved his camp on the seventh, according to his orders, another four miles nearer to Jack's cave. His camp was set up at Hospital Rock, the point from which Bernard had launched his attack on January 17. Jack was caught in an ever tightening circle, and the loss of his horses, even if Gillem did turn some loose, was a sign that he was under severe pressure. Mason was now two miles to his east. Gillem was three and a half miles on his west, and the south was a barren and inhospitable series of lava flows which the Indians knew well but did not want to live in unless they had to, for water was extremely limited in this section.

On Tuesday, the eighth, Jack sent word through Bogus Charley, Boston Charley, and Shacknasty Jim, that he would meet the commission at the peace tent if they would come unarmed. He promised that he would bring a delegation of six unarmed men to the tent, and the talks could start once more. Canby was dubious but was willing to go on. While the white men were preparing to leave, a signalman scrambled down the hill with a message from the officer on the lookout to inform Canby that Jack was up to his usual tricks. There were six Indians in the tent area all right, but at least twenty armed Indians had concealed themselves in the rocks to the north and south of the tent. With Winema's warning in mind, Canby refused to leave Gillem's camp.

When Dr. Thomas was talking to Bogus and Boston, he learned that Modocs were hiding in the council grounds; the minister turned to Bogus Charley and plaintively asked why the Indians were planning to kill the army leaders and the commissioners. Bogus sharply demanded, "Who said we were?"

Without hesitation, or any attempt to dissemble, Dr. Thomas answered, "Toby." Bogus at once denied any intention of harming the commission members and protested that the Modocs felt only friendship toward the negotiators. As soon as he was done talking

[55] Sacramento *Union* (April 12, 1873).

to Thomas, though, Bogus found Winema and gave her a tongue-lashing. He threatened her if she should ever repeat the story to the commissioners.

The frightened Winema went to her husband. He, too, realized that they were skirting very close to a tragedy and decided that they would stay as far away from the Lava Beds as they could.

On Wednesday another messenger from the Modoc camp came in and asked especially for Winema. She felt that they were calling her into the Lava Beds to kill her. The talks had reached such a stage the officers thought a messenger should go to Jack. They urged the Indian girl to make the trip in spite of her fears. General Canby promised her that there would be an immediate attack on the Stronghold if any attempt were made to harm her, and she was authorized to tell Jack and his warriors that not only was this the case, but also that the signal officers would keep her under close watch while she was gone. Meacham gave her his horse and a coat and she left after bidding a sorrowful farewell to her husband and child, whom she might well be seeing for the last time.

Riddle went up on Signal Rock, about two hundred yards south of the cavelike rock shelter used by his family for a campsite during the negotiations, and watched his wife riding through the lava rocks. He used the field glasses of a signal officer until she had disappeared into the Stronghold itself. During the several hours while she was talking to the Modocs, tension was high. Riddle was extremely restless. He caught sight of Dr. Thomas, walked over to him, and even threatened to kill the minister if anything happened to his wife as the result of Thomas' talking to Bogus Charley. About dark, however, to everyone's great relief, Winema was seen making her way back to Gillem's camp.[56]

She reported that, as soon as she had gone into the Stronghold, she was subjected to insistent demands that she identify the person who had warned her of the plot against the commissioners. She had no intention of betraying William (also called Weuim, or the Wild Gal's Man), so at first she tried a convenient prevarication by saying that she had dreamed about the plot. Even Curley Headed Doctor could not deny this might be possible, for the cornerstone of his

[56] Riddle, *Indian History*, 78.

religious teaching was that spirits came in dreams and communicated with the living. Apparently there was not enough conviction in her voice though, for after asking some pointed questions, they finally forced her to admit that she had been informed by a flesh and blood person in the camp, but she would not tell who it was.

Their threats grew so loud that she told them that Canby had promised an attack if anything happened to her, and that she was being watched. The fact that the signalman's binoculars could not see through stone barriers was possibly unknown to the Modocs. Since they were unready for battle, they changed their tactics.[57] They told her to go back and take a message to Gillem or Canby that the Modocs would not surrender. They were afraid to come out, but if the troops were taken away, they would leave the Stronghold.[58] The military not only knew this, but feared an Indian flight would occur, and they were equally determined that Jack was not going to leave the Stronghold except as a corpse or a prisoner of war.

After Winema returned, Canby and Gillem held a conference with their officers. Gillem, who had never been in the Stronghold, scoffed at the hesitation of his officers to attack. His sarcastic comments irritated them, particularly since they did not like him anyway. He rashly told his staff that "half a dozen men could take the Stronghold." To Mason and Green, this was a slap for their caution, and Mason asserted that a third of the command would be killed the first day of an attack. In the light of subsequent events, this was, of course, as untrue as Gillem's remark. Bernard agreed with Mason, and both spoke with the authority of men who had fought toward the Stronghold in January. Green was not willing to go as far as the others in their dislike for their superior, for he knew it would not cost that many casualties, but he did agree that a fight would be tough. The younger officers had very little idea of how difficult it would be, and those who had arrived since January urged action as promptly as possible. The waiting for the commission to make peace had frayed their nerves. Lieutenant Thomas Wright brashly asserted that he and Lieutenant Eagan could together go into the Lava Beds and round up all the hostile Modocs in fifteen minutes. Canby said very little; he listened to the heated talk, and kept his own counsel.

[57] Meacham, *Wigwam and War-path*, 455.   [58] *Gillem Report*, 5.

The private soldiers, who were not consulted, were not quite as eager as their officers for combat. Their votes were registered in the number of desertions taking place. As spring came closer, the number of those A.W.O.L. increased. The last straw occurred during Easter Week, when the cook for the officers' mess deserted. The Peace Commission was drafted into K. P. duty, and for a couple of days, Meacham prepared the meals and Dyar washed the dishes. Ministers received special treatment in those days, and Dr. Thomas was asked only to invoke divine blessing upon Meacham's culinary efforts before each meal.[59]

On Thursday, Meacham made a trip to Mason's camp at Hospital Rock. This required a boat trip around the Stronghold and took all day. He was gone, therefore, when the decision was made by the other commissioners to go again to the council tent on Friday. Jack had selected a different set of men from the usual group to find what the commission would do. Boston Charley and Hooker Jim were there, and they were old-timers. By now the soldiers were even calling them by name. With these two was a comparative stranger, Rock Dave, and Weuim, who had warned Toby. While the Indians were walking along the trail leading from the Stronghold to Gillem's camp, they met Dr. Thomas, who was in the rocks to the east of Gillem's, engaged in a private prayer session. To him, Boston Charley professed a change of heart and suggested that the Modocs were now ready for peace. Dr. Thomas was overjoyed; in his simple faith he believed that his prayers had been answered and that the Indians were being converted. He took Boston to Canby and cried, "God has done a wonderful work in the Modoc camp!"[60]

Canby was somewhat more skeptical but also hopeful. He sent the Riddles back to the Indian camp with an offer to conduct future negotiations under observation of armed men from each camp. The Modocs refused to carry on any talks under such conditions. Riddle then delivered another message from Canby, saying that if they would accept a reservation in a warmer climate, there would be amnesty for all, even the murderers. Canby had written this offer on a piece of paper, hoping that this would particularly impress the

[59] Meacham, *Wigwam and War-path*, 457.
[60] *Ibid.*, 463.

Indians. When Riddle handed the note to Jack, the Modoc snarled that he could not read it anyway and threw the paper to the ground. Riddle then left and came back to Gillem's camp with predictions of tragic events in the future.

He reported that the Indians were repairing their outpost and were piling rocks at strategic points in the Stronghold. They had also killed several head of cattle and were drying the beef, obviously in preparation for a fight. Riddle ventured the opinion that they had gone as far as they were going to go, and unless the army would be willing to concede them some reservation in the traditional Modoc country, there was going to be a fight, and soon.

In the absence of Meacham, his report was delivered to the commissioners. Thomas was presiding, and he overruled Riddle's pessimistic predictions. In a mood of rare exaltation, he stated his conviction that the Indians were willing to make peace and that the commissioners ought to make every attempt to meet them and extend the hand of peace. He gave as evidence of peaceful intent the fact that five men and four women had come in to camp that very morning and had professed a desire to stop the fighting. Since this delegation proposed a new conference for the next morning, Good Friday, at which five representatives from each camp could meet unarmed in the Lava Beds east of the tent, Thomas felt that they should accept the invitation. The whites could show their faith in the Modocs by going unarmed. By a vote of those present, the decision was made to go the next morning and talk to Jack, but with the reservation that the talk had to take place at the tent.

When Meacham returned from Mason's camp in the afternoon, he was told that the commission, along with Gillem and Canby, would make a delegation to meet Jack and his representatives the next day. Thomas informed him that this was an answer to prayer, but Meacham blurted out, "God has not been in the Modoc camp this winter! If we go, we will not return alive." Thomas reprimanded his fellow Methodist for the obvious lack of faith.

At nightfall, Boston Charley told Thomas that he wanted to stay in camp all night. Canby gave his permission, and Boston climbed the hill to the Riddle's cave, where he slept until Friday morning.[61]

[61] Yreka *Union* (April 19, 1873).

Early the next morning, Bogus Charley came in to camp from the Stronghold and joined Boston to give him news of the Stronghold.

During the night, in the Modoc camp, the war party finally decided upon their course of action. They felt they had to force Jack to reopen the fighting. If the five leading whites would come to the tent, as they had been invited to, an act of violence would set off a fight which would be conclusive and victorious. They convinced themselves that the three commissioners and Canby represented the leadership of the army, and if all of these were killed, the army would be withdrawn. Actually, this was how the Indians would have operated. When their leaders fell in battle, they quit fighting. Curley Headed Doctor and his followers decided that if the five men were eliminated, there would be no further moves to force the Modocs to surrender.

In a general meeting held after dark on Thursday night, all the Modocs—men, women, and children—gathered around the fire built in the council grounds circling Jack's cave. They seated themselves inside the rock wall that marked its boundaries on the gentle slope above the rostrum rock. John Schonchin and Black Jim led the discussion that night.

After mounting the rostrum rock, Schonchin explained that there had been enough meetings between peace commissioners and Modocs. The army was growing in strength and moving ever closer to the Stronghold. Something had to be done. Black Jim then took Schonchin's place and bluntly proposed to murder the whites. Weuim then asked Jack what he thought of the idea, and Jack took the rostrum.

In a speech of considerable length, Jack said that he was in favor of quitting and going to Yainax. Scarfaced Charley agreed with him. Schonchin again took the rostrum and said the Modocs had no choice. Since white men had been killed and settlers murdered, it was certain that the Americans would never let all of them go free; someone would be hanged without a doubt. He was probably right, for the Oregonians were determined that there had to be a wholesale execution after the war to teach other Indians that ceded lands were for whites alone.

Black Jim talked again and said that the whites did not have to negotiate. They had artillery now. Indians in the camp had seen it. The army was close enough to use it effectively. The Modocs could hope to win only if they did something that would turn the tide running against them into a different direction.

Jack took the rostrum once more, and, as their leader, said that the murder of the commissioners at the tent the next day must not take place. While he was still speaking, the war party made a dramatic move. They had prepared for Jack's objection by bringing a shawl and headdress such as Modoc women wore. Those nearest Jack jumped up and seized him, forcing the surprised Indian to his back on the very rock where he had been speaking. Contrary to hazy notions about Indian "chiefs," in Modoc society the "chief" is leader only so long as he commands the loyalty of the majority. If the war party could make him lose face by dreadful insults, he would be deposed, and the rebels could pick their own leader to carry on the war. The shawl and headdress were forced on the struggling Jack, and while they held him down, his opponents taunted him with cries of "Woman! Coward! Whitefaced squaw!" They said he was no longer the roaring bull, the true Modoc. He was frightened by the white man. Deliberately they kept up the din while Jack became more and more ludicrous in his women's garments.

In only a few moments, however, Jack managed to throw off their restraining hands. He leaped to his feet, flung the shawl and bonnet from him, and with a dramatic and impassioned voice said that if they wanted a leader in murder, they could have one. It would mean that he would die, and probably all of them would die, but if that was what they wanted, then he would show them how a murder should be carried out. As leader, he claimed his right to kill General Canby.

The delighted conspirators fell in with Jack's mood. Each clamored for a chance to kill a white man, but Jack pressed his advantage and named his own assistants. In case he failed to kill Canby, the fanatical Ellen's Man of the Hot Creeks was to take over and finish the job. If he hit the General, Ellen's Man could have the honor of administering the *coup de grâce*. Black Jim asked and received the right to kill Gillem. For his assistant, he was given a young boy of feeble intelligence, but one who would take orders. Before this

178

event nothing is known of this Indian except his name—Slolux. As head of the commission, Meacham deserved to be killed by an important Indian, so Schonchin John was detailed to shoot him. Hooker Jim was to help. Dyar was the target of Shacknasty Jim and another inconspicuous Indian of the war party named Barncho.

Someone raised the question of killing Frank Riddle, but it was decided that he was not to be touched. Meacham says that Scarfaced Charley promised to be in the rocks, and while he would not prevent the killing of the others, he announced that if either Riddle or Winema were hurt, the killer would have to answer to him personally.[62]

After an additional discussion, it was decided to make a complete massacre of the whites. While the commissioners in the west side were being killed, Miller's Charley, Curley Headed Jack, and another Indian who was never positively identified by the whites, were to try to persuade Major Mason to come out from Hospital Rock so that he could be killed too.

When the final plans had been completed the council broke up. Curley Headed Doctor summoned the faithful to a ghost dance. All night the dragging rhythmic stamping of the dancers could be heard by the sentries in Gillem's camp. As there had been other dances in the Stronghold before, no one in the army camp paid attention to this one.

Sometime in the early morning, two Indians stole quietly out of the Stronghold, almost bent double under their awkward load of rifles. These were Barncho and Slolux, who were to come out of the rocks after the peace talks had commenced to arm the assassins. They reached the tent and concealed themselves behind one of the many small knobs of lava about one hundred yards from the council tent. There they spent the rest of the night and most of the next morning in patient concealment, resting as much as possible before taking up the important business of the day.

[62] Meacham, *Wigwam and War-path*, 464–66; Riddle, *Indian History*, 72–74.

VII

TREACHERY

GOOD FRIDAY MORNING was the day the Modocs had set for the murder of Canby and the commissioners.

When the intended victims got out of bed they saw the day promised well to be a beautiful one. The sky was an intense blue as the April sky in the Lava Beds country can be. The air was clear, and the men on Signal Rock could easily see movement in Mason's camp where the soldiers were preparing their breakfast on the other side of the Stronghold. The snow had left the hillsides, and the wild flowers were beginning to bloom. It was the kind of a day that made a man feel good to be alive.

The peace commissioners prepared their own breakfast, as they had been doing for several days. Dr. Thomas invited Boston Charley to eat with them, and Boston accepted. He ate from Thomas' plate and drank steaming coffee from Thomas' cup. After breakfast, Bogus joined the others, and the two Modocs urged the commissioners to get to the tent as early as possible.

To show his own belief in the good intentions of the Modocs, Thomas gave both Boston and Bogus Charley a new outfit of clothes to wear to the conference. Boston circulated around the camp for a while as the commissioners were preparing themselves to go to the tent, and the soldiers talked to him about the trouble between the Indians and the government. He predicted that there would be no more fighting, but said that the conference would work something out; at the time, however, he knew that the council in the Stronghold had decided on the murder of Canby and the others. The soldiers put him down as friendly, almost harmless, and certainly an unimpressive looking Indian. He was only about five feet tall, and his clothes and cap were "a little worse for the wear."[1] Perhaps that was why Thomas gave him a new pair of pants and a new shirt.

After a time, Canby sent Boston and Bogus back to Jack to tell him that the commissioners would come to the tent, but no farther. If the Indians wanted to talk, the whites were ready. In a short time, the two Modocs came back, and said that Jack had agreed to meet Canby and was already at the tent with five unarmed men.

When Boston came to Meacham's tent, he was distressed to see that Meacham was changing his boots. At breakfast the commissioner had put on a pair of new boots, but they were not comfortable, and now he was changing them for his old pair. Boston Charley urged Meacham so persistently to wear his new boots that at the time it struck the white man as peculiar enough for him to remember the incident. He did not know why Boston Charley was concerned with his dressing arrangements, although probably he had a pretty good idea; later he remembered Boston's talk. In any event, Meacham paid no attention to the urging of the Indian and wore his old shoes.

Frank Riddle was waiting for Meacham to emerge from his tent. Riddle had not slept too well and in moments of wakefulness thought about the council for that morning in the light of the warning his wife had brought. He came to Meacham as soon as he got up to see whether the proposed meeting could be postponed, canceled, or at least held with an armed guard close by. Meacham agreed with him that a conference would be dangerous because, at the critical stage which the discussions had reached, the Indians were under severe pressure. The gradually closing army on both sides of them would very easily provoke them to a rash and violent action.

Next, Meacham and Riddle went to talk to Thomas and Dyar. They found that Thomas had already gone to Gillem's tent for a final consultation to decide what the commissioners would say to the Indians when they reached the council tent. Riddle and Meach-

[1] Maurice Fitzgerald, "The Modoc War Reminiscences," *Americana*, Vol. XXI, No. 4 (October, 1927), 498–521.

am asked the colonel's permission to enter, and were invited in. To their surprise, they found that Gillem had not yet dressed. He was very ill, and they heard him tell Thomas that he was sorry, but he wouldn't be able to go out with the others to the council tent. Gillem listened silently to Riddle's warnings of disaster.

Meacham suggested that since Gillem was sick, possibly none of them should go, or if they did, that they should go armed. He asked that at the very least, John Fairchild be armed and sent into the rocks at a discreet distance from the tent to cover them. While Meacham was making this suggestion to Colonel Gillem, Canby entered the tent. Delayed briefly by a talk with Major Green, Canby missed Riddle's pessimistic predictions, but he did come in early enough to gather the substance of the conversation.

Canby was no coward and he had great faith in the ability of the army to beat Indians. He treated Riddle's fears with contempt and said that field glasses would be ample protection. Men stationed on Signal Rock would watch any movement made by both parties. Were the Indians to commit any hostile acts, it would take only a few minutes, he thought, for Gillem's forces to come over and catch any trouble makers, or for Mason to advance on the Stronghold from the east. If Indians were seen sneaking through the rocks, they could easily be detected and intercepted.

Meacham suggested on the basis of warnings by both Riddle and Winema that if any treachery became evident, the Americans should agree to anything the Modocs asked for and get back to camp as quickly as possible. Canby refused even to listen to any arguments in favor of such double dealing. The General said, "I have dealt with Indians for thirty years, and I have never deceived an Indian, and I will not consent to it—to any promise that cannot be fulfilled."[2]

Thomas gave his private opinion that Riddle and Toby were unreliable and very likely to exaggerate for the effect they could create. It is true that Riddle was almost entirely illiterate and not very prepossessing in appearance. His wife was known to be a Modoc, and some whites considered her in league with her kinsman, Jack. Meacham and Dyar dissented from Thomas' opinion and said they thought they should go armed, even if they carried

[2] 43 Cong., 1 sess., *House Exec. Doc. No. 122*, Trial of the Modoc Prisoners, 161ff.

only concealed weapons. To this Thomas objected at once. He said that they must keep faith with the Indians, in thought as well as in deed. Canby agreed with him so strongly that Meacham and Dyar subsided. "The importance of the object in view justifies our taking some risk," the General said.[3]

Riddle listened to the exchange of ideas, shrugged, and said that if they wanted to go to their deaths, he couldn't stop them. He was free from responsibility, for he had warned them what would probably happen. He did defend his wife, saying that he had lived with her for twelve years and she had never yet deceived him. The commissioners then separated to make last moment preparations before going to the peace tent.

Thomas went to the sutler's store and paid his bill. He admitted that there had been predictions that he would be killed if he went to the council, and if he did not return, he wanted to be sure that he left no accounts unpaid. Canby stood waiting for a moment, speaking to his orderly, Scott, and to Monahan, his secretary. He then joined Thomas, and the two of them began walking away from the camp on the foot trail. They walked slowly along through the Lava Beds, talking together, and disappeared a short time after eleven o'clock. Thomas was heard to say, "I am in the hands of God. If he requires my life, I am ready for the sacrifice."[4]

Boston Charley mounted a horse, tucked his rifle under his arm, and followed them. He rode along with Canby and Thomas until they reached the tent.

Meacham and Dyar hurried to join Canby and Thomas. Sitting on the blankets of his tent, Meacham pencilled a short note to his wife:

You may be a widow tonight; you shall not be a coward's wife. I go to save my honor. John A. Fairchild will forward my valise and valuables. The chances are all against us. I have done my best to prevent this meeting. I am in no wise to blame. Yours to the end.
Alfred
P.S. I gave Fairchild six hundred and fifty dollars, currency for you.
A.B.M.

[3] *Report of Commissioner of Indian Affairs, 1873*, Meacham report.
[4] Meacham, *Wigwam and War-path*, 469ff.

He then asked Fairchild to deliver the note, his personal effects, and the money to his wife in Salem, if he didn't return alive. Dyar also gave Fairchild some money for his wife, who was at the Klamath Agency. Fairchild was whittling on a stick when they approached him, and he nodded agreement to their request without saying much.

As they walked toward their horses, Meacham asked Dyar why he was going if he felt that they would be killed. Dyar answered, "If you go, I am going. I will not stay if all the rest go."[5]

As they were climbing into their saddles, Oliver Applegate, who had returned from Yainax, slipped a derringer into Dyar's pocket. Neither said a word, but both looked at each other. Meacham saw the interplay and surreptitiously placed a derringer in his own coat pocket. The two men then mounted. Toby also was on horseback, weeping loudly and bitterly. After one last protest to Meacham, she bade her small son goodbye and rode out of camp with the others. Frank Riddle walked beside his wife's horse. The little cavalcade followed the lake shore to the council grounds.

Bogus Charley waited in camp for a few minutes after the commissioners left, checking to make sure that no soldiers were following. The Modoc was met by Fairchild, still whittling, who asked him what was going to happen. Bogus assured him that nothing was wrong. He was again asked by Fairchild whether he was sure. Bogus denied emphatically that any mischief was in his mind. He then left and ran as quickly as possible through the rocks so that he could get to Jack before the whites arrived.

Many soldiers scrambled up Gillem's Bluff that morning to watch the activities. They had no glasses, but in the clear morning air the tent was plainly visible and tiny figures could be made out with little difficulty. Most of the men anticipated no trouble. They had some time on their hands and sat or laid idly on the hillside with a blade of grass in their teeth and speculated whether the commissioners might expect any results from this conference.

While Jack and the other Modocs waited for the commissioners, Jack began to waver in his resolution of the night before. Ellen's Man proposed that he fire the first shot at Canby, but Jack reversed

[5] *Ibid.*, 471ff.

his position, and hastily reasserted his right to kill the General. Bogus, who had reached the killers, snorted at the conversation and said he would kill them all if the others were afraid. "Kill these men," he cried, "and the war will stop. It will scare the soldiers away."[6]

Then silence came across the Indians, for the commissioners were in sight.

Thomas was neatly dressed in a light gray tweed suit. Canby had on his army uniform. Meacham, Dyar, and Riddle were dressed in nondescript old clothes that the Modocs didn't particularly want. As the white men walked and rode up to the Indians, the Modocs stood up to greet them.

The commissioners knew that the Modocs had agreed that there would be five unarmed Indians there to meet their delegation. When the Americans arrived, they saw that there were actually six, and with Boston and Bogus, there were eight. Bogus Charley and Boston quite openly carried rifles, which they had had with them in the army camp that morning. The others, presumably, were unarmed.

The white men knew Jack, for they had seen his squat form many times in previous conferences. Gray-haired John Schonchin was standing beside him. Hooker Jim, tall, muscular, heavy, stood beside Schonchin. Ellen's Man stood to Hooker's right, short, and fat and soft looking, but a tough one in a fight. To the right and just behind Ellen's Man, on the lake side of the group were Boston Charley and Bogus. Both were still holding guns. To their right, on the end of the Modoc group, were Shacknasty Jim, hair parted in the middle, and Black Jim with a "Dutch Boy" haircut—bangs in front, and the hair hanging just below his ears at the back. They were standing carelessly around a small sagebrush fire to the north of the council tent. Jack had also built a sagebrush fire on the east side of the tent around which they all gathered as soon as the whites came. This had the effect of putting the tent between the conferees and the signal officers in Gillem's camp, who also found their work made more difficult by the sagebrush smoke that wavered back and forth across the scene, sometimes obscuring the grounds altogether.

General Canby opened the conference by taking from under his arm a box of cigars which he had brought out in lieu of a peace pipe.

[6] *Ibid.*, 478ff.

He handed one to each Indian and each white man. All lit their cigars except Dr. Thomas. During this brief ceremony, they shook hands all around, a ceremony which the Indians considered an absolute essential before any talk could commence.

Canby seated himself on a stone in front of the tent and turned himself so that he was directly facing Captain Jack. Meacham had remained sitting on his horse for a while, but after an interval he slowly dismounted, although he did not tie his horse. He saw that the five Modocs had grown to eight, and two of them were obviously armed, although none was supposed to be armed when he was near the tent. Canby ignored the rifles of Boston and Bogus, so Meacham sat down beside the General, facing John Schonchin. Winema then got off her horse, tied it to a sagebrush, and seated herself on the ground slightly to the left and in front of Meacham. Thomas stood for a while at the side of Winema, then moved back of Meacham and seated himself on the ground. Dyar did not sit down, but stood beside his horse, which he left slightly south of the council tent. He was ready to run at the first sign of trouble. Riddle left Winema's horse behind that of Thomas, but walked up and stood behind his wife and Meacham.

Just as the talks were about to begin, a man was seen walking toward the council ground along the trail through the rocks. The Indians became very much agitated. They did not know whether he would be added to the group, whether he was armed, or whether their plot might have been discovered. Canby noticed their excitement, and in some annoyance, asked Dyar, who was still standing, if he would mind riding back to tell the visitor that this was not a public gathering. Dyar returned, saying that it had been a civilian named Clark, who said he was out looking for a horse that had strayed away from camp. He had hastily retired when he was told to stop trying to visit a meeting between Jack and Canby.

By this time it was between 11:30 and noon, and the council was formally opened with the usual oratory. Meacham began to talk. He referred to the fact that the Modocs were the ones who had asked for the resumption of conversations and said the whites wanted to know what they had in mind. Jack replied with his standard request to have the soldiers leave the Lava Beds. The women and children were afraid of them, he said. Meacham replied that Canby couldn't send the soldiers away, but they could be used to protect the Modoc women and children at Willow Creek or at Fairchild's ranch near Cottonwood camp until a home could be provided for the Indians. The men could remain in the Stronghold until a new reservation, satisfactory to all concerned could be found. To show his sincerity, he placed his hand on John Schonchin's shoulder while he talked, but the Indian indignantly moved away from his touch.

Before Jack could make a formal reply to this proposition, Hooker Jim walked over to Meacham's sorrel horse (actually borrowed from Fairchild) and began to tie him to a sagebrush. Very ostentatiously, he removed Meacham's coat from the saddle and tried it on, as though he were selecting a new overcoat at a store. The talking stopped, and the delegates turned to watch him. He ignored them but looked at Bogus Charley and asked, "Bogus, you think me look like old man Meacham?" At that Hooker Jim strutted around for a moment or two, saying, "Me old man Meacham now."

No one minded if the Modoc wanted to play-act like a small child trying on his parent's clothes, but there was a chilly feeling in Meacham's viscera and a premonition that Hooker Jim was actually planning to acquire both his coat and his suit of clothes after his premature and imminent demise. Meacham decided to make a joke of it and handed Hooker Jim his hat, saying, "Take my hat, too." Hooker was about as humorous as a rattlesnake, and considerably more dangerous. He looked at Meacham with a glitter in his eye and said, "I will by and by. Don't hurry, old man."

Dyar was so jittery that he thought the moment for trouble had come. He walked behind his horse, ostensibly to tighten an imaginary stirrup, but actually to have something between himself and the Indians if shooting started. Riddle also moved behind Winema's horse, and she changed her position from sitting in front of Meacham to lying prone on the ground. She yawned with elaborate casualness, as though she were just too sleepy to stay sitting up any longer.

Canby didn't look at Meacham, though the commissioner tried to catch the General's eye to warn him that the Indians were up to no good. Canby knew that. He had dealt with Indians before and thought the best way out was to go on with the conference and get their minds off any evil schemes they had.

He therefore made a friendly speech in which he said that the President had the sole authority to send the soldiers away. He had personally always been a friend to the Indians, and they trusted him wherever he had gone. There was every reason for the Modocs to trust him, too, and he wanted them to do it.

It was then Thomas' turn to talk. He had been sitting, and he did not stand up but moved slightly forward so that he was on his knees in the position of prayer. He delivered what could be described as a short sermon, advising the Indians to change their religious beliefs and to trust the white men, asserting, too, that Canby was an honorable and good-intentioned man.

When he finished, Jack spoke again, reiterating what he had said. If the soldiers were removed, the Indians would talk about leaving the Stronghold, but not before. He was seconded by John Schonchin, who said he believed it in the power of the commission to give them the Willow Creek valley, between Van Bremer's and Fairchild's ranches, and to do it immediately. He admitted that neither Dorris nor Fairchild had told him this, and since their farms were near the creek, they would have to abandon their ranches if a reservation were set aside for the Modocs there. Unless Canby would promise then and there to take the soldiers away and give the Modocs the Willow Creek basin, Schonchin announced that he would talk no more.

Riddle and Toby had not yet finished translating Schonchin's remarks when Jack jumped suddenly to his feet and announced in a loud voice that he had to leave for a moment to answer a call of nature.[7] No one was embarrassed, for all were accustomed to the forthright ways and speech of the Indians. This seems to have been a signal to the patiently waiting Slolux and Barncho. As Jack returned to the group he uttered a peculiar call, and immediately the two boys came out of the rocks, armed to the teeth. In highest alarm, Meacham cried, "Jack, what does this mean?" He was never answered.

[7] Mason Report to Headquarters, June 13, 1873, S.F.P., D.C., 1873, #1251.

Jack said something in Modoc about which there has been a dispute. Whether he said "Attack!," "A-ta!,"[8] "Ut wih kutt!,"[9] or "Ot-we-kau-tux!,"[10] as various writers have claimed, will be difficult to prove now. They all agreed that what he meant was, "All ready!"

It was exactly twelve minutes after noon.[11] Jack pulled a revolver from under his coat and pointed it at General Canby, who sat as though he were transfixed, looking at it. Jack pulled the trigger, and the gun failed to fire. Why Canby didn't leap to his feet and attack the Indian or run, no one will ever know. He did neither. He continued to sit there for the split second it took Jack to recock the pistol, and this time the gun discharged. Canby went down, shot just below the left eye. If he had not been touched again, he would have died as the result of this wound.

To the amazement of everyone, the soldier managed to struggle to his feet and started a lurching run toward the army camp. He had actually covered almost forty yards when he tripped and blindly fell to the ground. Ellen's Man had picked up one of the rifles from Barncho and came up behind Canby. He shot him again as he lay on the ground. Jack drew a knife and stabbed Canby once in the throat. The two Modocs then pulled the army uniform from Canby's body. Ellen's Man took his watch. Only when this was finished did they turn to look at what the others were doing about their assignments.

When Jack gave his signal, Boston Charley leaped toward Dr. Thomas with the rifle that he had brought with him. He shot Thomas in the chest as the minister leaped to his feet. Thomas was able to run only a step or two before he collapsed to his knees. He leaned upon his right hand, looked up at Boston, and gasped, "Don't shoot again, Boston, I shall die anyway."

With scorn, Boston replied, "Why don't you turn the bullets? Your medicine is not strong."

Thomas tried to get up, and as he struggled to his feet and began to run, Boston allowed him to go only a few steps, then tripped him. The Indian sneered, "God damn ye, maybe so you believe what

8 Mason Report, #1251.
9 Riddle, *Indian History*, 90.
10 Meacham, *Wigwam and War-path*, 492.
11 Mason Report, #1251.

squaw tell ye, next time." There never was to be a next time. Some-one then placed a rifle to Thomas' head and shot him dead. Meacham later identified the second Indian as Bogus Charley, but at the trial Bogus satisfactorily established that he had hurried to the Strong-hold the moment trouble began.

The body of Thomas was stripped of its grey tweed suit. Steam-boat Frank, who was not in on the killing, left Scarfaced Charley, who was watching, and came out of the rocks long enough to take Thomas' coat.

As Canby and Thomas were being killed, Meacham leaped to his feet and started to run backward, frantically reaching for his derringer. As he did so, John Schonchin, pulled both a pistol and knife from his clothing and advanced toward the white man. In his panic, Meacham failed to cock the gun, and when he pulled the trig-ger, nothing happened. The sight of the gun stopped Schonchin, and undoubtedly saved Meacham's life. Schonchin paused for a moment, and Meacham had time to see why the gun had failed to fire. He retreated over the rough ground a short way past the bodies of Canby and Thomas. When Schonchin fired, he missed, but the bul-let passed through Meacham's whiskers. The Modoc began to fire wildly and was joined by Shacknasty Jim, Barncho, and Slolux, who all began to fire rifles. The closest shot took away part of one of Meacham's ears.

Running backward, Meacham couldn't see where he was going, and he tripped over a large rock and went down. With a shout of triumph, the Indians closed in for the kill. Meacham raised the der-ringer for his single shot, but before he could fire, a ricocheting bullet hit the rock by his face and glanced across his forehead, knocking him senseless.

At once Shacknasty Jim leaped upon him and began to remove his clothes. Slolux placed a rifle at Meacham's head and was about to make sure that he was dead, when Shacknasty Jim impatiently pushed him away. He probably didn't want to get the clothes dirty, for he said, "You needn't shoot. He is dead." and went on strip-ping Meacham.

Boston Charley came over from Thomas' body while Shack-nasty Jim was yanking at the clothing and said he was going to take

Meacham's scalp for his shot pouch. He made a slice in Meacham's forehead, cut around the one ear, and began to tug at the skin.

When the firing started, Dyar turned and ran, with Hooker Jim following him in hot pursuit. After only covering a few yards, Dyar succeeded in drawing his derringer from his coat pocket, and he turned and pointed the pistol at Hooker Jim. The Indian stopped abruptly, turned, and ran from Dyar instead. The agent was not interested in conducting a one-man counter attack, and continued to run for the army camp as fast as his frightened legs would carry him. Black Jim also started in pursuit of Dyar, but turned and helped the others remove Meacham's clothing. Hooker watched Boston trying to take Meacham's scalp and offered the comment that if Meacham's bald head would produce a scalp, Boston was welcome to it.

The whole pack was frightened away from the body of the unconscious commissioner when Winema suddenly cried, "The soldiers are coming!" Most assuredly they were not, but it frightened the Indians, and they left Meacham alone.

Winema herself had not been hurt. When the shooting started, Slolux struck her and knocked her down. Possibly this was to protect her, but probably the blow was delivered in the excitement of the moment. She was in no danger, for Black Jim and Jack both ordered Slolux to let her alone.[12]

Her husband also was in very little danger. Barncho, Shacknasty Jim, and Ellen's Man all started for Riddle, but seemingly only to chase him away, for he ran, and they didn't follow. They probably remembered Scarfaced Charley's warning. Riddle took no chances. He was just one jump behind Dyar in running toward Gillem's camp and safety.

Jack apparently felt that Winema had seen soldiers. He ordered his followers to run, and they quickly moved back to the Stronghold to prepare for the fight that they now knew was inevitable. Laden with the clothing and possessions of their victims, they must have made a ludicrous sight as they came into the Indian camp, but with the knowledge that there was real trouble ahead, few of the Indians were laughing. Only the war party could feel good about

[12] 43 Cong., 1 sess., *House Exec. Doc. No. 122*, Trial of Modoc Prisoners, 145.

the affair. They had won complete control of the camp, and although Jack was still the leader, he did as they said.

Meanwhile, on the east side of the Stronghold, the men at Mason's camp knew nothing of these events. Miller's Charley, and Curley Headed Jack, with another Indian said to have been Comstock Dave, gingerly approached the Hospital Rock base under a flag of truce. While many Indians had come and gone in Gillem's camp, almost none of this moving back and forth had taken place at Mason's, and the sentry was suspicious and truculent. He called for the Officer of the Day, who was Lieutenant William L. Sherwood of the Twenty-first Infantry. Since Sherwood did not understand the Chinook jargon, the speech most commonly used during such negotiations, Lieutenant W. H. Boyle, who was familiar with Chinook, asked to go with him to find what they wanted. Sherwood and Boyle's orders were that if any Indians wanted to talk to Mason they could meet him beside the sentry post.[13]

Curley Headed Jack was the spokesman. He asked whether Boyle was the "tyee," which is to say the leader of the military force on Hospital Rock. Boyle said that he was not but that he had been sent to find what the Modocs wanted. The Indians invited the two officers to come closer so that they could hear better. Since the two white men were not armed, they refused to go any farther out into the Lava Beds. They were already outside of the area which was under the protection of the rifles of the pickets. They told the Indians that they were going back to the sentry. The Indians began to talk very fast, and the officers were more and more puzzled as to what was going on. Obviously, the Modocs were not saying anything of importance, and after listening to them for a time, the two men broke off the conversation.[14]

Just as they turned away from the Indians, one of the Modocs seized his gun, which he had laid in the grass and opened fire. By reflex action, the two men began to run, dodging and weaving through the boulder-strewn field. Boyle yelled to Sherwood to separate from him so that they would have a better chance of distracting

[13] Boyle, "Personal Observations."
[14] Mason Report to Headquarters, June 10, 1873, S.F.P., D.C., 1873, #2773.

the Modoc fire. Sherwood quickly dashed up the hill, as Boyle ran toward the lake shore. Not thirty steps from the point of first fire, Sherwood was hit, and in a moment more he was down.

Boyle continued running, and the Indians concentrated their fire on him. He saw the sentries running toward him, firing as rapidly as they could aim and reload, and he fled toward them for protection. When the Indians saw the sentries coming, they broke off their fire and went back to the Stronghold. The frightened Boyle went into camp to report to Mason, while the sentries went out to find Sherwood. They found him alive but mortally wounded. He died the Monday after he was shot.

It was the firing on Sherwood and Boyle that alerted the signal station at Gillem's camp. The men who were still there had come back after a midday meal, and were taking it easy on the hillside when sounds of shooting were heard beyond the Stronghold. A moment of agitated signaling brought the news that the Modocs were attacking under a flag of truce and that Sherwood had been shot.

The signal officer, Captain Adams, scribbled a note, and a man ran down the hill to Colonel Gillem's tent to give him the message that the commissioners with Canby were in serious danger if the Modocs were reopening the war. Gillem read Adams' message, then sent for Dr. Cabaniss and asked him to take a note to Canby as fast as he could, saying that Mason's camp had been attacked, and that he should break off the conference. He delayed long enough to write the note because the Modocs knew enough English so that a shouted warning would precipitate a disaster.

While he was still writing, the killing at the peace tent began. The men in camp, who had heard the news of Sherwood and Boyle and were milling around in confusion, distinctly heard the firing not two miles west of them. Major Biddle, who had climbed the hill to see what was happening at Hospital Rock and was holding a pair of field glasses, swung them to the tent and shouted, "They are firing on the commissioners!" Adams himself ran down the hill this time and gave the message to Gillem.

The news raced through the camp like a grass fire, and all was turmoil and noise. The disorder ended almost immediately with the continued bawling of the sergeants, "Fall in!"[15]

A bugler blew an assembly. Men rushed to seize their arms and ran to their company assembly points. Miller's company and Eagan's company were ready first; and Major Throckmorton, behind Eagan, had his men in ranks in only a few minutes. The cavalry that was on the west side, seized its carbines and prepared to advance with the infantry and artillery companies. Momentarily they expected orders from Gillem. So far the orders of the junior officers had been largely automatic and spontaneous.

Gillem was ill, and the excitement seemed to make him powerless. He hesitated so long, that an inexcusable delay resulted while the officers waited helplessly for orders and the men grumbled in the ranks. The delay ended only when Major Biddle ran down the hill to see why the men weren't moving; he found Gillem paralyzed by indecision. What he said to the Colonel, Biddle never reported, but he came out and stated that Gillem had ordered Major Thomas to stay in camp and guard the artillery, while the rest were to march out to rescue the commissioners, if possible, or to capture their killers.

The men advanced quickly enough. Some say they marched at double time. It was certainly much faster than their advance had been on January 17. The improved visibility, the now familiar terrain, and the strain and excitement of the previous half hour all contributed to their speed.

No Modocs disputed their advance. Before they had gone far, the soldiers passed Riddle and Dyar, who ran by them, shouting that the Indians had killed the others. No one stopped the two survivors, and everyone believed that all the rest were dead. Even though Dyar reached camp exhausted and in a state of shock, he managed to get off a telegram to Washington telling of the murders.

In about half an hour, the soldiers reached the site of the killings. They found Winema sitting beside Meacham, who must have presented a frightful sight, since he was bloody, unconscious, and clad only in red flannel underdrawers. The bodies of Canby and Thomas were lying where the Indians had left them when Winema called

[15] Trimble, "Reminiscences," from Brady's *Northwestern Fights and Fighters,* 287ff.

that the soldiers were on the way. The naked bodies gleamed white in the rocks, except where they showed blood stains from the wounds they received.

Assuming that all three men were dead and seeing that Winema was all right, the soldiers advanced a few hundred yards farther toward the Stronghold. The Modocs did not attack, but the soldiers began to make preparations for defense against an expected assault. The officers knew that many soldiers would be hurt if they advanced much farther, for they were already past the point where the Modocs had begun to resist in January. The entire strategy since that defeat, was based on a prospective artillery offensive against the Indians, and it would have been foolish to have mounted a major attack without artillery preparation since the guns were ready. The men were ordered to halt and they retreated to the tent.

The surgeon gave each body a swift examination. He found Canby and Thomas quite dead, but Meacham was still breathing. More than that, he was beginning to regain consciousness. Dr. Cabaniss used the standard army remedy for shock and gave Meacham a stiff shot of brandy before calling for the stretcher. Meacham took one gulp, and although he was almost dead, he mumbled a weak protest.

"I can't drink brandy. I am a temperance man!"

He had "taken the pledge" years before, and even at this crucial moment he rallied enough to express his scruples.

"Stop your nonsense!" snapped Cabaniss. "Down with it! Down with it!"

Meacham drank. Probably he had to take the pledge over again after he felt better, but he was helped enough so that he survived a stretcher trip back to the hospital at Gillem's. Most of those who saw the shambles of his half-scalped head assumed that he had been shot through the brain, but examination showed that although his injuries were extensive, Boston Charley's knife had made only superficial wounds. The scars left on Meacham's scalp actually became his meal ticket in later years. He went on the lyceum circuit, and at the climax of his lecture on the Modoc War, Meacham would show where he had almost been scalped; he would then exhibit Shacknasty Jim, who had been near by, and Winema, who had saved his life.

This was a sentimental age. When young Scott, Canby's orderly, saw the broken and naked body of his commander, he flung himself sobbing upon the corpse and set up a tremendous howl of rage and grief. This does not seem to have been considered unmanly behavior in 1873, as only passing mention was made of it.[16]

By three in the afternoon, clouds had formed in the West, and a light snow began to fall. No one was now on the hill by Signal Rock. The overcast added to the drama of the scene. Atwell, the reporter, lifted Scott from Canby's body and covered the corpse with his own coat. The tent was then cut into strips as shrouds for Canby and Thomas, and the procession started back to camp, while Atwell mentally composed a story for his newspaper.

When they reached Gillem's, Atwell began to write. The other reporters, however, had to wait until they could talk to someone who had been out to the tent before they could write their stories. The press representatives realized that this would be the biggest story of the war. Never before had a band of Indians killed a regularly commissioned general of the army. The story could not be too long, or some competitor would get to the Yreka telegraph and scoop the nation. "Bill Dad" Atwell hired Tickner, who knew the road to Yreka better than anyone else, to ride there with his story. Others tried to outrace Tickner, but he beat them, and the account of the murders first went out through Atwell's newspaper in Sacramento.

During the night, coffins were nailed together, and plans were made for taking the bodies to Yreka for embalming and to Portland and San Francisco for burial. Military plans were already made and had only to be put in motion. On the next day, or on the day following that, punishment for the Modocs would be meted out, it was confidently believed. Gillem passed the word to his subordinates that since Donald McKay was coming down with Warm Springs scouts the next day, they should wait for them before the attack began. The one thing no one suggested was a further parley with Jack and his Modocs.

Saturday morning hostilities began when a group of Indians shot at a sentry on duty. That jittery young man promptly ran back to

[16] Meacham, *Wigwam and War-path*, 501–505; *Gillem Report*, 5.

his camp. From the eastern side, Mason sent out a scouting party into the Lava Beds south of Hospital Rock. When the party had gone between four and five miles to a point somewhere between Juniper Butte and the Three Sisters Buttes, a few Modocs, who had been trailing the soldiers, fired at them from long range. Those who were leading the march stopped and ran back to the main force in a panic. Lieutenant E. R. Theller, of Company I, Twenty-first Infantry, who was in charge of the scouting party, ordered the men to charge, and the Indians moved aside and into the lava flow to their west, an area which the Americans were reluctant to enter. All that day and part of Easter Sunday morning there were occasional shots fired by both groups, but no casualties resulted.

Gillem sent word to Mason to break off any action on the east side. He wanted a concerted attack made from both sides of the Stronghold as soon as McKay, the scout, arrived. Mason protested that the Indians should not be permitted forty-eight hours peace after the murders. He asked Gillem for permission to move toward the Stronghold during the night after Easter Sunday; then he could wait for the general signal to advance into the center of the Modoc defenses. Gillem expressly forbade it. Everyone had to wait for McKay.

To the Modocs, Easter weekend was an exciting and triumphant three days. The only fly in their ointment was a quarrel over the division of spoils taken from the whites on Friday. Jack demanded and got Canby's uniform, but Ellen's Man kept the watch, much to Jack's disgust. Bogus Charley and Boston Charley kept Thomas' possessions, while Shacknasty Jim, Hooker Jim, and John Schonchin divided Meacham's clothes. Jack felt that since Hooker Jim had let Dyar escape, he was not entitled to anything. Jack also made an enemy in Curley Headed Jack, because he insulted him for letting Boyle get away alive.[17]

Curley Headed Doctor began a victory dance Friday night to prevent the troops from attacking the next day. All night he danced, and those who cared to do so danced with him. Canby's scalp was added to the medicine pole to add strength to the work of the shaman. No troops appeared Saturday from the camp by the bluff, and

[17] Meacham, *Wigwam and War-path*, 509.

Mason's scouts had marched south instead of west. The doctor's medicine seemed very strong, for Curley Headed Doctor had advised murder and a resumption of the war. His advice had been taken, and no harm had come to a single Indian as the result. On he danced. Through Saturday night the Indians danced, and the dancers became more and more ecstatic as they convinced themselves that both the army and the United States government were powerless. The dancing continued through Easter Sunday, and on Monday the Modocs were still dancing.

On Easter Sunday all was quiet in the army camp at Gillem's Bluff. The men probably had no real affection for Canby while he was alive, but after his murder everyone was distressed. Some of the soldiers had undoubtedly cursed him roundly during the previous two months of misery and inaction, but now each felt a personal loss, and many indulged themselves in outbursts of rage against the Modocs. About noon on Sunday, the coffins were placed on the shoulders of a few picked men and were carried up the face of the bluff to the wagon ambulances waiting at the end of the "mule trail." An escort was detailed for each body—Canby's was Scott and the adjutant, Anderson. They were taken to Yreka and embalmed, then publicly exhibited before being taken away. Thomas was to be buried in San Francisco, while Canby would have funeral services in Portland; then he would be taken to Indianapolis for final interment.

A few hours after the bodies were taken away, McKay and his Indians arrived at Hospital Rock and Mason's camp. Word was sent immediately to Gillem that the scout had come and the attack on the Stronghold could begin.

The Warm Springs Indians had been authorized as early as March 22. Gillem and Canby both agreed that in case of renewed fighting, it would be best to let Indians fight Indians. In January, Wheaton had asked for Indian scouts and auxiliary soldiers to replace the Klamaths whom he did not trust, and Canby suggested Warm Springs Indians then. They were not called into service when the orders came to negotiate rather than fight, and the scouts were discharged with little or no compensation and told that perhaps they might be used some time again.

As one means of putting pressure on the Modocs, Canby decided in mid-March to enlist the discharged Warm Springs Indians and bring them down. He would tell the Modocs, as he did, that their enemies were on the way. He felt that this might terrify them into surrender. It did not.

Canby had a great deal of confidence in Donald McKay, whose ancestry endowed him with an unusually wide acquaintance among the Indians in the Northwest. McKay's father was one of the early fur-traders who operated out of Fort George, at Astoria, until he was drowned while crossing the Columbia in a canoe during a storm. McKay's mother was a Chinook woman. Throughout his life, McKay had been working either in the fur trade, or as scout or interpreter for the army on frequent expeditions against hostile Indians.

While the whites had confidence in McKay, the Warm Springs Indians did not. At once a difficulty came up when McKay got to the Warm Springs Agency before the recruiting officer did, and let it be known he was to be their captain. Agent Smith had enlisted one hundred candidates, but they all said they would refuse to serve if McKay were their leader. Some of them had served with him during the Snake War, and they accused him of swindling them out of much of their pay. No Indian could write enough to keep accounts or army records, but they thought they knew the amount they had coming, and they knew when they did not get it. It was only natural that they should lay the blame at the door of the man who kept the records. They did not prove their case, but they continued to dislike McKay.

The Indians had their superintendent wire Canby asking that they be permitted to pick their own leader. Canby replied that McKay would lead or he would select other Indians as his scouts, because the men the Indians wanted were either too young and inexperienced, or else they were not available.

McKay knew he was not liked and tried to get a different group of Indians from those whom Smith had enlisted. His choices, however, were not even on the agency. They had abandoned the farming life and the Christian religion and had drifted across the Columbia for the free life of hunters and for the religion of Smohalla. In the past, some of the agents had arbitrarily and excessively punished them for their views, and now they had left the reservation—a situation potentially the same as the one that had made Captain Jack an outlaw.

There were several such situations in the Northwest at this time, and it was essential to the plans of expansionists that the Modocs not be permitted successfully to defy the policy of the government, or there would be other Modoc wars. This was without doubt the motivating force behind Governor Grover's insistence upon Modoc defeat, punishment, and exile.

When the Christian Indians on the Warm Springs reservation found that they had to go with McKay or not at all, they accepted him, but were not cheerful about it. Army pay compensated for putting up with someone they disliked, however, and on the morning of April 4, they started the long hike toward Tule Lake.

There were seventy-two of them. Thirty-two were Wascos, twenty-four were Warm Springs, eleven others were called Teninos, and there was one Umatilla, one Nez Percé, one Snake, and one Simcoe (Yakima). Interestingly enough, the last man was a Modoc. The Snake was young Paunina, son of the old warrior who had fought the whites so hard in the '60's.[18]

Gillem and Canby expected them on April 10, but road conditions and their slow marching pace held them up for three additional days. They arrived only after Canby was dead.[19]

[18] Louis V. Caziarc to Headquarters, Department of the Columbia, April 6, 1873, S.F.P., D.C., 1873, #583; April 10, 1873, #617; Caziarc to Canby, April 4, 1873, #1641.

[19] For details of the murder of the commissioners, compare also Bancroft, *Oregon*, II, 609ff.; *Gillem Report*, 5ff.; *Report of the Commissioner of Indian Affairs, 1873*, Meacham Report; Report of Klamath Agency #75; Warm Springs Agency #72; Siletz Agency #74; 43 Cong., 1 sess., *House Exec. Doc. No. 122*, Trial of the Modoc Prisoners; Portland *Oregonian* (April 14, 1873); Meacham, *Wi-ne-ma*, 63–64.

Captain Jack (Courtesy Western History Collections, University of
Oklahoma).

Gillem's Camp and Tule Lake (Courtesy National Archives).

Captain Jack's Cave in the Lava Beds (Courtesy National Archives).

Howitzer battery in the Stronghold (Courtesy National Archives).

Mule-borne stretcher devised during the Modoc War (Courtesy National Archives).

VIII

RETALIATION

ON THE MONDAY MORNING following the murder of Canby, the usual bugle calls awakened the soldiers in their tents in preparation for the battle to avenge him. At once the Warm Springs Indians held their customary religious service, and by the time they were through, the soldiers were preparing for the attack on the Stronghold. This attack was to be successful, but by the time it was over the Indians were gone and the soldiers had captured only rocks.

The attack began when Gillem ordered McKay's Indians to leave Mason's camp telling them to move to the south along the route toward Juniper Butte taken by Theller two days before. They should be in position early Tuesday morning to turn across the extreme south end of the lava flow known then as Black Ledge, and today as the Schonchin flow. This is very rough terrain—much more so than the direct route from either Gillem's or Mason's camps to Jack's council ground. The objective was for the Warm Springs Scouts to be in position by Tuesday night so that they could attack from the south on the fifteenth, while the main army would attack from both east and west along the lake shore. The plan was good, but Mason did not put it into action.

On the west side, the Coehorn mortars were placed on the backs of pack mules and taken after dark to a point from which a bombardment of the Stronghold would be possible. Rations for a three day's campaign were cooked and packed.

The Indians in the Modoc camp knew that an attack was on the way and that the Warm Springs Indians had arrived. Curley Headed Doctor continued to dance, assuring his followers that no soldier, white or Indian, would cross the red tule rope that marked his magical boundary.

The bodies of Canby and Thomas reached Yreka on the same Monday the attack began. Canby's body was laid in state in the little mining town, and everyone for miles around took an informal holiday. More than a thousand people filed by the remains. In the afternoon almost two hundred school children were dismissed from their classes to march by the dead General in columns of two. Emotions in the street became more and more unstable. A resolution was passed at an informal town meeting on the sidewalk that there should be no further conferences with the Modocs. Secretary Delano, who had approved the formation of the Peace Commission, was denounced for not ordering the war continued, and he was hanged in effigy. For once, Californians and Oregonians were united on the way the war should be carried on.

On Monday, also, Dyar's telegram of information regarding the murders of Canby and Thomas reached Washington, D. C. His conclusion was that "Peace cannot be made with these men."[1] Meacham had recovered enough to send a brief account of the killings. "We believe that complete subjugation by the military is the only method by which to deal with these Indians," he said.[2]

The wrathful General Sherman ordered the Modocs exterminated. The War Department promptly received many suggestions for achieving this objective. One man suggested poison gas.[3] Another thought snipers placed strategically among the rocks could destroy the Modocs and avoid needless bloodshed to the whites. This seems like an intelligent suggestion in the twentieth century, but by the ethical standards of the nineteenth century, the plan was dismissed as unsportsmanlike because men were expected to march

[1] Telegram, Dyar to Clum, April 13, 1873, *Oregon Superintendency, 1873,* Office of Indian Affairs.

[2] Meacham to Delano, April 16, 1873, *Oregon Superintendency, 1873,* Office of Indian Affairs.

[3] A. Hamilton to Delano, April 17, 1873, *Oregon Superintendency, 1873,* Office of Indian Affairs.

into battle in a steady and upright line. Another suggestion, probably the result of watching a traveling company present a couple of Great Danes chasing Eliza across the everlasting ice of "Uncle Tom's Cabin," was to send "bloodhounds" to the Lava Beds and let them destroy the Modocs. Another more intelligent, if impractical, suggestion was to equip the soldiers with body armor to stop the low muzzle velocity bullets the Indians fired. Actually about all the men had to do was to advance steadily, without armor, and depend for their protection on the abysmally bad marksmanship of the Indians.

Only a few dissenting voices were raised to Sherman's orders. The admirable Lucretia Mott sent a telegram to President Grant deploring Sherman's threats to exterminate the Modocs. She and her friends blithely shrugged off the murder of the peace commissioners as an incident totally unrelated to the peace policy they advocated. They blamed it rather on the whole system of war-making, in which peace was always made after victory by a general with a victorious army at his back.[4]

If Pennsylvanians like Miss Mott censured the government, there was no doubt that Oregonians blamed both the Indians and the slipshod methods of the Interior Department for the killings. The general attitude in the West was "I told you so." Flags at Jacksonville hung at half mast. In Astoria, an indignation meeting was held and a resolution was adopted against any further dickering with the Modocs. Governor Grover made plans for calling out the volunteers once more.

General Sherman ordered a replacement for General Canby in the person of Colonel and Brevet Major General Jefferson C. Davis, who was stationed at Fort Townsend, Washington Territory. Davis was a competent officer, a West Point graduate, and a veteran of the Mexican and Civil Wars. Davis had no use for the Confederacy. He had been stationed at Fort Sumter and was particularly bitter because his name was exactly the same as that of the President of the Confederate government. During the war, he had been the victim of a celebrated squabble between civilian and army authorities.

[4] Lucretia Mott to President Grant, April 19, 1873, *Oregon Superintendency, 1873,* Office of Indian Affairs.

In the midst of the fighting in Georgia, while serving under Sherman, Davis' troops were hampered by the growing volume of slave refugees who insisted that he give them protection. Finally, the number of non-combatants grew to the point that he could hardly move. He ordered the freed men to leave his army, for Confederate cavalry under General Wheeler was very close, and Davis could not fight encumbered as he was. When the freedmen refused to leave, Davis marched his men across a bridge at Ebenezer Creek, and then ordered the bridge destroyed, a move which left the Negroes on the other bank. Wheeler's cavalry caught the Negroes before they could cross the stream and killed many of them, driving others to a death by drowning in the creek. A tremendous roar went up through the North when Davis' action was known, and he had to be relieved of his command in order to appease public opinion.

Davis was transferred to a number of obscure posts, and at the end of the War was sent to America's version of Siberia. He was ordered to Sitka, then the capital of the wild and almost unknown Alaska, which Seward purchased from the Russians. He received the transfer of that Territory from the Russians, and for a few months acted as whatever government there was for the whole corner of the continent. After a time he was quietly transferred back to the States, but he was left in the extreme northwest corner of Washington. Now, Sherman, his old commander, ordered that he be given another chance to command troops in the field.

At once, Davis left for Yreka and the Lava Beds, but the trip was a long one the way he had to go. Until he arrived, Gillem, too sick to be efficient, was left in command.

Gillem called a conference of his officers to outline final plans for the attack scheduled for the morning of April 15. After the officers had heard what they were to do, they adjourned for a brief period of sociability before returning to their units. In their tents, the young officers told stories, drank toasts to each other and sang songs like:

> *Then stand by your glasses steady*
> *The World's a round of lies—*
> *Three Cheers for the dead already*
> *And hurrah for the next who dies!*

At two o'clock in the morning of April 15, Major Green began actual hostilities from Gillem's camp by sending two companies of cavalry to what is now known as Hovey Point, about a mile west of the Stronghold. This point of land is a peninsula that juts into the lake almost three quarters of a mile beyond the direct route between Gillem's camp and the Modoc camp. The plan was that if the fighting repeated its course in January and the Indians came out of their Stronghold to engage the troops crossing the Lava Beds in skirmishing line, the cavalry could rush out of their concealed positions on the point, and cut off, capture, or destroy a considerable number of Modocs. Captain David Perry had recovered sufficiently from his January wound to be able once more to command his Troop F, and with him was Lieutenant C. C. Cresson, commanding Troop K, First Cavalry. Both troops left their horses in order to fight as dismounted infantry when the time came for combat. Their movement was executed perfectly in a windless and starry night. Well before dawn they were concealed and waiting for the infantry to begin its attack from the west.

Some of the infantrymen left behind decided informally during the night that an auspicious way to begin the battle would be to kill a Modoc, which so far no one had been able to do. A group of them left camp and hid in the rocks a few yards east of Gillem's camp. Long Jim had come over to the camp without any particular reason and found his treatment much different after Canby's death than it had been before. He was seized and held as a prisoner of war. The soldiers then induced the guards to let him try to escape so that they could kill him. They knew that outright murder of a prisoner would bring repercussions, but no one could be blamed for killing an escaping prisoner.[5]

The guards ostentatiously withdrew from their duty by pretending to go to sleep. They expected Long Jim to run at once, but he did nothing of the kind. The guards then began to talk over some way to induce him to try to "escape," but they did not finish their conversation, for the Indian suddenly leaped over the rock wall and fled for the Stronghold. Those who had plotted his death opened fire, but Jim kept running. A moment more and the men

[5] Meacham, *Wigwam and War-path*, 519.

in the rocks began to shoot at him. Still Jim ran on. The darkness closed around the flying figure, and the cursing soldiers realized that they had missed him. Someone, obviously, had been neglecting target practice.[6]

When daylight came, the inevitable bugles sounded once more, and the men prepared for battle. When breakfast was over, equipment checked, and last letters written, the men were ready to advance. The sun was up by the time that the troops under the field command of Captain M. P. Miller of Battery E, Fourth Artillery began to march. Besides Miller's own battery, temporarily commanded by Peter Leary, there were Batteries K and M, under Harris and Throckmorton, and two companies of the Twelfth Infantry—Company E under Thomas Wright and Company G under C. P. Eagan.

Half an hour later, at 8:30, the attack was well advanced, but the men moved with extreme caution. Miller ordered Leary and his own men to lead the advance. All troops in this movement were expected to perform as infantrymen. Accordingly, after the men had marched about half a mile toward the Stronghold, Battery E was shifted from an advancing column to a skirmish line, moving at right angles to the rest of the advancing men. The other troops were held until Battery E had gone another half mile. In case the Modocs were in the rocks and planned an ambush, Battery E was to be expendable. The knowledge that Perry was hiding on Hovey Point well beyond them gave the men some confidence that if trouble came, they would not have the difficulty that Perry himself had had in January.

The Modocs were as unhurried as the soldiers. When they saw their enemies coming, they stripped themselves of most of their clothing and bound themselves with rawhide bandages to protect their bodies as they crawled over and through the rocks. Then they moved leisurely into position while the women and children practiced an elementary civilian defense by huddling for safety in the caves and rock shelters of the Stronghold.[7] Stones were piled in front of each entrance to protect those inside from flying bullets or rolling cannon balls. These barriers may still be seen at the edge of some of the rock shelters.

[6] *Ibid.,* 521.   [7] *Ibid.,* 522.

By ten o'clock in the morning, the columns had moved past the spot where Canby and Thomas were murdered and along the lake shore for almost another mile. They were over two-thirds of the way to the outer defenses of the council ground and so far had neither seen nor heard a Modoc. The advance was much easier than it had been in January when the Indians had started killing Americans soon after they began to attack.

When Battery E reached the base of Hovey's Point and Perry's dismounted cavalry, they left Perry's command to remain in reserve, to keep the lake shore free from Indians and to prevent any possible flanking movement from the north. Perry stayed in this area until midafternoon.

The surface of the ground is very rough for the next quarter of a mile, and the advance slowed down. It would have slowed anyhow, for the strain of knowing that either the Indians must open fire soon or give up without firing a shot, an unlikely event, built up an almost unbearable tension in the men. There was another delay while Miller brought up the rest of his troops to join Battery E, then extended them to the south so that all units formed a single skirmish line. The two infantry companies were placed beside the lake with the artillery batteries on their right and the whole line extended south into the Lava Beds. Battery E was still in the most exposed position, for it was on the extreme right with its flank "hanging in the air."

When this maneuver was completed and Battery E began to advance toward the Stronghold once more, the first shots of the battle were fired. Eight Modocs had left the main group of their warriors and had crawled into the Lava Beds to prevent the soldiers from swinging around the Stronghold and making a junction with Mason's men. They understood Gillem's plan and were trying to prevent it from succeeding.

Jack did not have enough men to mount a major assault on the overwhelming numbers of soldiers moving toward him. He knew that only a defensive action had any chance of success. His men had orders, therefore, not to expose themselves needlessly, but to fire at long range in order to delay the soldiers as much as possible.

The first shot of the battle was an accident. A soldier fell, and his rifle discharged. One of the eight Modocs responded with a "Wow-ow-ow" sound, made by saying "wow" and patting his mouth with his hand. Immediately after the shot and the signal, the Modocs began to fire at the men of Battery E.

When the "ping" of the Modoc rifles was heard, the slowly advancing line stopped marching. The officers shouted commands to continue the advance, but the men either could not or would not listen to them and took cover instead. The officers, moving from position to position, urged two or three men here and a dozen or more there to start toward the Stronghold. This took time, and the men were in no hurry. By about noon, however, the attacking force had reached a point perhaps a thousand yards from the medicine flag flying just outside of Jack's cave.

At this point the rough terrain at the southeast corner of Hovey Point becomes a long, twisting, funnel-shaped shallow draw, fairly wide by the lake, and narrowing as it moves inland. The right flank was ordered to stay in the low depression and keep in contact with the balance of the troops who were supposed to continue the attack through the rough country between them and the lake. Battery E was to advance as fast as it could, but to move from cover to cover with one group firing at the Indians while another moved its position slightly toward the Stronghold.

By the time everyone knew his orders, the afternoon was well advanced. The eight Indians were extremely successful in slowing down the advance. They were as effective with their long-range sniping as a company of machine gunners would be at the present time. It took the four hundred men almost six hours to move half a mile against only eight men, who were firing slowly and cautiously, and whose accuracy was poor. Casualties were extremely light. An accounting made of the injuries incurred on the first day showed that three men had been killed and six had been wounded out of the entire attacking force on the west. Battery E, which had the most exposed position, lost two dead and three wounded during the entire fight. Wright's infantry company suffered no injuries at all. It would have been hard for them to have been hurt, for they were many hundreds of yards north of the Modoc snipers. Their positions, however, did not make them move eastward any faster.

No civilian was hurt, although one feared he was to be a casualty. A sutler from Gillem's Camp, Pat McManus, saddled a mule to ride to the front to see how the soldiers were making out. While he was carelessly riding south of the troops, he came within range of Steamboat Frank, who shot McManus' mule. The Irishman leaped behind a rock and stayed there while Frank periodically sent a bullet his way to keep him quivering with fright. The soldiers saw that he was safe as long as he stayed behind his shelter and did nothing to relieve him from his predicament.

When McManus tried to walk back to camp after dark, he was almost killed by the sentries left behind to guard the camp. "Dry up there," shouted the enraged and bedraggled Pat. "It's me! Don't you know a white man on his knees from an Indian on his belly?"[8]

Colonel Gillem was not unhappy about the way his plans were proceeding. Toward the end of the afternoon, when the advance had slowed to a turtle-speed, Gillem went out to look over the field. He turned to John Fairchild, who was with him, and said, "Mr. Fairchild, this is a splendid day's work. How long did it take General Wheaton to get this far?"

Fairchild looked around, and drawled, "General, I do not remember exactly, but as near as I can judge it was about twenty minutes."[9]

This, of course, was not true, but Fairchild shared the general dislike for Gillem and took this way to show it. Gillem turned on his heel and left the rancher. Their relations after that were extremely chilly.

The extreme caution shown by the advancing troops greatly encouraged the Modocs. On every previous encounter with the troops, the soldiers broke off the action and returned to their camps when darkness came. Usually, there were many days before any further action occurred. Jack assumed that the whites would again withdraw from their positions as soon as night came. He thought that if he could prevent the troops from breaking through his western defenses, they would go back to camp and the next day, should they come again, he could use the same tactics.

[8] *Ibid.*, 525.
[9] Thompson, *Reminiscences*, 116.

To Jack's dismay, the troops did not do as he expected. The officers ordered the men to stay where they were for the night and surround themselves with small rock fortifications. They should then rest on the ground and be prepared to advance into the Stronghold the next day.

It may be imagined that the men were not pleased with this order. The ground is full of sharp lava stones about the size of a man's fist, increasing occasionally to the size of a loaf of bread. There are no flat sides, and like ice-bergs they are imbedded far more deeply in the ground than their protruding points indicate. Even if the largest were dug out of the ground, the earth itself is volcanic material packed hard by weathering. The men slept—if they could sleep at all—either on large holes in the ground or on the sharp, pointed rocks. This may account for the fact that the rock protection they built around themselves was sometimes very thick and high. During a long, sleepless night, a man can pile a considerable number of rocks round himself, and if he has help, the pile may be almost awe-inspiring. The Modocs did not shoot a man that night, for the soldiers were much too well protected.

Perry's cavalry had taken very little part in the action on Tuesday morning, but during the late afternoon and early evening they moved forward. They passed through the men in the advanced positions, and in the dusk seized the heights at the extreme northwestern edge of the Stronghold from which the Modocs had poured such annoying fire in January. Doubtless this gave Perry great satisfaction, for during the January encounter he had been wounded by an Indian firing from one of the strong-points in the area now in his possession.

On the east side of the Stronghold, while the men from Gillem's camp were inching their way toward Jack, Mason's Twenty-first Infantry Battalion, Bernard's Troop G of the First Cavalry, and the seventy-two Warm Springs scouts had done almost nothing. Grandiose plans had been laid for these units to swing to the south and make a junction with Miller's artillery-infantry and to cut the Modocs from any possibility of escape toward the hills. Gillem sent Mason word on Monday, "Can you be ready to advance tomorrow morning?" and Mason answered, "I want to get my first position at night. I am ready to move tonight." Gillem then told him that he could take his first objective at the same time Perry marched to Hovey Point, but that he was to keep under cover and not to move until everyone on both sides of the Stronghold was ready. McKay's Indians were to be on the left, or southern flank, in order to meet Miller's men. These auxiliaries were specifically ordered to wear uniforms so that soldiers advancing from the west should not mistake them for hostiles.

The orders were clear enough. Mason put the Twenty-first Infantry of three companies under Captain George H. Burton. Troop G was under its usual commander, Captain Bernard. Jackson's Troop B was also attached to him, and McKay was told to report to Bernard for orders as well. A small detachment of Battery A, Fourth Artillery was held for special orders to be brought up later.

About midnight, Mason broke camp. Before daylight on Tuesday, his troops were in their positions before the Modoc Stronghold. Their line started at the lake itself, and ended about half a mile south of the shore. Instead of McKay's Warm Springs Indians marching to the Schonchin flow, as originally agreed upon, Mason had him place his men in concealment next to the white soldiers. By the time daylight arrived, everyone was safely behind rock fortifications built to conceal and protect their positions from enemy observers and fire. They were about a third of a mile east of the Modoc line of defense. Mason says in his report that "the men had so covered themselves . . . that it was impossible for the enemy to discover our exact location."

As morning came and the soldiers from the west were advancing, Mason had the artillery under Chapin moved into position, and the battery opened fire toward the Modocs. They were so far from the Stronghold, however, that few shells exploded in the Modoc camp. The bombardment was futile because nothing whatever was done to follow it up. Mason made the incredible statement that, "I did not however follow them, as it was no part of my plan to expose anyone unnecessarily." Gillem had given specific orders that Mason was to send the Warm Springs Indians to the south and these scouts were to join Miller's Battery E. In direct disregard to orders, Mason refused to budge.

Why Mason did this can only be surmised. It is true that none of the officers in the fight were of the dashing type. There were no "charges up San Juan Hill" in the Modoc War. Nevertheless, the officers, while not brilliant, were usually obedient. Mason must have detested Gillem so much that he wanted the failure of Gillem's plans to bring discredit on his commander. Gillem certainly suspected such a motive, for when he found Mason had disobeyed him, his denunciation of that subordinate was sarcastic and bitter.

During the night between April 15 and 16, batteries on both sides of the Stronghold kept up a steady bombardment of Jack's positions. The first mortar to fire on the west side failed to function properly, and the shell landed only about fifteen feet from the nearest of Perry's cavalry. As it lay on the ground, sputtering, hissing, and spinning about, a few men jumped to their feet in panic and started to run. Perry shouted for them to lie close to the ground. Fortunately they obeyed him, and when the shell exploded, no one was hurt.

Every fifteen minutes the guns would be fired. Although no damage was done to the Indians, the noise kept them awake and nervous. Finally the exasperated and sleepless Indians crawled as close as possible to the soldiers squirming on their beds of sharp lava rock, and the two forces called back and forth to each other "in plain if not classical English, names unfit to print."[10] The soldiers firing at the Indian voices would be answered with shots and jeering insults about their poor marksmanship and poorer ancestry.

By the end of that night, the men had eaten most of their rations, and they were hungry and tired. Gillem was optimistic, however, for he felt that this day would see the capture of Jack's band. He did not know yet that Mason had disobeyed him the day before. Of course Mason's men had suffered no casualties, but neither had the Indians. By Wednesday morning, most of the Modocs had shifted to the west side to resist Green's advance when it should begin.

Gillem sent Mason the message, "We will endeavor to end the Modoc War today. Try and join Col. Green's right. Let us exterminate the tribe. Push when Green attacks. I will be over this A.M." Mason sent him a message in reply, "The Indians are on our left and

[10] Fitzgerald, "The Modoc War Reminiscences," *Americana*, Vol. XXI, No. 4 (October, 1927).

rear. We have to fight them, but will do all we can to help Green."
The Indians were not behind him, but it gave him an excuse for
failing to move to the south. No attack was made from that direction.

Early in the morning Green got in touch with Mason by signal,
and the two officers improvised a plan to join their forces, which
were now separated by only a few hundred yards along the shore
of Peninsula Bay at the north of the Stronghold. It was not until
mid-morning that Gillem finally discovered that Mason had failed
to move on Tuesday and during the night had advanced less than
three hundred yards. He was so enraged that he countermanded
Mason's and Green's agreement to meet along the lake shore, and
ordered them to follow the original plan to make a junction to the
south. The officers paid no attention to his orders, and successfully
carried out their junction by the lake. This was effected without the
loss of a single man.

Combining the two groups was not a bad idea, for it cut the
Indians from their water supply. On the other hand, the failure to
join at the south of the Stronghold left a huge gap in the army lines
through which the Modocs could escape whenever they wished.

All that day pressure was maintained from the north, and the
men slowly advanced into the Stronghold only stopping now and
then to build rock fortifications, which are still plainly visible after
more than eighty years. By late afternoon, they had pushed their
lines forward along a quarter-mile front to a point less than fifty
yards from the gap in the rocks leading to the center of Jack's headquarters. If they could charge through and over the rock barriers,
there would be some bitter hand-to-hand fighting, but with the
superiority in numbers, the Indians would be beaten.

Encouraged by the hope for early victory, the soldiers built
another set of six-man forts along a ridge just outside the inner camp
of the Modocs; here they spent the night. As they had done the
night before, three men watched from each barricade, while three
rested as best they could. Twice during the night, there was a brief
flurry of fighting as the soldiers repulsed attempts of the Indians to
break through to the lake and water, which by now they needed
desperately. The Modocs could not afford the luxury of charging
a superior force; in their eyes not a single Modoc was expend-

able. Unless Curley Headed Doctor could produce some kind of miracle, the Modoc situation would reach the critical stage within a few hours.

The army's hope for victory rested on its ability to prevent the Modocs from escaping to the south and breaking into open country, or into the Schonchin flow where they could continue fighting; here the Modocs could find water in the ice caves and seepage pools. Green sent orders to Miller that Wednesday should be spent connecting his right with any Warm Springs Indians he could find. Miller's men, who were not enthusiastic about attacking across the rough ground to the south of the Stronghold, sent back word that the ground was "unpassable," which, of course, was not the case. Halfheartedly they crawled to the south. Miller finally ordered his men to turn and move east across the base of the Indian position. The soldiers had not advanced as far as he thought they had and his men succeeded only in exposing themselves to flanking fire from the Modoc snipers at the southwest corner of the Stronghold.

A bugler and one private soldier were killed here, and seventeen men of Battery E, which had been on the extreme right for two days, took refuge in a crater of broken rock. Miller joined them. He ordered his tiny command to throw up rock shelters for themselves, and they stayed where they were for several hours. Meanwhile, the entire force, extending from Miller and his seventeen men to the lake shore, had no commander; Green didn't know where Miller was or what he was doing. Eventually Miller decided that the Warm Springs scouts had been driven back and that no more efforts should be made to close the ring around the Stronghold. He then gave orders for retreat, a command which the seventeen men obeyed with alacrity.

The net result of this day's work along the west side was that the Americans were not as far advanced at the end of the second day as they had been at the end of the first, except along the lake shore which Gillem had specifically ordered not to be attacked.

In spite of the fact that Mason and Green had disobeyed Gillem, their action had a good result. They completely destroyed Curley Headed Doctor's power. Soldiers from Green's command crossed the magic red tule rope that the shaman had placed as a guarantee that no one would enter the Stronghold, and they kept advancing, although at a snail's pace. During the second night, an Indian was finally killed although Curley Headed Doctor had asserted that no one protected by his magic would be.

A cannon ball which had failed to explode attracted the attention of one Indian; he tried to defuse it by pulling the detonator with his teeth. The resulting explosion summarily removed the Modoc's head. Another cannon ball made a direct hit on the council fire and scattered the burning brands. The yells of terror and rage in the Indian camp were plainly heard by the soldiers in their rocky beds along the lake shore.

Since the Indians had lost a man, and Curley Headed Doctor's medicine had failed, the medicine flag was abandoned as worthless and left for the soldiers. The dispirited Modocs allowed Jack again to become their undisputed leader. About nine o'clock in the evening, he ordered one last attack to try to get water, and that attempt ended in failure. No Indian objected, therefore, when during the night of April 16, the shortage of water in the Modoc camp forced Jack reluctantly to order the evacuation of the Stronghold that had served him so well for almost five months.

To cover the withdrawal, Jack had a brisk fire directed at the army positions a few minutes before midnight. No damage was done, and no one was hurt, but every Modoc man was in action. The soldiers convinced themselves that the Modocs were not only alert, but were planning an assault on their lines that might materialize momentarily.

For the rest of the night the Modocs maintained some fire from their outposts, but after midnight the fire slackened. A few Indians yelled insults at the troops as they had done the night before. Jack left a small rear guard to keep firing while his women, children, and able-bodied soldiers crept out through the gap in the lines between Green and Mason. A low depression leading from the Stronghold into the Schonchin flow was the escape route of the Modocs, and while they were never more than four or five hundred yards from the troops in advanced positions, no one knew they had gone until late in the morning. The Warm Springs Indians said later that they had heard children crying during the evacuation, but they did not report these sounds to their superior officers.[11] Mason stated in his report that no one knew the Modocs had left until about 11 o'clock Thursday morning. Gillem ordered a pursuit, but the men advanced at their usual crawling pace, a rate which would have taken them many days to occupy the Schonchin flow.

Ellen's Man is credited with the next Modoc expedient to throw the troops off balance. He suggested that the Indians try a diversionary attack on Gillem's camp, in the hope that the men on the west would rush back to defend their headquarters. Accordingly, Hooker Jim and a handful of picked men were sent on a wide detour of the advancing troops to raise a row behind their lines. Gillem had left Lieutenant Grier, the quartermaster, and a small guard in camp to watch for just such an attempt. When Hooker appeared, Grier alerted the garrison and issued arms to the crowd of civilian hangers-on who were still in camp. He then sent to Green for help, but the Major refused to fall in with Jack's schemes. Hooker Jim had to leave with nothing accomplished.

On their way back to the new Indian camp, about noon on Thursday, Hooker's men overtook two newspaper reporters, and a nineteen year old Yreka boy named Hovey. Hovey was leading a mule loaded with supplies for the men now in the Stronghold. Since he had no idea that Modocs were behind him, the young packer took no precautions. Hooker Jim shot Hovey, and the reporters ran for their lives. The Indians stripped the body, mutilated it in the usual ways, and crushed the head flat with rocks.[12] The reporters ran back to camp, and their wild yells announced Hooker Jim's minor victory. The result of his raid was that the civilian packers refused to carry supplies out to the lines.[13]

The soldiers, meanwhile, were told to stay in the original Stronghold and fortify it so that the Modocs would be unable to retake it. As they occupied the cracks and caves, they found the dwelling places of the Modocs. There were animal bones everywhere. Some of the Indians had constructed temporary lodges in the little basins

11 Boyle, "Personal Observations," 28–29.

12 Portland *Oregonian* (April 19, 1873); Doris Palmer Payne, *Captain Jack, Modoc Renegade*, 198; Riddle, *Indian History*, 103.

13 William Simpson, *Meeting the Sun: A Journey All Around the World*, 364.

that occurred throughout the entire area. Others had cleared stones from the bottoms of the few caves, and were living there. A few other families had found shelter under an overhanging rock in a deep, rocky pit near the council ground. Twice the soldiers encountered Indians who had been left behind in the retreat. One old and wounded man was killed, and the report has it that his body was scalped. This was divided about eight ways and shown as evidence that a number of Modocs had been killed. Even the eyebrows were taken and kept as a scalp. Another report tells of an old woman found by the soldiers. She asked to be taken prisoner, but was shot by a Pennsylvania private on orders from his company commander.[14] Not many Modocs were killed on April 17, but they had lost their magic and their Stronghold.

The Modoc evacuation of the Stronghold was a great victory for the army. The only trouble was that no one knew where the vanquished had gone. The Modocs withdrew their women and children in good order and were just as dangerous in their new location as they had been in their old one. Although they had almost no water in their new camp at the edge of the Schonchin flow, there were small seepage pools in a few of the caves and ice in some others. Game was plentiful, and they were in no danger of starvation. There was now the probability that the Indians would scatter to the winds and spend the summer in hit-and-run raids from Goose Lake to Yreka to Yainax.

Gillem had to find the Modocs, and quickly, or their water shortage would force them into the open country. Rounding them up would then be a slow and difficult task. He ordered the cavalry to make a circuit of the entire Lava Beds to ascertain whether the main body of Indians had left or were still inside. Until they could report, he ordered camps maintained in the Stronghold, at Medicine Rock, at Scorpion Point, and at the base of Gillem's Bluff, while the Warm Springs Indians were ordered to camp on Hovey Point, the peninsula jutting into the lake just west of the Stronghold. Each camp was ordered to prevent the Indians from getting water in the lake so that the cavalry could run them down when they tried to go

[14] Fitzgerald, "The Modoc War Reminiscences," *Americana*, Vol. XXI, No. 4 (October, 1927), 516.

south. If the Modocs could be forced into the open to fight, the army would almost certainly destroy them.

The soldiers, however, did not always keep the Indians away from water. Furthermore, Indians were sighted, from time to time, standing at the edge of the Schonchin Flow, or even moving close to camp to look over the army installations. On several occasions, camp fires were seen.[15] No one doubted that there were still Indians in the Lava Beds, but what Gillem had to know was whether the main body had escaped to raid the settlements.

On Friday, April 18, after the occupation of the Stronghold, the Modocs made a direct appearance near Gillem's camp. They tried to entice the soldiers into an attack by mocking the artillery companies. A group of Indians would come out a few hundred yards from camp, set their guns on the ground as though they were a battery of mortars, and when Scarfaced Charley would yell, "Fire!" they would discharge their guns into the air so that the bullets would come into camp from a descending trajectory. The soldiers did not attack them, no one was hurt, and the Indians left after a few shots had been fired.

As this band left, another small group made a fast break for water. The soldiers saw them dash to the lake, but made no effort to intercept them. Even when the Indians plunged into the water and splashed and bathed in it briefly, no one tried to stop them.[16] The soldiers reported this to Gillem, but he did nothing. Although the men grumbled, Gillem continued to wait for Perry to return from his sweep around the lava flows. The Colonel insisted that he didn't know where the Modocs were. A small platoon of soldiers moving from the Stronghold to Gillem's camp did discover the Indians' location. They began to chase a group of Modocs, but when the Indians formed into a position for fighting, the soldiers stopped their advance and ran pell-mell for the safety of Gillem's headquarters.[17]

Inside the camps, therefore, there was little activity except for the building of forts in the Stronghold and the caring for wounded men in the general field hospital at Gillem's camp. Mason brought

---

[15] Boyle, "Personal Observations," 32.
[16] *Ibid.*, 34.
[17] Meacham, *Wigwam and War-path*, 546.

all of his wounded from Hospital Rock to Gillem's on the seventeenth. He moved a few men from the Stronghold to Scorpion Point late on Friday.

It seemed so quiet to Gillem that he took a walk of several miles from his headquarters to the Stronghold and on to Hospital Rock. He said when he arrived that he had not seen a single Modoc, which is probably true. The Indians were much farther south than the lake shore except for occasional forays.[18]

Friday was also the day for Canby's funeral in Portland and Thomas' funeral in San Francisco. Canby had been taken from Yreka to Portland in a zinc coffin placed inside of a wooden box. At his funeral many Protestant clergymen participated. Parts of the service were taken by a Methodist, a Presbyterian, and an Unitarian clergyman. At least six other ministers were present who took a modest part in the memorial. An honor guard was sent from Fort Vancouver. After it had lain in state, Canby's body was shipped to Indianapolis for burial.

Thomas' funeral was held in San Francisco at the Powell Street Methodist Church. Six thousand people were reported to have viewed his remains. General Schofield's staff officers attended the funeral. The Governor of California, and the Mayor of San Francisco paid their public respects to his memory. The reporters at the funeral counted forty-five ministers present—one from as far away as Chicago. The army sent six generals, six colonels, and at least three captains whose names were considered important enough to record.[19]

The day after the funerals, headquarters at the Presidio heard the disturbing news that while the Stronghold had been captured, no Indians had surrendered. New companies of troops were hastily ordered to the Lava Beds to prevent the Modocs from scattering. All California posts were stripped of troops. Captains Hasbrouck and Mendenhall with two new companies of troops pushed rapidly toward Tule Lake while the hundreds of troops that were already there watched the Indians come to water, or saw their fires, or wondered when they would be sent after the Modocs again.

[18] Boyle, "Personal Observations," 32.
[19] Portland *Oregonian* (April 19, 1873).

The inactivity ended Sunday when the Modocs shifted their zone of operations and attacked a supply train moving between the Scorpion Point camp and the Stronghold. Lieutenant Howe, in charge of the train, had twenty men in his escort force, and the Indians were driven off, but not until they had killed one soldier and wounded another.[20]

Not long after this skirmish, McKay came in and reported that his scouts had "discovered the Modocs" four miles south of the old Stronghold in the Schonchin lava flow. He reported seeing about forty men. There had not been much mystery about the Indians' position, but now it was officially known, and Gillem was almost compelled to do something to acknowledge McKay's report. Even the private soldiers were complaining that the Colonel was afraid, for he kept too many men on guard duty at the headquarters camp.

Another reason impelled Gillem to act. Rumors snowballed throughout the south central Oregon country. Every cloud of dust or every fire seen at night became a band of Modocs out to kill and burn. Yainax seemed to be the incubator of many of these rumors. Indians on the reservation reported Modocs visiting their friends and trying to recruit reinforcements for Jack. The hostiles bragged to the Klamaths and Old Schonchin's band alike of their victories and asked for co-operation in driving the army out of the Indian country.[21] Rumor also reported twelve to fifteen Modocs a day run to earth and killed.[22] There was no truth at all in the last rumor. The number reported visiting at Yainax was probably false as well, but there was undoubtedly some visiting back and forth between the "wild" Indians and the "tame," reservation Modocs.

Both Mason and Green went to Gillem to urge an attack after McKay reported the number and location of the Indians. Their urging became more pointed when Perry returned from his circuit of the Lava Beds and reported no Modocs outside of the lava flows.

Perry had had a difficult time. Many of his horses were sick with an "epizootic," which had been epidemic among animals throughout the nation during the winter. Many of his best mounts were dis-

[20] McElderry Report, S.F.P., D.C., 1873, #2273, 20/D.C. "B".
[21] Meacham, *Wigwam and War-path*, 557.
[22] Portland *Oregonian* (April 23, 1873).

abled by the disease.[23] It took him almost four days to make his patrol. His camps had been established at Van Bremer's, Ball's, and at Dry Lake, about ten miles south of Scorpion Point. The evidence he brought in confirmed that of McKay and made essential some kind of movement against the new camp south of the Stronghold.

On Thursday the twenty-fourth, the Modocs did not appear. Although Gillem had not admitted officially that they were near him, he decided that some method should be used to get artillery into position to shell the lava caves and pinnacles in the lava flow. No one knew whether artillery could be moved to the general area where the Modocs had last been seen. Possibly a location could be found where the mortars could be set up to command the entire flow, which is less than a mile wide and not much more than five miles long. This part of the Lava Beds is much rougher than the old Stronghold had been, and no one wanted to move infantry through here if artillery could force the Indians out.

The bustle of military preparations for a thrust against the Indians attracted the attention of curious people who wanted to see what a war looked like at close range; at that time they could walk into the Stronghold without danger to themselves. Men came from as far away as England to see the battle fields.

One English globe-trotter left a delightful account of his impressions of the army camp. His transportation stranded him at Yreka, for when the teamsters heard that Hovey had been killed and that the Modocs were still at large, many of them flatly refused to move a wagon into the Tule Lake Basin. The Englishman then hitched a ride with a courageous and tough driver who refused to quit. When the two men reached Gillem's camp, the Englishman's first reaction was one of amazement at the picturesque profanity of everyone in the camp. He had never heard anything like it.[24] As he sat in camp, he also watched a cameraman at work recording the war in a medium just coming into use.

Muybridge, a San Francisco photographer and a friend of Leland Stanford, came up to take photographs and to develop them on the spot. The camera expert took stereoscopic views to provide three

[23] Portland *Oregonian* (April 19, 1873).
[24] Simpson, *Meeting the Sun*, 364–80.

dimensional views of the Stronghold, the Warm Springs Indians, Gillem's camp, of grinning groups of officers standing in the Stronghold, sitting in the stone forts, or walking through the lava trenches that had caused the troops so much difficulty in moving forward in January and during the third week of April.[25]

Reporters were everywhere. The soldiers did not mind. They talked to the English writer, posed for Muybridge, and were interviewed for the papers back home. Some of the soldiers had no one to write to, for they were immigrants almost fresh from the ships from Europe. Some of them, enlisting under assumed names, hoped that they would not have to fight very hard and that they would be able to desert and go to San Francisco now that they were in the West. All of these found the camp visitors and the flood of hangers-on from Redding or Yreka entertaining and pleasant.

When plans were completed for a thrust against Jack and his warriors, the visitors and the men in camp were almost in the spirit of a picnic as they watched the artillery reconnaissance leave for its patrol.

[25] Fitzgerald, "The Modoc War Reminiscences," *Americana*, Vol. XXI, No. 4 (October, 1927).

Loa-kum-ar-nuk, Warm Springs Indian scout (Courtesy National Archives).

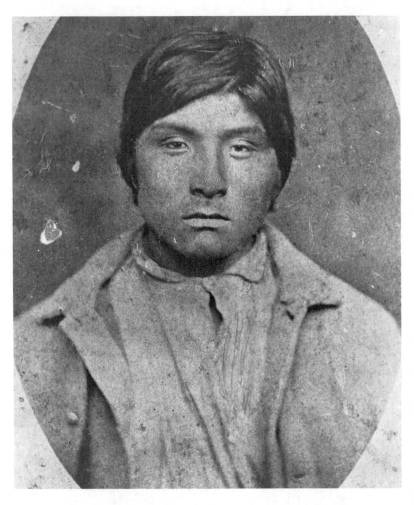

Boston Charley (Courtesy Western History Collections, University of Oklahoma).

Curley Headed Jack, Wheum, and Buckskin Doctor (Courtesy Western History Collections, University of Oklahoma).

Shacknasty Jim, Steamboat Frank, Frank and Toby "Winema" Rid⟨⟩
and their son Jeff, and Scarfaced Charley (Courtesy Kirk Collecti⟨⟩
Oklahoma Historical Society).

Captain Jack's family: his young wife Lizzie, his sister Mary, and his older wife, and his daughter (Courtesy Western History Collections, University of Oklahoma).

IX

THE THOMAS-WRIGHT MASSACRE

SOUTH OF THE LAKE SHORE, into the region where the Modocs had fled after they abandoned their Stronghold, the volcanic basin of the Lava Beds begins to tilt upward. It rises gently for the first six miles, but for the next six miles it becomes steeper and steeper. About twelve miles from the lake, the flattened beds give way to the steep hillsides of the Medicine Lake range to the south, with elevations of more than thirty-five hundred feet above the lake shore. Between Tule Lake and the Medicine Lake ridge, the volcanic activity which produced the lava flows through which Captain Jack's people hunted, hid, and fought, has laid down a pattern of cinder or pumice buttes and fumeroles, protruding through layer after layer of lava flows.

Into the plateau of lava just south of the Stronghold, the Modocs made their first retreat. The first of the pumice buttes lies just beyond their new rallying point. Near here, the Warm Springs scouts found them, and toward this butte General Gillem ordered the scouting party to take a howitzer to find whether the butte (now named for a private Hardin in the Modoc-fighting army), could be used as an artillery position.

The reconnaissance was largely Green's idea, but he received Gillem's approval before the orders were issued. Green ordered Captain Evan Thomas, who had missed most of the fighting for the Stronghold, to command the patrol. Thomas took his A battery of the Fourth Artillery and Battery K commanded by Lieutenant

Albion Howe. One of the Twelfth Infantry companies, E, under Captain Thomas F. Wright, was added to the artillery companies.

These officers were very young; most of them had parents with a military record. Thomas Wright was the son of General George Wright, former Indian fighter and commander of the Department of the Columbia. General Wright was drowned only a short time before the Modoc War broke out. The son, a West Point graduate, had served through the Civil War, both in the cavalry, and as a Major of the Sixth California Infantry. By the end of the war, the youthful soldier had received brevet rank through colonel and was given the permanent rank of first lieutenant. At the time of the Modoc War, he was a captain. He had contracted an excellent marriage not long before he came to the Lava Beds and he seemed to have a brilliant military career ahead of him.

The other officers were also young men. Albion Howe was a major of volunteers during the Civil War, but was now an artillery lieutenant in the regular army. He was the son of a former colonel in the army, and like Wright had also been married to the daughter of an army colonel just before he was sent out to the Modoc fight. Lieutenant Arthur Cranston was thirty and had a wife and child in Washington, D. C.; Lieutenant Harris was twenty-seven, a West Point graduate of the class of 1868.

Wright was the only one who had lived in the West, and while the other officers had had considerable experience fighting in the South under approved nineteenth-century battle conditions, they were not experienced Indian fighters. Their men were "Bowery boys from Chatham Square, striplings from the farms of Connecticut, Pennsylvania, Ohio, but especially from every country of Europe."[1] For thirteen dollars a month these men were expected to obey orders even if they meant death on a rocky lava shelf in northern California. Almost none of them knew or cared anything about their comrades-at-arms. "Few among them felt they were their brothers keeper; the Good Samaritan spirit scarcely existed." Some of the men had been officers during the Civil War; because they had been in some kind of trouble, they had re-enlisted under assumed names as a way to spend a few months or years until their failings

[1] DeCost Smith, *Indian Experiences*, 248.

had been forgotten. A few were said to have been Confederate veterans. Enlisted men were considered beneath the notice or concern of their officers, and the casualty reports scarcely took note of them. Officers were mentioned by name; sometimes non-commissioned officers were mentioned; privates were almost never listed. If they died, they were buried, frequently without a marker of any kind, and they wore no identification unless they had pinned notes on their clothes saying who they were. If they were unfortunate enough to be killed, frequently these scraps of paper would be discarded, and they were interred simply as unknown dead. There they lay, unmourned, in uncared-for graves, many times lost to the knowledge of their loved ones. These were not soldiers to lead in some Homeric struggle or some "Charge of the Light Brigade." They certainly were not willing to "Do or die."

On the morning of April 26, those men who had written to friends or relatives gave their letters to other soldiers to be mailed home and shook hands with those whom they were leaving in camp. Wright had written to his wife the evening before "to amuse her," he said.[2] After breakfast, the soldiers lined up in a double column ready to march south toward the low pumice butte they could see about four and a half miles distant.

Sixty-four officers and men were assembled for the patrol; with them were H. C. Tickner, the guide; Louis Webber, chief packer; and his two assistants. The assistants were in charge of the mules that carried the food, medical stores, stretchers, and spare ammunition. Dr. Semig, a civilian physician, was attached to the group in case a fight developed and someone needed aid. Donald McKay and twelve Indian scouts were ordered to leave their camp at Hovey Point and to meet the column advancing under Thomas' leadership at the base of the sand butte. Both groups were scheduled to arrive there around noon. At seven o'clock the order to march was given.

Pat McManus, the camp sutler who had nearly been killed during the second Stronghold fight, started to go with them, for he wanted to see what the country looked like toward the hills. When he paused momentarily to find something in his tent, Winema unbridled his horse and drove it away. When McManus returned and

[2] Simpson, *Meeting the Sun*, 382.

found what she had done, he was furious, but she informed him calmly that she was doing it "for the sake of your wife."[3]

After the marching column had covered about a mile, the formation changed. The infantry company deployed as a skirmish line running east and west at the front of the advance. Directly behind them marched the two officers, Thomas and Wright, and Tickner, the guide. The two artillery batteries led by Harris and Howe were marched in a column of two's like the stem of a letter "T". Behind the column was a tiny rear guard consisting of one non-commissioned officer and three men, commanded by Lieutenant Cranston. Dr. Semig walked with them.

For a time, no flankers were sent to look for Indians. The soldiers had seen the Indians in the lava flow to their east while they were still in Gillem's camp, and they knew that they were there. As time went by and no evidence of Modocs was seen, the men became more and more nervous. After a time flankers were ordered out, but they gradually drew back toward the main column, though Lieutenant Cranston repeatedly ordered them to march at a distance from the main body of soldiers. One non-commissioned officer, Sergeant Romer of Battery A, finally left the column and walked toward the west by himself, and acted as the only flanker on that side. The bulk of the soldiers closed into a tight bunch, and the officers were too inexperienced to realize that they would all be in serious trouble if they should actually encounter hostile Indians.

Thomas' orders were to move cautiously, not to start a fight; he was to fight only if the Indians attacked. He obeyed the order for caution admirably, for the rate of advance was less than a mile an hour. He delayed mainly to allow McKay and his scouts to catch up, but McKay apparently did not want to join the group, for he moved south even more slowly than Thomas' command.

The country through which Thomas led his column lies between the formidable Schonchin flow where the Modocs were and an even rougher area known as the Devil's Homestead, which begins as a lava fan about a mile and a half south of Gillem's camp, then narrows to a strip of lava along the bluff. Between these two flows the terrain is broken by knobs and ridges of lava protruding through

[3] Meacham, *Wi-ne-ma*, 66.

the topsoil at frequent intervals. This soil lies on top of a much older formation, and bunch grass and desert shrubs cover most of the area through which the men had to march. They had to be careful not to stumble on the small, sharp edged stones that lay loose on the ground thicker than on a New England hillside, but the route was otherwise not too difficult. About three miles from camp is a tiny lava flow which comes from a series of fumeroles known as the Ross Chimneys. This flow is as rough as the Devil's Homestead, but it can easily be avoided.

Men at the signal station watched the soldiers for the first three miles south of camp, and they saw that the Warm Springs Indians had not joined them. About eleven o'clock Captain Adams on Signal Rock lost sight of the marching column which passed around a particularly high ridge of lava. About all Adams could report was that the expedition was doing well, the cannon and supplies were moving, and that they had encountered no Modocs. During the time they could see the men, they received several messages from Thomas saying that he had found no Indians.

For nearly two hours the army headquarters had no way of knowing what had happened to the expedition. Presumably Thomas was continuing his advance, for no disturbance had been heard, and at the short distance of four or five miles, the sound of rifle shots would have been easy to detect. Few people in the camp worried about three companies of soldiers and a platoon of Indian scouts plus several civilians who were moving against only forty Modocs. They didn't expect Thomas to catch Jack and make him surrender, but neither did they expect anything serious to happen to his men.[4]

Although the signal station lost contact with Thomas, the Modocs kept him under observation. Jack detailed Scarfaced Charley to take twenty-four of his men to watch the movements of the soldiers. Quietly moving along the lava ridges and through the cracks of the Schonchin flow, the Indians kept pace with the slowly moving troops, although the route they had to use was much more difficult. About noon the movement of the whites and the Indians converged to the point where the two groups of fighting men were

[4] F. A. Boutelle, "The Disaster to Thomas' Command," (from Brady's *Northwestern Fights and Fighters*) 306.

less than half a mile apart, though the soldiers did not know that the Indians were that close to them. Scarfaced Charley ordered his men to abandon the lava flow and take positions on the top and at the sides of the butte which was the obvious objective of the soldiers. Jack himself came over and joined them.

As the Indians climbed the back slopes of the butte and concealed themselves in two or three rocky outcroppings on the northern slopes of Hardin Butte, the soldiers arrived. The crater on this butte faces the southwest, but on the north slope there is a small depression which in the 1870's was covered with a good stand of desert mahogany. On either side of the depression is a low ridge on which the Indians found ample cover.

The troops marched past, the Indians concealed on their west and east, completely oblivious of the fact that they were marching into an ambush; they continued toward the main body of Scarfaced Charley's Modocs stationed at the top of the butte about two hundred feet above them. As the Modocs lifted their guns to begin the battle, they were astonished to see the soldiers halt, break ranks, and sit down for lunch. The artillery companies and infantrymen were joined by the packers, guides, and officers. The men opened their packs under the tree-like mahogany shrubs and proceeded to eat. No one seems to have thought about putting out sentries, or about separating the troops. They were bunched together like children at a school picnic. Some of the men even had their shoes off, resting their feet only a few minutes after their halt.

Wright did say to Thomas that when no one saw any Indians it was time to start looking for them. Tickner assured Thomas, however, that they were "not within fifteen miles of Jack's camp;"[5] even though fires had been seen a few days before along the edge of the Schonchin flow. As the men took their ease, waiting for McKay's arrival, Thomas, Lieutenant Harris, and two signal men started to climb the hill toward Scarfaced Charley's hiding place. They wanted to signal back to Gillem's camp that they had seen no Indians and were about to return. As Thomas started up the hill, Wright ordered two men to climb the little ridge to their east to scout for Indians who might be coming across from the Schonchin flow. Jack

[5] Yreka *Union* (May 10, 1873).

was concealed in the lava outcroppings on this ridge, and when he saw them coming, he prepared to fire.

The soldiers plodded up the slope, oblivious of their danger. After they had walked about two hundred yards, Jack saw that his hideout was the objective of the two soldiers. The Indian leader and a companion then fired at the climbing soldiers; these shots were the first intimation any of the men had that they were being watched.

At the sound of the two shots, Thomas stopped climbing the main hill, and as the men with him started running down the hill, he stopped them long enough to send the message to Adams at headquarters, "We have found the Indians, they are behind the bluff." This was the only message received from Thomas. Before the report was completed, firing became general, and the army officers were much too busy trying to control their panic-stricken men to send Gillem any more news.

At first the Modocs fired at relatively long range, and the damage was comparatively slight, for they were not expert marksmen. As more and more of the Indians ran from the top of the hill to the little ridges on either side of the hollow where the army had rested, the officers soon realized that they would be completely trapped and exposed to short-range fire. The only way out of this cul-de-sac was to make a run for it between the flanking fire from the Indians or to make a frontal assault up the hill and drive the Indians from the top. As has been indicated, these soldiers were not of the stuff which sent the British up Bunker Hill. Without waiting for any orders, many broke and ran in pell-mell rout. The officers tried to rally some of their men but they were quite unsuccessful.

As soon as Thomas reached the others, he ordered Wright to take his infantry company and charge the Indians who were firing from a rocky ridge about six hundred yards north and west of the butte. He hoped that this diversion might allow the rest of the troops to escape in that direction. The company started, but when the Indians turned their fire toward them, most of the soldiers broke and ran. Captain Adams, anxiously watching from the signal station to learn what caused the firing, saw the running men and misinterpreted their movements. He sent word to Gillem that he had counted fifteen men coming through a rock gap north of the butte, and that the men looked all right. He reported Thomas retreating in good order. That report was as inaccurate as it could possibly be.

Charley detailed some of his men to follow the retreating infantry and to kill as many soldiers as they could. When one of the Indians picked off Wright, all semblance of organization stopped. The rest of the soldiers ran as far as they could before they stopped exhausted or were knocked down by the Indians. Some made it to Gillem's camp, bruised and limping, but over this area of several square miles of lava outcroppings and basins, many others were killed or wounded.

Cranston volunteered to take some of the men and drive away the Modocs who were killing Wright's infantry to their north. Thomas gave his permission to try, but only five men responded to his request for volunteers. Besides Cranston there were three men from Battery A, and two men from Wright's infantry company who had come back to the rest. The six men ran out of the mahogany thicket, but when they turned westward to give Wright some help, they were themselves surrounded and killed to a man.

It was evident that the army's situation was hopeless. Thomas, Howe, Dr. Semig, and Tickner, the guide, took all of the remaining men, now numbering only about thirty-five, and followed Cranston and Wright, with the hope of continuing directly north for Gillem's camp. Dr. Semig found two more men from Wright's company who were slightly wounded, and stopped to dress their wounds. Yelling Modocs pursued the jittery soldiers closely; the Indians left the slopes of the butte and were soon outrunning the stumbling troops. Tickner ran away from the main army, and the Indians let him go. The rest, thinking they were again cut off, turned toward the west and the prospect of more defensible ground.

When Thomas and Howe got to the ridge Wright had been ordered to take, they could find no trace of him or of his company. Wright's body was actually only a little way from them, and with him were those who had died under his command. The rest of Company E was on its way back to the headquarters camp. Thomas saw that there was no hope of finding reinforcements and shouted loudly for Wright in the hope that he might hear him and join them. All he heard in reply was a flurry of shots from the rapidly assembling Modocs. Thomas then looked around and chose a hollow filled with small rocks and sage brush about fifty yards from the ridge. He considered charging the ridge itself, but looked at his demoralized men, changed his mind, and was reported by a survivor to have said, "I will not retreat a step farther. This is as good a place to die as any."[6]

He ordered his little command of about twenty men into the hollow and told them to shelter themselves as best they could. The Indians above them poured a deadly fire on the cowering and poorly concealed soldiers. Here Thomas was killed with most of the rest of his soldiers. Although Dr. Semig was not killed he was so seriously wounded that the Modocs believed him to be dead and did not fire at him again.

About three o'clock in the afternoon, through some momentary and unexplained impulse, Scarfaced Charley broke off the attack. He called down to the helpless men below him, "All you fellows that ain't dead had better go home. We don't want to kill you all in one day."[7]

McKay, meanwhile, still had not reached the butte where he was to have joined Thomas. When the firing began, the Warm Springs Indians turned toward the ridge that Wright was trying to take, but were forced to take cover when stragglers from Wright's company began to meet them. The soldiers were in such a state that they failed to notice who these Indians were. All they saw were dark faces, and they dashed behind cover and began to fire at McKay's men. No amount of yelling helped, for the frightened soldiers were not listening. Tickner ran into the scouts when he left Thomas, and both he and McKay later alleged that they tried every way they could to identify themselves to their erstwhile allies. Every time anyone exposed himself, he would be fired on. When they saw that shouting was useless, the scouts raised their United States army hats —which was about the only uniform they had—and finally sneaked out and captured a bugler of one of the artillery companies. McKay said this frightened man was forced to blow all of the calls "from reveille to tattoo," but nothing helped. The soldiers fired at everything that moved or that they heard.

[6] *Ibid.*
[7] Meacham, *Wigwam and War-path,* 572; Bancroft, *Oregon,* II, 621.

Later in the afternoon a quaking sergeant of artillery was seized by McKay's Indians; he was sure that his hour had struck. McKay told him to take the bugler and go to Wright's men and tell them that the Indians in the rocks near them were friendly. Instead of doing as they had been told, the sergeant and the bugler both fled for Gillem's camp the moment they were away from the Warm Springs Indians. In the state the soldiers were in, McKay's men could probably have gone to Thomas' aid if they had wanted to, but they said later that all they could do to avoid the shots of their own troops was to stay under cover and wait for darkness.

The first stragglers from the attack reached headquarters between one-thirty and two o'clock. This was remarkable time. Understandably their speed was faster in retreat than in advance, but they made the four miles back to camp in less than an hour, an excellent speed over the rough country they had been crossing. Panic proved that the lava beds were not "unpassable," for men with sufficient incentive.

The arrival of the beaten soldiers was the first indication Gillem and Green had that Thomas was not making an orderly withdrawal. In the next few minutes, other terror-filled men ran into camp, incoherent with shock and fright. All they could say was that Thomas had been in a fight and that they had been cut off from his command. Since Gillem knew that Thomas' force outnumbered the Modocs nearly two to one, he was not particularly alarmed and did not order a relief party out. For his failure to send help, Gillem was severely censured, and almost immediately afterward was relieved of his command.[8]

When the sergeant and the bugler released by McKay arrived, however, they were able to give a relatively clear account of what was happening to the men west of the sand butte. Not until then did Gillem realize that Thomas was in need of help.

He ordered Green "to take all the available men in camp and proceed to the assistance of Captain Thomas." Green found about sixty-five men from three cavalry companies ready for immediate duty. Adams signalled to Mason's camp in the Stronghold, who sent

[8] Boutelle, "The Disaster to Thomas' Command," *Northwestern Fights and Fighters,* 306.

Jackson, Kyle and Miller with a pickup force of cavalry and artillerymen from there.[9]

By now it was almost four o'clock in the afternoon. Because of
Scarfaced Charley's unexpected generosity, no more soldiers were
killed or wounded, but the survivors still out by the buttes urgently
needed medical aid. Dr. McElderry, acting chief surgeon, asked
Gillem to be sure that a physician was sent out with Green, and
Gillem told him that Mason would send out one of his three doctors.
He did not order Mason specifically to send one, however, nor did
he check to see if Mason had independently sent medical help. In the
excitement, Mason failed to order a doctor out, with the result that
the rescue columns moved south with no medical facilities at all.

By the time the rescue columns had joined forces, darkness was
settling down. The rest of McKay's Indians came from Hovey Point
and joined the other soldiers after dark. The need for relief was so
acute that the men continued to advance even after night had come.
In the blackness, the leaders of the column became confused and
finally admitted that they were lost. A man from Thomas' command
who had run back to camp joined them, for he was ordered back by
Gillem to act as a guide, but the closer he came to the scene of the
battle, the more bewildered he became until fright made him utterly
worthless as a guide.

At last the situation became so bad and the danger of plunging
over a rocky bluff and injuring the men became so acute that they
were ordered to halt and build some kind of small fortifications until
morning could permit the search to go on. About midnight, five men
lost from the Thomas–Wright command wandered into Green's
position; two of them were unharmed. The three injured men were
sent back to Gillem's with two Indian guides, while the two remaining were asked whether they could guide the rescue party to the
survivors of the battle. They said they could, but they proved to be
utterly incompetent as guides. Before an hour or two had passed,
they admitted that they were as confused as Green's men were.
The rescue force spent the balance of the night gathering rocks and
piling them into small circular fortifications.

While the men under Green's command encamped, uncomfort-

[9] Green Report, June 22, 1873, S.F.P., D.C., 1873, #2773, 1/D.C.

ably, west of the butte, stragglers continued to return to Gillem's camp. Almost every one had a different story, but all agreed that Thomas had suffered a frightful beating.

Those left on the battlefield after the defeat spent a terrifying night. Almost all these men had been severely injured, and they expected to meet a painful death at the hands of the savages when morning came. Actually, the Modocs had left them, and they were in no particular danger. To the anxious ears of the soldiers, the noises of "piling rocks" (being made by their rescuers) sounded like the preparations of Indians for some horrible torture after dawn broke Sunday.

When light came, orders were given for selected men to leave the temporary forts and to look for survivors of the previous day's encounter. Sergeant Boyle of the First Cavalry left his position on the ridge to the west of the butte, which had been the objective of both Thomas and Wright, and made a brief circle of the area immediately adjacent to the rifle positions. He reported seeing bodies not a hundred yards from where Green's men had spent the night.

Lieutenant Boutelle was also looking for injured men, and when he and Boyle met each other in front of the lines, they checked back to the point where Boyle had seen the bodies. There they found Lieutenant Harris and Dr. Semig both badly hurt but alive; the other officers were dead. Most of the small command in the lava basin were also dead, but a few, like Semig, could be saved if prompt medical aid was given.

A request for the doctor brought the information that there was not a single surgeon in either Green's or Mason's party. The first order of business became sending for a doctor, who could also bring stretchers to move the wounded. It took time to signal for aid, and it took much longer for the surgeon to gather his equipment and start for the battle site.

All the men could do was use their limited knowledge of first aid and continue the search for other bodies. The search was undertaken with some trepidation, for the Modocs were watching in very plain sight, just out of rifle range. No one knew whether they would attack again or not. With the element of surprise gone, the Modocs did not care to attack, and they made no hostile moves. Their presence, however, unnerved the jittery troops, and the tired and frightened rescue company was not much better off than Thomas' command had been. Boutelle hazarded the guess that "a few shots from the Indians would have caused the entire abandonment of the wounded in a wild race to camp."[10]

Fortunately, the Modocs did not fire, and the work of finding the survivors went on. Wright was found with four others, all dead, some distance to the north of Thomas. The bodies of Cranston and his five companions were not found until about ten days later.

When Boutelle began to give Dr. Semig first aid, he tried to make conversation as he examined the injuries. Semig was not in a conversational mood, but he told Boutelle where he had been hurt and stated pessimistically that he was certain his foot had been injured so badly that he would die from gangrene. When Boutelle looked at him, he told the doctor that while his foot was hurt so severely that it would probably have to come off, he was not so dangerously wounded that he would die. In his pain, Semig replied with considerable irritation, "Boutelle, do you think I'm a damned fool? I'm a doctor." Boutelle was right, however. Although Semig did lose his foot, he survived.[11]

Others were not as fortunate. When Dr. McElderry received orders to aid the wounded, he got his supplies on pack mules and started for the scene of the disaster with five men for an escort. Though it was now broad daylight, he too got lost. Exactly where he went is hard to say, but he probably swung too far to the west and got behind the rough formation in the Ross Chimney flow which lies south and west of the Thomas battlefield. He reported that he was stopped by this wide belt of lava rock and had to leave the pack train with the guard. He took one Indian and one other soldier with him and what medical supplies he could carry in packs. They crossed the lava slowly and carefully. When he reached grass country again, he cautiously walked toward the soldiers ahead, and reached Green's rescue force just after noon on Sunday.

Before the wounded had been cared for, a storm darkened the

---

[10] Boutelle, "The Disaster to Thomas' Command," *Northwestern Fights and Fighters*, 311.

[11] *Ibid.*, *Northwestern Fights and Fighters*, 309.

sky over the mountains to the south. It turned cold, and flurries of snow were blown in from the hills. Freezing rain fell constantly until after dark. The men of Green's command were ordered to pick up the stretchers that had come out with the original force, put the surviving wounded on them, and carry them back to the hospital in Gillem's camp. Some of the dead were also carried to camp, but others were either not yet discovered or were buried where they were found because of the difficulty in bringing them out.

The loss was appalling. Thomas' force had lost almost as many men in two hours as the entire army had lost thus far in the war. Battery A had nine dead and four wounded, Battery K lost five killed and five wounded. The infantry company lost seven dead and seven wounded, and in addition three men from other units not engaged in the fight who had gone along for the hike were wounded and one was dead. The citizen packer was also killed. As usual, the Modocs suffered no losses.[12]

A thing to be remembered about such casualties was that the units involved were weakened as their numbers were reduced. Replacements were slow in arriving, and some units had not been reinforced since they had gone into action. Infantry companies, or cavalry troops of less than thirty effective soldiers were becoming common. The army's only solution was to move in additional units from other posts. Weakened or not, these companies had to get out of the lava beds or they would be exterminated.

The men walking out of the battle area when darkness fell on Sunday night were led by McKay and the twelve Indian scouts under him. Nine different details of men were organized to carry the stretchers with the wounded.

Some alarm was felt when the Modocs began to build fires in the lava flow to the east, for the soldiers thought the fires a signal for attack. The Indians did nothing to stop the relief force, however. As they moved around the fires, they could be plainly seen, and in the imagination of the soldiers, their movements were transformed into a dance of fiendish glee over the suffering and death they had caused. The Indians contented themselves with following the sol-

[12] Official casualty list, June 12, 1873, S.F.P., D.C., 1873, #1230; E. W. Stone to Headquarters, April 29, 1873, S.F.P., D.C., 1873, #742.

diers closely to see that they did not attack the camp, which contained their women and children.

Attack was about the last thing in the minds of the soldiers. They were cold and miserable and frightened. The work of carrying the stretchers over the rough ground was difficult, and again and again the bearers called for relief. Soon the column began to cross much rougher country than they would have entered in daylight. They even walked for a while across lava where huge boulders had to be moved aside to clear a trail through which the men could carry the wounded. Probably they had wandered into the Ross Chimney flow.

After they had gone through, they found the two mules that Dr. McElderry had left that morning, and the animals set up a tremendous noise. Two or three shots from the distant Modocs were fired to prove that the Indians had heard and were alert if some mule train were moving up to attack. The combination of fire and the shattering noise of the alarmed mules stopped the army in its tracks. Down the soldiers went in the darkness and freezing rain to defend themselves, but nothing further broke the silence; after some delay while some of the dead were placed on the mules, the column began to move forward once again.

The night was so black that a person could not see the man in front of him. The soldiers adopted the expedient of tapping the shoulder of the man in front in order not to wander from the column. The guides had no one to follow, and they had no idea where they were. The stretcher bearers stopped and rested whenever they had a good excuse, and sometimes they stopped without any excuse. Progress was so slow it appeared they would not reach the camp until morning.

Around midnight the storm grew worse. The rain and snow flurries now definitely became driving snow, accompanied by a strong, cold wind. The wounded men on the stretchers had been more than thirty hours with only rudimentary care. The roughness of their handling and the pain from their wounds combined to make an unbearable ordeal. It is a tribute to their conditioning that more of the wounded did not die of shock during that dreadful night.

At three o'clock in the morning the men were still on the trail. The cold had removed the last vestige of courage from many of the soldiers, and these tried to avoid helping to carry the stretchers. What had been a largely voluntary service at first was undertaken only after repeated orders by the officers. Eventually some of the men refused to carry the stretchers even in the face of direct, repeated, and loudly shouted orders accompanied by torrents of profanity.

By dawn the weary column found itself closer to the old Stronghold than to Gillem's camp, so they walked toward that for shelter. The men were bone-weary and covered with a two-day's growth of whiskers which were whitened by the snow. Since they had not taken enough warm clothes when they started out, now they were thoroughly chilled. Their food and water had been inadequate for a thirty-six hour expedition, and much of what they had taken out had been given to the wounded. An army went into the Lava Beds; a motley group of straggling, disorganized and exhausted men returned.

Since the hospital was at Gillem's camp, Green's relief force was ordered to take the wounded there before they disbanded for rest. Surprisingly enough, only one of the nine wounded men died after camp was reached. The last of them was brought in about six o'clock, Monday morning.[13] Lieutenant George Harris had been shot in the back, and while his wound was serious, it would not have killed him had it not been for the carelessness and roughness of his treatment while his bearers crossed the lava the day before.

At that, Harris did not die until sixteen days later. An interesting sidelight to the way affairs were handled in the 1870's is the story that when the casualty notice reached his mother in Philadelphia, she, with no one's permission, boarded a train for San Francisco, took a local to Redding, found a stage to Yreka, hired a supply wagon to the top of Gillem's Bluff, and came riding into the army camp at the foot of the bluff on the back of a mule she had borrowed from a packer. Her heroic trip was in vain, for Harris died about twenty-four hours after she arrived. In the sentimental age when the war was fought, this journey was heralded far and wide as a worthy example of maternal devotion. (One cannot help wondering what army hospitals would do today if the mothers of the injured men

[13] Miller Report, June 22, 1873, S.F.P., D.C., 1873, #2773, 6/D.C.

came walking into field hospitals over the world to interfere in the direction of the treatment of the wounded!)

Perhaps the only profit gained from this patrol was the knowledge that the pack-horse stretcher designed to bring men out of difficult terrain was an instrument of torture. The surgeon wanted no repetition of the medical bungling, and he devised a kind of reclining chair to place on a mule's back to bring out injured men from any future debacle like the Thomas–Wright affair. The specially designed litters came too late to help in this campaign but some publicity pictures were taken of the new stretcher, and everyone felt comfortable about knowing that some measures had been taken to care for the wounded.[14]

Gillem was so disgusted at the miserable performance of the troops who fled that he was in favor of discharging the "cowardly beefeaters." Davis, however, who had not yet arrived, insisted that they should be kept, trained, and made to fight so that they could retain their own self-respect and regain the respect of the Indians.[15]

While the troops from Gillem's camp were recovering from their harrowing two days against the Modocs, new reinforcements arrived at Scorpion Point. Captain H. C. Hasbrouck came in on Monday with a fresh troop of cavalry, and after the losses and demoralization of the weekend, his reinforcement was extremely welcome. His men were tired after their long ride, but their high morale made them, among troops in the Modoc country, exceptional men indeed. Morale among the older troops was at the lowest ebb which it had reached thus far in the war.

Jackson's men returned to the Stronghold on Tuesday, completely exhausted, and not at all eager to fight any more Indians. Hasbrouck came over to the Stronghold to reinforce the other cavalry there, while the Warm Springs Indians went on another scout to find, but not to fight, Jack and his men.

In Salem, the Governor of Oregon hurried his plan to recall the three companies of volunteers who had been discharged in January and those who had been enlisted since then. At the same time he

[14] McElderry report to Green, June 30, 1873, S.F.P., D.C., 1873, #2773, 18/D.C.; Trimble, "Carrying a Stretcher Through the Lava Beds," *Northwestern Fights and Fighters*; Gillem Report.
[15] Davis to Headquarters, May 4, 1873, S.F.P., D.C., 1873, Vol. III, 198–200.

stated that the only people who evidently knew how to fight Indians were the settlers, and the Oregonians had allowed about all the time they dared for the army to defeat the Indians and capture the murderers. By the last week of April the volunteer companies were declared ready, and ordered to the Lava Beds.

Company C, under Joseph H. Hyzer, recruited sixty-five men from Jacksonville and Roseburg. Company D, under Thomas Mullholland, recruited forty-three from the Goose Lake country and west to Klamath Lake, while Company E, under George R. Rogers, raised forty-one men from the Willamette Valley.[16] Although they were not welcomed by the army, they came without invitation and were on Tule Lake by mid-May.

No one knows what Jack did immediately after Thomas was beaten. Undoubtedly the Modoc morale was as high as that of the army was low. A San Francisco newspaper versifier tried to express Jack's reaction:

    "I'm Captain Jack of the Lava Beds
    I'm "Cock o' the walk" and chief of the reds.
    I kin "lift the ha'r" and scalp the heads
    Of the whole United States Army."[17]

[16] 43 Cong., 2 sess., *House Exec. Doc. No. 45.*
[17] Fairfax Davis Downey, *Indian Fighting Army,* 151.

X

FORCED RESISTANCE

San Fran Cal Apr 30 1873

To Col J C Davis
LAVA BED VIA YREKA

I WISH YOU TO STUDY THE SITUATION CAREFULLY AND LET ME KNOW IF POSSIBLE WHAT IS NECESSARY TO BE DONE   LET THERE BE NO MORE FRUITLESS SACRIFICES OF OUR TROOPS   THERE CAN BE NO NECESSITY FOR EXPOSING DETACHMENTS TO SUCH SLAUGHTER AS OCCURRED ON TWENTY SIXTH   ASCERTAIN WHO IS RESPONSIBLE FOR THAT AFFAIR   IF THE TROOPS OR THE NUMBER OF WHITE OR INDIAN SCOUTS & GUIDES AT THE LAVA BEDS ARE NOT SUFFICIENT TRY TO INFORM ME HOW MANY MORE ARE NEEDED   WE SEEM TO BE ACTING SOMEWHAT IN THE DARK

J M Schofield
Maj Genl[1]

WHEN DAVIS READ this telegram, he had already determined to close out Gillem's military career in the Lava Beds. There was little doubt as to the person ultimately responsible for the Thomas–Wright fiasco. This disaster, on top of the escape of the Modocs from the Stronghold, was more than Gillem's reputation could stand, and while he was not relieved of his command by Davis the moment he arrived, the commanding officer personally took over the immediate direction of military operations and sent

[1] Telegram, Schofield to Davis, S.F.P., D.C., 1873, #1946.

241

Gillem back to San Francisco before the month was over. The whole army hierarchy had finally been shocked into realizing Jack's wiliness and endurance.

Sherman sent word to Davis that if he needed the entire Fourth Regiment of Infantry from Arkansas he could have them. A batch of raw recruits from New York was due to arrive in San Francisco any day, and they, too, were offered to Davis. One disadvantage of this reinforcement was that many of the men he already had were little better than raw troops, and more of the same would not help much.

Wheaton was moved by the Thomas–Wright defeat to make a sarcastic comment about Gillem's leadership. "They don't seem to have driven Capt. Jack out of the Lava Beds with twice the force and more guns than we asked for . . . ," he said. "Gillem promised to send for me if any hostile operations became necessary, but he has not done so yet—G. scouted the idea of using Artillery, said the 1st Cav— would show us how to take Lava Beds—after 3 days fighting he calls for aid and 300 more men are sent—how funny— . . . After what has occured [sic] I think Cal– will not be so much inclined to find fault with our withdrawing for more men and Artillery in Jan."[2]

Davis' main difficulty was to find enough troops who were willing to fight so that he could put a force into the field. When he actually took over the direction of affairs on May 2, he found an army organization on paper, but the men lacked confidence in themselves and in their leaders. Davis' first task was to rest and re-equip the men and to help them regain some of their confidence. Until that was done, he had only the Wasco and Warm Springs Indians and the fresh troops that had come in since Thomas was killed who could be sent into a fight. The veteran soldiers were good for garrison duty, but that was about all.

During the week after their victory at the sand butte, the Modocs found living in the lava flow increasingly difficult. Their water shortage became more and more severe, and Jack told them to look for water in some of the lava-tube ice caves east of Schonchin flow. About the time Hasbrouck arrived at Scorpion Point, Jack and his followers shifted their camp across the lava, Counting women and

[2] Letter, Wheaton to O. C. Applegate, May 2, 1873, Applegate Collection.

children, he had about 165 persons with him, and at the moment these were taking his orders, although there was still latent factionalism within his band.

For three days the Modocs spent their time in or near the shelter of an ice cave between the lava flow and Juniper Butte. This cave is now known as "Captain Jack's Ice cave" because the Modocs lived there. In this cave, the Indians obtained water by chopping the ice with an axe, putting it into a sack, and carrying it to their camping spots. This is not a large cave, however, and there is a definite limit to the time that it will supply drinking water for 160 people. When the ice was exhausted, the Modocs used the ice from Frozen River cave a quarter of a mile away.

When that water was also gone, Jack shifted his people to Caldwell Ice Cave, in the higher country about four miles to the south. They stayed at this spot for about five days more and finally exhausted the ice and water supply in this cave. None of these caves is fed by a spring. They are formed from seepage through the lava rocks, and while the rocks are very porous, the rate of water formation is quite slow. When the ice was gone, it would have taken months or even years to replenish it.

About Thursday, the eighth of May, Jack moved his band once more. This time they went east of Caldwell Cave and passed behind three large pumice buttes to a point nearly ten miles east of any spot he had yet occupied. Now, they were almost due south of the army camp on Scorpion Point. The band camped on the shores of a dry lake bed and probably obtained water from wells dug in the sand.[3]

While Jack was moving from cave to cave and from camping place to camping place, the army lost track of him. The Warm Springs scouts went out on April 28 and spent five days trying to locate him. They did not return until Saturday, the third, a day after Davis arrived at Tule Lake.

When Davis heard that the scouts were unable to locate the Modocs, he declared that, while the Lava Beds made formidable obstacles to troop movements, they were not insurmountable. When

[3] For the Indian movements, see digest of interview between J. D. Howard, (Klamath Falls, Oregon) and Peter Schonchin, October 29, 1928. Record on file at Lava Beds National Monument, Tulelake, California.

he could bring his troops back in condition to fight, he planned to send them into action. He also announced that he would try to put an end to the Modoc War with one blow. As soon as it was ready, the army was to stay out until they found the Indians. It would not do to leave Captain Jack at large. Davis, however, did not know that the Modocs were in real trouble over their water supply.

On Sunday, the fourth, Davis sent an informal patrol into the area of Thomas' defeat. Several Indian women were in camp, and he rounded up One Eyed Dixie and one other Modoc, telling them to go out and find where the other Modocs were. The two women spent three days in the higher country to the south before returning; they not only reported that the Indians had left the beds, but that they had also found the bodies of Cranston and his five companions and would lead a burial party to the location. Preparations were made immediately to send out a party to bury the dead that the women had found, but last minute delays held up the burial detail for several days.[4]

Wednesday, the Warm Springs scouts came in again and said that they had found indications which showed the Modocs were somewhere in the southeastern part of the Lava Beds. Some of the officers doubted this report, for always until then the Modocs had been either in the center or the northern parts of the lava flows.

All doubt disappeared quickly, however, for in the afternoon, a train of three wagons carrying supplies to the camp on Scorpion Point was jumped by a band of fifteen to twenty Indians. Two infantrymen and one cavalryman of the escort were wounded, but not so much that they couldn't run away with the others. The Indians seized the wagons and found that they contained a variety of materials.

Official reports say very little about this "Second Battle of Scorpion Point." The casualties could not be ignored, and they appear in the official lists, but Davis dismisses the affair with a single line in his report to headquarters. It is evident that no one was very proud of himself, and it is equally noticeable that the troops were in no condition, mentally, to stand up and fight when they heard a Modoc yell followed by a few rifle shots.

[4] S.F.P., D.C., 1873, Vol. III, 214.

To this day, there is a rumor persisting that a shipment of whiskey was seized by Modocs somewhere between the Stronghold and Scorpion Point. Another account places the encounter near Lost River.[5] Probably the best account of this battle comes from a story told many years later by Peter Schonchin.[6]

According to this account, the Indians captured a wagon train at the east side of the Stronghold—certainly near the site of the May attack; they poked through the tool boxes of the wagons looking for something to break the heads out of the supply cases and barrels. To the surprised delight of the Modocs, they found that the soldiers had been escorting several kegs of whiskey. They seized some tin cups and proceeded to drain the contents of the kegs. In a very short time, the attacking force was gloriously drunk. If a determined counterattack had been made, the Indians might have been rounded up with ease. No soldiers appeared, though, and as the party got more and more boisterous, the Indians abandoned whiskey drinking for chasing the horses, still hitched to the wagons, through the rocks at the side of the road. The terrified beasts plunged across the rough ground with the driverless wagons bouncing and lurching behind them. In a moment there were three runaway teams, and the wagons were smashed to bits before the horses kicked themselves free. The Indians then turned back to the whiskey, which they had unloaded before running the horses away, drank what they could, broke the rest of the barrels to keep anyone else from having any, and went reeling through the lava in the direction of their camp.

If this Scorpion Point fight was the one which Schonchin describes, the reception of the escort when they came into camp without the whiskey supplies can only be imagined. Whiskey or not, eventually Lieutenant Boutelle and twenty-five cavalrymen rode out to the scene of the fight but found no Indians. They did round up the horses and bring them in. The only point of the affair that can be judged with accuracy was that the soldiers had been beaten again.

Davis could not afford to permit his whole jittery army to run away every time they encountered the Indians. Therefore he deter-

[5] Edith Rutenic McLeod, "Two Kegs of Whiskey," *Westways*, Vol. XLIV, No. 6 (June, 1952).

[6] Interview Peter Schonchin by J. D. Howard, September 5, 1924. Digest on file at Lava Beds National Monument, Tulelake, California.

mined to send out a scouting force under a leader who had not yet been in action and whose men were confident that they could beat the Modocs if they met them. To Captain H. C. Hasbrouck, therefore, was given the task of taking B Battery of the Fourth Artillery and of moving towards the spot in which the Modocs were presumed to be camped. He was to see whether he could find them and whether he could get enough efficiency out of his men to fight if he did. With Hasbrouck were the veteran officers, Jackson, Kyle, and Boutelle. Troops B and G of the First Cavalry were ordered to support Hasbrouck's battery, even though their previous battle record had not been good. McKay's Warm Springs scouts were sent along to help find the enemy.

On the day that Hasbrouck left with five days' rations, prepared to look for Indians in the direction that the scouts had found signs of Modoc camps, a small detachment was also sent out to bury the bodies of Cranston and his companions. The wary burial party saw no Indians, but they didn't delay long about the interment of their comrades. As soon as the task was over, they rushed back to Gillem's camp; it didn't take them any thirteen hours to return.

Hasbrouck used most of Friday in getting to Dry Lake. The cavalry and Indians were camped at the Lake, while the artillery was placed about a mile from the water in a little thicket of juniper and mahogany shrubs. At the time, this body of mud and alkali was known officially as "Sorass Lake," and so appears on the reports. Some of the more prudish members of officialdom spelled it "Sourass Lake" for politeness' sake.[7] Whatever it was called, all agreed that its water was unfit to drink.

After his soldiers had pitched camp, Hasbrouck put his men to digging wells in the hope that when they filled, the water would be drinkable. His disappointed and sweating men reported that no water came into the wells, and they had gone down about as deep as they could without shoring up the sides of the excavations. Hasbrouck, therefore, had to announce that the next day part of his command would ride the seventeen miles back to Scorpion Point to bring some potable water for the expedition. This detail was expected to leave camp at dawn.

[7] Thompson, *Reminiscences*, 120.

The Modocs kept a close watch on Hasbrouck's advance. The maneuver of the troops indicated that the Americans suspected where Jack was. If it came to a direct attack on the Modoc camp, the outnumbered Indians would not stand much chance against the troops. On the other hand, if the Modocs made a surprise attack as they had against Thomas or the whiskey train near Scorpion Point, there was a good chance that the soldiers would panic, and another notch could go into Jack's gun.

When the two bodies of soldiers separated to their camps, Jack realized that he had a golden opportunity to wipe out another section of the army. He made preparations at once to attack as soon as conditions were ripe. His men moved silently around the lake when it became dark enough to escape detection, taking up positions on a ridge about four hundred yards from the eastern camp and between the soldiers and Scorpion Point. If the troops tried to escape, they would run either into the mud along the lake shore or directly into the point blank fire of the Modocs.

Just before dawn, Jack gave a signal, and his men began to crawl closer to the sleeping army camp. The first warning that Indians were around came when a dog belonging to Charley Larengel, the boss of the pack train, began to growl deep in his throat. The second time he did this, Larengel became alarmed and went to the officer of the guard, saying that there were Indians around somewhere. When the officer asked him how he knew, Larengel told him that his dog had growled into the darkness. The soldier laughed at him and told the packer to go back to bed.

Larengel insisted so vehemently that he knew what he was talking about that the guard finally consented to warn Hasbrouck. He woke the officer and told him that the "unduly alarmed" boss of the pack train kept insisting that the Modocs were near.[8]

What Hasbrouck said to him was not recorded. Probably he was much too busy in the next few moments to say much of anything, for just then the Indians struck. In working their way through the usual lava cracks, the Modocs had natural protection from the rocks. Suddenly they let out their frightening yells and opened fire. As usual, the first reaction of the soldiers was to run.

[8] *Ibid.*, 121.

Demoralized and sleepy, the soldiers rushed out of their tents and headed for the lake. Two of Jackson's troop of cavalry were killed almost at once, and three or four more were wounded. As they ran in panic, three more fell, one wounded fatally. The Modocs came on at a dead run, firing as they advanced. To the soldiers, it seemed that the Thomas affair was about to be repeated with themselves cast in the leading roles as the victims. Jack was seen, clad in Canby's new uniform, on the ridge to the north of the army camp. Even in the half-light, those who saw him reported that they could clearly see that he was directing the would-be massacre.

Adding to the confusion, the horses broke away when the firing began and stampeded toward the open country. Hasbrouck roared for his officers to come to him and swiftly issued verbal orders which they were to carry out before the Indians actually overran the camp. Boutelle was ordered to try to circle the Indians and get help from the distant artillery camp. Kyle was told to take what men he could and go after the horses before the Modocs captured them. Jackson was ordered to go to the lake shore where the men were huddling in confused terror and to try to rally his men to make a stand until help came from the artillery camp.

By dint of considerable profane exhortation, the officers stopped the panic, and the non-commissioned officers took over. The sergeants of shaky Troop B got the cavalrymen into a skirmish line, and on their left, Troop G took a position under the command of Lieutenant Moss. They had no horses, but probably wouldn't have used them if they had. Fighting as infantry was hazardous, but the cavalry had learned by bitter experience that a horse and rider is a much larger target than an Indian behind a rock and that a disabled horse will put a man out of action as effectively as a bullet wound for the rider. Accordingly, the soldiers charged on foot toward the Indians in the rocks.

The first rush of the men advanced them about two hundred yards before they took cover. The surprised Modocs saw that they had miscalculated somewhere. This "routed" force still had teeth. While the Indians paused during a moment of uncertainty, the soldiers came out of their cover and began to advance once more. As they fired on the Modocs, a chance shot struck Ellen's Man and wounded him fatally.

Now it was the turn of the Modocs to retreat. Surprise was gone, and they were facing a determined, angry, and advancing band of men who acted as though they were trying hard to compensate for past failures.

As the troops moved steadily forward, the Modocs got their second shock. They had the unpleasant experience of being fired on from the rear. McKay and his Warm Springs Indians had outflanked them and were working in to cut them off. The fighting now became savage, and although it was brief, two Warm Springs Indians were killed and one wounded as the Modocs broke through them and escaped, carrying the unconscious body of Ellen's Man with them. By the time the artillerymen arrived, the battle was over; the Modocs were in full flight.

Hasbrouck sent word for McKay to take up the pursuit, for the Indians were retreating faster than his men could follow. The scouts mounted horses which Kyle's men had recovered and took out in hot pursuit of their enemies. Even though they were mounted, they captured no Modocs. They were able, however, to drive away the herders from the Modoc horses, and they captured twenty-four pack animals and most of the Modoc supplies, including powder, ammunition, and even some blankets. These were given to the Warm Springs Indians as spoils of battle.[9]

When the battered and shaken Modocs had made good their escape, they took stock of their situation and found it serious. Before this, in every engagement, they had come out stronger than they had gone in. The arms and ammunition thrown away by retreating soldiers or taken from the bodies of dead men abandoned on the battlefield had supplied the Modocs until now with a fairly steady source of equipment. In this encounter, however, they had lost almost all of their military stores, and of course they had no factories to make more nor any credit to buy powder and ammunition. The loss of the twenty-four animals did not put them all on foot, but it was a serious blow to their pride and financial standing. In losing these horses in addition to those captured by Bernard in January and by Biddle in March, they had lost most of their mobility. Perhaps

---

[9] Brig. Gen. H. C. Hasbrouck, "The Last Fight of the Campaign," *Northwestern Fights and Fighters*, 322.

their most demoralizing blow was the serious injury to Ellen's Man. The Modocs were not accustomed to bear losses, and his wound was a shock to them.

While the Modocs had been winning, the morale in the Indian camp had been high, but these losses brought out all the latent jealousies among the factions of Jack's followers. The simmering jealousies came to a head when Ellen's Man died in the afternoon. Since he had been no friend or supporter of Jack, his friends accused Jack of deliberately placing Ellen's Man in the front rank so that he would be killed. In the quarrel that followed, others stated their firm belief that Ellen's Man was the best strategist among the Modocs and that his death doomed their cause to certain defeat.

The body of the dead Indian was taken to a little clearing about three and one-half miles west of the lake. There a pit was hollowed out of the ground, and brush and logs were put into it. The body of Ellen's Man was placed on top of the pile and the fire was lit. As the flames consumed his body, the Indians saw the watch that he had taken from Canby's body slip into view; it was burned along with the body of the man who had helped kill the General.

When the cremation rites were over, the Modocs went back to the main body of their people. Here they found that the row between Jack and the Hot Creeks had grown to ferocious proportions. Bogus Charley, Hooker Jim, Shacknasty Jim, and Steamboat Frank all denounced Jack for the death of Ellen's Man. This group had been among the most vociferous of the war party in the Stronghold during the peace negotiations and had opposed any concessions to the white men. Now that things were going badly, however, they said they were going to leave camp. Ten of the Hot Creek band said they were going with them,[10] for they feared they would be sacrificed in any future fight Jack had with the army.

It is not known how Jack reacted to the desertion. Just at the moment, the army was not pursuing him and perhaps he imagined that some days would go by before they would make any more hostile moves. He certainly did nothing to prevent Hooker Jim and the others from leaving, although he probably could have done nothing to stop them.

[10] Meacham, *Wigwam and War-path*, 579.

Hooker Jim and his thirteen followers and their families mounted their horses and rode almost forty miles to get completely out of the war zone. They stayed in traditional Modoc country but moved west to the head of Butte Valley, about twelve miles directly south of present-day Dorris, California. They hid in a camp site on the slopes of Sheep Mountain, a peak that stands almost two thousand feet above the surrounding country. Jack's band rode west only a few miles, and camped on Big Sand Butte, just at the edge of the lava flows.

Hasbrouck, meanwhile, began his delayed trip back to Tule Lake and water. The battle he fought in the morning prevented his men from going on the special trip, and he decided that the entire force should withdraw, taking their dead and wounded with them. Because he had only twenty gallons of water left for his wounded men, he gave orders that no uninjured man was to drink anything; all water was reserved for the wounded.

In spite of the fact that he knew the Modocs were in trouble (he did not know how bad their situation really was), his need for water was greater than his desire to pursue the beaten enemy. Camp was struck Saturday afternoon, and the next few hours were spent in going back to Tule Lake with the casualties from the morning's fight.

For a change, his men were quietly exuberant. They were hot and tired and thirsty, but they had beaten the Modocs in a standup fight and had captured much of their supplies. That was something no one else had done, and they felt triumphant. One more fight, they said, and the war would be won.

XI

SURRENDER

THE SOLDIERS spent the ten days following their victory at Dry Lake in chasing the scattered bands of Modocs.

Hasbrouck sat in camp all day Sunday, making out reports which included suggestions that a cavalry column be supported by infantry and artillery. Davis was willing to try this plan and he sent orders to Colonel Mason to take the available forces and head toward Sorass Lake to meet Hasbrouck, who was to try once more to kill or capture Jack Monday morning. The orders were carried out and resulted in the eventual capture of the entire Modoc force.

In order to help accomplish this, another camp had been set up across the bay from Scorpion Point on what was called the "Island," now known as the Peninsula.[1] The "Island" is approached by a neck of land leading down from Bloody Point across Tule Lake and is still a prominent landmark. Here Hasbrouck took his wounded, and here also he turned in his jaded horses. In his report, he stated his opinion that horses were more of a hindrance than a help and asked permission to march his cavalry back to Sorass Lake as infantry. Early the next morning, while he was getting supplies preparatory to leaving, Mason went over to Davis at Gillem's camp to discuss the necessary steps to take in case of a battle.

Before daybreak Monday morning, Hasbrouck left the Peninsula with his marching cavalry column and swung to the east in order to approach Sorass Lake from the ridge at the base of the hills

[1] William S. Brown, *California Northeast, The Bloody Ground*, 98.

between Tule Lake and Clear Lake. Mason also left Monday morning, taking three artillery batteries and three of his Twenty-first Infantry companies. He formed them in a hollow square among the lava flows beyond the Stronghold. To prevent any surprise such as Thomas had met, Mason spread the formation to cover almost three quarters of a mile on each side.

Progress was very slow, although somewhat better than the rate of advance during most of the battles. Hasbrouck had to march his men almost seventeen miles along the bluffs at the eastern side of the valley south of Tule Lake. This area is not as rough as the Lava Beds, but the rocks make marching difficult. In addition, Hasbrouck had to carry his supplies, for now not only did the soldiers carry food and medical supplies, but they also had a pack train with water kegs. The supply services were organized so that a fresh water train would come into camp every twelve hours.

Mason had a shorter distance to cover than Hasbrouck, but he had difficult country to cross. His route took him just east of the Schonchin lava flow and Captain Jack's ice cave. His objective was a prominent pumice butte at the base of the foothills about eleven miles to the south. This butte is distinctive inasmuch as it is not covered with brush or timber as most of the others are. From this sand butte, he planned to swing east and meet Hasbrouck somewhere west of Sorass Lake. Hasbrouck gave his opinion that Jack would probably be on the sandy butte observing any movements from the army camps; the chances were good that they could have their fight near the butte.

By noon, Mason's 150 men stopped to rest and eat in the vicinity of the row of small craters known today as the Three Sisters Buttes. After their stop, the men formed into their hollow square formation once more and headed for the sandy butte (now called Big Sand Butte), which was about four and one-half miles away. Beyond the Three Sisters, the scrub juniper gets thicker, and although the lava crevices are not as frequent as they are at the lower elevations, the men had to cross an ancient flow in order to reach the sand butte. The upshot of it all was that Mason's men did not reach their objective at the base of the Butte until almost 3:30 P.M.

Just as Hasbrouck had predicted, Jack was there, and his Modocs could be seen on top of the bluff as Mason's force approached. This almost perfectly round Butte has its summit almost four hundred feet above its base. The first two hundred feet make for very difficult climbing. The slope approaches a 30 per cent grade, and there is no cover except a few blades of bunch grass. As long as the Modocs held the top and could fire on the climbing soldiers, losses were bound to be prohibitive, and Mason had already proved in the second Stronghold fight that he was not one "to expose my men unnecessarily."

When Hasbrouck arrived, the two leaders considered plans to force Jack from the top of the butte. It was so late in the day that both men felt there was no point in trying to rush the hill with troops already tired from a hard day's march. Jack would keep. When their men were rested, the chances for success would be much greater than if they ordered their weary troops into a fight and suffered heavy casualties.

Mason took his men to a point a mile or more back from the butte and went into camp for the night. Hasbrouck camped a little closer to the butte, but on the southwest side in order to force Jack to stay between them. McKay left his scouts during the night and went back to the Peninsula camp, for he had been sick all day and was exhausted after the long march.

It is possible that Jack would have fought if the Hot Creek band and Hooker Jim had still been with him. His effective fighting force was now only thirty-three men, however, and the combined army force was close to ten times that amount. Probably he knew that he could inflict some losses on any force climbing the butte, but his actions in the past have shown that he was not a barbarian. Even at this late date, if he could have found a way to escape the gallows it is almost certain that he would have surrendered. He continued to defy the whites mainly because he realized that his murder of Canby had made him an outlaw, and that once in the hands of the army he could consider himself a dead man.

During the night, accordingly, he abandoned his position on top of the butte and began defensive measures in the kind of terrain that had hitherto given him his greatest success. He shifted his position from the top of the butte to a position a few hundred yards to the

north and west in the lava flows at the base of the hill. He expected
the army to fight him the next day, and his men were ready in the
strongest position his limited forces could take.

Mason was the first to discover that the Modocs had moved. He
too recognized that here in miniature was another situation com-
parable to the Stronghold on the lake shore, and that an advance into
the lava fields in this dry country should not be undertaken lightly.
He told Hasbrouck that Jack's position was now even stronger than
it had been the day before. As the two men consulted, they agreed
that a frontal attack without some kind of reconnaissance would be
folly. Yet, attack they must.

Normally they would have been right. As it happened, however, Jack's band was now virtually destitute. They had almost no
water, their food supplies were low, their weapons were in deplorable condition, and their clothing was almost completely worn out.
Jack's only hope was to meet the army in a fight from strong defensive positions, and to force them to retreat to the camps along
the lake so that the Modocs could get more water and food in preparation for the next crisis. The very delay in attack, a stratagem
which had previously saved him, now worked against him. Every
hour the food and water supplies got lower and lower, and in a day
or two they would be completely gone. Jack did not dare force the
attack, for he lacked manpower. All he could do was wait, and he
could not afford to wait.

Wednesday morning, Hasbrouck and Mason put their troops
into formation for the attack and had a last minute conference. They
waited until the Warm Springs Indians came back with a report on
Jack's precise location and a suggestion as to the best means for taking the Modoc positions.

The Indians were much longer returning from this patrol than
they had expected to be. When they reported to Hasbrouck, they
said they had taken the extra time because they could not find
the Modocs. They did not want to come back until they were
sure, but they were almost certain that the Modocs had left the
lava flow altogether.

Hasbrouck couldn't be certain that this was true since the scouts
themselves were indefinite. If this move out of the lava were some

new strategic ruse of the Modoc leader, any advance into the rocks would probably result in the deaths of those men who first encountered the Indians. Hasbrouck asked for volunteers for a reconnaissance, and Lieutenant J. B. Hazelton of the Fourth Artillery, and twenty-six men were selected to gamble their lives against the possibility that the Modocs had really gone. The chance paid off, though, and by afternoon the men returned, having scouted the lava field thoroughly; they reported that there were no Modocs in the rocks.

The sense of futility struck Hasbrouck and Mason. Time and again, after escaping the army's attempts to surround them, the Modocs had turned to inflict heavy damage on the next patrol coming within their reach. If the army leaders were not careful, their names would surely head the next list of casualties. They were extraordinarily cautious, and it was not until late in the day that their trackers found the trail of Jack's band heading southwest along the Tickner road. After following it for eight miles until they lost their way in the mountains, they returned to their temporary camps near Big Sand Butte.

The distress of the troops was increased not only by the uncertainty of the Indians' position, but also by thirst. In their pursuit, they had lost some of their water kegs, and as a result were in very short supply. Mason took his command back beyond the Three Sisters to Juniper Butte for his next camp. This put him into the Lava Beds once more and only a few miles from Tule Lake where fresh water was easy to get.

Hasbrouck sent back for his horses. If he had to chase Jack, he did not want to move through the mountains on foot. The animals did not reach him until Friday evening about sundown. It had been almost a full week since the fight at Sorass Lake and Jack was still at large. The army did not know any more about how it was going to capture him than it did a month earlier.

On Friday, Davis sent for Mason and told him to leave his camp at Juniper Butte and go back to the Stronghold. When Mason arrived, he was told that since the Modocs were so far away there was little point in maintaining a watch over the old fortifications. Their camp was to be broken up, and on Sunday, Mason took his men into Gillem's camp. The addition from the Stronghold brought the number of men at Gillem's camp up to full strength once more. Company E, Twelfth Infantry had been sent to Fort Klamath as an escort for the wounded from the Thomas–Wright and Dry Lake fights, who were hospitalized there.[2]

While Mason was bringing the infantry back to the lake, Perry had gathered his cavalry; in accordance with his orders he began to scout the ridges west of the lake, looking for some way to cut off Jack's band from his escape routes. Perry went to Van Bremer's ranch and found no sign of Indians. On Saturday, as his troops were riding to the south and east, they met Hasbrouck's scouting force riding westward. Neither had seen an Indian, and each was somewhat dismayed to meet the other and to discover that Jack had eluded them again. They rode down to Antelope Springs to get water, for Hasbrouck's men had used up their entire supply; then both troops rode back to Van Bremer's where they spent Saturday night.

Sunday morning, the nineteenth, Perry and Hasbrouck dismounted their men and formed into skirmish lines to fight once more as infantry. In this way they sacrificed mobility, but they were better able to find signs of Modocs. Their plan was to spend Sunday exploring the valley south of Van Bremer's in search of Modocs. At the end of the day they would swing together in a pincer movement and perhaps catch some Indians in a trap. Since every sign they had seen indicated that the Modocs were traveling west, the Indians were almost certainly in one of the valleys or on the ridges that separated them.

Perry marched down the east side of the valley, and Hasbrouck's men marched along on the west side opposite Dome Mountain. Jackson with B Troop of the First Cavalry followed the marching columns down the valley with the Warm Springs scouts. These men were mounted and rode down the valley floor, either to block the Modocs if any attempted to escape between the two marching columns or to run up quickly and give aid if one of the troops flushed any Modocs.

Hasbrouck and his marching men had not gone more than a few miles when they crossed a fresh and distinct Indian trail. Like the

[2] Davis to Gillem, May 15, 1873, S.F.P., D.C., 1873, Vol. III, 208.

proverbial hounds on a scent, the men became excited at their discovery. They thought that Jack could not be far away. As usual they were wrong.

What they actually had found, though they did not know it, was Hooker Jim's band, which had come from its safe camp on Sheep Mountain to see what was going on in the valley. If Hooker Jim had stayed on the mountain, the soldiers might not have found him for weeks, but by coming out of his hiding place, he betrayed himself.

Hasbrouck ordered his men to follow the fresh trail. As soon as they started up the steep ridge to their west, the Indians opened fire. No one was hurt, but at once the soldiers ducked behind cover and would not move.

The sound of the rifle shots brought the Warm Springs Indians and Jackson at a gallop. Hasbrouck ordered Jackson and his mounted men to follow the Indians and bring them in if they could. A "hot pursuit" of the Indians took Jackson almost eight miles along the ridge opposite the Van Bremer place, and finally the harassed Modocs scattered among the juniper trees. Ten of their number were captured by Jackson, but he took no men. Five women, five children, and a small number of horses and blankets comprised the sum total of his success for the day's effort. When Jackson returned to Hasbrouck, he claimed to have killed two men, but no bodies were found. Subsequently all Indians were accounted for; obviously his claims were on a par with other such assertions. Jackson was again indulging in wishful thinking.

The horses of the cavalrymen were completely tired out. Jackson was told to return to Van Bremer's with his captives while Hasbrouck and Perry looked for the rest of the Indians. No one informed Lieutenant Hazelton, who was separated from the others, of the day's developments, and he proceeded on an independent scouting operation south of the Willow Creek valley where the fight had occurred. At dark he was still several miles to the south, and he camped for the night in the hills. He did not bring his men in to Van Bremer's until the next day; he had seen no Indians.

The Modocs with Hooker Jim had not expected to be attacked, and in their flight they doubled back until they were north of the point where the skirmish began. They met a teamster carrying the mail to Gillem's camp, and fired on him; the teamster immediately turned back. On Monday, this man asked for an escort, which Hasbrouck furnished him in the form of Lieutenant Boutelle and twenty men. Hasbrouck himself marched over to Fairchild's ranch with his company and camped there on Monday night.

Hasbrouck still did not know that Jack was not with these Modocs. His reports indicated that he thought all the Modocs were still together, and as a result of these reports, Davis sent Mason and the infantry to Van Bremer's ranch to go to Hasbrouck's aid if they should be needed. Mason arrived there on Wednesday.

Even before Mason came, however, Hasbrouck pressed the search for the Indians. On Tuesday, the twentieth, the horses were saddled, and Hasbrouck's company prepared for a riding patrol. As they were leaving, Fairchild asked to speak to Hasbrouck. Fairchild said that the captured women had told him that their men wanted to surrender but were afraid for fear that the soldiers would kill them out of hand. The women told Fairchild that Hooker Jim's band had been coming in to arrange for a surrender when they saw the approaching troops on Sunday. Before they could signal their intent they were attacked. Hasbrouck was skeptical of this claim, but he agreed that a new effort to get the Indians to give up was worth a try and said he would hold up his search if the women would go out and bring their men and the others with them.

The women were warned that the surrender would have to be immediate and unconditional. The army did not propose to be deceived again by the Modocs as it had been through March and April when one promise after another was made and broken with no explanation. With Hasbrouck's assurances that the men who gave up would not be murdered on the spot, the women went out to find them.

The Indians hiding in the hills did not believe their women at first and refused to give up. The women came back in and told Hasbrouck that they could not get the men to surrender, but they thought that if they had a little more time, they would succeed. Davis was informed of developments, and he was also told that it looked as if the Indians were stalling again. He issued orders that after Wednesday night any Indian found with a gun in his hand would be shot at sight. If they would surrender, they would be treated as prisoners of war.

On Thursday, the twenty-second, the Modocs sent word that if Fairchild would go out to protect them, they would come in. Fairchild believed them and went out to meet them. Davis came up from Tule Lake to follow developments and to be present if the Indians appeared. Hasbrouck's and Perry's men were there as well. Gillem came in with some additional troops during the day. Mason was instructed to move from Van Bremer's to Fairchild's.

About sunset, Fairchild rode in with the Indians. There were probably five hundred soldiers present to witness the surrender. To this array of troops were added the usual hangers-on. Everyone was disgusted when they saw that Fairchild had not brought in the expected number of prisoners. Close inspection showed that he had only about a dozen men and a few women with him.

The Modocs were destitute. Their horses were sorry looking nags, skinny and lame. The men were wearing portions of United States Army uniforms taken from the bodies of the dead in the month before. The women were still wearing clothing taken from the homes of settlers the previous November, and these clothes were badly faded and worn with crude patches holding them together. Both the men and women had daubed their faces with pitch as a sign of mourning for their defeat.

They were a silent and distrustful lot as they came into the army camp. The men followed Fairchild closely, and they were in turn followed by their women. The children came in last. As many youngsters were piled on top of the horses as the ponies could carry.[3]

Davis was standing at the door of his tent; as the Indians came up to him, he stepped forward. Each man dismounted and laid his rifle at Davis' feet, until all twelve adult males had given a token of their surrender. Davis asked Bogus Charley, who spoke the best English of anyone in the group, where the others were. Bogus said Jack and his party had separated from theirs. Davis and the other

---

[3] The pursuit and capture of the Indians is taken from accounts and reports by Hasbrouck, *Northwestern Fights and Fighters;* Mason Report, #1251; *Gillem Report.*

officers then asked where Hooker Jim was, since his was obviously the band they had chased on Sunday. Bogus replied that both Hooker Jim and Boston Charley were dead. Steamboat Frank, Shacknasty Jim, and Curley Headed Doctor nodded in agreement. Davis took Bogus and the leaders into his tent to question them about the rest of the Modocs.

While they were talking, a commotion outside aroused Davis' attention. As he lifted his head to hear better, the flap of his tent was thrown violently aside and a panting Indian tumbled in, throwing himself on the floor at Davis' feet. In a moment the frightened face of Hooker Jim lifted itself and looked at Davis. The astonished officer asked him why he had not come in with the rest and why he had told them to say that he was dead. Hooker admitted that he had stayed outside the army camp to see whether the rest of the party were murdered. Since no harm had come to them, he thought he would take the chance to surrender; not trusting the soldiers, he ran past them at full speed and threw himself on the mercy of the army leader.[4]

The Modocs were shown a campsite and were promised that no harm would be done to any of them during the night. The Warm Springs Indians, who were on guard duty, frightened their prisoners badly, however, by honing knives on their moccasins whenever they saw one of the Modocs watching them.[5]

Davis had already informed General Schofield that the Modocs had left the Lava Beds and admitted the possibility that they might be out raiding before the month was out. The Oregon settlers were told what had happened. By the end of this third week in May, the three companies of volunteers called into service by the Governor of Oregon came into the Lava Beds to help in the search for Jack's band. The possibility that Jack might turn south—indeed he was headed south when last seen—caused the Governor of California to send in some volunteer soldiers to help in the capture of the remaining Modocs. In reality, Jack had gone east of Clear Lake, but no one knew this just yet.

With considerable energy, Davis reorganized his plans and troop

[4] Bancroft, *Oregon*, II, 627.
[5] Sacramento *Union* (May 24, 1873).

dispositions. Green was placed in charge of all cavalry forces. At least these were able to act for the job they were best prepared for—ranging swiftly over large areas of country looking for Indians. Mason was given command of all infantry stationed at Van Bremer's and Fairchild's, and Captain John Mendenhall was placed in charge of all foot batteries of artillery, which were told to leave the Lava Beds and go to the Peninsula camp on the east of Tule Lake.[6] Gillem was sent back to the San Francisco area.[7] Mason was given instructions to have his infantry act as guards over the prisoners.[8]

The burning question was how to find Jack and the other thirty-seven Modoc fighters still at large. Actually even these were not all together, but were divided into two or three groups with several families entirely on their own. Since the military authorities did not know this, they assumed that they were all armed, dangerous, and ready for trouble.

Bogus Charley, Steamboat Frank, Hooker Jim, and Shacknasty Jim told Davis while he was questioning them the next day that they were fairly certain about Jack's location. When they were questioned further, the four men gave their opinion to Davis that they could lead the soldiers directly to Jack. Davis was convinced until then that the Modocs had gone south of Fairchild's and were in the vicinity of McCloud. The leaders from the Hot Creek band who were prisoners disagreed. They told Davis that Jack would be either at Willow Creek in the canyon east of Clear Lake, at Coyote Springs southeast of Clear Lake, or at Boiling Springs on the Pit River. There was also the possibility that Jack had gone as far as Goose Lake, although the Hot Creeks said that was not likely. After some discussion among themselves the captive Modocs agreed that the Willow Creek hideout was the most probable spot.

Several moves were made to capitalize on this information. Jackson was ordered to take his cavalry from Fairchild's to Scorpion Point in case Jack should be in that vicinity. Jackson moved around the head of Tule Lake on Friday. The whole camp at Fairchild's was made ready to shift east of the Lake so that the men could be

[6] Davis to Gillem, May 19, 1873, S.F.P., D.C., 1873, Vol. III, 210.
[7] Special Orders 59a, May 21, 1873, S.F.P., D.C., 1873, #1257, 5/D.C.
[8] Davis to Mason, May 24, 1873, S.F.P., D.C., 1873, Vol. III, 213.

closer to Jack if Hooker Jim's guess proved accurate. Hasbrouck marched more slowly than Jackson, but got to Scorpion Point on Sunday, and on the following Wednesday, Perry came into the Scorpion Point camp. When he came, the headquarters moved from Fairchild's as well.

During the period of waiting for the army to transfer its base, the usual rumors swept the army tents. Saturday the men saw Major Hoyt order four horses to be specially shod for a secret expedition. They observed a sense of suppressed excitement and whispered conversations among the younger officers. At noon, several of these men left with their Springfield rifles on their shoulders and cartridge belts around their waists. Although nothing was said, the men were sure that something "big" was afoot. That night, a sense of anticlimax settled upon the soldiers when the officers returned and were overheard discussing the success of a secret duck-hunting trip.[9]

On Sunday, Davis left Fairchild's, but he took a different route from that of the cavalry. With two armed civilians and five soldiers, he started for Scorpion Point with the four leaders of the Hot Creek Modocs, who claimed to know Jack's hiding place. The party did not go around by the ford and the north side of the lake but struck directly over the ridges and Gillem's camp, crossing the Lava Beds past the Stronghold at the south of the lake. They did not reach Boyle's camp on the Peninsula until Monday. There were some who thought traveling and camping in Hooker Jim's company was dangerous, but the thoroughly chastened Modocs offered no harm to anyone.

By Tuesday, Davis was convinced that the four Modocs could be trusted with the job of locating Jack. The soldiers gave Bogus Charley, Hooker Jim, Steamboat Frank, and Shacknasty Jim four days rations and told them to find their erstwhile leader. The four Indians spent the day scouting south of Tule Lake and past Horse Mountain in the direction of Clear Lake.

Since they were sure Jack had gone along the road leading toward the Applegate ranch, Hooker Jim suggested that Jack might not be running at all, but was perhaps planning a raid in retaliation for the activities of Ivan and Oliver in the early stages of the war.

[9] Sacramento *Union* (May 29, 1873).

Perry's First Squadron, with Jackson's troop and Hasbrouck's mounted artillery battery, were sent to Applegate's posthaste on Friday, not only to protect the ranch but also to run Jack to earth if he was in that area. The trip was almost thirty-two miles, and part of it was made through a most unseasonal snowstorm.

As Bogus Charley and his companions approached the place where they thought Jack might be, they were met by four Modoc sentries whom Jack had posted to watch for soldiers. In this way the Hot Creeks discovered that their guesses had been correct. The sentries accompanied the four Hot Creeks until they were about a quarter of a mile from Jack's camp, then abruptly left them. The Modocs in camp came out and formed themselves into a rough line to look over their visitors whom they had not seen since the big quarrel after the Sorass Lake fight. Jack came out, finally, and told the four spies that they might stay in camp, but since they had deserted him after the May 10 fight, they would have to give up their guns and be his prisoners. Hooker Jim refused to allow himself to be disarmed, and all four of them held their guns during the entire talk that followed.

Jack asked why they had come. He recognized the horses belonging to John Fairchild, and he wanted to know where the four Indians had got them and whether the whites had sent the four men to find him. Hooker Jim and the others told him that they had surrendered along with the rest of their faction and that they had been well treated. They advised Jack to give up too.

Jack grew violently angry. These men were the leaders of the group that had put the shawl and woman's hat on him in April when he had talked just the same way. Now these hypocrites were telling him to give up when it was certain that he would be hanged if he did. He declared hotly that he would never surrender and that if he died it would be with a gun in his hand, not with a rope around his neck. He told the four renegades that they could go back and live with the whites if they wanted to, but if they ever came back within gunshot, he would shoot them like dogs.

This was turning the tables for fair. Curley Headed Doctor and Hooker Jim had said almost the same thing to Jack when he had tried to begin peace negotiations back in February. The Hot Creeks did not know how to answer the angry chief, and finally Bogus Charley asked if Jack would leave so that he could talk to his friends without interference. Jack said that such a talk was out of the question. It was they who should leave and at once.

Scarfaced Charley spoke up at this point and announced that he was going to visit with the four in spite of Jack's order. This was something new. Charley and Jack had been very close during the entire trouble, and his defiance of Jack indicates that there must have been some quarreling between the old friends under the stress of humiliating defeat and hunger. Scarfaced Charley told Bogus that most of the twenty-four men with Jack were tired of fighting, running, and starving, and they wanted to quit living like animals. Bogus turned to him and said earnestly that the soldiers were already on the way and that the Warm Springs Indians were with them. An unnamed Modoc bitterly asked Bogus whether he was there to guide the soldiers. Bogus refused to answer, but said instead that the soldiers were coming whether they were guided or not. Jack growled about talk which he had forbidden, but nevertheless Bogus and Scarfaced Charley continued for a long time. When Bogus returned to Davis he reported that Jack's band was disintegrating and that many of them would surrender as soon as they could sneak away from their leader.

On their way back to Tule Lake, the four Modocs met Jackson and Hasbrouck, who told them to wait at Applegate's, for Davis would be there at once. Meanwhile Davis had restored Wheaton to field command after Gillem had been sent back to San Francisco. Wheaton was with the troops again, and he wanted to be on the grounds for the final act of the affair if he could manage it. Jack would either surrender or die within the next few days.

On Thursday, the soldiers who had reached Applegate's were made ready for attack. They knew by this time their enemy's strength, for the Modoc spies had faithfully informed them that they had only twenty-four opponents, and some of them were wavering in their loyalty to Jack. Quickly the soldiers moved to the place where the four scouts had said they could find Jack's band. The Hot Creek Modocs went with them and acted as though they had been in the service of the United States during the whole war.

They warned the troops of a possible ambush, but added that, with the proper precautions, such an attack could be prevented.

When the soldiers had reached a point three miles from Jack, Green divided his force into three detachments and gave each a squad of Warm Springs Indians. Hasbrouck and part of the troops took the north side of the canyon and were guided by Hooker Jim. Green and most of the rest of the men took the south side of the valley, guided by Steamboat Frank. Fairchild and the other two Modocs with the Warm Springs Indians moved up the floor of the creek valley.

The members of Jack's band did not have so keen a watch out as they had had the day before, and the troops were within a mile of his camp when four of Jack's sentinels were seen. The troops halted, and at the advice of Steamboat Frank, twelve men under Lieutenant Bacon were sent around and over a little mountain that permitted the troops to approach Jack's camp almost unobserved. The Warm Springs Indians were within three hundred yards of Jack's camp when three men came out and yelled to them to stop. They asked why so many men had come. Obviously not wanting to fight, the Modocs hoped to talk themselves out of their predicament.

Fairchild, Bogus, and Shacknasty Jim then tried to induce one of them to come close and surrender. The man who came out into the open proved to be the "deceased" Boston Charley. Boston laid his gun down at Fairchild's feet, and the Warm Springs Indians also laid down their guns to relieve Boston of any fears he might have had that he would be murdered on the spot. The usual handshaking ceremony took place, and then the conversation began. All troop movements were halted until it could be seen whether Boston would surrender, and whether others of the band would come with him. More Modocs began to draw closer, and things looked encouraging.

Steamboat Frank went over to his horse; as the animal moved away from him, the hammer of Frank's gun caught in a shrub. The gun fired. Although after a moment's startled silence the conversations with Boston Charley went on, the other Modocs hiding in the outskirts thought that Boston had been shot, and all scattered like frightened jackrabbits. Boston was told by Major Green to try to round them up again, to see whether they could be induced to surrender that evening or the next morning.

As Boston left the Fairchild party, he ran straight into the arms of Hasbrouck's men. They did not know what he was planning to do and did not believe him when he told them. He was just one more Modoc to be taken out of action. He was seized, made prisoner, and escorted to the rear. Fairchild and Major Green waited for more than an hour and a half for Boston to come back. When nothing was heard from him, Green sent Donald McKay to discover what had happened to the Indian. Finding that Boston had been captured, McKay went over to Hasbrouck to get the Modoc released so that he could bring in the others who had run away. By the time the mixup was unsnarled, however, all the Indians except a few women had disappeared completely. Boston came back at dark and told Fairchild that "Queen" Mary and some children with the other women would surrender. These were rounded up, but nothing more was accomplished that day.

Friday, the thirtieth, everything had to be done over, except that by now the Modocs had scattered to the four winds, and they had to be discovered and assembled in groups of two or three. Most of the Indians ran in the direction of Yainax. They followed a dim trail through the high country north of Clear Lake, along the timbered ridge and down the rocky slope leading into the Langell Valley.

The troops doggedly followed the route of the Modocs, and about one o'clock, Fairchild and his party struck a fresh trail. They followed it about six miles to the northeast and were rewarded by the sight of three men who answered their hail but kept on running. The Modocs turned into a canyon and hid when they saw Fairchild was coming after them. Later in the afternoon the other soldiers flushed another small band of Modocs; but thirteen of Jack's men, including Jack himself, ran into the same canyon and also hid.

The Warm Springs Indians discovered the hiding place of this group, and Jack fired a few warning shots in the general direction of the scouts, but missed by so wide a margin that it is doubtful whether he actually intended to hit anyone. The Warm Springs

Indians and Modocs then carried on a long range conversation, which Dr. Cabaniss, the surgeon, joined. Scarfaced Charley came down off the hillside and told Cabaniss that they wanted to give up, for they were ravenously hungry and very tired. Cabaniss and Charley went back to the hiding Modocs, who were quiet but extremely uneasy while they approached. Cabaniss talked directly to Jack and made every effort to persuade the leader to lay down his arms.

Jack wanted to know what they would do with him if he surrendered. The doctor was not authorized to say, but he did make Jack promise that all Modocs would surrender in the morning. It was night then, and the women were weary. Jack complained that no one had either food or clothing; Cabaniss left with the promise that he would return with food and clothing.

When the surgeon returned to the soldiers and told them of his talk with Jack, he was given both encouragement and supplies. The army pulled back five miles to Wilson's ranch in the Langell Valley in order to reassure the Modocs while Cabaniss negotiated. The doctor and One-Eyed Mose carried the supplies back to the Modocs. Food and some clothing were distributed, and Cabaniss remained in the Indian camp all night.

When the surgeon got up in the morning, he found that Jack had pulled out very much earlier. He had given an excuse to the other Modocs that he was going to find a better camp on the bluff, but they knew that he didn't yet dare to surrender and couldn't bear to watch his followers give up. The other Indians were completely exhausted and figured they might as well quit then as later.

Scarfaced Charley was the first one to reach the military camp. He laid down his gun, and it was gravely accepted. Scarfaced Charley had done all his fighting in the open, and although he had killed a good many soldiers with Thomas and Wright, it was believed that no one had been killed by him except in fair fight. He was not treated as a "war criminal" and had nothing to fear for his life. All he would lose by surrender was his liberty.

John Schonchin, who came in next, was in a different frame of mind. He had been among the most vociferous of the war party and was credited with numerous crimes. He had also helped to murder

Canby and Thomas. In all probability he would be hanged, and the fact that he surrendered showed the mental condition that he was in. He was extremely gloomy as he laid down his gun. Nevertheless, he had had enough; he would fight no more.

Nine or ten other Modocs came in one by one and gave up their arms. There were about a dozen altogether who surrendered this Saturday morning. Most figured that they would be hanged or shot on the spot, but nothing dramatic happened. They were taken to Lost River where the rest of the army was encamped and told that they should also camp there. They were not given their rifles back.

On Sunday, June 1, Fairchild and a Lieutenant Taylor with sixteen men for an escort took the prisoners to General Davis, who was staying at the Applegate ranch on Clear Lake. Davis was pleased, of course, to get this band of prisoners, but the biggest game was still at large.

The soldiers could practically smell the end of the campaign, and the whole affair turned into a sort of hunting party. Major Trimble was in charge of the searching troops this morning, and about ten miles farther out from the camp, the searchers struck Jack's trail. They found that Jack had doubled back, had left the Lost River and Langell's Valley, and had run for the Willow Creek hiding place where Steamboat Frank and Bogus Charley had first found him. About five miles up this creek, a Modoc stepped out of the brush and everyone halted. This Indian proved to be Humpy Joe, a hunchbacked half-brother of Jack's. The Modoc asked for Fairchild, and the scout with Trimble's party told him that Fairchild was not there. Joe was warned that the place was surrounded and that Jack had better give up before someone lost his life.

Trimble took a guide and with Humpy Joe went to the creek to call to Jack. For an instant there was no answer, then Jack stepped out on a little ledge of rock holding his rifle in his hand. He still said nothing, but looked at Trimble, who climbed up to him and asked for the gun. Jack then asked whether Fairchild was there; when he was told that the rancher was not, Jack handed over his gun to Trimble. He was reported to have made the undramatic comment that "Jack's legs gave out."[10]

[10] New York *Times* (June 17, 1873).

Effectively, this was the end of the Modoc War. Not all of Jack's Modocs were captured, but they were so few and so scattered that they no longer constituted a threat to the taking of the Lost River Valley by the ranchers. With Jack, John Schonchin, Bogus Charley, Scarfaced Charley, Hooker Jim and the other leaders already in the hands of the soldiers, and Curley Headed Doctor completely discredited by the series of disasters that had overtaken them, the others would not defend what they had fought to keep any longer. Their immediate job was only to find enough food to keep themselves alive.

When Jack himself called two other men who were still with him, they came out of hiding along with their women and children. Two of the Indian women were Jack's own wives, and one of the children was his. He walked over to the Warm Springs Indians, and the general handshaking ceremony that the Indians liked so well was then performed. There was a brief conversation among scouts and prisoners, but Jack did not feel talkative; Humpy Joe did most of the talking for both of them.

All the Indians were then mounted behind Warm Springs Indians and taken on the ten mile ride to Davis' camp.

It was reported that all the way to the Clear Lake camp, the Warm Springs Indians sang a song of victory, which grew in volume as they approached Davis' headquarters. By the noise, the men in camp knew something had happened, and they came out of their tents to see what it was. Jack's arrival, therefore, had something of the nature of an ancient Roman triumphal procession. The soldiers were lined up along the trail, and the captives were taken between the lines of curious soldiers while the Warm Springs Indians continued to sing. When Jack reached the camp, he was silent and dignified. The only break in his composure occurred when he saw Fairchild. He bowed to that white man from the back of the horse he was riding but said nothing; otherwise he ignored the staring eyes of the curious soldiers. When the cavalcade reached Davis' tent, the scouts ranged themselves in a long line and delivered their prisoners to the general. Jack and his younger wife were allowed to change their clothing before they were interviewed, but beyond that the whites made no concessions.

It was late Sunday afternoon, and Davis ordered that Jack be taken at once to the blacksmith and fitted with leg shackles to keep him from running away again. He was ordered fastened to John Schonchin.

When the two head men were separated from the other Modocs, there was instantaneous alarm. All of the prisoners feared the worst, and at once they jumped to the conclusion that Jack and John Schonchin were being led to their execution. Six soldiers were detailed to escort them to the blacksmith, and no one explained either to Jack or to the other Modocs what was to happen. When the little party passed John Fairchild on the way, the agitated Jack asked what was going to happen to him and where they were going to take him. Fairchild did not give him a direct answer, but said it was all right and that neither man would be harmed. Jack then went with the soldiers a little less reluctantly.

Fairchild suggested to an officer that since neither John Schonchin nor Jack spoke English, it would be better if an interpreter explained what was happening. Since Bogus Charley and Jack were not now on speaking terms, Scarfaced Charley was drafted as an interpreter.

Scarfaced Charley relayed the news to Jack that he was to be shackled. Jack and John Schonchin complained bitterly, saying that no one had mentioned this possibility to them when they surrendered. The two men were told that protest was useless, for their surrender had been unconditional. In gloomy silence the two Indians submitted to the indignity, and for the rest of their short lives they were linked together by bands of iron. Both Jack and John had no illusions about their ultimate fate. Bogus Charley predicted freely that all of the Modocs would be hanged.

As soon as the excitement of Jack's capture died down, Davis sent orders to Mason to bring all troops still at Fairchild's ranch and march the infantry to the Peninsula camp, now in charge of Lieutenant Boyle. Davis would join them as soon as he could bring the captives and troops from Clear Lake. The Hot Creek band of Hooker Jim's followers were to be brought to the Peninsula with the others so that all the prisoners could be kept together.

Not until Friday, the 6th, did the troops and their Modoc

prisoners arrive in Boyle's camp.[11] Things were thoroughly confused as Jack and Davis' soldiers arrived, but it didn't take long to bring some order. Acting under orders from the commanding officer, the carpenters began constructing a gallows to hang the ringleaders of the resistance. At this time two new problems were dumped at Davis' feet.

The Oregon volunteers, whom Grover had called into service after the Modocs had escaped from the Stronghold, did not reach the Lava Beds in time to participate in any of the final battles. But they did arrive in time to round up the few Modocs not taken at Cottonwood Creek or those who gave up with Jack in the Langell Valley. Old Indian fighter Ross was again appointed as "General" of the one hundred fifty volunteers, and he made his headquarters in the Langell Valley. Hyzer's company went toward Goose Lake, not only to look for Modocs, but also to look for additional recruits. The main service of this volunteer company was that they met Mulholland and some of the regulars and furnished them supplies. In their own eyes, however, their most important service came when they overtook a dozen Modocs looking for someone to receive their surrender.

The clash between state and federal authority flamed up again. Hyzer delivered the prisoners to "General" Ross, and wired Grover with characteristic frontier modesty, "The Modoc War was ended by the Oregon Volunteers at 12 o'clock last night."[12] Grover replied at once congratulating the settlers and ordering Ross to pick out any murderers of white men and turn them over to the Jackson County sheriff for execution.

When Davis heard of this exchange, he sent an escort to bring *all* Modocs to the base camp as prisoners of war. His message told Ross that these Indians were not to be tried by civil courts, for the state had no jurisdiction over them. Any trials that were conducted were to be by court martial. At first Ross ignored Davis' position and orders.

When the Oregonians tried to identify the murderers who had been indicted, they found themselves in difficulty at once. Using

[11] Wheaton report to Headquarters, October 5, 1873. S.F.P., D.C., 1873, #2773.
[12] Sacramento *Union* (June 6, 1873).

standard procedure, they showed the Indians to some of the widows of murdered settlers, including the Boddys. Although the women had given the names of the Modocs they met in November, they were unable to identify even Black Jim, the best known of the Modocs whom Hyzer had captured. If they couldn't recognize anyone as prominent as he, the chances of their knowing some of the less important Indians were poor indeed.[13]

Ross must not have been completely bloodthirsty, for he told Davis since he couldn't identify the killers he could take over all the prisoners, murderers and all. Davis reassured him that there would be some executions, for the gallows was being built, and seven or ten Indians would be executed before the day was over.[14] Thus, the first problem was resolved.

Davis honestly believed that the best way to end Indian resistance throughout the frontier was to execute the ringleaders of the Modoc War as quickly as possible as examples to other desperate red men. Subject only to the countermanding of his orders by higher authority seven or more men were to die at sunset Friday. Being a dutiful officer, he had wired Sherman and Schofield of his plans, and when he got their reply, he was faced with his second problem.

Both Schofield's office at Pacific Headquarters and the War Office in Washington were concerned over the legal question of trial for the murderers and the nature of a trial court. Until this technicality could be settled, there were to be no hangings or shootings.[15] In a wire to Davis, Sherman authorized the leaders to be hanged only when properly identified and convicted, and he also authorized Davis to spare the Hot Creeks who had helped capture Jack if in his judgment it was wise to encourage Indians to betray rebels.

Davis was greatly annoyed by this second jolt of the day. As he read the telegram, he blurted out in the hearing of some civilians, "If I had any way of making a living for my family outside of the army, I would resign today!"[16] He sat down and wrote a protest to headquarters against allowing lawyers to interfere with operations

---

[13] Thompson, *Reminiscences*, 121.
[14] Bancroft, *Oregon*, II, 632.
[15] Telegram, Sherman to Davis, S.F.P., D.C., 1873, #1968.
[16] Thompson, *Reminiscences*, 127.

in the field, "Your dispatch indicates long delay in cases of these red-devils which I regret. Delay will destroy the moral effect which their prompt execution would have upon other tribes as also the inspiring effect upon the troops."[17]

Davis then went out to the prisoners and relieved his feelings by delivering a tirade against the Modocs. He charged that ever since the white men began to travel through or settle in the country, the Modocs had been known as a merciless band of robbers and murderers. He then turned directly to Jack and said: "Even among your Indian neighbors you are known as a domineering and tyrannical tribe. Old settlers in the country report as many as three hundred murders committed by your people. . . . For these many crimes no adequate punishment upon the guilty, even as a tribe or individually has been made. . . . A few years ago, regardless of these acts of treachery, the government gave you a reservation of land for a home, where, if you chose, you could have remained and enjoyed the annual bounties of the government unmolested. . . . You all went upon the reservation and part of your tribe has remained, but you and your band seemed to have preferred the warpath. You left the reservation, you spurned the kindness of the government, and even resisted the soldiers in the execution of their duty in forcing you to the reservation. . . . Now that I have recounted your history and that of your tribe, the recent acts of yourself and band, I will close this interview by informing you that I have this day directed that you and your confederates, members of your band, be executed. . . . While I was preparing a list of those I intended to execute, a courier arrived from Washington, saying, "Hold the prisoners till further orders."

If Davis was angry at the delay over the executions, the Oregonians in camp were even more furious. Not long after Colonel Davis returned to his tent, and while he was talking to several men, the correspondent for the New York *Herald* rushed in and blurted that Mrs. Boddy and Mrs. Schira were trying to kill the Indians. A quick investigation showed that Mrs. Schira had a double edged knife in her hand which she was trying to use on Hooker Jim. Mrs. Boddy had a gun which she did not know how to cock. Davis dis-

17 Davis to Headquarters, S.F.P., D.C., 1873, Vol. III, 217.

armed the women, and in the process got his hand cut by Mrs. Schira, who apparently recognized Hooker Jim as one of the men who had killed her husband.[18]

The Modocs in captivity must have been a subdued lot that Friday night. The gibbet was almost completed, and if they were not convicted by one court, the Oregonians had no intention of allowing any double-jeopardy clauses in the Constitution to prevent them from hanging those they wanted to hang. In addition, the prisoners had to witness the celebration of their humiliation by their enemies, the Warm Springs Indians.

That night, with the army as an interested audience, the scouts put on an informal dance-history of the war. The entire war was acted out in pantomime. First, the Warm Springs Indians portrayed the Modocs before the war started. They showed the Indian women toiling under their loads; the actors took the parts of the soldiers and fought the battle of Lost River. They pretended to struggle through the fog-shrouded lava fields in the January battle for the Stronghold. They showed the soldiers being surprised, slain, and stripped of their clothing by the triumphant Modocs. Each of the major battles was depicted. The Modocs were finally driven out of the Stronghold. Wright and Thomas were killed, the Battle of Sorass Lake was fought, and finally the flight and capture of the scattered bands was shown. All of this was accompanied by drum beats, with yells of the Indians for supplemental sound effects. A sort of chanting in recitative interpreted the actions in the dance. The dance lasted for hours, with only the light from the flickering camp fires built to illuminate the pageant ground. The effect of the barbaric scene was such that those who witnessed it never forgot it. Everyone was there and all sat in fascinated attention.[19]

Most of the following day was spent waiting for some official decision as to the best legal way to hang some Modocs. The judge advocate for the Department of California sent his opinion that a court martial could apply only where there was statute law, which certainly did not exist for the Modocs. Only by the application of

[18] Thompson, *Reminiscences*, 128–30.
[19] Don C. Fisher, "A Brief History of the Modoc Indians and Their War Fought in 1872–73," Unpublished typewritten MS, Lava Beds National Monument, Tulelake, California.

some sort of a common law of war could the Modocs be tried, and that before a military commission. Another smaller point was whether this was a real war or only a "police measure." If the Modocs were not citizens—and they certainly were not that in 1873—then they were not answerable to any laws either of the United States or of the State of Oregon. Custom decreed that acts of treachery or attempts to kill a man already disabled were punishable by death. Beyond that, none of the Indians could legally be tried in an American court for what was not construed to be a crime under their own rough code of laws. A formidable array of precedents was cited to support this conclusion.[20]

This legal decision was considerably different from the suggestion by bluff old General Sherman that Davis should shoot the leaders, hang the murderers, put the rest of the men in Alcatraz, and disperse the women and children among other Indian tribes so that in a generation or two of intermarriage the Modoc identity would be completely lost. Even Sherman bowed to an opinion by the Attorney General of the United States, who wrote the President, also on Saturday, that the "common law of war" precluded hanging the Modocs without trial. Precedent was also cited mentioning trials of some parole violators during the Mexican War and also others who were recaptured during a battle in which they fought after their surrender, parole, and exchange in the Civil War. The murderers of Lincoln were tried by a military commission. The conclusion reached was that the only crime the Indians had committed during the entire war was a violation of an implied truce. Even savages considered this a crime. Those who fired on Sherwood and Boyle and killed the peace commissioners on April 11 were to be tried, and if found guilty, they were to be executed. Since no one else, by Modoc standards, had committed any crimes, they were to be treated simply as prisoners of war.[21]

When the news of the decisions to postpone the hangings reached the citizens of Oregon, there was a great deal of grumbling about federal interference. Even the troops were angry that the hangings had been put off. The upshot of it all was that a group of

20 Curtis to Schofield, June 7, 1873, S.F.P., D.C., 1873, #2145.
21 43 Cong., 1 sess., *House Exec. Doc. No. 122*, 86.

disgruntled settlers determined to lynch a few Modocs to express their disapproval.

An undetermined number of Modocs were still at large. There were probably at least a dozen. Four of these came in to Fairchild's ranch in the early part of the week and gave themselves up, along with their wives and children. They were sent to the Peninsula at once. John Fairchild's brother James drove the mules which pulled the wagon loaded with this group of newly surrendered prisoners. They started on Saturday, the seventh, over to Boyle's camp to be with the other prisoners. No attempt had been made to keep this information from anyone, and they became the objects of the lynching plot.

As the wagon crossed the Lost River ford, it was met by some of Hyzer's volunteers—the majority of whom had been recruited in the Klamath country. Fairchild identified himself, and was allowed to go on with the prisoners. Hyzer's men turned to the west, while Fairchild drove east.

As the wagonload of captives reached Adams Point, perhaps seven miles beyond where Fairchild met Hyzer's men, two unidentified persons rode up to Fairchild and stopped him. They might have been settlers; if so, Fairchild covered up for them, because he swore he had never seen them before, and he knew every man in the Klamath Basin. Fairchild's assertion that they were strangers gave strong support to the charge that they were members of the volunteer forces from some other part of the state. Whoever they were, they were not in uniform. This meant little, for none of the volunteers wore uniform clothing.

The two men ordered Fairchild to get down from the driver's seat; when he objected they forced him to do so at gunpoint. While one man kept Fairchild covered, the other cut the traces of the mules and drove them away from the wagon. By this time, the terrified prisoners were sure their hour had come. In the case of four of them, this belief was justified.

The two white men fired into the wagon at almost point-blank range. Little John, Tee-He Jack, Pony, and Mooch were killed outright. Little John's wife was also shot for good measure, but this seems to have been an accident. She was not fatally wounded, and she lived to tell the tale, although she could not identify her husband's murderer any more than Fairchild could. While Hyzer was absolved of all responsibility, he made no effort to determine what the shooting was about or to apprehend the white men who killed the Indians. It would probably have been too much to expect Oregon volunteers to arrest any white man for the killing of an Indian in early June, 1873, no matter how flagrant the murder.

A squad of ten artillerymen and a non-commissioned officer did come when they heard the disturbance, and remained to guard the wagon against further attacks. Word was then relayed to Davis, who quickly sent an officer with fifteen men to bury the dead Indians on the spot and to bring the others in to the Peninsula.[22] He made no effort to catch the killers but the deed had the effect of separating further the army and the civilian population in their attitude toward the Modoc prisoners.

This was a violent age. Reconstruction in the South was still running its course, and sudden death in the mining camps of California or Nevada was not uncommon. The desperadoes of the middle border were making names for themselves from Texas to Minnesota. Lynching was not considered a crime by many people, even though most men disapproved of settling a personal quarrel with a gun. The murder of the unarmed Modoc prisoners may have shocked the humanitarians in Philadelphia, but it did not ruffle the frontiersmen. There was never any investigation, official or unofficial, and it is unlikely that the killers could have been convicted of anything more serious than a breach of the peace.

Superintendent Odeneal made a half-hearted attempt to get Dyar to investigate the murders, but Dyar made all sorts of excuses. Public opinion was the main reason. "It would be better for a stranger to the people of this section to take the case in hand," he said. He cited the difficulty in gathering evidence. He claimed that his duties at the agency took all his time. Obviously some kind of unknown pressure was put on him to prevent an investigation. Odeneal took the hint and never mentioned the embarrassing matter again.

[22] Davis orders to Green, June 8, 1873, S.F.P., D.C., 1873, #2773, 3/D.C.

President Grant received a new spate of letters from the indignant Philadelphia and New York friends of the Indians. One man with heavy sarcasm intimated that it would be a splendid idea to have the Warm Springs scouts "employed to kill and scalp the white ruffians of Oregon," although deploring an application of Sherman's policy announced for the Modocs. The writer thought it would be wrong to order "utter extermination of all the border ruffians of Oregon, and the women and children belonging to them."[23]

Those who denounced the Oregonians were as intemperate in their charges as the westerners were against the Modocs. The charges stated that the settlers were really responsible for the murders of Thomas and Canby. They urged that the murderers be found, tried by a jury of some other than Oregonians (who would naturally acquit them) and be executed with Jack on the same gallows. Another denounced both Davis and Gillem for their harsh treatment of the prisoners.[24]

To Davis' credit, he refused to be stampeded by the hot tempers and denunciations that rattled around him like spent grapeshot. Probably he was toughened by the withering criticism he had endured during the Civil War. To his discredit, he did absolutely nothing to apprehend or punish the murderers of his prisoners. He decided to avoid further trouble by taking the surviving Modocs to Fort Klamath under heavy military guard and holding them there until they could be tried and the guilty ones punished.

Meanwhile, some of the cavalrymen, deciding that the war was over, made plans to flee from the Lava Beds. There had been intermittent desertions throughout the entire campaign, but these men all left at once. They were apprehended after only a short period of A.W.O.L. and promptly became parties of the first part in a court-martial proceeding charging them with "theft to the prejudice of good order and military discipline," and desertion. This charge meant that they had stolen their horses and gear when they tried to desert. All of the culprits pleaded guilty and were sentenced to

---

[23] Letter, George M. Coates to President Grant, June 11, 1873, *Oregon Superintendency, 1873,* Office of Indian Affairs.

[24] *Oregon Superintendency, 1873,* Office of Indian Affairs.

seven years at Alcatraz; during this time they had to wear a ten-pound ball attached to their left leg by a three-foot chain. So much for military jurisprudence in the nineteenth century.

On Wednesday, the eleventh, Davis ordered Jackson back to Fort Klamath with Troops B and K of the First Cavalry, to build a stockade and shelters for the use of the prisoners until the military commission could assemble. At this time, he had forty-four men, forty-nine women, and sixty-two children in his custody. There were only about three Modoc men still uncaptured, and they were either unimportant, or if needed (like Miller's Charley, who had killed Sherwood), they would likely be picked up in a few days or weeks.

Jackson went to Klamath and built a stockade 100 feet long, by 50 feet wide. He used twelve foot logs, sunk three feet in the ground as a fence. Roughly a third of the space had another fence across it. The Hot Creek band was to be placed in the smaller area, while the Lost River band (Jack's) were to be in the larger area. This work was to be completed as quickly as possible, for Davis wanted to start for the Fort with the prisoners and the troops not later than the next Sunday. Davis certainly did not plan to have his prisoners rattling around when they got there. The space allotted to each person averaged four feet by eight feet. This was enough room for each Indian to lie down to sleep but that was about all. In this tiny area, arrangements had to be made for cooking, living, visiting, sleeping, and all toilet and sewage facilities. It was a true concentration camp.

By Saturday, the fourteenth, Davis was ready to move the prisoners and the troops. The prisoners, traveling under the escort of Mason's Twelfth and Twenty-first Infantry to Fort Klamath, were placed in wagons for a journey of several days. Many of the prisoners were shackled together as Jack and John Schonchin were. During the first night, Black Jim and Curley Headed Doctor, who had been ironed together, thought they saw a chance to make their escape. They began to run, but were instantly pursued by soldiers. Their flight was short, however, for the chain between them caught on a sagebrush and tripped them. Black Jim came up with a bloody nose. The two Modocs sat and nursed their bumps, cursing all the while in a mixture of English and Modoc obscenities. They received scant sympathy from the soldiers and were kept from further mischief, for their chain was fastened to a stake pounded into the ground. The prisoners once secured, the soldiers went back to their other duties.[25]

Another prisoner made a more successful attempt to escape. Curley-Headed Jack, one of the three men who killed Lieutenant Sherwood, somehow got a gun and hid it under his clothing. He knew that his chances of acquittal were almost hopeless, and he was determined that he would not permit himself to be hanged, for the Modocs believed that strangulation would prevent the soul from leaving the body.[26] While the attention of his guards wandered, he quickly pulled the gun out and shot himself through the head.

The sound of the shot brought the infantrymen on the dead run, but when they saw that the Indian had killed himself they dug a grave, gave him an unceremonious burial in an unmarked grave beside the road, and then moved on.[27]

These two incidents were all that marked the serenity of the trip to Fort Klamath, and by the end of the third week in June, the prisoners were in the stockade.

Since not all of the remaining soldiers would be needed for guard duty and since the officers felt the need to cut military expenses as quickly as possible, they decided to march several of Green's cavalry units and the Twenty-first Infantry commanded by Mason back to Fort Vancouver. Five troops of cavalry and three of infantry with Battery E of the Fourth Artillery started a long, six-hundred mile hike to headquarters by way of eastern Oregon and the Columbia Valley. This trek would not only get the men to Vancouver cheaply but it would also quiet and overawe any of the other Indian bands of the Columbia Plateau who might be encouraged to start trouble by the example of the stout defense put up by Jack's microscopic army.[28] This was a big parade, but was not an outstanding success as far as subduing the Indians was concerned. The Snakes who had abandoned the Yainax station were not induced to come back, and

[25] Riddle, *Indian History*, 151.
[26] McLaughlin, *My Friend the Indian*, 330.
[27] Meacham, *Wigwam and War-path*, 604.
[28] *Ibid.*, 581; Bancroft, *Oregon*, II, 634; Special Orders 56a, June 19, 1873, S.F.P., D.C., 1873, #1381.

no one tried to force them to come. Apparently no settlers wanted their range. The Nez Percés living in the Wallowa Mountains were definitely not overawed. The white settlers did want their range, and those Nez Percés who fought back four years later defeated some of these very same troops. David Perry, a captain by 1877, had the dubious distinction of being the first regular officer to be beaten by Chief Joseph.

All of the artillery except Battery E, and Hasbrouck's Battery B were left at the Peninsula camp under Captain John Mendenhall, but they began at once to carry out orders which transferred them to San Francisco. By the end of June there were neither soldiers nor Indians in the Lava Beds.

XII

TRIAL AND SENTENCES

WHEN THE CAVALCADE REACHED Fort Klamath, the prisoners were put into the stockade at once, where they were to stay until their leaders could be tried and punished. The most important men, including Jack, Boston Charley, Black Jim, John Schonchin, Slolux, Barncho, and seven others were placed in the fort guardhouse. Miller's Charley was still at large, and Curley Headed Jack was a suicide. The identity of the third man in the Sherwood killing could not be learned. The "Modoc Bloodhounds," Hooker Jim, Bogus Charley, Shacknasty Jim, and Steamboat Frank, were allowed to stay outside of both prison and stockade as a reward for their services. Scarfaced Charley was also given his freedom, probably out of respect for a tough antagonist who played it according to the white man's rules. He was required to stay on the Fort grounds but was otherwise free to go and come as he pleased.

The guardhouse where Jack was kept was a small, stout building thirty feet long by forty feet in width. It was divided in such a way that there were two small cells at one end. One of these housed the young men, Barncho, Slolux, and Boston. The other contained the quarters of Jack and John Schonchin. Black Jim stayed outside the cells in the large "tank" room with the seven other Modocs. While these were not murderers, they were still considered dangerous enough to keep in confinement. Around the walls of this room were placed bunk beds, upon which the Indians could sleep, sit, or talk.

By the end of the month of June, all doubts were resolved about which Indians the commission should try. Identification by Mrs. Boddy was necessary before any convictions could be obtained in a civil court for the murders committed against the civilians in November. She was thoroughly confused. She had identified some who were not there and had shown herself unable to identify Black Jim, who was almost undoubtedly among the killers. In addition, because of the growing antagonism between civil and military authorities, the President's cabinet and the army gave scant consideration to the desires of Governor Grover of Oregon and his advisers.

On the thirtieth of June, the United States Attorney General ruled that only the actual killers of Canby and Thomas should stand trial. Sherwood's killers were to be ignored, even if Miller's Charley should be caught later.

Colonel Davis wanted to get one thing cleared up before the actual trial began. He had heard rumors during and after the fighting that the Klamaths and Schonchin's band at Yainax were encouraging the men of Jack's band to fight, all the while protesting their loyalty and devotion to the white men. He called for Allen David, Old Schonchin, Jack, and John Schonchin for an interview on the last Thursday of June so that he could clear up some rumors before the following Wednesday when the trial was scheduled to get under way.

With Toby Riddle as interpreter, Davis questioned each man sharply. Allen David did not always give direct answers to the questions put to him but kept protesting the good intentions of the Klamaths and their loyalty to the whites. He denied knowing that any Klamaths furnished ammunition to the Modocs. He denied that any Klamaths molested the Warm Springs Indians while they were serving with the army. He denied sending any messages to Jack while the fighting was going on around the Stronghold.

Old Schonchin also denied any improper negotiations with Jack. He admitted keeping some money for his brother John, but did not know where it had come from. Jack said that both Boston Charley and William had insisted that Old Schonchin brought a message from the Klamaths encouraging the murder of the commissioners, and promising help if they were killed. Bogus Charley and Steamboat Frank had also said this was so, and Bogus had been the one who told Davis. Schonchin denied it outright, and that was that. Jack had not talked himself out of responsibility for the murders. The best he could do was to act like a small boy pointing a finger at another child and saying, "He told me to do it." Jack was an adult, however, and he could not escape the consequence of his killings by charging that Allen David or Old Schonchin had put him up to it. He did succeed in sowing some doubt in the minds of the whites about the reliability of the Klamaths and Schonchin's band.[1]

Lieutenant Colonel Washington Elliott of the First Cavalry came to Fort Klamath for the trial in order to act as senior officer on the military commission. The judge advocate for the California area, Major H. P. Curtis, came with him. Other than these two, the trial court consisted of the men who had fought Jack. Mendenhall, Hasbrouck, Captain Robert Pollock, who had been commanding officer of the supply base at Fort Klamath during the fighting, and Second Lieutenant Kingsbury of the Twelfth Infantry made the balance of the court.

It is difficult to evaluate the trial that followed. In some ways, the Modocs were victims of gross injustice. They were given no counsel, and they understood very little English. As a consequence, charges could be made against them which they would not even understand, and although they were allowed the right to cross-question the witnesses, this privilege did Jack little good, since he couldn't speak the language of the court. This glaring inconsistency struck even the contemporary, prejudiced mind. On the other hand, the court leaned over backward to permit the Indians to bring any shred of information to light that might help their case. The court overlooked breaches in regular procedure, since it seemed to be making an honest effort to ascertain the truth and was not too much concerned with protocol. It was evident to the Indians that they were going to be hanged, and several of them turned defiant or hopeless and virtually refused to defend themselves. Those who did participate defended themselves rather poorly and worked through interpreters who have been accused of incompetence. The transcript of the trial is clear enough, however, so that the accusation of incompetence does not seem to hold up.

[1] Report of Davis' interview with Indians, June 26, 1873, S.F.P., D.C., 1873, #2161.

The first day the court met, proceedings were stopped because arrangements had not been completed. Court recessed over the Fourth of July holiday, then met again on Saturday, July 5.

Everyone in the area was present. Only the six Modocs who had actually participated in the murder of Canby and Thomas and who had not served the army in helping to round up their fellows were made defendants. Proceedings were naturally drawn out, for each item of business had to be interpreted to the Indians. They listened to the calling of the commission into session and the minutes of the first meeting. The defendants were then asked whether they had any objection to the members of the trial court. Just what would have been done if an Indian had objected was never decided. The Modocs were in a state of apathy at the time, however, and raised no objection to anything proposed to them.

Since no objections were heard, the commission members swore each other in (which ceremony was duly interpreted to the Modocs), and the trial was under way. Frank Riddle and Toby, his wife, were sworn in as interpreters and paid $10 per day while the trial lasted. The Modocs were asked who their counsel was to be, a rather silly question, for they had had consultation with no one. Since they admitted they had no counsel and no one was assigned to defend them, they were presumed to act as their own lawyers.

The charges were read; each was charged with murder in violation of the laws of war, (Canby and Thomas) and assault with intent to kill in violation of the laws of war, (Meacham and Dyar). Each prisoner was asked how he pleaded, and each stood up and replied, "Not Guilty" to all counts.

Frank Riddle was called as the first witness. It seems peculiar that a court official should also be a witness for the prosecution, but this was almost in the nature of an inquest rather than a trial. The only trouble from the Modoc point of view was that the inquest also had the power to determine guilt and to pass sentence. Riddle's testimony added nothing that had not been known. It merely made this information a matter of the official record. He told a little of the military organization of the Modocs, grading it from Jack the "chief," through Schonchin the "sergeant," Black Jim, a "watchman," to Boston, who was nothing more than a "high private."

Barncho and Slolux were described as "not anything." He told of his visits to the lava Stronghold, Toby's warnings, and Canby's refusal to take precautions against treachery. He said his own warnings were unheeded by both Canby and Gillem. He testified as to the speeches delivered at the fatal conference, stated that he had seen the Modocs armed, and that instead of the five men promised, there were eight in sight with two more armed men in the rocks behind him. He admitted that he had run as soon as the shooting started and had not looked back, so beyond this time his testimony could no longer be that of an eyewitness.

His wife was then called, and she also gave her account of the warnings, concluding her testimony by telling what happened after her husband started to run. The Modocs did not question her testimony. When she was done, Dyar was called, and he identified the prisoners as those who were present when the attempt was made on his life.

The next day, the Indians told their story to the court.

First to testify were the four Modocs who had helped run Jack down. They gave evidence for the prosecution. They had been promised virtual immunity by Davis and were willing to testify against their former associates. They had also been reassured by the specific statement, "You will not be hurt—you shall not be hurt."[2]

Shacknasty Jim was first. Since he did not think he would be hanged, he admitted quite freely that he had been at the council on the Thursday night before the murders. He further admitted that he had been present when Canby was killed. Steamboat Frank denied being at the killing, but said he had watched it from the distance of about a quarter of a mile. Bogus Charley confessed that he had been present when Canby was killed. Hooker Jim also admitted participation, and each implicated Jack along with the others who had been there.

Hooker Jim was almost plaintive when he was asked whether he was a friend of Captain Jack. "I have been a friend of Captain Jack, but I don't know what he got mad at me for," he answered. The Court asked, "Have you ever had a quarrel or fight with him?" Hooker replied, "I had a quarrel and a little fight with him over to

[2] 43 Cong., 1 sess., *House Exec. Doc. No. 122*, Trial of the Modoc Prisoners.

Dry Lake, beyond the Lava Beds." Desertion and leading a man's enemies to help capture him were apparently not reasons for anger in Hooker Jim's way of thinking!

William said that he overhead Jack and John Schonchin planning to kill the commissioners and warned Winema about it. William has been described by some writers as a friend of Jack's, but if that were true, he showed it in a peculiar way. He cheerfully helped put the noose around Jack's neck by testifying that the Modoc leader had been planning the murder for more than a week before it happened. The actual evidence seems to prove that Jack agreed only the night before the killings took place. This was a small point, however, and did not affect the basic evidence that the murder was thoroughly premeditated.

Neither Jack nor his fellow prisoners cared to cross-examine any of their accusers. They sat in glum silence. During most of the trial, Slolux sat with his head in his arms and his face on his chest. Sometimes he slumped to the floor and slept. The amazed white spectators could not understand a man so indifferent at a trial for his life that he could sleep, and they assumed that he was half-witted. Barncho was almost as indifferent. He refused to sit with the others, but sat or lay on the floor, and unless he was spoken to, he said nothing during the entire trial.[3]

The last witness for the prosecution was A. B. Meacham. When he came in to the courtroom, Jack offered to shake hands with him, but Meacham refused, signifying that he was not in a forgiving mood for the attempt on his life. This was the first time the two had met since John Schonchin's bullet had knocked Meacham senseless.

Meacham explained the events of the council at which Canby was killed. He told where each person stood or sat, and gave the general tenor of all of the talks. For a man who had almost had his brains blown out, he seemed to have a remarkably keen memory about details up to the very moment when he was knocked down and unconscious. Since the Indian prisoners did not deny any of his allegations, nor did they cross examine—if they knew what cross-examination meant—the presumption is that his account must have been accurate. Certainly it agreed with that of the other witnesses.

[3] Curtis to Gen. J. M. Schofield, *House Exec. Doc. No. 122*, 199.

That night, Meacham went to the guardhouse to see Jack and the others. Again he refused to shake hands but talked to them about getting a lawyer. Jack shrugged and said, "Everybody is against me; even the Modocs are turned against me. I have but few friends. I am alone." Then he looked at Meacham, and said, "Meacham, you talk for me."

If the victim of an assassination plot had served as the attorney for the defense, he would have created a sensation. Meacham was actor enough to realize the dramatic possibilities and was sorely tempted to accept the offer. There was already intense interest throughout the country in the case, and such a development would give Meacham untold publicity for the lecture tour that he was contemplating. He went to the judge advocate and offered to serve the Modocs. The judge told him that the court was willing if the Modocs were.

More calm thought and a conversation with his doctor and some of his friends changed Meacham's mind, however. He decided that it would be prudent neither for his health nor for his reputation among the unforgiving Oregonians if he, as a white man, dared speak in defense of the killers. He backed away from the task. Jack once said, "I cannot talk with the chains on my legs. My heart is not strong, when the chain is on my leg." The chain was still on his leg, and after Meacham changed his mind, Jack still had no one to defend him.

On Tuesday, the fourth day of the trial, the final two witnesses for the prosecution were called. Neither had very much startling testimony to give. Lieutenant Anderson of the Fourth Artillery testified as to General Canby's full name, his rank, and what he was doing in the Lava Beds. Dr. McElderry testified as to the nature of Canby's wounds, establishing the fact that the gunshots killed both him and Thomas. Neither had died from natural causes!

No questions from the Modocs.

Jack was offered the chance to produce witnesses on his behalf. He put three on the stand, Scarfaced Charley, Rock Dave, and One-Eyed Mose.

Scarfaced Charley was the first to be called. His testimony did have something to add. His remarks provided no real defense of

Jack, but he did indict the Klamaths and Allen David. If the Modocs were going to be punished, Charley was going to do his level best to see that they had some company. He gave names, places, and dates.

Link River Jack was accused of bringing the Modocs "powder and stuff" before the January fighting began. During the battle of January 17, ten Klamath scouts brought ammunition and guns. He got eighty percussion caps from another Klamath. He reported that Allen David told the Klamaths to fire into the air and that the Modocs agreed not to shoot any of them. One Klamath gave powder to Ellen's Man. Another gave Jack twenty caps. Little Link River John was captured by Modocs and allowed to go free after he had told them that the Yainax Modocs were in favor of wiping out their relatives in the Lava Beds. He said that in the January battle the Klamaths separated from the soldiers in the fog and successfully concealed themselves from the passing soldiers. The Modocs then moved around the flank of the troops to a spot where they could talk and trade with the Klamaths. He backed his testimony with the fact that while the losses to the white soldiers had been relatively severe, not one single Klamath was wounded, missing, or dead at the end of the day's fighting.

Dave's testimony was short, but he criticized Allen David. He had been visiting at Fairchild's, he said, after Meacham came to organize the Peace Commission. He claimed that David sent word to him that he was sorry the Modocs hadn't told the Klamaths there was to be a fight in November or they would have sent down a delegation to take part in the soldier-shooting party. The only reason the Klamaths had not helped was that "a white man" had told them that Jack had burned one of their tribe alive. There was additional irrelevant material, having little to do with Jack's part in the murder of Canby, but the court allowed the Indians to introduce even hearsay evidence in order that they might feel they had presented their case as favorably as possible.

Mose merely repeated that Link River Jack, a Klamath, had given some caps to him, to Ellen's Man, and to Barncho after the November battle. This was again utterly immaterial and irrelevant, but there does not seem to be any reason to doubt that at least some of the charges might have been true. There were plenty of soldiers who had also asserted that the Klamaths were not to be trusted. Others insisted just as stoutly that not one Klamath had turned against the whites. Probably the argument will never be settled.

At last, Jack himself was given a chance to speak. After some hesitation he got slowly to his feet and looked around at the court and the spectators. He said at last, "I don't know how white men talk in such a place as this, but I will do the best I can."

The judge advocate told him almost kindly, "Talk exactly as if you were at home, in a council."

There is a tradition fostered by romantic writers that the last speech of a defeated Indian leader should be a moving, eloquent oration about his fathers, the new ways of life and the spirits of the departed Indians brooding over the great cities that would arise in the red-man's land. Jack's speech ignored this tradition. In fact, it was not so much a speech as a cry of distress, rage, and frustration because everything he had ever done had failed. As a child about to be punished for misdeeds, Jack tried to shift the blame for his actions to someone else.

First he blamed Jackson for precipitous action in opening fire at the Lost River camp in November. Jack said he told Bogus to stall for time until he could get some clothes on, for he was in bed when the soldiers came. (If he had wanted to, Jack could have put on full dress complete with white tie during the time Jackson waited for him to put in an appearance.) He had intended Ivan Applegate, Dennis Crawley, or Henry Miller to speak for him, he said. He declared further, that he still had not intended to fight after the Lost River affair until the Hot Creeks came into camp in early December. He asserted that they were not only terrified by the near lynching, but also that they were among the most urgent in forcing him to fight. He said if Fairchild had come right away, war might still have been avoided, but Fairchild did not come until just before the attack on January 17.

Jack claimed that the civilian, Nate Berwick, told him that the commissioners were trying to get the Indians to come to the tent unarmed so that they could murder them. He did not give details, however, about the time of this conversation. An Indian woman claimed that Meacham was going to burn Jack alive on a pile of logs at Fairchild's ranch. The Modoc complained that the whites always thought an Indian chief was a monarch of some kind. He said he certainly was not boss of the Modocs. He bitterly attacked Hooker Jim for always wanting to fight. He tagged him, along with Bogus, Steamboat Frank and Shacknasty Jim, who had joined the army to save their own necks, as the real villains of the Modocs band. It was they who should be hanged and not he, he said. With that, he sat down.

Schonchin's statement was very short. The burden of it was that the Klamaths were very bad Indians and everything he had been accused of doing was the result of some nefarious Klamath activity somewhere in the background.

The others had nothing to say.

Major Curtis, the judge advocate, made a short speech in which he denied Jack's allegation that Jackson had really started the war by his November attack. Then he adjourned the court for the members to retire and consider a verdict and the sentencing, both to be done the next day.

During the evening, a lawyer named Lewis, arrived from Colusi, California. He said he wanted to offer his professional services to the prisoners. Since he had known they were to be tried, and the papers had carried the dates and names of the trial court for over two weeks, it seems that Lawyer Lewis was not overzealous to see justice done, or he would have been there when the trial started. Jack certainly would have given him his chance for the national limelight, for the Modocs would have accepted anyone willing to defend them.

The following day, court reconvened, and the military commission announced that all six defendants had been found guilty on all counts. This was not a surprising verdict. Least of all were Jack and his associates surprised. Jack had expected to be hanged ever since his killing of Canby. White men always hanged some Indians after unsuccessful uprisings had been quelled, and Jack knew that he was doomed before the trial began. His main bitterness was that the four "Modoc Bloodhounds" had been exempted. The proverb that "misery loves company" applied in full measure to Jack.

The judge advocate announced that there would be no further

trials, because those who had helped capture Jack were to be rewarded with liberty so that other Indians could see that in time of Indian war they could literally "get away with murder" if they turned against their own people. If such knowledge were widely known, any Indian leader would have less chance of holding his own followers when things started going wrong.[4] (Apparently, however, the followers of Sitting Bull and Joseph never received the word from Curtis' arguments.)

The end of the matter was simply that all six defendants were sentenced to be hanged, and the date for execution was set for the following October 3. With the sentencing, the court adjourned sine die. The prisoners were taken back to their guardhouse, and the other Modocs remained in the stockade. The military and federal government then retired into their metaphorical cyclone cellars to sit out the storm of disapproval that was bound to arise on all sides from those who didn't like the way the trials had been conducted.

The storm was not long in coming. The Oregonians were satisfied with what had been meted out to Jack but were furious that the other indicted murderers had escaped without even a trial. Their complaints rent the skies. Governor Grover wrote and spoke about the injustice of allowing murderers to go scot free. Oregon editorial writers denounced the military commission.

What the President and the Secretary of the Interior really dreaded more than the bitter comments by the Oregonians—who were far away—was the formidable barrage of objection they knew would be laid down by the humanitarian organizations in the East. They did not have long to wait. As soon as the word of the verdict got to the newspapers, the letters and petitions began to come in.

A former citizen of the Rogue River Valley, one John Beeson of Philadelphia, a member of the National Association to Promote Universal Peace, filled the Quakers of that city full of stories of how the troubles around Jacksonville in the 1850's had been incited and resolved. Each time there was a meeting of this organization, a memorial would be directed to Grant or Delano (the secretary of the interior), giving advice in handling the Modoc problem. The

[4] 43 Cong., 1 sess., *House Exec. Doc. No. 122;* Meacham, *Wigwam and Warpath,* 607–35.

embarrassing part of their petitions was that while their factual material was frequently badly garbled, their conclusions often made sense. "To subject the fate of the Modoc chief to the decision of a Military or any other commission chosen from the party in the wrong cannot be otherwise than extremely unjust," stated a resolution from New York.[5]

Three days after sentence was passed, a Philadelphia meeting requested Grant to exercise clemency for all the Indians, pointing out that even after the Civil War no one had been executed as a war criminal. This was not quite true. The petition was signed by the president of the Universal Peace group, and also by its strong-minded vice-president, Lucretia Mott.[6] Alfred Love, the president, made a special trip to Washington, and it was only with difficulty that Grant avoided a meeting with him.

Another group meeting in New York, the American Indian Aid Association, pointed with some asperity to "the ridiculous farce of administering justice by erecting the gallows by General Davis before the trial begins; the unprecedented reading to the accused Modocs their indictment and sentence of death from the same paper." They also denounced "the fallacy of assuming that the extinction of the Indian race is owing to manifest destiny."[7]

As time went by and it became evident that somebody was going to be hanged, the tenor of the petitions coming to Washington changed. Requests were received asking that some of the Modocs be sent East for adoption and education. Certain members of the Quaker church also asked for an uncondemned Modoc who could be brought to Philadelphia as a show-piece for demonstrating their good works.

Petitions came even from California asking for executive clemency. One such petition arrived from Elisha Steele, now the sheriff of Siskiyou County, which was also signed by John Fairchild and the war correspondent for the Sacramento *Record*, who signed himself "Bill Dadd the Scribe."

[5] Cooper Institute petition, June 30, 1873, *Special File Modocs, 1873*, Office of Indian Affairs.

[6] Petition signed July 12, 1873, *Special File Modocs, 1873*, Office of Indian Affairs.

[7] *Special File Modocs, 1873*, Office of Indian Affairs.

"Bill Dadd," or H. Wallace Atwell, also requested in a separate letter to the Secretary of the Interior that he delay execution until the trial records could be examined. He denounced Riddle, particularly, for being illiterate and incapable of understanding English himself; therefore he was unable to make the Modocs understand exactly what was being said to them. He charged that Toby, Riddle's wife, continuously shielded her own relatives in the proceedings—though this accusation does not stand up in view of the fact that Jack was her uncle and she made no attempt to shield him. All Atwell wanted was an investigation and review by people who lived neither in California nor in Oregon.[8]

The heat contained in these contrasting petitions tended to neutralize them in the minds of the officials in Washington. Grant tried to be agreeable, and was willing to do what would be most acceptable, but he felt he had to present any change in policy to his cabinet, and Secretary Delano and Secretary of War Belknap were unwilling to yield to pressure.

The only successful petition was one from the War Department itself, requesting an executive commutation of sentence for Barncho and Slolux. Major Curtis, the commission judge, wrote the office of the Judge Advocate General in Washington,

I would like to have said a word in favor of lenity toward Barncho and Sloluck. The others were all involved deeply in the plot to murder, consulted about it with each other and acted as ringleaders, I have no doubt. Barncho and Sloluck, however, I regard as common soldiers, who obeyed orders in being present, or rather within hail, and whom it will be an unnecessary outlay of national vengeance to put to death. They both took no visible interest in the trial, and I doubt if they understood it. Sloluck sat with his hands over his face, and much of the time on the floor, apparently asleep. He is quite a boy, at least in looks. Barncho was little better. Neither of them, I believe could have taken any prominent part in the war, or in anything. One of them knocked down Mrs. Riddle and seized her horse, but did no injury.[9]

[8] Steele, Fairchild, and Atwell, July 30, 1873, *Special File Modocs, 1873,* Office of Indian Affairs.

[9] Curtis appeal, 43 Cong., 1 sess., *House Exec. Doc. No. 122,* 190.

While the President was reaching a decision, affairs continued as usual at Fort Klamath. Guards were detailed to watch the condemned prisoners and those in the stockade. Somewhat more spacious quarters were provided for the women and children as the weeks went by. Toward the end of July, it became necessary to issue clothing to the prisoners, for their possessions were badly worn when they were captured, and in the following two months they didn't improve any. This request created a minor crisis among the government bureaucrats and kept the secretaries of Fort Klamath busy for days.

Wheaton made a formal request for permission to issue new clothing. The Portland army headquarters forwarded the letter to the Secretary of War. He did not pass on it, but the clothes were furnished anyway. An order had to be sent directing the Modocs to wash their old clothes; the ones that were beyond repair were to be buried, since they were literally lousy. Some two weeks after this momentous decision was reached, the War Department wired approval of an issue of supplies and directed that the costs be assessed against the Indian Bureau. The Bureau promptly retorted that, "The said Indians are under the control of the War Department as prisoners of war, and whatever expense there may be incurred in clothing or in feeding them should, in the opinion of this office, be borne by that Department." Finally, the unhappy President of the United States settled the trivial issue by directing that the Indian Bureau pay for the clothing.[10]

This high-level squabble did nothing to relieve the boredom of the men at the post. Something had to be found for them to do. This last week in August, therefore, Colonel Wheaton ordered that Captain Hasbrouck should go back to the Lava Beds with fifteen men and bring in the bodies of the victims of the Thomas-Wright fight in April. The captain took nine artillerymen, six infantrymen, two wagons, five pack animals, and Donald McKay as a guide.

He was gone for eight days. Monday, they traveled twenty-five miles and Tuesday made the old Lost River ford. Wednesday, they reached the site of Gillem's camp, and on August 28, they did the job they had been sent out to do. Thirteen bodies were exhumed

[10] *Special File Modocs, 1873*, Office of Indian Affairs.

near the sand butte, but only nine of these were identified. Hasbrouck then returned and went to the Stronghold, where he recovered the body of an Oregon volunteer, along with that of an unidentified cavalryman, both of whom had been killed in January. All of the bodies, except that of Cranston, were interred in the cemetery by Gillem's camp and the graves marked of all who could be identified. Since it was not considered fitting that Cranston, an officer, should be buried with the common soldiers, his body was returned to Fort Klamath. On Friday, Hasbrouck went over to Fairchild's ranch and was met by a very hungry and weary Modoc. It proved to be Miller's Charley who had remained a fugitive until the trials were over. He was in distress, but his waiting had paid off, for he was in no danger of being tried for anything—not even the murder of Sherwood, of which he was guilty. He was escorted to Fort Klamath two days later, and was put in the stockade with the other prisoners on Monday, September 1.

On September 9, Grant received another of the series of petitions requesting amnesty for the Modocs. This time it came from Baltimore, although the wording was clearly Quaker.[11] Whether he had only now had enough or whether he had been making up his mind over a long period of time, Grant acted at last by issuing an order the next day, modifying the death sentences of two of the six Modocs by commuting the punishment of Barncho and Slolux to life imprisonment at Alcatraz Island.[12]

The order was duly transmitted to Wheaton, but he was told that no Modoc might know that any of the prisoners was to be spared. Only on the actual day of the hanging would Barncho and Slolux know of the change in plans. The other prisoners were to be given no hint. Grant ordered finally that when the executions were over, all Modoc survivors were to be sent East into exile and were not to be told where they were going.[13]

September slipped by. The soldiers were drilled each day to give them something to do, and the rest of the time, they policed the grounds, as soldiers have done probably since the days of Alexander

[11] Petition to Grant, September 13, 1873, Office of Indian Affairs.
[12] General Court Martial Orders, #34, September 12, 1873, S.F.P., D.C., 1873, #2312.
[13] Headquarters to Wheaton, September 22, 1873, S.F.P., D.C., 1873, #2381.

the Great. The Modoc prisoners were visited by the other Modocs of Old Schonchin's band at the Yainax station, who were free to come and go, sometimes to the number of fifty a day. They were easily handled. Neither visitors nor prisoners proved to be at all difficult.[14] At night the sentries paced to and fro around the stockade, with the quaint touch of having a single lighted candle set on a post for illumination.[15]

As summer faded into autumn, preparations for the execution began to take shape. The post carpenter, Hiram Fields, erected a stout gallows large enough to hold all six prisoners, even though only four of the nooses were to be used.[16] The scaffold was thirty feet long, built of dressed pine logs a foot in diameter. Four stout posts were put in the rear to support the platform, and the trap was set to reach two posts in front. The beam supporting the ropes was very high and completely separate from the platform and trap. There were no "thirteen steps" at the side. The condemned men were expected to climb up a ladder at the front of the gallows.

By way of mental cruelty, Wheaton ordered six graves dug in front of the guardhouse, just outside the parade ground fence. In this way, he hoped to bring a measure of punishment not ordered by the War Department to Barncho and Slolux. The graves were left where the prisoners could entertain themselves by looking into the holes they could expect shortly to occupy. Wheaton's excuse for digging six was that if only four were dug, questions would be asked, and there had been orders given that no publicity should be made of the commutation in sentence until the day set for the execution.[17]

September ended while the soldiers continued to haul an accumulation of refuse from the camp grounds, and to return with stone for fireplaces and chimney flues from a ten-mile-distant rock quarry. It also saw the usual goings and comings of officers, couriers, paymasters, and the conduct of all the multitude of army post

[14] Wheaton report, September 1, 1873, *Fort Klamath Letter Book*, VIII, Office of the Adjutant General.

[15] Robert Pollock to Headquarters, June 19, 1873, *Fort Klamath Letter Book*, VIII.

[16] James Williams, *Life and Adventures of James Williams.*

[17] Wheaton report, September 30, 1873, *Fort Klamath Letter Book*, VIII.

doings. The event that overshadowed all of this trivia, however, as October arrived was the impending execution of Captain Jack and his associates for the murder of Thomas and Canby.

XIII

THE DAY OF RECKONING

A S THE DAY for the execution approached, the army re-laxed its regulations somewhat and permitted the families of the condemned men to visit them in the guardhouse. Under guard, the six men were even allowed to visit their friends inside the stockade.

The final decision by the President had not been given to the prisoners, but several still hoped that they would escape the noose. They dreaded hanging far more than death itself. However, the graves dug outside their prison gave them little hope for a reprieve.

On Thursday, the second of October, Colonel Wheaton, accompanied by a chaplain with interpreters Oliver Applegate and Dave Hill, the Klamath leader, made the official call to the prisoners to inform them that they were to be hanged the next day. The proceedings were opened by a general handshaking. The chaplain then gave the Indians a short religious talk which might have comforted a white convict in a death cell but was probably unintelligible to a group of non-Christian Indians. Nevertheless, the prisoners listened to him politely.

When the chaplain had finished, Wheaton asked him to tell the Modocs that President Grant would not pardon them. The priest did so, and Applegate and Hill interpreted his announcement as they had the previous talk by the priest. In accordance with Wheaton's decision, Slolux and Barncho were not told that they were to be spared.

After a painful silence, Jack was the first to speak. He blamed the young men of his band for forcing him into the war and the killing. He complained that he had expected to be pardoned when he surrendered and denounced the four "bloodhounds" who had run him to earth. "I feel that while these four men—Bogus, Shacknasty Jim, Hooker, and Steamboat—are free, they have triumphed over me and over the government," he said.[1] (He did not remember that when he surrendered, he had no choice, and no promises of amnesty were made.) He asked whether there was any further hope of pardon left. Wheaton replied that there was not. When he was asked if he had any final request to make he said, "I should like to live until I die a natural death!"

The Colonel then asked him whom he should like to see lead the Modocs after he was gone. He refused to name anyone, except by indirection. He is reported to have said, "I cannot trust even Scarfaced Charley." The indication was that if he could trust anyone, Charley would be the man; accordingly, Wheaton appointed him "chief" immediately after the execution.

After Wheaton and Jack had finished talking, Slolux spoke to the extent of denying any part in Canby's murder. Barncho also denied any part in the crime. They were not telling the truth, of course, and what they expected to gain, or whom they expected to convince by such childish denials is hard to say.

Black Jim suggested that he would make a good leader for the Modocs, and if the white men would please pardon him, he would take good care of the survivors of Jack's band. Captain Jack shook his head impatiently at such nonsense, and Jim then went on to say, "I am afraid of nothing. I am not afraid to die."

Boston Charley was silent until that moment. Now he spoke. He had become irritated at the streak of cowardice in his fellow murderers. "When I look on each side of me, I think of these other men as women. I do not fear death. I think I am the only man in the room. I fought in the front rank with Shacknasty, Steamboat, Bogus, and Hooker. I am altogether a man, and not half a woman. I killed Dr. Thomas, assisted by Steamboat and Bogus. . . . I would like to see all my people and bid them good-bye today. I would like to go to the stockade to see them."

[1] Meacham, *Wigwam and War-path*, 638.

Boston was asked why they had killed Canby. He talked quite freely, saying that in spite of all the fair words, presents, and good treatment, the Modocs continuously feared treachery. They hoped that by killing their leaders, the other white men would give up and go home. He conceded that it was the younger men who forced the issue and prevented Jack from stopping the murders.

Schonchin John was the last to speak. He asserted that he, too, was firm and resolute, but requested that his son Peter be left to live at Yainax with his uncle. He blamed Odeneal for everything, "the murder of Canby, for the blood in the Lava Beds, and the chains on my feet." He said, as the translators reported it, "I was an old man, and took no active part. I would like to see those executed for whom I am wearing chains. . . . My heart tells me I should not die—that you do me a great wrong in taking my life. War is a terrible thing. All must suffer—the best horses, the best cattle, and the best men. I can now only say, let Schonchin die!"[2]

The chaplain then said a prayer, which was translated to the Indians. While he prayed in English, Applegate put it into the Chinook jargon, and Hill rendered it into Modoc. How much the Indians got is again doubtful, for communication with these Indians was always difficult.

Friday was the day set for the execution. During the night, dozens of visitors arrived. The execution of Jack was a gala event to many of the citizens, and the few hundred white men that lived in the Modoc and Klamath country made a strenuous effort to be present. All the soldiers stationed at the Fort were required by orders to witness the execution, and in addition, the sheriff of Jackson County was there to serve Wheaton a warrant requiring him to deliver to the civil courts of Oregon any indicted Modoc not tried or executed. Any Klamath Indian who wanted to watch was permitted to do so. Even some Snakes were present. All the Modoc prisoners were required to witness the punishment of their leaders, and the four turncoats were given a vantage point so that they could see all that happened.

At half-past nine in the morning, the soldiers lined up in front of the guardhouse, and the officer of the day entered the prison. He

[2] *Ibid.,* 643.

unlocked the cells and ordered the condemned men to come out. With their chains rasping along the floor, the six Modocs obeyed.

In front of the building, a four-horse team stood, hitched to a large wagon which held four coffins. The six prisoners were ordered to climb into the wagons. The records do not say whether they made any comment as to the discrepancy in the number of prisoners and the number of coffins. At any rate, Jack, Schonchin, and Black Jim each sat on a coffin, and the three younger men who had been cell mates sat side by side on the fourth. When everyone was seated, the driver moved his team the few yards to the gallows escorted by the beat of the muffled drums of a column of marching troops from Battery B, Fourth Artillery, Companies E and G from the Twelfth Infantry, and Company F from the Twenty-first Infantry.

When they arrived at the scaffold, the troops parted, and the team drove directly to the north side of the gallows where the ladders to the platform had been placed on the posts.

Wheaton ordered the men to get out of the wagon and climb to the scaffold. As each man prepared to climb the ladder, the blacksmith removed the shackles from his ankles. Jack was the first up the ladder, and he took his place beneath one of the nooses. Schonchin, then Boston, and Black Jim followed. Slolux and Barncho were left sitting on the coffins, and since no one told them to climb to the gallow's platform, they were quite content to remain where they were. The reporters seated at a table by the foot of the scaffold wrote of each event as rapidly as they could.

The four men on the platform were led forward slightly to the drop, and Corporal Ross of Company G, Twelfth Infantry placed the noose around Jack's neck, after cutting some of his hair back so that the rope would encircle his neck better. Corporal Killien did the same for Schonchin, Private Robert Wilton for Black Jim, and a Private Anderson for Boston Charley.

As the ropes were adjusted, a settler from Goose Lake called out, "Jack! What would you give me to take your place?" Quick as a flash Jack turned toward him and grimly replied, "Five hundred ponies and both my wives!" Wheaton was probably not much amused by this bit of macabre joking. Perhaps he did not understand what they said.

Seats were provided for the men on the gallows, and they were requested to sit with the ropes around their necks. First, Captain Hogue, the executioner, bid each of them a brief farewell. The finding and sentence of the trial court was read and translated to each of the condemned men. Finally the order for their execution was read to them. As this was being translated, the adjutant prepared to read another paper. Immediately after Dave Hill had translated the order to the men on the gallows, the second paper was read, commuting the death sentences of Barncho and Slolux to imprisonment for life at Alcatraz Island.

It was about ten-twenty.

Again the chaplain offered a prayer. As Dave Hill finished putting the last of it into the Modoc language, Hogue flashed a handkerchief as a signal, an axe cut the rope holding the drop, and the Modoc murderers fell to their deaths. Boston and John Schonchin drew their legs upward convulsively for an instant in their fall, but Jack and Black Jim seemed to die instantly. Captain Hogue felt the pulse of each, and at ten-twenty-eight pronounced all of them dead.[3]

At the moment of the drop, the Modoc prisoners groaned in sympathy for their leaders. The crowd began to mill about as the bodies hung at the end of the ropes, and after about half an hour, the executioner ordered them cut down. Only then did the spectators begin to disperse. The four bodies were placed in the coffins, the two surviving convicts were seated on the wagon bed this time, and the rest of the Modocs returned to their quarters.[4]

As soon as the soldiers had left, the ropes that had executed the killers were removed, unraveled, and sold to souvenir hunters for five dollars a strand. Some of the hair Ross had cut from Jack's head was picked up and sold for whatever the traffic would bear.

Friday afternoon the coffins were lowered into the graves, and all six of the holes were filled with earth. That night, someone, never identified, opened Jack's grave and put his body on a freight wagon headed for Yreka. Since nothing had been done to preserve the corpses, haste was essential. As soon as the wagon arrived at Yreka,

[3] Yreka *Union* (October 11, 1873); Sacramento *Union* (October 6, 1873).
[4] Report, Wheaton to Headquarters, November 1, 1873, *Fort Klamath Letter Book*, VIII, Office of the Adjutant General.

Jack's body was embalmed, and then in somewhat less haste it was sent to Washington, D. C. Rumor insisted that it was used for a time in a sideshow, where it was exhibited for 10¢ a look.[5] It is impossible to determine the truth of this charge. Sideshow or not, eventually the remains were taken to the museum of the Surgeon General's office in Washington, reduced to a skeleton, and for many years displayed as a specimen of Indian anatomy.[6]

Jack's body arrived at Yreka only about one jump behind the news of his execution. An ambitious reporter had hired relays of horses between Fort Klamath and Jacksonville; as soon as the Indians were dead, he started riding for the nearest telegraph station. Wheaton had prepared his reports in advance, and the reporter took the official notices along with his newspaper story. By half-past seven on Friday night, this 1873-model pony express rode into Jacksonville and sent the story to the army and the waiting public in Yreka and over the entire country.

On Monday, when Wheaton entered his office, he was met by the sheriff of Jackson County, who had been there since Friday. The sheriff had bench warrants and a writ of habeas corpus to serve on the army commander. The warrants demanded that Scarfaced Charley, Hooker Jim, Curley Headed Doctor, Long Jim, One-Eyed Mose and two or three others be turned over to the sheriff for civil trial in Jacksonville. The writ commanded that Wheaton appear with the men on October 15, to show why they were held at Fort Klamath instead of being sent for trial in Jacksonville.

Brusquely, Wheaton refused to honor either writ or warrant on the ground that the Indians were prisoners of war under jurisdiction of the federal government and that no state had any claim to them.[7] Governor Grover complained at once to Davis in Portland and demanded that the army hand over its prisoners.[8]

Davis supported Wheaton's position, and at once sent word of Grover's actions to Washington and the President. At a cabinet meeting, the Secretary of War told Grant and the others the desires of the Governor of Oregon. There was a brief discussion weighing

[5] Riddle, *Indian History*, 197.
[6] Gatschet, *Klamath Indians*, lxxiv.
[7] Wheaton to Headquarters, October 6, 1873, S.F.P., D.C., 1873, #2350.
[8] Grover to Davis, S.F.P., D.C., 1873, #2310.

the relative importance of states rights and federal authority. With no one there to plead the case for Oregon, the cabinet arrived at its conclusion quickly and sent orders to Davis:

Shown by the Secretary of the President in Cabinet today. It is understood, the orders to send all the Modocs to Fort D. A. Russell, as prisoners of war, given the 13th September 1873, will be executed by Gen. Schofield, and no further instructions are necessary.

Grover did not get the prisoners.

When the final disposition of the Modoc prisoners was settled, Wheaton ordered that the rest of the plan should be carried out. Captain H. C. Hasbrouck and his light battery B, Fourth Artillery, were given the task of guarding the prisoners. They left Fort Klamath on Sunday, the twelfth, in wagons obtained from Jacksonville. Hasbrouck's job was to take 153 men, women, and children to Redding and the railroad.[9]

Wheaton gave orders that no one, prisoner or newspaper reporter, was to know the destination of the Modocs, at least until they reached their first stop in Wyoming.

The trip by wagon took longer than the trip by rail. When the Indians and their guards arrived in Redding, Barncho and Slolux were given special guards to take them on to San Francisco and Alcatraz. The other Indians were put on the east-bound train.

There is no record of the reaction of the Modocs as the train left the Redding station. It is very doubtful whether any of them had ever been on a train before, and the fear of the unknown, added to the knowledge that they were leaving their ancestral homes forever, probably depressed them deeply. It certainly broke their once proud spirit, for never again is there any record of even the meanest or cruelest of them causing any trouble to the Indian agents.

When the Indians reached Wyoming, new orders were waiting for them to go to Fort McPherson in Nebraska. Hasbrouck turned over a total of 39 men, 54 women, and 60 children to the command-

[9] Report, Wheaton to Headquarters, November 1, 1873, *Fort Klamath Letter Book*, VIII.

ing officer of that post on October 29, a little more than two weeks after they had left the stockade at Fort Klamath.[10]

They remained at Fort McPherson on a temporary basis only until the middle of November. Orders arrived which moved them once more. They were taken to Baxter Springs, Kansas. They reached this point on November 16, and were allowed to stay there only a week. The agent at Baxter Springs recommended that the Indians be removed from there, for he said it was "a notorious place for corrupting Indians." His suggestion was that they be taken to Seneca Station on Shawnee land in the Indian Territory, where they could have a better chance of adjusting to a new environment.

Just before Thanksgiving and almost exactly a year after the war began, the Modocs arrived at their final stop at Seneca Springs on the Quapaw Agency. Here they were finally given a kind of shelter. A barracks was constructed at the extremely low cost of $524.40, from scrap lumber. Although the Indians were not carpenters, they built the shelter themselves with only one day's aid from three white men. The structure was put up only about two hundred yards from the Agent's headquarters so that they could remain under his direct supervision.[11]

Scarfaced Charley was now the leader of the Modocs. The twenty-two year old leader had no desire to continue, but was willing to do what needed to be done. Under his direction, the Modocs received blankets and clothing from a $15,000 appropriation to keep them through the winter. It was expected that the agent could make farmers out of them during the next summer season. Schools, of a sort, were provided for the Modoc children. The once hostile band was completely subdued.

The Modoc War was now officially ended. The soldiers had already scattered to their new assignments and stations in other districts and divisions. History had repeated its act of pulling different men from all parts of the United States and even from some foreign countries, compressing them together for a moment of time in a tiny area to fight a few battles, then like an hourglass, spreading them out again when the time and event was ended.

---

[10] 43 Cong., 1 sess., *House Exec. Doc. No. 122.*
[11] *Report of the Commissioner of Indian Affairs, 1873.*

Through the deeds of a few desperate men along a forbidding lake shore, more than a thousand people had been involved in warfare. Now it was over, and the participants in the war would never again be together. All would have in common, however, the memories of the parts they had taken in the Modoc War.

It was an expensive campaign for that period. Considering the number of Indians killed, it was almost as costly as a twentieth century war. Most of this was due to large scale profiteering, only part of which could have been legitimate. In the statements sent to the army are such items as soap at 50 cents a cake, iodine at 50 cents an ounce, $1.25 a quart for rubbing alcohol, $4.00 a pound for calomel. Horseshoeing came to $1.25 a shoe, and a blacksmith could easily make $35.00 a day. These prices were charged during times when many people were working for less than $2.00 a day in wages. Obviously there was money to be made in an Indian war. Teamsters charged $20.00 a day for their services. The Oregon volunteer officers put in bills for pay equal to that of officers in the United States Army, while privates and noncommissioned officers put in claims for $2.00 a day, which was almost four times what the regular army enlisted men were paid. At first the government refused to allow such bills, but politics intervened and eventually the federal government assumed the obligations.

John Fairchild did not lose any money on the war. His own pay for services came to $455, which was not out of line, but he rented horses and sold hay to the government to the tune of another $2,000 between November 30 and February 20.

The highest prices were paid for transportation of men—and women—and supplies from Redding to the Lava Beds. One William Hoog received payment of $118,132.86 for bringing men and supplies to the Lava Beds from Redding. Of course, the fact that the war was fought through the winter contributed heavily to the transportation costs. If the expenses were high, at least they were cheaper than if they had had to bring supplies over the all but impassable roads from Jacksonville.

The army did not include any of the pay of the regular force in costs charged to the conduct of the Modoc campaign. The direct expense for supplies, transportation, and services, exclusive of pay for the men, was over $280,000.[12] In addition to the costs incurred by Oregon and California volunteers, the total direct costs paid by the government were in the neighborhood of $420,000. Additional sums spent for indirect expenses such as pensions for the soldiers have not been officially determined. It may be safely estimated, however, that the total must have reached another $100,000.

The generalization can be made that considering the number of Indians involved in hostilities this was the most expensive Indian war that the United States ever fought. It was also the only war in which a General of the Army was killed by Indians.

[12] 43 Cong., 1 sess., *House Exec. Doc. No. 185;* 43 Cong., 2 sess., *House Exec. Doc. No. 45.*

XIV

AFTERMATH

T HE AVERAGE AMERICAN living in 1874 probably soon forgot the Modoc War. He took the attitude that it was over, the "renegades" were dead or in exile, and their fate served as a lesson to other Indians that the white man was not to be trifled with. His attention was soon diverted to new Indian wars with Nez Percés, Bannacks, or Sioux.

A chilling portent of things to come was evident as early as February 1873 while the Modocs were still in the Lava Beds. A small group of white settlers encountered a band of well-armed Indians in the vicinity of Summer Lake. When they asked the Indians why they were not on a reservation, the red men informed the settlers not too politely that they did not intend to live on a reservation any longer. The citizens threatened to bring soldiers and compel the Indians to go back. In reply, the Indians said that while they were "good Indians," they were not afraid of the soldiers. They could whip soldiers, because Captain Jack had showed them how.[1] Nothing serious came of the incident, for the Paiutes did not fight, though they did not go back to Yainax, either.

No one in the Modoc War gained much by his participation. The Indians were ruined. No white military heroes emerged, no political figures gained stature from it, and even Meacham, who tried to capitalize on his experiences by going on the lecture plat-

---

[1] Henry Fuller to Governor Grover, February, 1873, S.F.P., D.C., 1873, #941.

form, found that the public was not much interested in past happenings on the obscure frontier of northeastern California.

Meacham does give us what meager information we have about the immediate events following the exile of the Modocs to Oklahoma. Since he was going to tell the story of the Modoc War in the East, he needed some Indians for background and local color on the stage with him. In addition, he needed some words of the Modoc language—which he did not know—in order to give the impression that he had intimate knowledge of the people who had tried to kill him. He wrote Oliver Applegate in August, 1873, for "a few Modoc or Klamath sentences to *embellish* my lectures. . . . I hope you will take time to write them out with Plain Spelling and Pronunciation."[2] When he received his desired information, he went to Oklahoma to induce some Modoc Indians to join his lecture company. Accompanying him were Toby and Frank Riddle.

When the Riddles and Meacham arrived at Quapaw, they found some of the fiercest of the Modoc fighters engaged in a stern game of croquet! All of the Modocs seemed pleased to see him, and from time to time he used several of them, including Shacknasty Jim, Steamboat Frank, and Scarfaced Charley as ornaments to his speaking tours. He gave Toby Riddle the name of "Winema" and liberally interpreted it as meaning "The Little Woman Chief." (Of course she was not a chief, for the Modocs did not have women as their leaders, but the name has stuck with her, and there are those who think this was her original name.) Throughout 1874, 1875, and 1876, Meacham lectured intermittently in Missouri, Kentucky, New York, Philadelphia, and Washington, but with only indifferent financial success.

When he returned to the agency, Scarfaced Charley acted as the "chief" for about a year, but he refused to interfere with the customs of the Modocs. When the Quapaw agent demanded that he prevent his men from gambling their blankets and clothing away, Scarfaced Charley said he would do nothing to stop them. The Agent then deposed Charley, and appointed Bogus Charley to act as chief in his place.[3] Bogus remained in authority for many years.

[2] Meacham to O. C. Applegate, August 8, 1873, Applegate Collection.
[3] 43 Cong., 2 sess., *House Exec. Doc. No. 53.*

Scarfaced Charley died of consumption about 1890.[4] At that, he outlived many of his friends, for even by 1880 almost fifty of the exiles had died.[5] All of the Modocs suffered heavy mortality during their exile, and this was particularly true of the children.

The Modocs settled down fairly well, sent their children to school, had a small farm of 180 acres of cultivated wheat and corn land for the 150 survivors of the band, and the agent professed to be satisfied with their conduct and progress.[6] The rest of their 4,000-acre reserve was timber and prairie land.[7]

Many of the Indians took the names of white men after they went to Oklahoma, and it is difficult to know what happened to the old warriors in consequence. Slolux, for example, became known as George Denny. He was pardoned after serving five years of his life sentence at Alcatraz. He died at Quapaw in 1899. Long Jim kept his name, but lived only six years after he was removed from California. Three of the last four survivors took the names of Ben Lawyer, Henry Hudson, and Johnny Ball. How they were known in 1873 is not clear. Curley Headed Doctor died in 1890; Miller's Charley, the murderer who never came to trial, lived until 1912.

In 1909, the government allowed any of the Modocs who cared to do so to return to Yainax. A number did, and some of their descendants are still on the Klamath reservation. One-Eyed Mose, for instance, came back to Oregon, although he died only a year after his return. His wife, Artina, sometimes known as One-Eyed Dixie, survived him by many years. In the early 1880's, Steamboat Frank and Scarfaced Charley were converted to Christianity by a Quaker missionary.[8] Steamboat Frank decided to enter the ministry, but did not live long enough to be given an active pastorate, although he did conduct a few services on the reservation.[9] He died in Maine

[4] "The Last of the Modocs," The Bagley Scrapbook No. 2, University of Washington Library.

[5] James B. Fry, *Army Sacrifices, or Briefs from Original Pigeon Holes*, 253.

[6] *Report of the Commissioner of Indian Affairs, 1876.*

[7] *Northwestern Fights and Fighters*, 254.

[8] J. R. Gregg, *A History of the Oregon Trail, Santa Fé Trail, and Other Trails*, 282.

[9] J. P. Dunn, *Massacres in the Mountains: A History of the Indian Wars of the Far West*, 583.

in 1885. Hooker Jim died in Oklahoma in 1879. Winema lived until 1932, and Peter Schonchin until the 1940's.

The military authorities in the war did not long survive their enemies. Gillem was dead at the age of forty-five, less than three years after the end of the war. He never fully recovered from the sickness that plagued him during the campaign, and died in his native Tennessee. Davis, who outlived Gillem by four years, died at the age of fifty-one in Chicago. Wheaton survived his fellow leaders long enough to be retired as a regularly commissioned major general in the army. After the Modoc campaign, he was assigned to the colonelcy of the Second Infantry Regiment, and he retained this rank until 1892. He retired just before the Spanish-American War broke out, and died in 1903.

The civilians who were involved in the war lived longer than most of the Indians or their military antagonists. Dyar and John Fairchild both lived into the twentieth century. Fairchild was a minor official in Siskiyou County political circles for several years before his death. Steele, on the other hand, died in 1883 at the age of fifty-six.

When the student of the Indian troubles turns from men or events to generalizations, he is struck with the obvious fact that the most serious aspect of the Modoc War was that the government had clearly learned nothing from its experience. Even while Jack was awaiting execution at Fort Klamath, the civil government of Oregon expressed concern over the actions of certain Nez Percés of Joseph's band living in the Wallowa Valley of northeastern Oregon. The conditions existing in the Lava Beds that made Jack fight were identical with those in the Wallowa Valley during the balance of the decade of the 1870's. A treaty signed on June 11, 1855, had given the Nez Percés the Grand Ronde Valley and the Wallowa Mountains in addition to lands in Idaho. On June 9, 1864, certain Nez Percés splintered from the Wallowa bands and were induced to sign a new "treaty" surrendering the Wallowa country and all parts of their traditional hunting lands in Oregon. Joseph refused to recognize the validity of such a treaty, and continued to live in the Wallowa Valley, as Jack had continued to live along the Lost River.

The story of Chief Joseph has been told again and again and

needs no repeating, but a letter from Governor Grover to the Commanding General of the Division of the Pacific is so representative of the attitude that produced both the Modoc War and the Nez Percé War, that parts of it are worth repeating. Governor Grover was quite specific about his position.

If the Government shall admit that one sub-chief, out of more than fifty joined in council, can, by refusing his signature, or by absenting himself, defeat the operation of a treaty, the policy of making treaties would be valueless, and but few treaties would be binding. For there exists hardly a treaty with Indians west of the Rocky Mountains in which all the sub-chiefs and headmen joined and against which they have not positively protested. . . .

By the order of the General Land Office, bearing date May 28, 1867, the public lands in Wallowa Valley and vicinity were directed to be surveyed and opened for settlement. The surveys made under this order amounted to eleven townships. . . . Eighty-seven farms have been located and pre-emption and homestead claims have been filed thereto in the U. S. Land Office at La Grande. . . .

As the Indians have only the right of occupancy, and the United States have the legal title, subject to occupancy . . . the acts of the Government in surveying the Wallowa Valley and opening the same for settlement and the consequent occupancy of the same by settlers . . . and the recognition of these claims by the Local Land Office of the United States, would work a complete extinguishment of the Indian title by operation of the law, as far as the occupied lands are concerned. . . .

This State has already much of its best soil withheld from being occupied by an industrial population in favòr of Indians. The region of country in Eastern Oregon now settled and to which the Wallowa Valley is the key, is greater in area than the state of Massachusetts. If this section of our State, which is now occupied by enterprising white families, should be removed to make roaming ground for nomadic savages, a very serious check will have been given to the growth of our frontier settlements, and to the spirit of our frontier people in their efforts to redeem the wilderness and make it fruitful of civilized life. . . .

I learn that young Joseph does not object to going on the Reservation at this time, but that certain leading spirits of his band do object, for the reason that by so doing they would have to abandon some of their nomadic habits and haunts. The very objection which they make is a strong reason why they should be required to do so; for no beneficial influence can be exerted by agents and missionaries among the Indians while they maintain their aboriginal habits. . . . There are but seventy-two warriors in this band. . . .

Considering that the demands of Joseph's band were made during the period of the apparently successful resistance of the Modoc outlaws against the treaty stipulations with the Klamaths, and now the Modocs are subdued, it will doubtless be much less expensive to the Government and much more consistent with its general Indian policy, to induce Joseph's band by peaceable means to make their home on the Nez Percé Reservations, than to purchase the rights of white settlers now in the Wallowa Valley. . . .[10]

How wrong he was! To the average Oregonian, however, the logic of Grover's position was unassailable. His suggestion did not work, however. Joseph's Nez Percés refused, just as Jack's Modocs had, to go to the reservation. When trouble broke out, it was Perry and the First Cavalry, Wheaton, and others who had to make the first attempt to capture Joseph. They were dismally unsuccessful. Joseph's resistance, much more formidable than Jack's and covering a vastly larger territory, is better known than Jack's fight. It should never be forgotten, however, that both fights were part of the same policy that produced Indian war after Indian war in American history.

From the events of the Modoc War other conclusions may be drawn. While this war was not much different, except in detail, from other such wars, it serves as almost a perfect case study of American maladministration of its Indian affairs. Confined as the war was to a few square miles of territory, it is not difficult to see the whole grim course of events which time after time featured the relations between whites and Indians in larger areas.

If one wanted to duplicate the conditions that produced these wars, he should start with a primitive culture which had existed with minor changes for centuries, then suddenly expose it to a technologically superior culture such as the white traders represented. He should then subject this culture to a devastating disease like smallpox, and follow the epidemic almost immediately with white missionaries who would tell the aborigines that their age-old religious

[10] *Oregon Superintendency, 1873,* Office of Indian Affairs.

leaders were deceivers. While most of the survivors, such as the Indians of the mid-1800's, would not accept Christian teachings, they would agree, as the Modocs did, that the shamans were worthless, or such disasters would never have occurred. A return to the old ways of life, however, would be impossible. Some would try to be like the white men, some would become indolent and morose, while others would react violently in an irrational "nativistic" movement. Yet, even while this last group would resist the whites, they would already have themselves become so acculturated that they would be dependent on their enemies for their clothing, the food they ate, and even the very weapons they fought with.

One should then take a government that did not know where it was going or what it was doing. He should watch that government negotiate a treaty with several groups of people, like the Indians, who represented many points of view to which the government agents should pay no heed. He should watch a Senate of that government ignore the treaty for years, while a land office opened the lands for settlement, even though compensation had never been paid. If any protest took place from the dispossessed, he could watch troops move into the disputed land to end the protests of the original landholders. All that would be needed then to produce an explosion would be a dispute in the bureaucracy of the government which would lead to one department encouraging the Indians to resist, while a group of outsiders through desire for profit or through sentimentality furnished the most aggressive of the native population with weapons. A war would then be sure.

The result would also be inevitable. A few score, or even a few hundred men, hampered by their families, with no factories and no certain food supplies could never hope to resist an industrial nation of several millions. One battle, even a victorious fight like the Nez Percé victory at White Bird Creek, or the Sioux victory at the Little Big Horn, and the primitives could fight no more, for their supplies would be exhausted unless more could be captured. In the long run, only death or exile would be left for them.

So it was in the Modoc War, and so it would be again if the conditions that produced it were to be duplicated.

Today, the land of burned-out fires is much as it always was.

The lake has been drastically reduced in size, and the ancient bed is covered with grain fields crisscrossed by highways and railroads; yet on a foggy morning these fade away and the gray mist gives the appearance of water with all the ancient islands and landmarks clearly visible. The United States government has taken over most of the battle area as the Lava Beds National Monument. Trails take the visitor past the rocky fortifications in the Stronghold, through the Thomas-Wright field, and by the Gillem encampment. With only a few exceptions, these areas look almost as they did eighty years ago. In other more inaccessible areas, the student of the war needs to be a rugged hiker in order to follow the routes of the Indians and their American antagonists.

Outside the monument area and the lake basin, some of the old ranches are still farmed. Cattle and hay are still grown on the Van Bremer and Fairchild ranches, although these places have passed through several hands since they were first claimed and settled.

Traces of the old emigrant roads may still be seen if one knows where to look. Most of the land in the monument that the whites once wanted so badly, is now remarkable only for its extreme desolation and solitude. In summer a few head of deer and antelope graze through the lava fields. The bighorn sheep is gone. Rodents swarm through the rocks, while their enemies, the hawks and owls glide silently overhead.

APPENDIX I

A CHRONOLOGY OF THE EVENTS OF THE MODOC WAR

October, 1864	Treaty Signed with Klamath-Modocs
April, 1870	Jack Leaves the Reservation
November 29, 1872	The Battle of Lost River
December 21, 1872	The Battle of Land's Ranch
January 17, 1873	The First Battle for the Stronghold
January 22, 1873	The First Battle of Scorpion Point
January 29, 1873	Peace Commission Appointed
April 11, 1873	Murder of the Peace Commissioners and Lieut. Sherwood
April 14-17, 1873	The Second Battle for the Stronghold
April 26, 1873	"Thomas-Wright Massacre"
May 2, 1873	The Second Battle of Scorpion Point
May 10, 1873	The Battle of Dry Lake
May 22, 1873	Battle of Willow Creek Ridge
June 1, 1873	Captain Jack Surrenders
July 1-9, 1873	Trial of Modoc Leaders
October 3, 1873	Execution of Modoc Leaders; Exile of Jack's Band to Oklahoma
1909	Surviving Modocs Return to Klamath Reservation

APPENDIX II

The Army

Gen. E. R. S. Canby, commanding officer, Department of the Columbia, acting head, Military Division of the Pacific, murdered by Captain Jack, April 11, 1873.

Col. Jefferson C. Davis, Canby' successor as commanding officer, Department of the Columbia.

Lieut. Col. and Bvt. Maj. Gen. Frank Wheaton, Twenty-first Infantry, commander, District of the Lakes, director of the Modoc campaign from November to January 23, 1873, and after May 22, 1873.

Col. and Bvt. Maj. Gen. Alvan C. Gillem, First Cavalry, commander of Modoc campaign, January 23–May 22, 1873.

Maj. and Bvt. Col. John Green, First Cavalry, commanding officer, Fort Klamath, who sent Jackson to Lost River and started the war; field commander in Stronghold battles.

Maj. and Bvt. Col. E. C. Mason, Twenty-first Infantry, commander east side of Stronghold.

Capt. and Bvt. Col. David Perry, First Cavalry, Troop F, wounded January 17.

Capt. and Bvt. Maj. James Jackson, First Cavalry, Troop B, commander during Battle of Lost River.

Capt. and Bvt. Col. James Biddle, First Cavalry, Troop K, captured Modoc ponies in March during sweep of Lava Beds.

Capt. and Bvt. Col. R. F. Bernard, First Cavalry, Troop G, cavalry commander on east side of Stronghold; commanding officer during Battle of Land's Ranch.

Capt. and Bvt. Maj. Evan Thomas, Fourth Artillery, Battery A, killed
April 26.

Captain H. C. Hasbrouck, Fourth Artillery, Battery B (mounted and
serving as cavalry), commanding officer at Battle of Sorass Lake in
May; escorted defeated Modocs to Kansas.

Lieut. Geo. M. Harris, Fourth Artillery, Battery K, killed April 26.

Lieut. Thos. F. Wright, Twelfth Infantry, Co. E, killed April 26.

Lieut. Charles P. Eagan, Twelfth Infantry, Co. G, wounded and out of
action after April 12, 1873.

Sundry other officers and assorted non-coms and privates.

Civilians

Alfred B. Meacham, onetime Indian superintendent for Oregon, head
of Peace Commission.

Rev. Eleasar Thomas, peace commissioner, killed by Boston Charley,
April 11, 1873.

L. S. Dyar, Klamath sub-agent, peace commissioner.

A. M. Rosborough, judge of Superior Court, Yreka, California, peace
commissioner.

Elisha Steele, onetime Indian superintendent Northern California, Yreka.

John M. Fairchild, rancher, Cottonwood Creek, California.

Pressly Dorris, rancher, Butte Valley, California.

Oliver C. Applegate, Yainax sub-agency commissary operator, interpreter, head of company of Oregon volunteers.

Ivan Applegate, rancher, Clear Lake, California.

Jesse Applegate, rancher, Clear Lake, California.

Lindsay Applegate, father of Oliver and Ivan, sub-agent of Klamath
agency, co-leader of South Emigrant Road expedition.

Ben Wright, Indian fighter and agent after Rogue River War.

Bob Whittle and Modoc wife, Matilda, ferryboat operators on Link
River, interpreters.

Frank Riddle and Modoc wife, Toby (Winema), trappers and hunters
on Lost River, interpreters for Peace Commission and at trial of Jack.

H. Wallace Atwell, "Bill Dadd the Scribe," reporter for Sacramento
Record.

Sundry other volunteers, reporters, teamsters, sutlers, "laundresses," and
just plain kibitzers.

Modocs

Captain Jack, the leader.
Curley Headed Doctor, the shaman, leader of war faction.
John Schonchin, second in command.
Bogus Charley, messenger between Modocs and army, a "bloodhound" for army.
Peter Schonchin, son of John, last survivor of Modoc War.
Shacknasty Jim, a murderer, also a "bloodhound."
Scarfaced Charley, leader after Jack's execution, lieutenant under Jack.
Steamboat Frank, a "bloodhound," later a Quaker lay minister.
Boston Charley, hanged for the murder of Thomas.
Ellen's Man George, one of Canby's murderers, killed May 10, 1873.
Black Jim, hanged for murder.
Barncho, died in Alcatraz prison for part in murder.
Miller's Charley, killer of Sherwood, never brought to trial.
Curley Headed Jack, killer of Sherwood, suicide June, 1873.
Slolux, pardoned and exiled after term in Alcatraz prison.
One Eyed Watchman, killed in Battle of Lost River, November, 1872.
Hooker Jim, killer of settlers in November, a "bloodhound."
Mooch, murdered by settlers, June 8, 1873.
Little John, murdered by settlers, June 8.
Pony, murdered by settlers, June 8.
Wooley Jackey or Tee-He Jack, murdered by settlers, June 8.
Old Tail, killed during Battle of Stronghold, April 16, 1873.
Rock Dave, Big Ike, Long George, Long Jim, Humpy Joe, William (the Wild Gal's Man), Greasy Boots, Old Chuckle Head, One Eyed Mose, Lost River Old Man, Tule Lake Big Man, Butte Creek Man, and others.

BIBLIOGRAPHY

I. Unpublished Manuscripts

i. Miscellaneous

Bagley Scrapbook No. 2. University of Washington Library, Seattle.

Boyle, Lieut. W. H. Personal Observations on the Conduct of the Modoc War. (Handwritten MS.) Pacific MSS, No. A96. Bancroft Library, Univ. of Calif., Berkeley.

Canfield, David, and Crouch, J. Carlisle. Report of Preliminary Archaeological Reconnaissance, Lava Beds National Monument, November 18–December 4, 1935. U.S. Department of the Interior, National Park Service, typewritten report.

Fisher, Don C. Ben Wright. (Typewritten MS.) Lava Beds National Monument, Tulelake, Calif.

———. A Brief History of the Modoc Indians and their War Fought in 1872–73. (Typewritten MS.) Lava Beds National Monument, Tulelake, California.

Golden, John. Political Factions Among Three North American Indian Tribes; The Hopi; Klamath-Modoc; and Fox. (Typewritten MS.) University of Chicago.

Palmer, Joel E. Statement of Inhabitants of Southern Oregon and in Northern California in Regard to the Character and Conduct of the Modoc Indians. Also a Statement of Gen'l Joel Palmer on the Same Subject While He Was Superintendent of Indian Affairs in Oregon.

Statements of W. S. Kershan and Rev. Josiah L. Parrish. Pacific MSS, Bancroft Library, Univ. of Calif., Berkeley.

Ross, John E. Narrative of an Indian Fighter, Pacific MSS, Bancroft Library, Univ. of Calif., Berkeley.

Squier, Robert J., and Grosscup, Gordon L. An Archaeological Survey of Lava Beds National Monument, California, 1952. U.S. Department of the Interior, National Park Service, typewritten report.

———. Preliminary Report of Archaeological Excavations in Lower Klamath Basin, California, 1954.

ii. *National Archives, Washington*

Office of Indian Affairs, *Special File, Modocs, 1873.*
Oregon Superintendency, 1872 (selected documents).
Oregon Superintendency, 1873 (selected documents).
Office of the Adjutant General, Fort Klamath Letter Book, Vol. VII (selected pages).
Fort Klamath Letter Book, Vol. VIII (selected pages).
Camp Warner Letter Book, Vol. VII (selected pages).
Camp Warner Letter Book, Vol. VIII (selected pages).

iii. *Records of the San Francisco Presidio*

Department of the Columbia, 1872 (selected files).
Department of the Columbia, 1873 (selected files).

II. GOVERNMENT PUBLICATIONS

Annual Reports of the Commissioner of Indian Affairs to the Secretary of the Interior, 1870, 1872, 1873, 1876.
Congressional Documents.
    42 Cong., 3 sess., *Senate Exec. Doc. No. 29.*
    43 Cong., 2 sess., *Senate Misc. Doc. No. 32.*
    43 Cong., 3 sess., *Senate Exec. Doc. No. 39.*
    43 Cong., 1 sess., *House Exec. Doc. No. 22.*
    43 Cong., 1 sess., *House Exec. Doc. No. 122.*
    43 Cong., 1 sess., *House Exec. Doc. No. 185.*
    43 Cong., 2 sess., *House Exec. Doc. No. 45.*
    43 Cong., 2 sess., *House Exec. Doc. No. 53.*

43 Cong., 2 sess., *House Exec. Doc. No. 131.*
45 Cong., special sess., March 5, 1877, *Senate Exec. Doc. No. 1.*
Hodge, Frederick Webb, ed. *Handbook of American Indians North of Mexico.* 2 vols. Smithsonian Institution, Bureau of American Ethnology *Bulletin 30.* Washington, Government Printing Office, 1910.
Reports of the Commissioner of Indian Affairs, 1863, 1864, 1865.
Swanton, John R. *The Indian Tribes of North America.* Smithsonian Institution, Bureau of American Ethnology *Bulletin 145.* Washington, Government Printing Office, 1953.

III. NEWSPAPERS

Klamath Falls *Herald-News.*
Portland *Oregonian.*
Sacramento *Bee.*
Sacramento *Union.*
Yreka *Union,* 1872–73.

IV. BOOKS

Allen, James Michael. *Wi-ne-ma.* New York, Vantage Press, 1956.
Auble, C. C. *Historical Descriptions of Modoc County and Northeastern California.* Redding, Calif., Free Press Publishing Co., 1900.
Bancroft, Hubert Howe. *History of Oregon.* 2 vols. (Vols. XXIV and XXV of *History of the Pacific States of North America.*) San Francisco, The History Company, 1888.
Bland, T. A. *Life of Alfred B. Meacham.* Washington, D. C., T. A. and M. C. Bland, 1883.
Brady, Cyrus Townsend, LL.D. *Northwestern Fights and Fighters.* (American Fights and Fighters Series.) New York, Doubleday, Page and Company, 1909.
Brown, William S. *California Northeast: The Bloody Ground.* Oakland, Biobooks, 1951.
Carey, Charles Henry. *History of Oregon.* 3 vols. Chicago, Pioneer Historical Publishing Company, 1922.
———. *A General History of Oregon, Prior to 1861.* Portland, Metropolitan Press, 1935.

Cressman, L. S., and others. *Archaeological Researches in the Northern Great Basin.* (Carnegie Institution *Publication No. 538.*) Washington, Carnegie Institution, 1942.

Curtin, Jeremiah. *Myths of the Modocs.* Boston, Little, Brown and Company, 1912.

Dellenbaugh, Frederick S. *The North-Americans of Yesterday: A Comparative Study of North-American Indian Life, Customs, and Products, on the Theory of the Ethnic Unity of the Race.* New York, G. P. Putnam's Sons, 1900.

Downey, Fairfax Davis. *Indian Fighting Army.* New York, Charles Scribner's Sons, 1941.

DuBois, Cora. *The Feather Cult of the Middle Columbia.* (General Series in Anthropology, No. 7.) Menasha, George Banta Publishing Co., n. d.

Dunn, J. P. *Massacres in the Mountains: A History of the Indian Wars of the Far West.* New York, Harper and Brothers, 1886.

Evans, Elwood. *History of the Pacific Northwest, Oregon, and Washington.* 2 vols. Portland, North Pacific History Company, 1889.

Frémont, John Charles. *Memoirs of My Life.* Chicago, Belford, Clarke and Co., 1887.

Fry, James B. *Army Sacrifices, or Briefs from Original Pigeon Holes.* New York, D. Van Nostrand, 1879.

Fuller, George W. *A History of the Pacific Northwest, with Special Emphasis on the Inland Empire.* New York, Alfred A. Knopf, 1947.

Gatschet, Albert Samuel. *The Klamath Indians of Southwestern Oregon.* Washington, Government Printing Office, 1890.

Gaston, Joseph. *The Centennial History of Oregon, 1811–1912.* 4 vols. Chicago, S. J. Clarke Publishing Co., 1912.

Good, Rachel Applegate. *History of Klamath County, Oregon, Its Resources and Its People.* Klamath Falls, Oregon, 1941.

Gregg, J. R. *A History of the Oregon Trail, Santa Fé Trail, and Other Trails.* Portland, Binfords and Mort, 1955.

Grover, L. F. *Report of Governor Grover to General Schofield on the Modoc War, and Reports of Maj. Gen. John F. Miller and General John E. Ross to the Governor.* Salem, Mort V. Brown, State Printer, 1874.

Heizer, R. F., and Whipple, M. A. (eds.). *The California Indians. A Source Book.* Berkeley, University of California Press, 1951.

Hines, Rev. H. K. *An Illustrated History of the State of Oregon.* Chicago, Lewis Publishing Co., 1893.

Hittell, Theodore H. *History of California.* 3 vols. San Francisco, N. J. Stone and Company, 1898.

Horner, John B. *Oregon: Her History, Her Great Men, Her Literature.* Portland, J. K. Gill, 1921.

Hunt, Rockwell D. *California and Californians.* 4 vols. Chicago, Lewis Publishing Co., 1932.

Jocelyn, Stephan Perry. *Mostly Alkali.* Caldwell, Idaho, The Caxton Printers, Ltd., 1953.

Kroeber, A. L. *Handbook of the Indians of California.* Berkeley, California Book Company, Ltd., 1953.

McClure, James D. *California Landmarks, A Photographic Guide to the State's Historic Spots.* Stanford, Calif., Stanford University Press, 1948.

McLaughlin, James. *My Friend the Indian.* Boston, Houghton Mifflin Co., 1926.

Manypenny, George W. *Our Indian Wards.* Cincinnati, Robert Clarke and Company, 1880.

Meacham, Alfred B. *The Tragedy of the Lava Beds.* Washington, D. C., Bland Publishers, 1883.

———. *Wigwam and War-path, or the Royal Chief in Chains.* Boston, John P. Dale and Company, 1875.

———. *Wi-ne-ma (The Woman-Chief) and Her People.* Hartford, American Publishing Company, 1876.

Merriam, C. Hart. *Studies of California Indians.* Berkeley and Los Angeles, University of California Press, 1955.

Miller, Joaquin. *My Own Story.* Chicago, Belford-Clarke Co., 1890.

Mitchell, Hon. John H. *Indian Depredations in Oregon.* Washington, Government Printing Office, 1874.

Mooney, James. *The Ghost Dance Religion and the Sioux Outbreak of 1890. Fourteenth Annual Report* of the Bureau of American Ethnology to the Smithsonian Institution, 1892–93, part 2. Washington, Government Printing Office, 1896.

Nash, Philleo. "The Place of Religious Revivalism in the Formation of the Intercultural Community on Klamath Reservation," in *Social Anthropology of North American Tribes,* ed. by Fred Eggan. Chicago, University of Chicago Press, 1955.

Odeneal, T. B. *The Modoc War: Statement of Its Origin and Causes Containing an Account of the Treaty, Copies of Petitions, and Official Correspondence.* Portland, "Bulletin" Steam Book and Job Printing Office, 1873.

Odgers, Charlotte. *Jesse Applegate: Study of a Pioneer Politician. Reed College Bulletin*, Vol. XXIII, No. 2 (January, 1945).

Payne, Doris Palmer. *Captain Jack, Modoc Renegade*. Portland, Binfords and Mort, 1938.

Peters, DeWitt C. *Pioneer Life and Frontier Adventures: An Authentic Record of the Romantic Life and Daring Exploits of Kit Carson and His Companions, from His Own Narrative*. Boston, Estes and Lauriat, 1883.

Relander, Click. *Drummers and Dreamers*. Caldwell, Idaho, The Caxton Printers, Ltd., 1956.

Rensch, H. E. and E. G., and Hoover, Mildred Brooke. *Historic Spots in California*. 3 vols. Stanford, Stanford University Press, 1933.

Riddle, Jeff C. *The Indian History of the Modoc War and the Causes That Led to It*. D. L. Moses, 1914.

Schofield, Lt. Gen. John M. *Forty-Six Years in the Army*. New York, The Century Co., 1897.

Seymour, Flora Warren. *Indian Agents of the Old Frontier*. New York, D. Appleton-Century Co., Inc., 1941.

Shaver, F. A. *An Illustrated History of Central Oregon, Embracing Wasco, Sherman, Gilliam, Wheeler, Crook, Lake, and Klamath Counties, State of Oregon*. Spokane, Western Historical Publishing Co., 1905.

Smith, DeCost. *Indian Experiences*. Caldwell, Idaho, The Caxton Printers, Ltd., 1943.

Spier, Leslie. *The Prophet Dance of the Northwest and Its Derivatives: The Source of the Ghost Dance*. (General Studies in Anthropology, No. 1) Menasha, George Banta Publishing Co., 1935.

Splawn, A. J. *Ka-mi-akin, Last Hero of the Yakimas*. Portland, Binfords and Mort, 1944.

Simpson, William. *Meeting the Sun: A Journey All Around the World*. London, Longmans, Green, Reader, and Dyer, 1874.

Thompson, Col. William. *Reminiscences of a Pioneer*. San Francisco, 1912.

Underhill, Ruth Murray. *Red Man's America: A History of Indians in the United States*. Chicago, University of Chicago Press, 1953.

Verrill, Alpheus Hyatt. *Our Indians: The Story of the Indians of the United States*. New York. G. P. Putnam's Sons, 1935.

Victor, Frances Fuller. *The Early Indian Wars of Oregon, Compiled from the Oregon Archives and Other Oregon Sources*. Salem, Frank C. Baker, State Printer, 1894.

Williams, James. *Life and Adventures of James Williams, a Fugitive Slave, with a Full Description of the Underground Railroad.* Philadelphia, A. H. Sickler and Co., 1893.

Wilson, Hugh, Jr. *The Causes and Significance of the Modoc War.* Klamath Falls, Oregon, Guide Printing Co., 1953.

Winther, Oscar Osburn. *The Great Northwest.* New York, Alfred A. Knopf, 1950.

Wissler, Clark. *Indians of the United States, Four Centuries of Their History and Culture.* (The American Museum of Natural History Series.) New York, Doubleday, Doran and Co., Inc., 1940.

V. Magazine Articles

Anon. "The Modoc Massacre," *Harper's Weekly*, Vol. XVII, No. 852 (April 26, 1873).

———. "The Modocs," *Harper's Weekly*, Vol. XVII, No. 853 (May 3, 1873).

———. "Uncle Sam Hunting the Modoc Flea in His Lava Bed," *Harper's Weekly*, Vol. XVII, No. 854 (May 10, 1873).

———. "The Modoc War," *Harper's Weekly*, Vol. XVII, No. 855 (May 17, 1873).

———. "Funeral of General Canby," *Harper's Weekly*, Vol. XVII, No. 856 (May 24, 1873).

———. "Our Indian Allies," *Harper's Weekly*, Vol. XVII, No. 859 (June 14, 1873).

———. "The Last of the Modocs," *Harper's Weekly*, Vol. XVII, No. 860 (June 21, 1873).

———. "Captain Jack's Cave," *Harper's Weekly*, Vol. XVII, No. 861 (June 28, 1873).

Applegate, Lindsay. "Notes and Reminiscences of Laying Out and Establishing the Old Emigrant Road Into Southern Oregon in the Year 1846," *Oregon Historical Quarterly*, Vol. XXII, No. 1 (March, 1921).

Brown, J. Henry. "The Biggest Little War in American History," *Oregon Historical Quarterly*, Vol. XLIII, No. 1 (March, 1942).

Brown, William S. "The Other Side of the Story," *Overland Monthly*, Vol. LXXXII, No. 4 (April, 1924).

Bunker, W. M. "In the Lava Beds," *The Californian*, Vol. I, No. 2 (February, 1880).

Clarke, Samuel A. "Klamath Land," *Overland Monthly*, Vol. XI, No. 6 (December, 1873).

Churchman, Evelyn. "Story of the Pit River," *California History Nugget*, Vol. VII, No. 6 (March, 1940).

Dillon, Richard H. "Costs of the Modoc War," *California Historical Society Quarterly*, Vol. XXVIII, No. 2 (June, 1949).

Drury, Aubrey. "The National Monuments in California," *Motorland*, Vol. LXIX, No. 2 (August, 1951).

Fenton, William D. "Political History of Oregon from 1865 to 1876," *Oregon Historical Quarterly*, Vol. II, No. 4 (December, 1901).

Fenton, William D. "Father Wilbur and His Work," *Oregon Historical Quarterly*, Vol. X, No. 2 (June, 1909).

Fisher, Don C., and Doerr, John E., Jr. "Outline of Events in the History of the Modoc War," *Nature Notes* (Mimeographed pamphlet), Crater National Park, 1937.

———. "Saving the Early History of Klamath County," *The Oregon Motorist*, Vol. XI, No. 9 (June, 1931).

Fitzgerald, Maurice. "The Modoc War: Reminiscences of the Campaign Against the Indian Uprising in the Lava Beds of Northern California and Southern Oregon in 1872–73. A First Hand Account of the Murder of Gen. Canby," *Americana*, Vol. XXI, No. 4 (October, 1927).

Gatschet, Albert S. "Songs of the Modoc Indians," *American Anthropologist*, Vol. VII, No. 1 (January, 1894).

Hall, Jody C., and Nettl, Bruno. "Musical Styles of the Modocs," *Southwestern Journal of Anthropology*, Vol. XI, No. 1 (Spring, 1955).

Hendryx, James B. "End of the Modoc War," *Hunting and Fishing*, Vol. XI, No. 10 (October, 1934).

Howard, Maj. Gen. O. O. "Famous Indian Chiefs—Captain Jack: Chief of the Modoc Indians," *St. Nicholas*, Vol. XXXV, No. 7 (May, 1908).

Larson, Rupert L. "California Pocahontas," *Westways*, (October, 1942).

Lockley, Fred. "How the Modoc Indian War Started," *Overland Monthly*, Vol. LXXXI, No. 7 (November, 1923).

Maloney, Alice Bay. "Shasta was Shatesla in 1814," *California Historical Society Quarterly*, Vol. XXIV, No. 3 (September, 1945).

McLeod, Edith Rutenic. "Two Kegs of Whiskey," *Westways*, Vol. XLIV, No. 6 (June, 1952).

Nettl, Bruno. "North American Indian Musical Styles," *Journal of American Folklore*, Vol. LXVII, No. 265 (July–September, 1954).

Ogden, Peter Skene. "Journal, 1828–29," *Oregon Historical Quarterly*, Vol. XI, No. 4 (December, 1910).

Powers, Stephan. "The California Indians: The Modocs," *Overland Monthly*, Vol. X, No. 6 (June, 1873).

Rosborough, Alex J. "A. M. Rosborough, Special Indian Agent," *California Historical Society Quarterly*, Vol. XXVI, No. 3 (September, 1944).

Santee, J. F. "Edward R. S. Canby, Modoc War, 1873," *Oregon Historical Quarterly*, Vol. XXXIII, No. 1 (March, 1932).

Sargent, Alice Applegate. "A Sketch of the Rogue River Valley and Southern Oregon History," *Oregon Historical Quarterly*, Vol. XXI, No. 1 (March, 1921).

Scott, Leslie M. "Indian Diseases as Aids to Pacific Northwest Settlement," *Oregon Historical Quarterly*, Vol. XXIX, No. 2 (June, 1928).

Steele, Rufus. "The Cave of Captain Jack," *Sunset*, Vol. XXX, No. 5 (May, 1913).

Trimble, Will J. "A Soldier of the Oregon Frontier," *Oregon Historical Quarterly*, Vol. VIII, No. 1 (March, 1907).

Turner, William M. "Scraps of Modoc History," *Overland Monthly*, Vol. XI, No. 1 (July, 1873).

Vining, Irving E. "The Lure of the Lava Land," *Oregon, The State Magazine*, Vol. I, No. 1 (May, 1927).

Wells, Harry L. "Frémont and the Modocs," *The West Shore*, Vol. X, No. 3 (March, 1884).

———. "The Modocs in 1851," *The West Shore*, Vol. X, No. 5 (May, 1884).

———. "The Ben Wright Massacre," *The West Shore*, Vol. X, No. 10 (October, 1884).

Young, F. G. "Financial History of Oregon," *Oregon Historical Quarterly*, Vol. XI, No. 4 (December, 1910).

INDEX